SAINT AMBROSE: *His Life and Times*

SAINT

Succeeding centuries have seen the rise of misguided his-
orians, and there have been a number of "gibbons" whose
vritings on St. Ambrose still cloud his works and reputation.
n recent decades, however, he has received much fairer treat-
nent from the hands of historians like E. Bickel, R. Paribeni,
V. Ensslin, and Charles N. Cochrane. Of particular signifi-
ance is the observation which Hans Lietzmann made shortly
efore he died in 1942: "Ambrose was certainly one of the
reat men of human history, even before he became a bishop,
nd he by no means regarded his office as a sinecure when he
vas the pastor and the political confidant of three emperors.
'hat was also a fact of which the emperors themselves were
ery conscious. Theodosius was not wrong in giving way to
is man, in whom the classical dignity proper to the Roman
nse of what the state demands was combined with a pro-
undly earnest, Christian conception of the meaning of life."[2]
nd Henri Bremond, in an address on the occasion of his re-
ption into the French Academy, has pointed up the lesson
hich may be learned from reflection upon the life of St. Am-
rose and the age in which he lived: "The great controversies
the third, fourth, and fifth centuries broke out. There was
great stir about metaphysics, couched in Greek terms like
ypostasis and *ousia*, which enthralled the East but dismayed
e Latin world. To what purpose? Had the Church become
school? Had the kingdom of God become an academy? No,
uchesne answers with St. Ambrose and Newman. The truth
that God does not wish to save the world through syllo-
sms."[3]

This life of St. Ambrose was written to be read. The works
ed in the notes have therefore been limited to those that are
sential. It is the hope of the author that this study will in its
n modest way spread the fame of one who strove strenu-
sly for the good, especially through the example of his own
e, and who lived in an age no less tragic than our own. In
t, it is rather startling to realize how closely today's Iron

AMBROSE

HIS LIFE AND TIMES

by Angelo Paredi

TRANSLATED BY

M. Joseph Costelloe, S.J.

UNIVERSITY OF NOTRE DAME PRESS ∘ 1964

The present book was translated
from Angelo Paredi's volume in Italian,
S. AMBROGIO, E LA SUA ETÀ,
published 1960 by Editore Ulrico Hoepli, Milano.

Imprimi Potest: The Very Reverend John J. Foley, S.J.,
Provincial of the Wisconsin Province

Nihil Obstat: Joseph Hoffman, C.S.C.,
Censor Deputatus

Imprimatur:
✠ *Leo A. Pursley, D.D., L.L.D.,*
Bishop of Fort Wayne-South Bend

Library of Congress Catalog Card Number 63-19325
Manufactured in the United States of America

Preface

In an interesting novel that appeared in 195[...]
represents a conversation that took place at
near Trier between Helena, the mother of C
ervina, her daughter-in-law, and Lactantius, t
tian author who had been called to the impe
cate the young Crispus. In a corner of the
gibbon, a small Indian monkey, fretting wit
and chattering for fruit.

Helena mentions the atrocities committed
tians in the East and the sad days that th
But they are also glorious, Lactantius co
questions his sincerity. If they are so glo
not stay home in Nicomedia? To defend h
replies that there is need of "a special quali
just as one must possess "a special qualit
a humbler profession, it is true, but nonet
portance: "Suppose," he says, "Suppose t
come, when the Church's troubles seem
should come an apostate of my own trad
with the mind of Cicero or Tacitus and the
and he nods at the gibbon. "A man like th
again and again but what he wrote would
minds when the refutations were quite f

Curtain resembles the *limes,* or boundary, of the late Roman empire.

The plates and illustrations that have been included in this book should give something of the temper of the times in which St. Ambrose lived. In this English translation, which has been made from the Italian original published at Milan in 1960, it has been possible to clarify a number of details. These improvements are largely due to the publication of two more volumes of St. Ambrose's works by O. Faller in his critical edition in the *Corpus Scriptorum Ecclesiasticorum Latinorum* (LXXIII and LXXVIII). The author wishes to extend a special word of thanks to the Rev. M. Joseph Costelloe, S.J., the translator, for the care he has taken to check the sources from which this biography was written.

Angelo Paredi

Milan, The Ambrosian Library, Spring, 1963.

Contents

○

Contents

o

Curtain resembles the *limes,* or boundary, of the late Roman empire.

The plates and illustrations that have been included in this book should give something of the temper of the times in which St. Ambrose lived. In this English translation, which has been made from the Italian original published at Milan in 1960, it has been possible to clarify a number of details. These improvements are largely due to the publication of two more volumes of St. Ambrose's works by O. Faller in his critical edition in the *Corpus Scriptorum Ecclesiasticorum Latinorum* (LXXIII and LXXVIII). The author wishes to extend a special word of thanks to the Rev. M. Joseph Costelloe, S.J., the translator, for the care he has taken to check the sources from which this biography was written.

Angelo Paredi

Milan, The Ambrosian Library, Spring, 1963.

The present book was translated
from Angelo Paredi's volume in Italian,
S. AMBROGIO, E LA SUA ETÀ,
published 1960 by Editore Ulrico Hoepli, Milano.

*Imprimi Potest: The Very Reverend John J. Foley, S.J.,
Provincial of the Wisconsin Province*

*Nihil Obstat: Joseph Hoffman, C.S.C.,
Censor Deputatus*

Imprimatur:
✠ *Leo A. Pursley, D.D., L.L.D.,
Bishop of Fort Wayne-South Bend*

*Library of Congress Catalog Card Number 63-19325
Manufactured in the United States of America*

AMBROSE

HIS LIFE AND TIMES

by Angelo Paredi

TRANSLATED BY

M. Joseph Costelloe, S.J.

UNIVERSITY OF NOTRE DAME PRESS ∘ 1964

Preface

o

In an interesting novel that appeared in 1950, Evelyn Waugh represents a conversation that took place at a country estate near Trier between Helena, the mother of Constantine, Minervina, her daughter-in-law, and Lactantius, the famous Christian author who had been called to the imperial court to educate the young Crispus. In a corner of the terrace there is a gibbon, a small Indian monkey, fretting with its golden chain and chattering for fruit.

Helena mentions the atrocities committed against the Christians in the East and the sad days that they have brought. But they are also glorious, Lactantius counters. Minervina questions his sincerity. If they are so glorious, why did he not stay home in Nicomedia? To defend himself, Lactantius replies that there is need of "a special quality to be a martyr" just as one must possess "a special quality to be a writer," a humbler profession, it is true, but nonetheless of some importance: "Suppose," he says, "Suppose that in the years to come, when the Church's troubles seem to be over, there should come an apostate of my own trade, a false historian, with the mind of Cicero or Tacitus and the soul of an animal," and he nods at the gibbon. "A man like that might be refuted again and again but what he wrote would remain in people's minds when the refutations were quite forgotten."[1]

Succeeding centuries have seen the rise of misguided historians, and there have been a number of "gibbons" whose writings on St. Ambrose still cloud his works and reputation. In recent decades, however, he has received much fairer treatment from the hands of historians like E. Bickel, R. Paribeni, W. Ensslin, and Charles N. Cochrane. Of particular significance is the observation which Hans Lietzmann made shortly before he died in 1942: "Ambrose was certainly one of the great men of human history, even before he became a bishop, and he by no means regarded his office as a sinecure when he was the pastor and the political confidant of three emperors. That was also a fact of which the emperors themselves were very conscious. Theodosius was not wrong in giving way to this man, in whom the classical dignity proper to the Roman sense of what the state demands was combined with a profoundly earnest, Christian conception of the meaning of life."[2] And Henri Bremond, in an address on the occasion of his reception into the French Academy, has pointed up the lesson which may be learned from reflection upon the life of St. Ambrose and the age in which he lived: "The great controversies of the third, fourth, and fifth centuries broke out. There was a great stir about metaphysics, couched in Greek terms like *hypostasis* and *ousia,* which enthralled the East but dismayed the Latin world. To what purpose? Had the Church become a school? Had the kingdom of God become an academy? No, Duchesne answers with St. Ambrose and Newman. The truth is that God does not wish to save the world through syllogisms."[3]

This life of St. Ambrose was written to be read. The works cited in the notes have therefore been limited to those that are essential. It is the hope of the author that this study will in its own modest way spread the fame of one who strove strenuously for the good, especially through the example of his own life, and who lived in an age no less tragic than our own. In fact, it is rather startling to realize how closely today's Iron

Plates

o

beginning on page 441

I

Trier

o

The Roman empire in its decline. The Aristocracy. Trier. The childhood of St. Ambrose. Christian families and the deferment of baptism.

Both St. Ambrose and St. Augustine were convinced of the providential character of the Roman empire. In his *Commentary on the Forty-fifth Psalm,* the former notes that "the Romans, tired of civil war, conferred the *imperium* on Augustus Caesar, thus bringing to an end their intestine strife. But this also made it possible for the Apostles to travel throughout the whole world as the Lord Jesus had bidden them: 'Go forth and teach all nations.' "[1] And in a sermon preached some years later, St. Augustine echoes these same sentiments in the following terms: "Let the Church march on! The way is open; our road has been built for us by the emperor."[2]

Only a relatively few paid much attention to the Apostles as they walked along the imperial roads. But by the fourth century, Christianity had become so widespread that it almost constituted a state within a state. The crisis of the ancient world, in fact, coincides with its adoption of Christianity. The Roman empire, which to many different races seemed to be the ideal state, came to realize in time that there had risen within it, and still apart from it, a new spiritual community that was concerned about matters unknown to it before, matters that were outside the sphere of politics, foreign in fact to the interests of this world.

The goal for the historians of the Roman empire is the explanation of this slow separation of the inner from the outer community, the creation of a duality out of an indistinct unity. As one of the keenest observers of ancient history has observed, "the history of antiquity has meaning in so far as it develops and culminates in Christianity."[3] Our intellectual growth implies a realization of norms limiting the manifestations of our physical existence, but this does not mean that later years must be called "decadent" when compared with those of childhood. Similarly, the entrance of the Church into the public life of the fourth century does not mean that it should be blamed for the decline of the ancient world, as it was by the historians of the Enlightenment. It merits no such accusation, even if the first great flowering of Christianity as an organized society attracted into its own orbit, and away from that of the camp and politics, many of the most dynamic individuals and most brilliant minds of the age. Most of the outstanding men of the fourth century were men of the Church—Athanasius, Basil, Damasus, Ambrose, Augustine, and John Chrysostom, to mention but a few of those who are best known. And of all these, the most important for understanding the problem of the relationship between Church and State was the bishop of Milan, St. Ambrose.

St. Ambrose was born in Gaul, probably in 334, at a time when his father occupied one of the highest posts in the prefecture.[4] Since in the fourth century the prefect's headquarters were at Trier on the Moselle river, it is reasonable to suppose that St. Ambrose was born there. He received the name Aurelius Ambrosius, the first name being derived from the *gens Aurelia* to which his mother belonged, and the second from his father.[5] He was the third child in the family, a sister Marcellina, and a brother Satyrus having been born before him.

The *Ambrosii* were obviously Romans, but the Greek names (Soteris, Satyrus, and Ambrose itself) indicate that the family may have had Greek antecedents, though such names were quite common in the late Empire. But even if the family was originally Greek, it had been Romanized for several generations since it had numbered magistrates and even consuls among its members.

In the year 334, Constantine the Younger was also living at Trier. This prince, the eldest of the sons of Constantine the Great and Fausta, born in the year 317, had received from his father the government of Mauritania, Spain, Gaul, and Britain. Constantius, another son, had been given Asia Minor, Syria, and Egypt, while Constans, the youngest, had received Italy, Africa, and the Danubian provinces. But Constantine's death on May 22, 337, threw the state into a turmoil. Shortly after his death, nine members of the imperial family were murdered by the troops. A meeting of the three Augusti in 338 at Sirmium or Viminacium in Pannonia did not reconcile their differences with respect to the problems of succession. In the spring of 340, the twenty-three-year-old Constantius II suddenly left Gaul, crossed the Alps, and marched against his recalcitrant brother Constans. But when he arrived at Aquileia, he was ambushed and slain by agents of Constans. The latter then annexed Gaul, Spain, and Britain to the territory he already ruled.

Since Ambrose's father had been one of the slain Augustus's high officials, it is quite probable that his own fortunes were closely linked with those of the deceased monarch. The family would then almost certainly have left Gaul to return to Rome.

The high position held by his father, his own subsequent career in the government, the property which he possessed at the time of his election as bishop of Milan would all indicate that St. Ambrose belonged to the Roman aristocracy. At this time Roman nobles passed on the highest posts in the imperial bureaucracy as if they were hereditary rights. By a kind of tacit agreement, a son succeeded to his father's office. Inscriptions of the fourth century show that provinces were frequently governed by members of the same family. Even emperors who came from the lowest ranks of the army, and were themselves of foreign birth, did not meddle with this tradition since it assured them of experienced assistants.

For members of the senatorial class, posts in the government were a source of enormous wealth. In the general impoverishment that characterized the last stages of the Empire, when the middle class had almost entirely disappeared, the senatorial class was the exception. It was a class of great landed proprietors with vast domains scattered throughout the various provinces that had the appearance of small independent states. Some of the senators still lived in Rome or in other large cities, but the majority dwelt on their fortified estates surrounded by thousands of workmen and slaves. These could be armed to protect their property. This new nobility, in contrast with that of the age of the Antonines, was intellectually impoverished and had little real compassion for the masses bound by imperial edicts to the land or to their respective trades.

Among the nobles, especially among the Christians, there were, of course, obvious exceptions. One of these was Melania the Younger, the sole heiress of Valerius Publicola, who in his turn had been the sole heir of Valerius Maximus, prefect of Rome in 362. A few details from her life can throw some light on the position occupied by St. Ambrose and his family and explain why the Milanese church during the early Middle Ages could possess property in Liguria and Sicily.

Melania owned vast estates on both sides of the Po, and also in Apulia, Campania, Sicily, Gaul, Spain, Britain, and proconsular Africa. One, for example, had four hundred slaves and sixty-two houses for the *coloni*, or serfs. According to an estimate made by Rampolla in 1905, the annual return of these holdings would have amounted to 116,000,000 French francs.[6] When she was twenty years old, Melania, with the approval of her husband Pinianus, decided to sell the greater portion of her estates so that she could give the proceeds to the poor. At the same time she freed some eight thousand slaves. Considering the value of these slaves alone at this time, her generosity towards them must have represented a loss of many millions.

Melania's fortune, however, in comparison with that of Symmachus, who will appear quite frequently in these pages, was rather modest. He owned a house at Capua, three at Rome, three villas in the Roman campagna, twelve others in different parts of Italy, and lands in Sicily and Mauretania.

Another very wealthy individual was Sextus Petronius Probus. After passing through all the magistracies and being three times prefect of the praetorium, he finally asked for baptism at the age of sixty. Ammianus Marcellinus, who lived for some years at Rome, tells us that Probus owned estates in almost all the provinces, though "a private individual would not be able to say whether they had been justly acquired or not."[7] Similarly, Ausonius describes the holdings of his friend Paulinus of Bordeaux, later known as Paulinus of Nola, as "kingdoms."[8] As we shall see later, Paulinus, also the son of a prefect of Gaul, kept in touch with St. Ambrose through his letters. Before making himself poor for Christ, he could have been hailed as a prince since he owned entire towns and cities in Aquitania besides Nola in Campania and Fondi in Latium.

The fame and fortune of these noble Romans can give us some idea of St. Ambrose's own family. Already at the time of Diocletian, members of the family had held high offices in the state, as is clear from the saint's own words when speaking of the virgin Soteris, the martyr of the family: "She preferred the faith to the consulships and prefectures of her ancestors."[9]

From his palace at Trier, the prefect of Gaul had charge of

the administration of justice and the execution of the imperial policies throughout central Europe, from Hadrian's Wall built to keep the Picts and Scots out of Britain to the mountains of Morocco, and from the frontier formed by the Rhine and the Rhone to the Atlantic. The heavy taxes collected by the imperial bureaucracy in North Africa, the Balearic Islands, Spain, Gaul, Belgium, Germany, and Britain flowed to Trier. As the representative of the emperor, the prefect of Gaul promulgated his laws, watched over the governors of the various provinces of the prefecture, received appeals from provincial tribunals, and supervised the maintenance of the roads and the imperial post. He also had to provide the rations and pay of the armies stationed in his territories, though their command was entrusted to dukes and counts (*duces* and *comites*) who took their orders immediately from the emperor.

Under Diocletian, the hierarchy of the imperial functionaries had been divided into four classes, *illustres, spectabiles, clarissimi,* and *perfectissimi.* The prefects of the praetorium belonged to the first of these, the dukes and counts to the fourth. Under this same emperor the imperial authority was regarded as sacred, and extreme manifestations of respect, such as prostration, were introduced from the East. This court ceremonial was continued under Diocletian's successors. Thus, in 326, on the occasion of his twentieth anniversary as emperor, Constantine appeared in public wearing robes of silk and purple adorned with gold and gems, and bearing on his head a diadem of pearls.

Even the emperor's closest assistants now had to stand in his presence. From this custom came the name of *consistorium* for the sovereign's private council. State officials also shared in the sacred character of the emperor, and the closer they were to his person, the greater was the respect shown to them.

Thousands of lesser officials were needed to maintain the elaborate pomp, and thousands of secret service men (*agentes in rebus*) to secure the safety of the sovereign.

When Ambrose was born, Trier was one of the most important cities of the world. It had been founded by Augustus on the right bank of the Moselle near the place where the river becomes navigable for large vessels. The city itself was the focal point of eight Roman roads and at the center of the natural waterways formed by the Moselle, Saar, Sauer, Ruver, and Kyll rivers. Because of its strategic position, it gradually replaced Lyons as the capital of Gaul. It was destroyed by the Alemanni in 259-262, but then restored more magnificent than before. When Diocletian divided up the empire, Trier became the residence of Galerius Maximianus, the Caesar of the West. Even today numerous traces of the ancient Roman Treveri may be seen at Trier. Among the most impressive of these are the three levels, lateral towers, and inner court of the *Porta Nigra,* the remains of the two great baths, the bridges over the river, and the basilica of Constantine, now a Lutheran church.

Athanasius, the great bishop of Alexandria, lived in exile at Trier from 335 to 337. He had been unjustly condemned by the Arian bishops at Tyre, and then tried again at Constantinople by Constantine the Great. The emperor unfortunately believed the false charges of Eusebius of Nicomedia to the effect that Athanasius had tried to prevent the shipping of grain from Egypt to Constantinople. Flying into a rage, he sent him into exile at Trier.

At Trier, Athanasius found a flourishing Christian community. During his stay in the city he told the faithful about the Egyptian monks, especially about the most famous of them all, St. Anthony, who had gone into the desert about the year 270 after handing over to the people of his village his patrimony of two hundred and seven acres of good Egyptian land.[10] As a young man Athanasius had lived for some time with Anthony in the desert, and it may well be that Marcellina, Ambrose's sister, a girl of about ten at this time, may have heard him speak of this renowned Egyptian monk at her home in Trier.

From the *Confessions* of St. Augustine, we know that a chance discovery of a small monastery outside the walls of the city and the reading of the life of St. Anthony by Athanasius which they found there led two officials attached to the court at Trier to renounce the world. Not to be outdone in generosity, the two young women to whom they were engaged also consecrated themselves to God.[11] A further example of the flourishing state of monasticism at Trier is found in the life of St. Jerome. After completing his studies at Rome, he went to Trier about the year 365. The austerities practiced by the monks which he found there inspired him with a desire to adopt a similar mode of life.

It was in such surroundings, then, that St. Ambrose first saw the light of day, but he tells us nothing of his own childhood in his extensive writings.

To us it seems strange that he never mentions his mother in his works, something which is in marked contrast with the moving account which St. Augustine has left us of his own, St. Monica. It is not that St. Ambrose was insensible to a mother's love. As we shall see later, he could speak of it with feeling.[12] His silence is perhaps, at least in part, to be explained by a fine reserve, too Roman in character to treat of private matters in works for public use, such as were all his writings. Neither does St. Jerome ever mention his mother, though it is certain that she was a Christian.

Ambrose was the youngest of three children. His brother Satyrus was a few years older, and his sister Marcellina ten years older than he. One day when Ambrose was still an infant, the nurse who was watching his cradle in the court of the prefect's palace was astonished to see a swarm of bees swoop down and rest upon the eyes and lips of the sleeping child. Frightened, she called to some members of the household who were walking at a little distance. They came, and Ambrose's father and mother, and even his sister Marcellina, saw the bees enter and leave the mouth of the child without disturbing him. The bees then flew off and were lost in the blazing sun, as Ambrose's father exclaimed: "This child is destined for great things!"[13] Since bees had already deposited their honey on the lips of Pindar and Plato, and two centuries after their visit to Ambrose were to come down again upon the infant Isidore of Seville, this episode should almost certainly be taken as a bit of folklore symbolizing the future eloquence of the saint, which would be as sweet and nourishing as honey, and an instrument of wondrous deeds. This is the only incident of the saint's childhood recorded by his biographer Paulinus, but we may well imagine that his life passed pleasantly in the palace with its gleaming marbles and mosaics, its statues and colonnades, and its fountains and enclosed gardens. We can also imagine the delight that he and his sister and brother had as they stood on the banks of the Moselle and watched the clumsy barges pass by, loaded down with casks of Rhenish wine for distant ports.

The Christianity of the Ambrosii is demonstrated by the martyrdom of Soteris, already mentioned, who may have been the great-aunt of the bishop of Milan. In a discourse to the Christian virgins of that city, St. Ambrose described her martyrdom in the following terms: "Although she was extremely fair and of noble birth, this virgin preferred her sacred faith to the consulships and prefectures of her ancestors; and though she was ordered to offer sacrifice, she refused to do so. When the cruel persecutor ordered her to be slapped so that she might yield either to the disgrace or pain of the blows, this tender virgin lifted her veil from her head and bared her face, which she only uncovered for martyrdom. She willingly accepted the injury to her features so that what is frequently a source of temptation might be a sacrifice to martyrdom. She rejoiced that the threat to her chastity should be lessened by her loss of beauty. They could disfigure her face with blows, but they could not destroy the beauty of her virtue and the charm of her fair soul."[14]

A further proof of the Christianity of St. Ambrose's family

was the dedication which his sister Marcellina made of her virginity to Christ in a solemn ceremony at Rome on Christmas, 353. Though Ambrose could thus have applied to himself the words of St. Jerome, "From the cradle I was nourished on Catholic milk,"[15] neither he nor Jerome received baptism until much later in life. Jerome was baptized in 367 at the age of twenty, St. Ambrose in 374 at the age of forty. But such delays were not at all unusual. Rufinus was twenty-six at the time of his baptism, Paulinus of Nola thirty, St. Augustine thirty-three, and Satyrus, the brother of Ambrose, over forty. As may be deduced from the lives of Sts. Basil, Gregory of Nazianzus, and John Chrysostom, the same custom prevailed in the East. If these cases are to be regarded as exceptional, it is only because others waited still longer to receive the sacrament.

In the first book of his *Confessions*, St. Augustine asks why his own baptism had been deferred.[16] Among the various answers that might have been given for this lamentable practice was that during the centuries of persecution great heroism was required on the part of anyone with an official position in the Roman world to seal his adherence to the new faith through baptism. Since pagan cult practices were intimately connected with the exercise of public office, the holding of such an office was practically precluded by the promises made at the time of baptism. As a consequence of this, the men in many otherwise Christian families put off their baptism until old age so as not to be forced to relinquish their public positions. In the first half of the third century, Origen noted that there were many such instances of weakness and inconsistency.[17]

In the fourth century, when Christianity became a licit religion, and when whole areas were converted to the faith, the practice continued through force of habit, though there was also another important factor entering in—the severe penitential discipline of the early Church. Only the stoutest hearts could look forward without trepidation to the possibility of long years of penance for a single serious lapse. Baptism was therefore frequently put off until the passions of youth should have been dulled by time. An example for this was certainly found among the most prominent men of the state. Though Constantine raised splendid basilicas at Rome, Jerusalem, Constantinople, and elsewhere, and endowed the churches with gold and other precious gifts, he did not himself receive baptism until he was on the point of death. And this was the case with other emperors of the fourth century as well. St. Augustine recalls the fact that in the early years of the fifth century when there was a general alarm at Constantinople, all the people ran to the basilicas, which were now too small to hold the crowds, and desperately asked for baptism.[18] They even asked to receive the sacrament on the streets and in the squares. And St. John Chrysostom indignantly observes that baptism was not received with eager joy but with fear and trembling by those in the throes of their last agony, after hearing from their doctors that there was nothing more that they could do.[19]

In the fourth century, the children of Christian families were brought to the church for the ceremonies of the catechumenate, but few received the sacrament of baptism itself before reaching the use of reason.[20] Different ceremonies were used for enrolling the children among the catechumens. These varied from place to place. In Africa candidates were enrolled by making a sign of the cross on the forehead and placing a pinch of blessed salt, the symbol of wisdom, upon the tongue. In Gaul the ceremony consisted in the sign of the cross and the imposition of the priest's hands on the candidate, as was perhaps also the case in Rome and Italy in general. It was with these rites, then, that St. Ambrose was as a child initiated into the Christian mysteries.

When a catechumen finally decided to receive baptism, he gave his name to the bishop and thus became one of the immediate candidates, or *competentes.*

In the course of reflecting upon his early life, St. Augustine recalls the fact that he had been a catechumen as a child and deplores the deferment of his baptism:

> "When I was still a child, I had heard of the eternal life promised to us through the humility of Your Son our Lord God, descending even to our pride; and I was signed with the sign of His cross; and I was seasoned with His salt when I came from my mother's womb, who greatly trusted in You. When I was still a boy, You saw one day, O Lord, how I was suddenly taken with a pain in the stomach and fell so suddenly sick that I almost died. You saw, O my God, for You were my Protector, with what faith and earnestness of mind I begged the piety of my mother and of Your Church, the mother of us all for the baptism of Your Christ, my Lord God. My mother being much disturbed by this, since with a chaste heart and faith in You she was lovingly concerned for my eternal salvation, hastened to procure as best she could that I should be initiated and washed with Your loving sacraments. . . . But I soon recovered, and my cleansing was put off as if I needed to be defiled still further if I lived longer, since the guilt contracted by the stain of sin is indeed greater and more dangerous after baptism than it is before. . . . I beg of You, my God, for I would gladly know if it would please You, why my baptism was deferred, whether it was for my good that the reins of sin were loosened as it were or not. How is it that even now on all sides we hear it said: 'Let him alone, let him do what he wants since he is not baptized!' whereas if there is a question of bodily health we do not say, 'Let him be still further wounded, for he has not yet been cured?' How much better would it have been for me to have been quickly cured so that through my own diligence and that of

my friends my soul might under Your protection have preserved the salvation it had received from You?"[21]

In later years St. Ambrose might have made a somewhat similar, though less passionate, reflection. He came to look upon the years of his youth passed without the sacraments as a time in which "he had been lost."[22]

FLA(via) MAX(ima) FAVSTA AVG(usta)

Bronze coin. See H. Cohen, *Description historique des monnaies frappées sous l'empire romain,* VI (Paris, 1862), 183, no. 6

Fausta, born about 298, wife of Constantine in 307, mother of Constantius II, became enamored of Crispus, the son of Constantine and Minerva. When he refused her advances, she denounced him to his father, who had him executed in 326. When he later learned what had really happened, he had Fausta put to death in a bath tub of scalding water. See the sources cited by O. Seeck in "Crispus 9," *Realen. der class. Alter.,* IV (1901), cc. 1723-24.

II

Rome

○

The Ambrosii at Rome. Education in antiquity. The veiling of Marcellina. The usurpations of Magnentius, Vetranio, Nepotianus. Arianism. Nicea and the reaction to it. Athanasius. Gregory of Cappadocia. Sardica. The Council of Milan. Pope Liberius. George of Cappadocia. Constantius II at Rome. Rome in the fourth century: students, people, grain supply, games. The youth of St. Ambrose. Julian the Apostate.

The death of Constantine II at Aquileia in his unfortunate attempt to subdue his brother had as its immediate consequence Constans's annexation of Gaul, Spain, and Britain. The high officials who had served under Constantine II apparently shared in his misfortune. At least there was a new prefect of Gaul at Trier in the spring of 340. We have no inkling of what happened to St. Ambrose's father. Paulinus is our only source of information about him, and since he is not mentioned again in the *Vita Ambrosii*, we may presume that he must have died during the course of these months. At any rate, the family returned to Rome, where Ambrose remained from 340 to around 365, that is, during all of his boyhood years.[1]

When a son of a prominent family in antiquity reached the use of reason, he was as a rule handed over to the care of a pedagogue, a slave specially chosen to instruct him. The great wealth of the *Ambrosii* would make us believe that in St. Ambrose's case this choice was made with great care. Ancient satirists all too often describe the pedagogue as a conniving accomplice in the precociously vicious habits of their young masters, but this was certainly not always the case. In his *Hexameron,* St. Ambrose may have been thinking of his own pedagogue when he wrote: "Things which frequently offend or terrify cowards, the weak, and the impious are, on the other hand, useful for others, just as pedagogues are for children. They seem to be bitter, sharp, and troublesome. They are feared for the whippings they inflict; they check licentiousness and demand discipline; with their threats they restrain the minds of children so that they do not become dissipated; through their austerities they make their charges temperate, and more dedicated to the pursuit of praise than play."[2]

We may gain some idea of the ancient pedagogue from Mardonius, an old Scythian slave to whom Julian, the future Apostate, was entrusted at the age of six in the year 337. In his writings, Julian frequently speaks of Mardonius and describes him as being most diligent in taking him to school, in helping him to repeat his lessons, in guiding him in his choice of reading, and in inspiring him with a love for spiritual things. "Never let the crowd of your playmates flocking to the theaters," Mardonius advised him, "lead you astray so that you crave such spectacles. Do you long for horse races? There is one most cleverly described in Homer. Take up the book and read it! Do you hear others talking about actors and dancers? Let them be! The youths among the Phaeacians dance in a more manly fashion. And you have Phemius for a citharode and Demodocus for a singer. Moreover, in Homer there are many many trees which afford us with more pleasure than those we see: 'Even so near the altar of Apollo on Delos did I once see the young shoot of a date palm burgeoning.' And there is the wooded isle of Calypso, and the caves of Circe, and the garden of Alcinous. Know well that you can not see anything more delightful than these."[3]

Since Julian was of a somewhat sanguine temperament, we must not believe that he was always convinced by the Stoicism of Mardonius. He even confesses that he at times rebelled.

Because of the high rank of his family, the young Ambrose must have been saved from the humiliations of the *ludus litterarius,* the name at this time for an elementary school.[4] There were many of these in the cities, and from the second century on, they were also to be found in provincial towns. The state took no interest in them as such since they were in the hands of private individuals.

Such a school was usually located in some cramped and

Roman covered wagon

A bas-relief in the church of St. Mary of Saal near Klagenfurt.

narrow quarter, usually in a portico opening onto the street with a curtain to cut off the distractions of the passing traffic. From the ages of seven to thirteen, boys and girls were sent to such a school to learn the rudiments of reading, writing, and arithmetic. Though Quintilian and Augustine are separated by more than two and a half centuries, they substantially agree upon the sad status of teaching in these schools.

Poor devils who did not know how to make a more decent living acted as teachers, since their pay, at least in the first century, was ridiculously low: eight asses, or about twenty-five cents, per month from each student. From very early in the morning until noon, they had to keep their charges in check; and to hold the attention of their students, they had frequent recourse to a switch.

Quintilian, who did not himself approve of flogging, noted some of its disadvantages: "When children are beaten, the pain or fear frequently produce results of which it is not pleasant to speak and which are likely afterwards to be a source of shame, a shame which unnerves and depresses the mind and induces the child to shun and loathe the light. One is ashamed to note how scoundrels abuse this right of corporal punishment if guardians and instructors are not carefully chosen."[5]

The desperate monotony of these schools only deadened the energies of the poor students. There was no method in the teaching, or the method seems to us to have been somewhat irrational as when, for example, children had to learn the names of the letters of the alphabet in order before they were to see the way they were written. This same technique was used in learning writing and arithmetic. Long hours were spent in counting on one's fingers: one and two on the right hand, and three and four on the left. "One and one makes two, two and two makes four, was for me a hateful chant," wrote St. Augustine when reflecting on what he suffered in his first years at school.[6]

And his memories were really painful. "As a child I began to pray to You, my aid and refuge, and I broke the chords of my tongue praying to You; and small though I was, with no small entreaty I prayed to You that I might not be beaten at school. And when You did not hear me (which should not have been accounted as folly on my part), my elders, and even my parents, who did not wish me to fall into any evil, made sport of the whippings I received and which at the time seemed to me to be a great and grievous evil."[7]

Since the schools were so poor, it is not surprising that at the end of the fourth century Vegetius deplored the illiteracy of many recruits who could not even keep track of their military expenses.[8]

As a boy, however, Ambrose was more fortunate than Augustine, and he received his elementary instruction at home.

The grammar school, the second step in the educational system in antiquity, roughly corresponded to our modern high schools. In such a school, children were taught how to speak correctly and to read the poets. For several centuries the teaching of grammar at Rome continued to show the same predilection for Greek and Greek culture as it had at its origins. But for the age of St. Ambrose, there is some question about the status of Greek in the schools. From what St. Augustine has to say about it, Greek does not seem to have been seriously studied in Roman Africa in the fourth century. Even St. Jerome, who studied grammar and rhetoric at Rome from about 359 to about 367, had later to learn Greek by himself.[9] It seems certain, however, that at least in the aristocratic circles, from which St. Jerome was excluded in his youth, Greek studies were still cultivated. Most of St. Ambrose's sermons show a dependence upon Greek authors. In November, 384, St. Jerome wrote a letter to Paula to console her for the loss of her daughter Blaesilla, who had died at the age of twenty, already a widow after a marriage that had lasted only seven months. Among the many things which he found to praise in Blaesilla, who had never lived outside of Rome, was the fact that she had spoken Greek so fluently that one would have thought that she knew no Latin.[10]

In the grammar schools, the texts of the poets, especially of Homer and Virgil, were minutely analyzed. There were many questions about style, metrics, music, mythology, history, astronomy, and mathematics, but these were always in some way connected with the explanation of the text. After the *emendatio,* that is, the criticism of the text, came the *enarratio,* or commentary on it, and finally, the *explanatio,* or exegesis of the text, carried out rather pedantically line by line or phrase by phrase.

A student had to practice reading in a loud voice, memorize passages that had been explained in class, and write themes. These could consist in rendering poetry into prose so as to express the ideas of the poem in one's own words or in freely developing the text.[11]

"I was bidden," writes St. Augustine, "to memorize the wanderings of a certain Aeneas (while I forgot my own errors) and to weep for Dido, dead because she had killed herself for love. . . . The wooden horse full of armed men, the burning of Troy, and the ghost of Creusa herself was for me a most delightful spectacle of vanity. . . . I was given a task, troublesome enough to my soul, under the promise of a reward of praise or the fear of shame and whipping; namely, that I should make a speech on those words of Juno expressing her anger and her sorrow that she could not keep the Trojan king from going to Italy. I had heard that Juno never uttered these words, yet we were bidden to imitate the passages of these poetic fictions and to turn into prose what the poet had expressed in verse. And whoever showed the greatest signs of grief or anger according to the dignity of the person represented and the subject matter received the most applause."[12]

This type of teaching, turned wholly on the past, was bound to be heavy and monotonous. Its usual result was a culture that was formal and pedantic, without interest in research or disinterested speculation. The typical intellectuals of this age manifest a distressing lack of originality of thought.

We do not know if Ambrose took pleasure in these "vain studies" as Augustine candidly confesses of himself.[13]

The most famous teachers in Rome at this time were Donatus and Marius Victorinus. While St. Jerome prides himself in recalling them, they are never even mentioned by St. Ambrose.

In many of his later works, St. Ambrose shows that he was quite familiar with Virgil, Cicero, Sallust, and Seneca, and among the Greeks, Homer, Plato, and Xenophon. His quotations from Sophocles and Euripides, on the other hand, seem to be taken from Philo.[14]

A young Roman usually finished grammar school at about the age of fifteen or sixteen, or even later. He then passed under the tutelage of a rhetorician until he was twenty or more. These rhetorical studies would thus correspond to a certain extent with those taken in our universities.[15]

In almost every city of the empire there was a rhetorical school where the theory of eloquence was taught and where students gained practice in writing and delivering speeches in defense of some imaginary culprit or in praise of some fictitious individual, or he proposed solutions to hypothetical cases in court. This teaching ought to have been complemented by courses in philosophy and law; but, in the fourth century, law was only studied at Rome, Constantinople, and Beirut, and philosophy only at Athens. In an edict of the year 425 given by Theodosius II to the university at Constantinople, we discover that there were in the city three Latin rhetoricians and ten Latin grammarians, five Greek rhetoricians and ten Greek grammarians, one philosopher and two jurisconsultants.[16]

At Rome, therefore, Ambrose could take courses in rhetoric and law. These were precisely the studies which could prepare him for a career in the imperial service. Seneca, Petronius, Tacitus, and Juvenal all speak disparagingly of the schools of rhetoric. We can gain some idea of them by reading the treatises of the rhetorician Seneca. The reading is so tedious and deadly that the author himself in the last book confesses his shame, as though he had lost too much time on trivialities.

It cannot be seriously maintained that every form of scholastic teaching must inevitably be reduced to empty shams. Rather, it is necessary to say that the schools were languishing at this time because public life itself was languishing and there was no longer room in this despotic and chaotic world for thought. Those of a nobler character were finding an escape in religion. Petronius was of the opinion "that the young lose their judgment in school where they hear or see nothing of that which occurs in real life, but, instead, pirates chained to a beach, tyrants issuing edicts bidding sons to cut off the heads of their parents, and answers to oracles demanding the sacrifice of virgins to ward off the plague."[17]

When speaking of his decision to quit teaching rhetoric at Milan, Augustine is no less scornful: "I decided in Your sight not to break off violently but to gently withdraw myself from the teaching of eloquence where words were sold so that boys, not meditating on Your law, nor on Your peace, but on a flock of crazy lies and forensic battles, should no longer purchase from me weapons for their madness."[18]

Moreover, in addition to the insignificance of Symmachus, the extravagance of Ausonius, and the ignorance of Nonius Marcellus, there was the added factor that almost all the teachers of the fourth century were pagan.

The aversion which St. Jerome, and still more St. Ambrose, had for rhetoric, philosophy, and mathematics, is thus quite understandable. In his denial of any value to pagan thought and philosophy, St. Ambrose became almost fanatical. But this may have been a kind of reaction to the endless weariness which he had experienced in the rhetorical schools of Rome.

Music formed an integral part of the study of metrics. At this particular period there was a rage for music almost like the enthusiasm that is shown today for popular singers and instrumentalists. Ammianus Marcellinus lamented the fact that houses which in former times were famous for their devotion to serious pursuits now re-echoed with the sound of singing and the tinkling of lyres and flutes. Libraries were shut up like tombs and people amused themselves with lyres as large as carriages, hydraulic organs, and other instruments of enormous size.[19] In his writings, St. Ambrose refers to music and musical instruments and to contests held for singers and musicians.[20] He writes so technically about these matters that it is obvious that he had received an exceptional education in music. We shall see the practical consequences of this when we take up his reform of the liturgy of his church.

St. Ambrose's first biographer mentions only one incident that occurred during his youth. When the *sacerdotes,* that is, the bishops, entered the house of the Ambrosii, his mother and sister used to kiss their hands. The young Ambrose liked to joke about this manifestation of reverence still very common in Catholic countries in the south. He thought that the companion of his sister Marcellina should also kiss his hand "since," as he said, "he would also become a bishop."[21] This is an extremely valuable bit of information since it confirms the fact that the family was Christian and that it was visited by Pope Liberius.

On the feast of the Epiphany in 353, his sister Marcellina consecrated her virginity to God.[22] Her reception of the veil took place in the Vatican basilica. Before receiving the vow of the young woman and placing the veil upon her head with a solemn prayer, Pope Liberius delivered a touching exhortation. Later, when speaking to the virgins of Milan, St. Ambrose was fond of recalling that great day in which he may also have had a part. Marcellina continued to live at home as she had done before, but Ambrose must have noticed some change in his sister, not only in the greater modesty of her dress but also in her comportment and occupations, even though the Church at the time did not impose any greater obligations in the matter of prayer or the exercise of charity upon those who professed continence than it did upon the ordinary run of Christians.

Marcellina's consecration of herself to a life of virginity should be associated with the fervent spirit of asceticism that had been brought to Rome by Athanasius, the bishop of Alexandria. After he had been driven for the second time into exile in 339, he had come to Rome to be near Pope Julius and remained there for more than two years as a guest in the home of the patrician Albina. Athanasius already enjoyed great renown for his numerous adventures in his struggle with the Arians. Exiled first by Constantine and later by Constantius II, in the eyes of the people of the West he personified the faith of Nicea. He and the two Egyptian monks who accompanied him never tired speaking about the solitaries of the Thebaid and the prodigies they performed. The first center of monastic life in the West thus took shape in the luxurious palace of the Marcelli on the Aventine. Marcella, the daughter of Albina, was the first conquest of this propaganda of Athanasius. She was later joined by Asella, Fabiola, and Principia, other young women of the Roman aristocracy. The practice of continence and asceticism was not something that had been introduced by Christianity into the world, but the desire to imitate Christ more closely and to carry His cross gave a special character to Christian virginity that elevated it far above the continence of pagan philosophers. During this period, especially in the East, the ardent desire for a solitary and continent life became almost a contagion. St. Basil had to recall the fact that a Christian could not leave his wife to go and become a monk without first obtaining her consent.[23] St. Nilus, who went to live as a solitary on Mt. Sinai after having been governor of Constantinople toward the end of the fourth century, has left an account of his ardent desire for eremitical life and the anguish he experienced on leaving his wife and two small sons: "I took my children, still very young, by the hand and led them to their mother. Giving one of them to her and keeping the other near me, I then disclosed to her what I had in mind. The tone of my voice and the expression on my face made her realize that my decision was final. It would have been useless to try and dissuade me, and she did not attempt it. Seeing that she could not oppose my departure, she gave her consent, but not without anguish. She was choked with grief, and tears ran down her cheeks. . . . You know how painful is the separation of those who are lawfully married. It is a suffering no less terrible than that caused by a sword which pierces one to the quick."[24]

In the general context of decadent paganism, these immoderate religious aspirations can find their explanation and justification.

Three years before Marcellina received the veil, Ambrose must have witnessed the catastrophe that made the eternal city flow red with blood after the usurpation of Magnentius.

In January, 350, a conspiracy against Constans, the Augustus of the West, originated in Gaul. It was begun by Marcellinus, the *comes rerum privatarum,* or minister of finance.

Flavius Magnus Magnentius, a barbarian who had come into Gaul as a prisoner in the time of Constantine the Great and was then in command of a body of troops, was hailed Augustus at the end of a banquet at Autun on the night of January 17. Constans fled toward Spain, but at Elna, at the foot of the Pyrenees, he was overtaken and killed by assassins by order of Magnentius. The latter remained ruler of Gaul, and very soon gained acceptance also in the vicariates and provinces of Spain, Britain, Africa, and Italy. Only the army in Illyricum refused to recognize him. Instead, it proclaimed an old general Vetranio Augustus. Philostorgius tells us that this nomination was due to the quick wit of Constantia, sister of Constans, and of Constantius II, who persuaded Vetranio to don the purple to confound the plans of Magnentius.[25] Constantia was at this time the widow of Hannibalian, who had been killed in the murder of the relatives of Constantine in 337. In that year Vetranio asked her to be his wife, but Constantius II forbade the marriage.

Rome had also recognized Magnentius as Augustus when there occurred a new change of scene. Flavius Popilius Nepotianus, son of Eutropia, and consequently grandson of Constantius Chlorus, was at Rome, and had already been consul in 336. Being convinced that he had a greater right to the purple than the barbarian Magnentius, he gathered together a band of wastrels and gladiators and had himself proclaimed Augustus at Rome on June 3, 350. The usurper of Gaul sent a prefect of the praetorium against him.

Nepotianus shut himself up in Rome and raged against the supporters of Magnentius until the latter sent Marcellinus against him with a large force. With the assistance of a traitor among the senators, the latter succeeded in routing the Romans. Nepotianus was killed, and his head, impaled on a stake, was carried about the streets of the city. A savage repression of the revolt followed immediately with the slaughter of his followers, and among these was Eutropia.

In the fall of 350, after settling affairs in the East, Constantius marched from Antioch toward Constantinople to tend to the situation developing in the West. Magnentius sent Marcellinus to enter into negotiations with him. He asked to be recognized as Augustus, admitting his own inferiority to one who was a higher Augustus. He offered his daughter to Constantius in marriage, and asked in turn for the hand of Constantia, the latter's sister. But Constantius came to terms first with Vetranio with the promise of a pension. In secure possession of superior forces, he rejected the proposals of Magnentius. Later it was reported that his father, Constantine the Great, had appeared to him in a dream, bidding him to vindicate his brother Constans.

On September 28, 351, a great battle took place at Mursa, the modern Eszek, or Osijek, on the banks of the river Drava, between Hungary and Yugoslavia. After his defeat, Magnentius repaired to Aquileia. According to Sulpicius Severus, Constantius II, a sad and eccentric emperor if there ever was one, remained praying all during the battle in the church of the martyrs of Mursa, and the day after went to the field where it had taken place and wept to see the plain covered with tens of thousands of bodies.[26] In 352 Constantius invaded Italy, occupied Sicily, Africa, and Spain, and despite an unfortunate encounter at Pavia, succeeded in forcing Magnentius back into Gaul. Finally, Magnentius, after having been again routed at Mt. Saleon, committed suicide at Lyons on August 10, 353. Constantius II then became the sole Augustus of the Roman world.

At the time, Constantius was thirty-six years old, and infatuated with his imperial dignity. Small in stature, with twisted limbs, ugly, and rather ludicrous, he spoke little, and when he did it was in a low voice. As a persecutor of paganism and of orthodoxy, he numbered among his personal enemies the most prominent men of the age: Julian, Ammianus Marcellinus, Athanasius, and Hilary. Suspicious and given to intrigues, he was eminently successful in making himself hated by all. It may be, however, that he also had some redeeming qualities and that his sorry reputation is at least in part due to the fact that Christian writers could not pardon his Arian intransigency, and pagan writers in their turn his intolerance.

Arianism may be described as the translation into theological terms of an attempt to laicize and nationalize the Church.[27] In making Christ a creature no matter how sublime, it destroyed the mystery of the Blessed Trinity and at the same time undermined the mysteries connected with the life of Christ and the uniqueness of Christianity and the Church's claim to immunity from any interference on the part of the State in carrying out its functions as mediatrix between men and God. Arianism reduced Christianity to the level of every other naturally religious doctrine and, as a consequence, logically denied its own autonomy. Not without some reason it has been maintained that the empire should have instinctively favored Arius and his doctrine in order to regain what it had lost, that is, control over the freedom of the individual conscience which seemed to detract from the absolute power of the Augustus.[28] But if it would be going too far to attribute such an intuition to the political Arianism of Constantine the Great, it would be a still greater error to attribute it to his son Constantius.

But the latter was, at any rate, dominated in his relations with the Church by a group of Arian bishops.

In May, 325, some three hundred bishops assembled for the Council of Nicea (the modern Iznik in Turkey). Constantine had gone to the trouble of inviting them from all over the

Roman world, placing at their disposal the carriages of the public post. The council condemned Arius and his followers. Christ was defined as being of the same nature as the Father: ὁμοούσιος τῷ πατρί, *consubstantialis patri.* The formula is non-biblical and had been rejected some decades earlier by the Council of Antioch in their condemnation of Paul of Samosata, who had given it a Sabellian meaning; that is, he had taught that the Son is only a manifestation of the Father, not a person distinct from Him. But in 325 the Council of Nicea decided that the formula expressed their opposition to Arianism in affirming that Christ is God just as the Father is God and is in no sense inferior to Him. The Arian bishops were deposed, and Constantine sent them into exile. But in 328, only three years after the council, during which time Athanasius had become bishop of Alexandria, Constantine agreed to recall three Arian bishops from exile, Eusebius of Nicomedia, Marus of Chalcedon, and Theognis of Nicea. These were relying upon the favor and protection of Constantine's mother and sister.

Unfortunately, the teacher of a number of Arian priests and bishops and the source of their errors, Lucian of Antioch, had died as a martyr at Nicomedia under Maximinus Daia in 311-312. He had been buried at Drepanum on the eastern bank of the Sea of Marmara at the entrance to the Gulf of Nicomedia. The town was later known as Helenopolis from the fact that Helena had been born there. She had, moreover, a very great devotion to the martyr buried there.

This was the beginning of a very sad affair. The three Arian bishops that had been rehabilitated won over the sympathies of Constantine and used them to destroy the Council of Nicea. All the orthodox bishops were deposed and exiled one after another, beginning with the bishop of Antioch, the populous capital of the East. The espiscopal sees represented not only positions of great honor, but also of great material resources. Ever since Constantine in 321 had recognized the juridical status of the churches and their capacity to inherit, church properties, already common in the third century, were constantly being increased.

Then it was Athanasius's turn. After many unsuccessful attempts, the Arian cabal succeeded in bringing an accusation against Athanasius at the Council of Tyre in the summer of 335. He received an order to appear. With forty-nine Egyptian bishops who, however, were not able to participate in the deliberations because they were not invited, he went to Tyre.

There are always malcontents and all the more so when the one in command is as resolute as Athanasius. The principal charge laid against him was that he had broken the chalice of Ischiras, a self-appointed priest of the Mareotis, the region between Alexandria and the Libyan desert, who had arrogated to himself the right of celebrating the Eucharist in his village. Macharius, a priest, commissioned by Athanasius to visit the districts of the Mareotis, had forbidden this and had perhaps made use of some external sign to make the prohibition still more impressive. At the trial in Tyre, which was based on such trivialities, the Arians had civil servants and soldiers at their disposition. They decided to send six bishops to Egypt to make an investigation on the spot. Here, for the first time, there appear as members of this inquisition two young bishops of Pannonia, Ursacius and Valens. They will appear again later in the struggle with St. Ambrose. The six members of the commission behaved scandalously in Egypt. The priests and deacons of the Mareotis, who would have testified that Ischiras was not a priest and that no chalice had been broken, were not even able to get a hearing, while in the meantime the military escort of the bishop beat and killed the faithful, and the bishops themselves feasted on days of fast.

Athanasius realized that all that was sought at Tyre was his condemnation, so he departed. The council was still in session when a letter arrived from Constantine inviting all its members to come to Constantinople. On October 30, 335, when the emperor was returning to the city on horseback, he was suddenly confronted by Athanasius, who stopped him in the middle of the street and asked that he be heard along with his accusers.[29] The emperor gave his consent. The audience which followed has already been noted: it ended with the first exile of Athanasius to Trier.

In November of this same year Arius, also through the intervention of the emperor, was readmitted into the Church by means of an ambiguous profession of faith. But this could not be effected at Alexandria since the people rose up, causing Constantine to fear a rebellion. It was then decided that Arius should be readmitted at Constantinople, but on the evening before the reconciliation, while he was being conducted through the city in triumph, in the square where the porphyry column with the statue of Constantine stood, he felt himself suddenly stricken and entering a public restroom he died, as his bowels burst according to the account of ancient historians.[30]

To compensate themselves for the death of Arius, the bishops gathered at Constantinople condemned and deposed Marcellus of Ancyra because he supported Athanasius and Nicea.

Finally at noon, on Pentecost, May 22, 337, Constantine died in his villa of Ancyra near Nicomedia after receiving baptism on his deathbed from Eusebius, the Arian bishop of Nicomedia. On November 23, 337, Athanasius returned to Alexandria.

From the very beginning of his rule, Constantius II entrusted himself to the guidance of a group of Arian bishops. In 338, these bishops first sought to have the condemnation of Tyre in 335 and the results of that notorious inquest recognized by Pope Julius at Rome. But later, with Constantius's approval, they nominated a successor to Athanasius in the person of Gregory of Cappadocia, who was immediately consecrated bishop and sent into Egypt.[31] Even if Athanasius had been legitimately deposed, which was not the case, his successor should at least have been elected by the clergy and people of Alexandria, and then consecrated by the bishops of the province, as was the universal custom at this time. Philagrius, the prefect of Egypt and a personal enemy of Athanasius, received orders from Constantius to install the new bishop. On March 18, 339, he expelled Athanasius after storming a church in which some were wounded and others slain. The building itself was then set on fire and burned along with the neighboring baptistry. Four days later Gregory entered the city. Accompanied by soldiers he passed from one church to another to take possession of them. On Good Friday he had thirty-four people seized and beaten in a church because they had resisted him. Athanasius wrote a letter of protest to all the bishops of the world, and it forms one of the most moving pages in Patristic literature. He begins by recalling the Levite of Ephraim whose wife, according to the Biblical account, had been slain by the wickedness of the men of Gabaa. He placed her body on an ass, and coming to his house he cut it up into twelve pieces and sent a piece to each of the twelve tribes of Israel to arouse their indignation so that they might avenge the offense.[32] This is what Athanasius says they have done to his church. What has just happened surpasses all the horrors of the persecutions. This is what makes the pagans blaspheme and persuades them to believe that the consecration of bishops in the Church is no more than a question of bribery and violence on the part of the civil authorities. If the bishops remain silent there is danger that the evil will spread: their episcopal sees will become objects of trade and commerce. He then recalls the acts of violence, the murders, the violations of virgins, and the profanations and burnings of the churches.

Julius, the bishop of Rome, answered this letter by summoning a council to which he invited Athanasius. The council, which was assembled at Rome in 341, recognized Athanasius as the only lawful bishop of Alexandria. In the letter which Julius wrote to the bishops of the East to notify them of its decisions he placed his finger on the source of the evils—that discouraging lack of Christian spirit which the bishops manifested by their scandalous rivalry: "Dearly beloved, it is not in keeping with the Gospel for the decisions of the Church to be condemnations to death and exile."[33] Nevertheless, although he was recognized at Rome, Athanasius was not able to return to his see. In 342, Pope Julius together with the bishops Hosius of Cordova and Maximinus of Trier asked Constans, the Augustus of the West, to intercede with Constantius II. A council was agreed upon, to be held in 343 at Sardica in the Balkans, the modern Sophia. Ninety-four bishops from the West and seventy-six from the East came for the meetings, but the Arian bishops of the East refused to take part in them until Athanasius and Basil of Ancyra should have been summarily condemned. Hosius tried every means of compromise, but in vain. The Arians, confident in the support of Constantius II, suddenly left Sardica, and as they were leaving, they sent out an encyclical letter which condemned not only Athanasius but also Pope Julius and all his other supporters. The bishops who remained proceeded with the regular business of the council. The faith of Nicea was reaffirmed. Athanasius was declared innocent; the bishops who had usurped his see were excommunicated along with Ursacius and Valens. The final statement of the council was a solemn declaration of the right of the Church to its spiritual independence and the expression of a desire that the civil magistrates should not occupy themselves with matters about which only the Church could decide. In the matter of ecclesiastical discipline, the Council of Sardica ordered that an end should be put to the abuse of ordaining a rich layman, lawyer, or public official as bishop. Only one who was already within the hierarchy of the Church should be elected. Another abuse was the passing of a bishop from one see to another. Who was ever seen passing to a smaller or poorer church? Here was another proof of ambition and self-interest. Every bishop changing his see should be deposed and excommunicated. It was just at this time that

Valens of Mursa was doing everything he could to obtain the see of Antioch.

But since the bishops of the Orient, for the most part Arian, had taken no part in the council, the legislation of Sardica remained largely theoretical.

Constantius II fell under the ever increasing influence of the bishops of the East even though their former leader, Eusebius of Nicomedia, had died toward the end of 341. He put the imperial post at their disposal so that they could travel far and wide arresting bishops who had been reconciled at Sardica and persecuting their supporters. One of the leaders of the Arian faction was Stephen, bishop of Antioch. The scandal which occurred at Antioch on Easter, 344, can furnish us with some idea of their way of acting.

At Antioch, where Constantius II was busy making preparations for his war against the Persians, there arrived as delegates from the Council of Sardica, Vincentius of Capua and Euphrates of Cologne. They brought with them a letter from Constans asking Constantius II to permit the return of the exiled bishops to their own churches. But Stephen, the Arian bishop of Antioch, tried to discredit them with an ugly trick. The hotel in which the two orthodox bishops were staying was some distance from the others. Scoundrels hired by Stephen bribed a servant of the hotel. They procured a woman of the street and led her into the room where the bishop of Cologne was sleeping. The night was rent by the shouts of the surprised bishop and of the woman, who was dumbfounded at finding herself in the presence of an old man and bishop. The villains immediately ran into the room in order to be able to tell later what had happened. The bishops, however, had the outer gates shut at once, and the woman and those who had brought her were arrested. The following day Salianus, the head of the band given by Constans as an escort to the legates, came to the hotel and asked Constantius II for an inquest. Stephen was deposed. The Christian communities even in the East would have nothing to do with bishops of this kind.[34]

When after two years on the episcopal throne, Eusebius of Nicodemia died at Constantinople, his followers were extremely anxious to get as his successor the Arian Macedonius. But since the faithful were still loyal to their exiled bishop, Paul of Thessalonica, there was such an outbreak of violence in 342 that the general Hermogenes, a *magister militum,* was slain and his body dragged through the streets. Constantius II then hastened from Antioch to Constantinople. He drove Paul out of the city and punished the people by cutting in half the free distribution of grain which they had been receiving from the governor.

Meanwhile, on June 25, the intruder, Gregory of Cappodocia, died at Alexandria. Constantius then recalled Athanasius, but the latter put off his return for more than a year. He feared some trick and also wanted everything to be in order, one of the requirements being a return to the faith of Nicea. Eventually he decided to leave Aquileia. He passed through Róme, where the faithful rejoiced to see again the famous bishop who had been for years a guest of their church. He then went to Antioch, where he found Constantius II. The emperor swore that all the accusations against the bishop had been destroyed. Athanasius's reception at Alexandria on October 21, 346, was a triumph.

In the West, Ursacius and Valens, sensing the change of wind, came to Rome to offer their submission to Pope Julius. They abjured their Arianism and accepted Athanasius into their communion. The Council of Sardica had deposed them, but Pope Julius in his desire for peace restored them to their sees.

A kind of truce lasted from 346 to 350. Constantius was being continually threatened by the Persians and did not wish to antagonize his brother Constans, a Catholic and favorable to the Catholics. But when, through the usurpation of Magnentius, Constans was removed from the scene and, even worse, when Constantius II became the sole ruler of the Roman world after the death of Magnentius in August, 353, the sad effects of Caesaropapism were soon felt even in the West. This began with the removal of Photinus, the anti-Arian bishop of Sirmium. Though he was not orthodox, he was deposed and sent into exile. He was replaced by Germinius, an Arian bishop who came from Cyzicus. Athanasius was accused of having entered into secret agreements with Constans and Magnentius. In the meantime, on April 12, 352, Pope Julius died, and on May 17, his successor, Liberius, was elected.

Early in 353, while Constantius was at Milan, Athanasius sent Serapion of Thmuis with four other Egyptian bishops to the court. At this same time Athanasius received a letter from Constantius through an imperial messenger granting his request to be present *ad comitatum,* that is, at the court. Since Athanasius had made no such request he understood that his enemies had sent the prince a forged letter. He accordingly replied that he was ready to appear but he wanted an order to that effect. It did not come.

Towards the end of 353, Pope Liberius sent two legates, Vincentius and Marcellus, bishops of Campania, to Arles, where Constantius was spending the winter, to ask the emperor to summon a general council at Aquileia. Unfortunately, Ursacius and Valens were at this time living at the court and dominating it. They had already carefully renounced the retraction they had made at Rome to Pope Julius after their condemnation at Sardica. In general, the bishops of the West had not as yet taken any part in the Arian controversy. It was thus easy for Constantius to obtain the signatures of the bishops of Gaul to a condemnation of Athanasius at a council held at Arles in the fall of 353. Even the papal legates were induced to add their signatures to the condemnation. Paulinus, the bishop of Trier, was the only one who refused. Then, as Hilary of Poitiers observes with bitter sarcasm, "The other bishops judged him to be unworthy of the Church, while the emperor judged him to be deserving of exile."[35] On this occasion Constantius had the opportunity of showing his animosity to Pope Liberius by accusing him of ambition and intrigues. When the pope learned what had happened at Arles, he wrote another letter of protest renewing his demand for the summoning of a real council which would confirm the faith of Nicea and settle various other problems.

Constantius feigned consent. Instead of at Aquileia, the council was held at Milan between January and May, 355. There, together with a few bishops from the East, were assembled at least thirty bishops of the West. Pope Liberius sent as his legates Lucifer, bishop of Cagliari, the priest Pancratius, and the deacon Hilary. At Milan, as it had been at Arles, Constantius's first item on the agenda was the condemnation of Athanasius. Eusebius of Vercelli, however, asked that the bishops should first sign the creed of Nicea, and he brought out a copy of it for this purpose. Dionysius, the bishop of Milan, picked up a pen and was on the point of signing the parchment when Valens of Mursa rushed up and seized both pen and parchment, shouting out that such a procedure was inadmissible.[36] Such violence in a crowded church so distressed and angered the Catholics of Milan that it was thought best to transfer the place of meeting to the imperial palace.

Determined to carry the day, Constantius summoned the three orthodox leaders, Lucifer, Eusebius, and Dionysius. He tried to influence them with threats and promises, but in vain. Contrary to the other thirty bishops who capitulated, these three bishops remained steadfast and would neither condemn Athanasius nor deny the faith of Nicea.

As Athanasius wrote later, they believed that "exile was a part of their ministry." Lucifer was sent in chains to Germanicia in Syria, Eusebius to Scythopolis in Palestine, and Dionysius perhaps to a mountain village of Cappadocia, all being placed under the surveillance of Arian bishops. They were followed by the regrets and esteem of their flocks. Pope Liberius wrote a letter to commend and console them. The Arians invited to the see of Milan Auxentius, a Cappadocian who did not even know how to speak Latin, the language of his new subjects.

Pope Liberius remained to be dealt with. Constantius sent him a eunuch of the court with a letter asking for his signature to the condemnation of Athanasius. In his efforts to win over the pope, he sent along with the letter a number of valuable gifts. But Liberius refused to sign. The eunuch placed the gifts on the Confession, that is, on the altar over the tomb of St. Peter in the Vatican basilica, but the pope had them thrown out of the church. The prefect of the city was then ordered to seize Liberius and send him off to Milan. Ammianus Marcellinus writes that because of the populace, who were devotedly attached to him, the pope had to be spirited away at night, and that with the greatest difficulty.[37] St. Ambrose at the time was about twenty years old, and he must have shared in the popular dismay at the loss of Liberius.

A stenographic report of the dramatic encounter between pope and emperor in the imperial palace at Milan has been preserved. Since he continued to resist the condemnation of Athanasius, Liberius was sent into exile at Beroea (the modern Stara Zagora in Bulgaria), where he was kept under the watchful eye of Bishop Demophilus, one of the Arian leaders.

During this same year of 355, the nonagenarian bishop Hosius was summoned from Spain to the court at Milan. When the Arians were unable to win him over, he was dismissed by Constantius, who later wrote him a number of letters.

In the meantime measures were being taken in Egypt to secure the banishment of Athanasius. During the summer an imperial notary failed to overcome the resistance of the people and the magistrates. Another notary was then sent to Alexandria, but this time with troops and an imperial officer.

On the night of February 8, 356, while Athanasius was

celebrating a vigil with his people in the church of Theonas, the building was surrounded by soldiers. They broke down the doors and killed some of the faithful, but Athanasius managed to escape. After eight months of lay rule, the Church of Alexandria, on February 24, 357, received a new bishop, George of Cappadocia. The latter was the son of a Cilician laborer. He had held an administrative post at Constantinople but had been dismissed for his unscrupulous conduct. Later he engaged in a number of different occupations. For a time he provided various military installations with pork for the soldiers, and then he decided to enter the clergy of one of the churches in Cappadocia. About the year 345 he met Constantius and became such a good friend of his that he was told to visit Julian, who at this time was sequestered in the magnificent palace of Macellum at the foot of Mount Argaeus (the modern Erciyas Dagi) near Caesarea in Cappadocia.[38] After he had come to know George, the fifteen-year-old Julian decided that Christians fought each other like wild beasts. At his own home, not far from Macellum, George had a beautiful library. Julian was allowed to use it, and there he eagerly read the works of Origen and Eusebius of Caesarea along with those of pagan rhetoricians and philosophers, and among these latter the writings of Porphyry and Iamblicus in particular, the last of the Neoplatonists.

When Julian as emperor was informed of the murder of George at Alexandria in 362, he wrote to the prefect of Egypt to gather up the remains of his library, which he had come to esteem as a youth, and send it to him at Antioch.

After his appointment as bishop of Alexandria, George entered the city in February, 357, and succeeded in staying there for eighteen months.[39] He banished sixteen Egyptian bishops, sent those of the clergy who remained faithful to Athanasius to the mines, and forbade assemblies in the city. When Duke Sebastian, whom the emperor had nominated as his right arm, discovered that secret meetings were being held in the cemeteries, George reacted at once. He ordered the virgins and the other women to be flogged with thorned branches and the men to be banished. On the side he engaged in various business enterprises. He got control of the salt beds, the areas employed for the cultivation of papyrus, and even monopolized the funeral processions. In August, 358, the Alexandrians, tired of it all, attacked him in church. He fled and was not seen for another three years. Athanasius, in his turn, was wandering about the desert, but always secretly so as not to be taken by the agents of Constantius.

A successor to the exiled Liberius was appointed in the person of the Roman archdeacon Felix. He was consecrated in the imperial palace at Milan by three Arian bishops in the presence of three eunuchs who represented the people. Although he gained acceptance with a few of the clergy at Rome, most of the faithful refused to recognize him, regarding him as being nothing more than a heretic and intruder.

In Gaul, however, toward the end of 355, a return to orthodoxy was being set in motion through the efforts of Hilary of Poitiers. Hilary was a noble pagan convert living a holy life with his wife and daughter when, about the year 353, the bishop of the city died. Hilary was enthusiastically elected as his successor by the people of Poitiers. Upon the return of the bishops from Milan after the condemnation of Athanasius, Hilary realized that he would have to oppose their decision. But the Arian Saturninus of Arles in a council at Béziers, probably in the spring of 356, succeeded in quashing Hilary's opposition. Constantius was thus able to exile Hilary as he had earlier the other orthodox bishops. From 356 to 360, as a consequence, Hilary was banished to Asia Minor.

Constantius could now boast that he had subjected nearly all of the churches of the empire to his own theological tenets. In addition to his own victories over the bishops, his generals had defeated Magnentius and various German tribes. The emperor decided that it would be proper to go to Rome with a powerful force to celebrate his different triumphs.

In the fourth century Rome still preserved a great deal of her ancient splendor. Ammianus Marcellinus, Rutilius Namatianus, Themistius, Ausonius, and Prudentius all agree in singing her praises: Rome was the queen of the world, an ocean of beauty, the first city of the world.

At this time, Rome was still a very large city, though its population had somewhat declined from the 800,000 or so inhabitants that lived there during the flourishing period of the second century.[40] The *regionarii,* or rudimentary guides to the city, of this period list 1,782 *domus,* or private palaces, and 46,290 *insulae,* or apartments, each with five or six separate quarters for rent. These apartments were often five and six stories high, heaped up on dark narrow streets, without running water, and offering few conveniences to the masses of citizens. The homes of the wealthy, on the other hand, were well equipped and richly adorned with marble and mosaics.

Pagan priests banded together in sacred colleges drew large profits from the numerous temples scattered throughout the various regions of the city. Eleven huge public baths provided convenient social centers for thousands of the citizens. The Baths of Caracalla had some 1,600 marble seats for visitors, and the Baths of Diocletian almost twice that number. Connected with the baths were shops, gymnasia, libraries, and gardens, walks, and covered porticoes. And in addition to these large public establishments there were 856 smaller baths under private management. Then, too, there were the various fora with their arches, columns, temples, and basilicas. Among the most impressive of these was the Forum of Trajan with its enormous covered market, basilica used as a court of law, and column standing between two great libraries.

The Circus Maximus, which served as one of the sites for horse races, had seats for 150,000 spectators. The theaters of Balbus with 7,700 seats, of Marcellus with 14,000, and of Pompey with 17,000 were always active during the summer. Finally, there was the Colosseum with its 45,000 seats and standing room for 5,000 more. Throughout the whole of the fourth century it continued to be a site for gladiatorial combats and wild beast hunts.

Constantius entered the city on April 28, 357, and remained there until May 29. According to Ammianus Marcellinus, he rode into the city on a golden chariot gleaming with precious stones.[41] He was surrounded by a large military force. The soldiers of the different corps carried large banners, and their standards were adorned with gold and jewels. Cavalrymen dressed in Persian fashion with their whole bodies covered with armor were a particular object of attraction. Constantius himself, though he was hailed on all sides, remained in a statuesque pose, without turning his face either to the right or to the left. But this was typical of his constant endeavor to preserve the imperial dignity. As Ammianus notes on at least two occasions, Constantius was never seen spitting, blowing his nose, or wiping his mouth in public.

During the course of his stay in Rome, Constantius addressed the senators and nobles in the curia, and the people in the forum. He visited the sights of the city, the baths, the amphitheater, and the Pantheon; but when he came to the Forum of Trajan, "he stood fast in amazement," in the words of Ammianus, "turning his attention to the huge complex about him that beggars description and which will never again be imitated by mortal men." Ormisda, a brother of the king of Persia and a refugee at the Roman court from the time of Constantine, was standing near him at the time. When Constantius asked him what he thought of Rome, he replied that his greatest satisfaction was to have learned that even there men were mortal. As a memorial of his own visit, Constantius decided to erect a superb obelisk in the Circus Maximus. This was one which his father had previously brought from Heliopolis to Alexandria.

In his visit to Rome, Constantius was accompanied by his wife Eusebia and his sister Helena, the wife of Julian, who was at this time in Gaul. The Christian nobles at Rome thought that this would be an opportune time to ask for the return of Pope Liberius. Since this would have been a dangerous request for the men to make, it was made by a delegation of women dressed in all their finery. Among them may well have been Ambrose's mother and sister. They begged the emperor to have compassion on the city, deprived as it was of its shepherd and exposed to the ravaging of wolves. When Constantius replied that Rome already had a shepherd to rule her, they told him that no one entered a church when Felix was in it. Although he himself subscribed to the faith of Nicea, he communicated with those who denied it. The emperor is then supposed to have said that Liberius was about to return, and "better than before," that is, as an Arian. But the accuracy of this report is quite doubtful. At any rate, it is certain that when some time later Constantius sent a letter to Rome to inform the people that Liberius would return and would govern the Church there together with Felix, the people cried out in jest as they heard the letter being read by the prefect of the city in the circus: "This is good! Just as there are two distinct factions in the circus with different colors for each, so there will be a different bishop for each party in the Church." Their laughter then turned to anger, and all cried out together: "One God, one Christ, and one bishop!"

After two years, the rigors of exile caused the unfortunate collapse of Pope Liberius's resistance. He signed a formula of compromise (but which, however, did not deny the faith of Nicea), accepted the excommunication of Athanasius, and wrote letters to the bishops of the East and of Campania to intercede with Constantius for his return to Rome.[42] But the emperor left him waiting for another year. Finally, on July 29, 358, Liberius was able to re-enter Rome. He was given a triumphal reception. Felix had to withdraw to an estate he owned on the Via Portuensis. In the fall of this year, he attempted to occupy the Basilica Julia (Santa Maria in Trastevere) with some of his followers, but he failed to do so since the people themselves intervened. From then on he remained isolated until his death on November 22, 365.

During these eventful years, Ambrose was following the course of rhetoric at Rome, and we may well believe that he was passionately interested in the various shifts in Constantius's religious policy. Though he was a Christian, the emperor was a persecutor of both pagans and Catholics. Rome at the time was still two-thirds pagan, and the Catholic minority had little knowledge of, and still less sympathy for, Arianism.

While he was at Rome, Constantius had the altar of Victory removed from in front of the senate, giving as his reason the offense which this altar gave to the Christian senators. It had been placed at the entrance of the hall, and it was customary for senators before entering the building to burn a grain of incense upon it. The statue of Victory, on the other hand, stood at the end of the hall on a base about a yard wide, which can furnish us with some idea of the size of the statue itself. The latter was a noble war prize taken from Tarentum which Augustus had placed on its pedestal in the senate on August 29, 29 B.C. Before this venerated symbol, the senate swore fidelity to the new ruler, and each year before this same statue it offered prayers and vows for the prosperity of both the emperor and the empire.[43]

The majority of the older students at Rome were pagan. They came there from all over the empire. Their life, like that of university students at Athens and Carthage, was not exactly tedious. From the life of St. Basil, who was a student at Athens about the year 350, and from the writings of Libanius, Himerius, and Eunapius, we are well informed about student activities in this ancient Greek city, and they could not have been much different at Rome during this same period. There were student frays almost every day.[44] Newcomers were frequently treated to blows from clubs wielded by members of the different scholarly or athletic factions. The professors themselves had few scruples about mixing into the turmoil. Himerius, a famous professor of rhetoric, was once so seriously wounded that he had to postpone his lectures.

Some teachers, to secure a larger number of students, would entertain them with good dinners or even in some worse way. A new student was initiated with a solemn procession intended to parody the ceremonies at Eleusis.

St. Augustine in his *Confessions* has left a vivid description of university life at Carthage. Among the students was a group known as the *eversores*, or "spoilers," who preyed upon the simplicity of the newcomers.[45] Student life was so free that St. Augustine's mother found it necessary to exhort her son not to fall into fornication and above all not to commit adultery.[46] At Rome the students were no better than they were at Carthage, as Augustine found out when he arrived there in 383. He failed to collect the tuition that was due to him since the students were squandering it on other interests. St. Jerome, who studied rhetoric at Rome from 360 to 365, later spoke with regret of the errors of those years. In a letter written in 384 to a young girl with the rather strange name of Eustochium, he recalls the temptations that plagued him even in the desert:

> "How often, when I was living in the desert, in that vast solitude parched by the burning rays of the sun which gives a savage dwelling place to hermits, did I imagine that I was among the pleasures of Rome? I used to sit alone because I was filled with bitterness. My unshapely limbs were rudely clothed in sackcloth, and my skin from long neglect had become as black as an Ethiopian's. Tears and groans were my daily portion; and, if drowsiness ever overcame my struggles against it, my bare bones, which were scarcely knit together, clashed against the ground. Of my food and drink I shall say nothing, since even when they are ill, solitaries take nothing but cold water, and for them to

> eat anything cooked is regarded as self-indulgence. And yet, through fear of hell I had condemned myself to such a prison, where my only companions were scorpions and wild beasts, I often imagined that I found myself amidst bevies of girls from Rome. My face was pale and my body chilled with fastings, but my mind was burning with desires, and the fires of lust kept boiling up before me when my flesh was as good as dead."[47]

In another letter which he wrote in 375-376 to friends at Aquileia commending his young sister to them, he speaks of "the slippery path of youth" on which he himself "had fallen."[48]

The merry bands of students created such a turmoil with their none-too-innocent amusements that on March 12, 370, Valentinian issued an edict forbidding students from the provinces to continue their studies at Rome beyond their twentieth year.[49]

Still, the students could not have been so very much different from the rest of the people of Rome. We have already pointed out the enormous capacity of the theaters, the baths, and the circuses. The imperial grain supply had to provide free rations for more than one hundred and fifty thousand heads of families during the second century. If we take into account the fact that there must have been at least three or four members to each family, this means that at least half a million people were dependent upon the public dole. In addition to these there were the relatively few very wealthy senatorial families, mounting up to a few hundred at the most. Neither the very poor nor the very wealthy had any real work to do. Between these two classes were the businessmen, for the most part merchants and shopkeepers. Even these did not work more than seven hours a day during the summer and six in winter. Moreover, the actual working days during the course of the centuries had been greatly reduced by the introduction of new feast days. No people have had so many feasts as the Romans of the imperial centuries. During this period there were some one hundred and ninety obligatory feast days each year. Thus for every work day there was a feast day, except when there were two of the latter. And this does not include the extraordinary feasts such as those marking the arrival of Constantius at Rome in 357. To keep the people occupied and amused, new baths, theaters, and amphitheaters were erected in or about the city.

The circuses were thronged from morning till night. When there was a spectacle, there were as many as a hundred races a day. The gaily dressed crowds came to them in tens and hundreds of thousands. Sports parties now supplanted the ancient political factions. They were distinguished by the different colors worn by the horses and their jockeys. There were the Whites, the Greens, the Blues, and the Reds. Bets were placed in every part of the circus. The fans were so keen for their favorite horses that we find the names of the latter in the mosaics on the floors of the baths. On the floor of a bath in Numidia has been found the name of a horse that had been victorious at Rome. It may still be read today: *Vincas non vincas, te amamus Polydoxe*—"Whether you win or not, we love you Polydoxus."

Interest in the theater seems to have been somewhat less. During the Empire, and also in the fourth century, women appeared upon the stage, though they played mostly the part of mimes. Two types of drama were particularly popular. There were the highly tragic plays with violent plots such as the *Banquet of Thyestes* or the *Madness of Ajax,* and there were those of a romantic character. The indecency and morbid sensuality of the mimes and erotic plays were so bad that we shall see Ambrose obtaining a decree from Gratian freeing actresses who became converts from the obligation of continuing in their profession. It was obviously regarded as being incompatible with a Christian life.

St. Augustine spends a whole chapter of his *Confessions* describing the shows in the theater "full of portraits of my misery and of fuel for the flame that burned me."[50] The "tragedies" often became just that in reality since it became customary to substitute a condemned criminal for the actor at the end of the play. The torments thus ceased to be imaginary. In the tragedy *Hercules on Mt. Aetna,* for example, the hero actually died in anguish in the flames, and in the *Laureolus,* the mime was actually nailed to the cross. Aberrations such as these, which seem incredible to us, were tolerated for centuries. It is not surprising, then, that Ambrose and other Fathers of the Church did not hesitate to openly condemn such perversions.

The amphitheaters provided even worse spectacles. At times there were shows where the contestants fought with blunted weapons, or where chariots were drawn by wild animals, or where elephants wrote Latin phrases on the sand. But these were the exception. As a rule the combats were all too real. Thousands of Romans, from morning till evening for whole days together, were intoxicated at the sight of continuous slaughter and barbarous sacrifices. Already in the time of Nero, Seneca had protested against the debasing influences of such sights. At certain times the spectacles became even more cruel. Men and women were left naked in the arena as prey to wild beasts without any means of defense. Christians were often condemned to this penalty *ad bestias.* Among the most moving accounts of the early persecutions are the descriptions of the deaths of Perpetua and Felicitas in the amphitheater at Carthage and of Blandina and her companions in that of Lyons.

In 326 Constantine forbade condemnations *ad bestias,* but we do not know to what extent this edict was observed. Certain it is that the butchery in the amphitheaters continued throughout the whole of the fourth century. Toward the end of 393, Symmachus experienced one of the greatest disappointments of his life. He had made extensive preparations for the games which he presided over to celebrate the appointment of his young son as quaestor. One of the most sensational numbers on the program was to have been a battle fought by twenty-nine Saxon prisoners whom Symmachus had obtained at considerable expense. But on the very day of the feast the barbarians got an unfortunate notion into their heads. Without considering the resentment of the people or the popularity of the young quaestor, which was bound to be diminished by their act, they strangled each other with their "impious" hands. Typically, Symmachus consoled himself for his loss "by thinking of Socrates and philosophy."[51]

Just as the boys of antiquity tricked "their pedagogues, their teachers, and their parents with countless lies in their love for play and their desire to see frivolities,"[52] so a passion for the games in the amphitheaters obsessed their elders. Alypius, who had gone to Rome some time before Augustine to study law, "was incredibly carried away by his ardent longing for the gladiatorial shows. At first he utterly detested and opposed such spectacles, but one day he accidentally met some of his friends and fellow-students as they were returning from dinner. With a kind of friendly violence they dragged him off to the amphitheater even though he stoutly resisted. . . . When they had reached the amphitheater and taken the seats they could, the whole place was seething with the cruelest pleasures. Alypius closed the doors of his eyes and forbade his mind to indulge in such great evils. If he had only also stopped his ears! For when one of the contestants fell, a great shout of the whole crowd beat mightily upon him, and being overcome by curiosity, and prepared, he thought, to despise and overcome anything that he might see, he opened his eyes and was struck a deeper wound in his soul than the gladiator was in his body. . . . For as soon as he saw that blood, he drank in a kind of savagery, nor did he turn away but fixed his gaze upon it, and unawares drank in the Furies themselves, and was charmed with the wickedness of the fight and drunk with bloodthirsty joy. . . . He watched the sight, he cried out, was inflamed, and carried away from there such a madness that it spurred him on to return, not only with those who had dragged him there, but to run ahead of them and to drag along others as well."[53]

In his short work *On the Spectacles,* written in the very first years of the third century, Tertullian had pointed out the pagan origins of the different spectacles, circus, theater, and amphitheater, and had showed the Christians that it was their duty to refrain from such idolatry, hatred, and impurity. To those who claimed that Christ had not forbidden the games in His preaching and that the sun itself looks down upon them without being stained by the sight, Tertullian replied: "Yes, and the rays of the sun enter into the sewers, and are no less pure for that. Would that God did not see men sinning, so that we might all escape His judgment! But He sees lies, adulteries, frauds, idolatries, and the shows themselves; and it is precisely on this account that we will not look at them, lest the All-seeing see us. You are, sir, making a comparison at the same level between the criminal and the Judge: the criminal who is a criminal because he is seen, and the Judge who is a Judge because He sees. Outside the limits of the circus are we intent on playing the madman? Outside the gates of the theater are we bent on lewdness, outside the racetrack on arrogance, and outside the amphitheater on cruelty because outside the porticoes, the tiers, and the curtains God also has eyes? In no place is there ever any excuse for that which God has forever condemned."[54]

But the Christians of the fourth century were different from those of the time of Tertullian. St. Ambrose at Milan and St. Augustine at Hippo wore themselves out in trying to keep their people in church when the shows were going on. There was an even worse problem in Constantinople, a city without a tradition but predominantly Christian. St. John Chrysostom describes a Holy Week of the last years of the fourth century. On Wednesday a torrential downpour threatened to flood the fields with their ripening grain and even the city itself. The people kept chanting the litanies in the churches. Their prayers were answered, and the rains came to an end on Thursday. Greatly relieved, the people left the churches on Good Friday for the circus.[55] The following day, Holy Saturday, they flocked to the theater. And yet this was a Christian community which, if we can judge from the homilies of St. John Chrysostom, was as a rule quite fervent. It is not surprising then that as a youth Ambrose should have witnessed the combats of the amphitheater. In explaining a psalm when he was bishop of Milan, he recalled that one day when he was still young he had seen an athlete throw his adversary and kick him in the face as a token of derision.[56]

However, as a number of beautiful paragraphs in his sermon on the death of Valentinian II would seem to indicate, Ambrose's own youth was free from serious disorders. He praises the young who despite the storms of passion manage to preserve themselves in true sobriety. Because of the self-control and abstinence that the sweet yoke of Christ demands, it can be burdensome to youth, but those who will have borne it from childhood will experience its joys.

On the other hand, this same funeral oration could indicate the opposite as well. St. Ambrose notes that the time of youth is a slippery one. Yet this may simply be a rhetorical commonplace. In his writings he makes so few references to his early years that novelists are the only ones who can possibly discuss whether or not he passed his early years unstained. In a letter on the Arian persecution of Justina, St. Ambrose goes out of his way to note that women are the most serious source of temptation for men,[57] and in his treatise on the education of virgins, after praising a woman who trains those whom she has brought forth in pain to virtue, he goes on to answer an objection: "But you men say that a woman is a temptation to a man. Yes, this is true, and the more beautiful she is, the greater the temptation. . . . But it is not a defect in a woman to be what she was born. . . . We cannot find fault with the work of the divine Artist."[58] From this we can judge that his own outlook was quite normal.

In addition to the pagan, there was also the Christian Rome, with its still lively recollections of the numerous martyrs who had consecrated the soil about the city with their blood. Ambrose must have been particularly aware of this since the death of Soteris was well remembered in the family. Although he was still only a catechumen, he must have frequently visited the catacombs as others were accustomed to do. As we have already seen, St. Jerome together with his friends Bonosus and Rufinus of Aquileia studied at Rome between the years 360 and 365, and in his commentary on the prophet Ezechiel he tells us something of the practices of the Roman Christians at this time: "When I was studying literature at Rome in my youth, I was accustomed on Sundays to visit the tombs of the apostles and martyrs along with companions of my own age and with the same ideals. We frequently went down into the crypts cut deep in the earth, and all along the walls could be seen tombs. So great was the darkness that it seemed as if the words of the prophet, 'They shall descend alive into hell,' were being realized. A small opening allowed a shaft of light to descend from above, and this diminished a little the fear of the darkness. We walked on with slow steps, plunged as it were in a dark night that recalled Virgil's line: 'Horror and silence on every side terrified our soul.' "[59]

At this time Jerome, since he had not as yet received baptism, was, like Ambrose, only a Christian in desire and family tradition. But it is not likely that he was acquainted with Ambrose, much less on intimate terms with him. Like Augustine, Jerome came from a middle-class family which would have had few, if any, dealings with the aristocracy to which Ambrose belonged.

Even after the return of Pope Liberius to Rome, the struggle against the Arians only increased in intensity during the final years of Constantius's reign, and it had many repercussions within the Christian families of the Roman aristocracy. There is still extant from the year 356 a letter of Bishop Hosius of Cordova, who was at the time some ninety years old, in which he tells Constantius that he is worn out with the constant threats and continuous pressure being exerted by the emperor: "I have been a confessor from the very first, when a persecution broke out in the time of your grandfather Maximian; and if you will persecute me, I am ready again to endure anything rather than to shed innocent blood and betray the truth. But I cannot approve of your conduct in writing in this threatening manner. Cease to write thus; adopt not the cause of Arius, nor listen to those in the East, nor give credit to Ursacius, Valens and their fellows. . . . Cease to use force; write no letters, send no counts; but release those who have been banished. . . . When was any such thing done by Constans? . . . Remember that you are a mortal man. Be afraid of the day of judgment, and keep yourself unstained for it. Do not interfere in the affairs of the Church or give commands to us concerning them. . . . It is written, 'Render to Caesar the things that are Caesar's, and to God the things that are God's.' "[60] But in the end Hosius was exiled for a year to Sirmium, where his signature was also wrung from him.[61] During this same time Athanasius is even more outspoken in his *Apology for His Flight*, his *Apology to Constantius*, and his *History of the Arians for the Monks*. In these works the great champion of orthodoxy lists the many bishops who were being held in exile far from their large and influential sees. He condemns the tortures to which even the virgins of the Church had been subjected: "These worthy Arians who have slandered me, and by whom conspiracies have been formed against most of the bishops, having obtained the consent and cooperation of the magistrates, first stripped them, and then caused them to be hung up upon the rack and scourged on the ribs so severely three different times that not even real criminals have ever suffered the like."[62] Constantius himself is described as the precursor of the Antichrist: "For having put on the profession of Christianity, and entering into the holy places, and standing therein, he lays waste the churches, transgressing their canons, and enforcing the observance of his own decrees. Will any one now venture to say that this is a peaceful time for Christians, and not a time of persecution? A persecution indeed, such as never arose before, and such as no one perhaps will again stir up, except 'the son of lawlessness,' do these enemies of Christ exhibit, who already present a picture of him in their own persons. Wherefore it especially behooves us to be sober . . . lest this be that 'falling away,' after which he shall be revealed, of whom Constantius is surely the forerunner."[63]

Lucifer of Cagliari composed similar works. From about the year 356 is his *De non conveniendo cum haeretics*—"*On Not Associating with Heretics.*" In 359 appeared his *De non parcendo in Deum delinquentibus*—"*On Not Sparing Those Sinning Against God,*" and in 360 his *Moriendum esse pro Dei filio*—"*One Must Die for the Son of God.*" These bitter invectives were sent to the court in the hope that Constantius would amend his ways.

In his turn, Hilary of Poitiers in the spring of 360 wrote from Constantinople a scorching attack on the emperor in the form of a letter to the bishops of Gaul entitled *Contra Constantium imperatorem:* "It is now time to speak since the time to keep silent has passed. Let us await the coming of Christ since the Antichrist has conquered. Let the shepherds cry out since the hirelings have fled. Let us lay down our lives for our sheep since the thieves have entered in and the raging lion goes about. . . . Almighty God and Creator of all! would that You had granted me to live and make my confession in You and Your only-begotten Son in the days of Nero or Decius . . . since there would then have been no doubt that they were persecutors. . . . But now, instead, we fight against a deceitful persecutor, against a fawning adversary, against the Antichrist Constantius, who does not strike us on the back but pats the stomach. He does not condemn us so that we may be reborn to life, but he enriches us to lead us to death. He does not hurl us into prison so that we may be free, but he showers us with honors so as to enslave us. He does not tear our sides, but conquers the heart; he does not behead us with a sword, but slays our souls with his gold. . . . He confesses Christ so as to be able to deny Him. . . . He builds churches to destroy the faith. He always uses Your name, O Christ, in his discourses, yet he does everything he possibly can to destroy faith in You as being God equal with the Father. . . . I say to you Constantius what I would have said to Nero, or what Decius or Maxentius would have heard from me: 'You fight against God, you rage against the Church, you persecute the saints, you hate the preachers of Christ, you destroy religion. . . . You lie when you say that you are a Christian: you are a new enemy of Christ. Distribute the episcopal sees to your followers and substitute evil bishops for good; imprison the priests; send your armies into the fields to terrify the Church. . . .' The persecution of Constantius is a diabolical work. . . . He condemns to the mines the servants of the Lord. He has brought about the death of Paulinus, the saintly bishop of Trier. He spreads terror and confusion through the churches of Alexandria, Milan, Rome, and Toulouse, banishing the bishops, beating the priests and deacons, and profaning even the mystery of the body and blood of Christ."[64]

While this was going on, Ambrose was passing from youth to early manhood. With other members of his family he must have been saddened at the sufferings of the orthodox at the hands of the Arians. In the light of these sad events and the general persecution of Catholic bishops by Constantius, some of the demands and claims which Ambrose himself made later as a bishop cannot be said to have been excessive.

Here it will be well to summarize the Arian developments

during the last three years of Constantius's reign. In the summer of 357, the three Arian bishops Valens, Ursacius, and Germinius drew up a formula of the faith at Sirmium which aimed at avoiding the terminology of Nicea (*homoousios:* Christ is of the same nature as the Father) as well as that of the moderate Arians (*homoiousios:* Christ is like the Father). It was then presented to the bishops for their signature. Pure Arianism was to become the official doctrine of the state. But then the Eastern bishops split up into different factions. For some (the Anomoeans) the formula was not Arian enough, and for others (the Homoeousians, the moderate Arians), it was too Arian. Toward the end of 357 Leontius, bishop of Antioch died. When the psalms were chanted in church he had been accustomed to cough at the end of the "Glory to the Father," since the orthodox Christians wanted to say "Glory to the Father, and to the Son, and to the Holy Spirit," but the Arians, "Glory to the Father by means of the Son in the Holy Spirit." Both parties would listen to the bishop, but after the first words he would cough until the end.[65]

There had now been installed at Antioch as his successor a certain Eudoxius. He had not been elected by the bishops of the province but had obtained his post through the eunuchs of the court. In his preaching Eudoxius showed himself to be a thorough-going Arian. Basil of Ancyra then gathered a council at Ancyra before the Easter of 358. After this, he took a new moderate formula to Sirmium and had Eudoxius disowned by Constantius, who wrote a letter to the Antiochians.[66] They should not believe that he had nominated Eudoxius, and they should not trust certain ambitious individuals who changed their episcopal sees merely to increase their revenues. Basil and the other moderate Arians were thus making some advance toward the orthodox position.

In the summer of 358, Liberius was brought from Thrace to Sirmium. Hilary of Poitiers certainly interpreted Basil's formula in a good sense, and he looked upon the moderate Arians as his brothers. Probably Pope Liberius also extended his hand to Basil. In 359 the extreme Arians regained control of Constantius. Two councils were held. The first convened in May at Rimini, where some four hundred bishops were assembled. Constantius paid the expenses for all, including those incurred in traveling, though some bishops of Gaul refused this assistance as being improper. Only a minority, about eighty bishops, were Arian, but the prefect Taurus had received orders not to yield. After seven months of negotiations and threats, all the bishops capitulated and signed as Constantius demanded. At Seleucia in Isauria (modern Turkey) where one hundred and fifty eastern bishops were assembled, a quaestor of the sacred palace was charged with the task of reducing Basil and the moderate Arians, who constituted the majority, to obedience. Here less was effected than at Rimini. Finally, early in January 350, as a complement to Rimini and Seleucia, a council assembled at Constantinople, where Constantius was in residence, consecrated a new formula, that of Acacius. This omitted both the *homoousios* of Nicea and the *homoiousios* of Basil of Ancyra, that is, of the moderate Arians. This apparent compromise secured the supremacy of the Arians in the East to the time of Theodosius. But during these same months a new regime was set up in the West with the proclamation of Julian as Augustus at Paris (February, 360). The Church in the West was thus freed from the baleful intervention of Constantius and could at last breathe again.

Even though he was himself a pagan, Ammianus Marcellinus condemned Constantius for the trouble he caused the Church: "He stirred up many controversies, and, as these became widespread, he nourished them with contentious words. And since bands of bishops hastened here and there on the public post-horses to the 'synods,' as they are called, he cut the sinews of the courier-service as he tried to adapt the whole ritual to his own will."[67]

But under Julian the Church experienced still further persecution. The son of Julius Constantius and Basilina, Julian was born at Constantinople in 331. His father, Julius Constantius, was a half-brother of Constantine the Great who during the reign of the latter had had to wander about like the hero of the *Odyssey* to escape the jealousy of his stepmother Helena, who as a girl had worked in an inn.[68] Constantius Chlorus, of Serbian stock and the father of Constantine, had abandoned her after the birth of the future emperor in order to marry Theodora, the daughter of Maximinus. Basilina, Julian's mother, on the other hand, was a noble Christian whom Julius Constantius, a widower and by this time father of Gallus, had married in 330, when she was still very young. Julian could not have remembered his mother for she died when he was only a few months old, but he always preserved a tender regard for her.

In the dark tragedy in which six or seven members of the imperial family lost their lives, Julian also lost his father. He was only six years old at the time. He was then entrusted to the care of Eusebius, the famous Arian bishop of Nicomedia, who was also a relative of Basilina. At the end of 341 Eusebius died. The young Julian does not seem to have been at all close to him. After the death of Eusebius, Julian was sent with his brother Gallus to the imperial estate at Macellum. This was a delightful spot under the cloudy summit of Mt. Argaeus in the very center of Cappadocia and of Asia Minor. But it was also a prison. Far from everything which he had known and loved, separated from his fond pedagogue Mardonius, and under the constant surveillance of a band of eunuchs in the service of Constantius, Julian found his greatest consolation in the books of the palace. While there, from his tenth to his sixteenth year, he experienced a great enthusiasm for the intellectual life. His religious training was, however, in the hands of individuals who were not of a spiritual frame of mind themselves. Among these could be numbered George of Cappadocia, whose later boldness as Arian bishop of Alexandria we have already seen. Julian was baptized at Macellum, instructed in the sacred mysteries, and at a Mass on Easter received the Eucharist. He was even admitted into the clergy by being made a lector. As was customary at the time, when still only thirteen or fourteen years old, he read the Sacred Scriptures to the people in church, perhaps at Caesarea. Still more, he could read and did read other Christian writings in the sumptuous rooms at Macellum. He also had the opportunity to venerate the tombs of the martyrs in the neighboring cities, to visit the hospitals and the places of refuge which the bishops vied with each other in building.

He admired the great charity that existed among the faithful despite the desperate struggles that engaged their bishops. He himself practiced charity and understood its efficacy as a means of propagating the faith.

Toward the end of 347 he was able to leave Macellum to attend school at Constantinople and later at Nicomedia, where he became acquainted with Libanius. At this time Hellenism was enjoying a veritable renaissance. In Neoplatonic speculations, enthusiasm for the poetry and religion of ancient Greece was associated with the practices of the Oriental mystery religions, which in turn were explained in a symbolic sense and were carried out in secret societies. Aedesius of Pergamum, Maximus of Ephesus, and Priscus were more devotees of a mixture of magic and spiritualism than they were philosophers.

Julian now hesitated no longer in his choice between the ancient culture of Greece and the Church. When his brother Gallus became Caesar in 351, Julian was able to make use of the inheritance which he had received from his maternal grandmother and went in search of teachers of Neoplatonism and theurgy at Pergamum and Ephesus. It was perhaps at Ephesus that he renounced his Christian baptism in a crypt dedicated to Mithra. As one of his modern biographers has observed, "The apostasy of Julian is above all the act of a mystic deluded by the promise of heavenly immortality and beatific visions. . . . When he began to worship the ancient gods, he was carrying out a mystic vocation and obeying the guardian deities of his dynasty and the empire, and he let himself be guided by their voices."[69] In his writings, Julian makes frequent reference to his consecration to Mithra. He declares himself to be a faithful "soldier" of this god who is his "father." But more than this, he identifies Mithra with the sun god Helios, the highest expression of the supreme One in the philosophy of Plotinus.

In 354, after committing numerous atrocities at Antioch, Gallus was summoned to court by Constantius, but before he reached his destination he was murdered at Flanona near Pola. Julian then received an order to come to Milan. On his way he was able to visit Troy, where he met Pegasius, the Christian bishop of the city. While Pegasius was guiding him about the tombs of the heroes and the temples of the ancient Gods, Julian was surprised to see that their cult was still observed and that the bishop himself did not make the sign of the cross nor hiss through his teeth before the statue of Athena as Christians usually did. There were at this time numerous apostates from the faith, and for a variety of different reasons. Pegasius himself later became a pagan priest.

Accusations had been brought against Julian at Milan, and he had to wait six months before he obtained an audience. Eusebia, the wife of Constantius, finally intervened in his favor. She obtained permission for him to continue his studies at Athens. This proved to be a source of intense satisfaction for Julian, but he was able to remain at this ancient center of culture for only a few months in the summer of 355. There he met a number of famous philosophers. His passionate interest in the strange speculations of the Neoplatonists received an added incentive. He was initiated into the mysteries of Eleusis, which were explained to him as being the embodiment of the highest philosophical truths. At Athens he also made the acquaintance of a number of Christians, both teachers and students. Two of the latter became famous bishops: Basil of Caesarea and Gregory of Nazianzus. With the coming of fall, however, Julian was ordered back to Milan. He wept tears of desperation, begging the goddess Athena to let him die rather than permit his return to court. But he realized how futile it would be to resist the emperor and left without delay. In his own words, "Athena guided me wherever I went. She sent me Helios and Selene as my guardian angels."[70]

At Milan, on November 6, 355, Constantius crowned Julian with a diadem and placed the purple of a Caesar on his shoulders. The soldiers who had gathered for the ceremony beat their shields upon their knees as a sign of their own approval.

What did Julian think of the new honor? Gregory of Nazianzus, who had known him at Athens at this period, has left a rather terrible portrait of him with his restlessly moving head, his wild, wandering eyes, his shifting feet, his nostrils breathing hate and scorn, his proud and insolent face, and his constant paroxysms of uncontrolled laughter.[71] But this was a description which Gregory gave in later life, when he saw all the evil that Julian had effected in the false pursuit of an imagined good. We, on the contrary, are inclined to pity him, as Julian pitied himself once the excitement of the moment had passed. He well knew, as he had read in one of his favorite authors, Dio Chrysostom, that riches, an inherited throne, a crown and purple robe, and citizens and soldiers flocking together to hail one as a king bestow nothing more than a perilous power. And after the thunderous hurrahs he returned to the silence of the palace, where he repeated to himself a line from Homer: "By purple death I'm seized and fate supreme."[72]

Five years in Gaul, at Paris, and on the frontiers of the Rhine, proved that this Greek sophist who never spoke of Rome and whose heart was in Athens possessed great talent both as a military leader and as a politician.[73] After conquering the Alemanni in 356, in a second campaign in 357 he obtained an even greater victory at the Battle of Strasbourg. In 358 and 359 the Rhine again became safe for Roman commerce. Among his other accomplishments, Julian freed twenty thousand prisoners from German captivity. His own life was austere. As a loyal follower of Mithra he resisted every form of sensuality and showed himself kind and open to others. He would rise at midnight from his poor hard bed and, after a prayer to Hermes, would begin his work.

He did everything he could to diminish the hateful burden of the provincial taxes. He instituted a regime of strict economy, even going so far as to have everything that was superfluous removed from his table, while he ate the same rations as the troops. He was careful to see also that justice was administered impartially.

In February, 360, while Constantius was still occupied with his preparations for an invasion of Persia in the East, the troops at Paris acclaimed Julian Augustus. Reluctantly he was forced to accept the crown. In the summer of 360 he reconquered the last stretch of the Rhine to the sea, and sailing rapidly he returned up the river from Xanten to Basel. Negotiations with Constantius proved to be fruitless. Toward the end of 360, Helena, the sister of Constantius whom Julian had married in 355, died. The following year Eusebia, the wife of Constantius, also died. She had always favored Julian. The rupture between the two cousins was thus inevitable. In the summer of 361, Julian marched from Gaul toward the Danube. Then with a small fleet he sailed from Regensburg to Bonmünster. In early October he was at Sirmium. Pushing on toward Constantinople, he finally arrived at Nish in Serbia. From here he sent out a white paper to the principal cities of the empire in defense of his own actions. He asked them to choose between the two rivals, one of whom had expelled the barbarians from the frontiers and the other, Constantius, who had invited these same barbarians to take up arms against the forces under Julian's command. He also wrote a letter to the senate of Rome which was publicly read to it by the prefect of the city.

Ambrose, who was twenty-seven at this time, certainly heard the comments which the senators had to make on Julian's criticism of, and attacks upon, Constantine the Great and Constantius.

Julian was more fortunate in the measures which he took to bring the provinces of the West quickly into line. Since the two praetorian prefects had fled to Constantius, he placed Mamertinus in charge of Illyricum and Italy. He appointed Maximus, a senator, prefect of Rome, and was able to secure grain supplies for the city despite the fact that Constantius's lieutenants intercepted the regular transport of grain from Africa. He was thus able to check the revolts of the people which had disturbed the peace of the city even during the preceeding year.

But Constantius, after leaving Antioch to encounter Julian in the West, died of a violent fever on November 3, 361, at Mopsucrene (near Adana in modern Turkey). Like his father before him, he received baptism on his deathbed. His body was carried to Constantinople. To the Christians who accompanied the bier, it seemed as if they heard angels on the Taurus mountains singing the praises of the dead emperor.[74]

The leaders of the court in the East sought in vain for someone whom they could set up against Julian. Finally, about the middle of November, cavalrymen arrived at Nish bearing the official report of Constantius's death and the obedient submission of the eastern provinces.

The trials of Julian's brief rule of twenty months were all experienced in the East, but they had strong repercussions in the West, and especially at Rome, where paganism maintained its traditional position despite the laws of Constantine and Constantius in favor of the Christians. The aristocracy in particular was largely pagan. The Ambrosii, though Christian, were related to the powerful pagan family of the Symmachi, whose head at this time was Lucius Aurelius Avianius Symmachus, later to become prefect of the city in 364-365.[75] We shall see his son Quintus Aurelius Symmachus contending with St. Ambrose in a celebrated struggle over the altar of Victory in front of the senate.

Another famous family was that of Probus, of the Anician clan. This also was closely connected with the Ambrosii. Probus himself was the powerful protector of Ambrose and his brother in the early years of their careers. Through their family connections with the Symmachi, the Ambrosii were also on terms of friendship with the Nicomachi and the Albini. Volusianus, prefect of Italy in 355, and of Rome in 365, and cousin of the emperor Julian, was a member of the latter clan. In such surroundings paganism was a matter of vital import since it opened the way to public careers and to the rich revenues of the pagan priesthoods.

Moreover, there were thorny problems connected with family relationships and marriages. One would like to say that there were also intellectual and religious problems as well. But paganism, at least with respect to the traditional religion of Rome, was at this time practically dead. Interest in non-Christian religions was largely confined to the worship of Mithra, and this was carried out in an exotic fashion. Further, a marked decline in intellectual interests had set in. The best known writer at Rome during this time was the Quintus Aurelius Symmachus mentioned above. He was of the same age as Ambrose and highly esteemed by his contemporaries as a man of great talents. But his letters are almost too silly to read, and even his panegyrics show a depressing poverty of thought.

In the palaces of the Symmachi and of other Roman nobles, Ambrose as a young man must have often heard that paganism meant a love of tradition, of the charms of poetry, a cultivation of the classics (Nicomachus Flavianus and Praetextatus in these very years were having the ancient texts transcribed and emended), a passion for ruling, and something which was not necessarily identified with the degradation of the amphitheater and with the immorality of the stage and baths. But Ambrose must also have felt the poverty of this ideal, the painful void, its radical inability to furnish an answer to the problems of the world and of the human soul.

These great pagan lords, so enthralled with the past, eagerly followed the various steps which Julian took to restore the old religion. And, as Ammianus tells us, he began "with plain and formal decrees ordering the temples to be opened, victims to be brought to the altars, and the worship of the gods to be restored. And in order to add to the effectiveness of these ordinances, he summoned to the palace the bishops of the Christians who were at odds with each other and the people who were also at variance, and politely advised them to set aside their differences and each without fear or opposition to observe his own beliefs."[76] The bishops who had been exiled by Constantius were thus able to return to their sees.

Ammianus believed that the emperor had acted in this way to increase the conflicts among the Christians and thus render them less harmful. The actual result of his efforts was, however, quite different from any such intent. In various places, with the apparent approval of the emperor, the pagan reaction to Christianity became violent, and in some cities of the East, Christians were even tortured and put to death.[77]

Julian's next effort in the restoration of paganism was the creation of a priestly organization modeled after the hierarchy of the Church. He wrote "pastoral letters" to the new pagan bishops to encourage them to give good example by the austerity of their lives and their acts of piety and benevolence. They were also ordered to preach in the temples. But as has been well observed, "all these ascetic and devotional regulations, this new mystical hierarchy, were in reality unprecedented innovations, though they were set forth as being a return to the old deities. . . . The ministers of the new order repaired the sanctuaries, re-erected the statues, renewed the splendor of the old processions, listened to the oracles speaking again in the whisperings of the forests and the murmur of the fountains, re-established the power of the sun and stars, and mounted the pulpit to preach philanthropy by appealing to the authority of Homer and Plato. But no matter how hard they tried, when the priests who organized these displays of empty splendor turned from the altar to see what effects their zeal was producing, they frequently met the indifferent gaze and smiling banter of a public that was indifferent to the sad plight of the temples."[78]

During the first months of his reign, although he openly favored paganism, Julian remained reasonable and tolerant toward the Christians. His abolition of the exemptions and privileges of the Christian clergy may be regarded simply as a part of his general policy of economic, political, and social reform. "But after the spring of 362, he yielded to new influences. We can see the sectarianism of a theocrat gradually replacing the prudence and moderation of an enlightened monarch."[79]

On June 17, 362, Ambrose could have seen the new scholastic laws posted up at Rome. With these ordinances, which were published simultaneously in all the cities of the empire, Julian manifested his open opposition to Christianity. Anyone seeking a post as teacher or professor would have to secure a statement from his local senate attesting his good character, and this would then in turn have to be ratified by the emperor. A circular letter sent out by the emperor explained how this decree was to be interpreted. Those who instruct the young should not have opinions that are irreconcilable with the exercise of their profession. Their integrity must be above reproach. To claim to admire the classics and at the same time to look upon them as being nothing more than inventions of the devil shows a lack of logic and frankness. It means that one has sold himself for a few coins and he is thus not worthy of the office of teaching. Christian teachers are free, and they need not change their own opinions, but they ought to make a choice. Either they should cease teaching what they do not take seriously or, if they wish to continue teaching, they should begin to teach by their own example.[80]

Julian's attitude was thus that of one who believed that the paganism of the classics studied in school was still alive, whereas by this time it was really dead and buried, its only survival being purely literary.

The law seemed to be innocent enough and without any great significance, but in reality it was cruel and revolutionary since up till this time the schools of the empire had enjoyed full liberty.

Many Christian teachers preferred to abandon their chairs rather than to deny their faith. Among these were Prohaeresius at Athens and Marius Victorinus at Rome. The latter, "a teacher of very many noble senators," was so famous for his eloquence that a statue had been erected to him in the Forum of Trajan. In 355 he became even more renowned when he was converted "to the wonder of Rome and the exaltation of the Church."[81]

Even among the pagans there were those who deplored Julian's narrow-mindedness. His great admirer Ammianus Marcellinus condemned the scholastic law as being "inhuman and deserving to be buried in everlasting silence."[82]

Julian's next move was the composition of a polemical work, *Against the Galileans*, that is, against the Christians. In writing it, he drew upon the lessons which he had learned from his teachers as a youth and his own experiences as a Christian. He criticizes the biblical narratives. In commenting on the first pages of Genesis, for example, he criticizes the account that God wished to create woman in order to give man a helpmate like himself: "A wonderful helpmate, who does not only not help him, but who betrays him!" He compares Moses with Plato, denies the prophecies of the Old Testament, and maintains that with the exception of St. John none of the evangelists would say that Christ is God, and he speaks sarcastically of the sacraments. In the next century Cyril of Alexandria wrote that many lost their faith through reading the works of Julian.[83] Though they had been written in Greek, Ambrose would have seen them in the hands of the more ardent pagans.

In June, 362, Julian left Constantinople for Antioch, where he remained until March, 363, when he set out on his last campaign, his ill-fated expedition against the Persians. Antioch at this time was a brilliant and luxurious city whose inhabitants gave themselves over freely to every kind of pleasure and amusement. They found Julian, with his shaggy beard that marked him as a philosopher, and his austere and studious habits, little to their liking. Even the pagans found him irksome and excessively devout. They were further irritated by the fact that while the poor of the city had great difficulty in finding enough to eat, Julian slaughtered herds of cattle and hundreds of birds in his sacrifices to the gods. And his soldiers so stuffed themselves with meat and wine that they had to be carried from the temples to their quarters on the shoulders of passers-by. The resentment of the Antiochians, however, only sharpened the ill humor of the emperor. He accordingly attacked them in his bitterly sarcastic *Misopogon*, or *"Beard-Hater."*

He excluded "the Galileans" from administrative offices and positions in the provinces on the pretext that their own law forbade them to make use of the sword. Several miles from Antioch there was a resort by the name of Daphne, rich in springs and pleasant groves. It had once been famous for its oracle of Apollo, but in more recent years it had drawn crowds of Christians to the tomb of the martyr Babylas, who was buried there. In August, 362, Julian visited the temple of Apollo and found it in a lamentable condition despite the wealth of the town. He saw only one poor priest there, and he happened to be sacrificing a goose from his own flock. The emperor decided to restore its voice to the oracle by purifying the surrounding area. He ordered the bones of St. Babylas to be transferred to the common cemetery of Antioch. The Christians, however, turned this translation of his relics into a triumphal procession. On the night of October 22 the temple of Apollo was destroyed by fire. The Christians were accused of arson, though the fire may have been started by lightning. In revenge, Julian ordered most of the splendid Christian basilicas of Antioch to be stripped of their treasures and closed, and he burned down the chapels at Miletus that had been erected in honor of the martyrs. During this same month of October he sent orders to Egypt to have Athanasius, who had returned seven months before to Alexandria, expelled since his presence there was prejudicial to the city: "During my reign that infamous wretch has dared to baptize Greek women of high rank!"[84]

In different cities during the course of these months violence broke out against the Christians, not because the emperor had issued specific orders to this effect, but because it was known that he would condone it. Many churches were sacked and profaned, and Christians were murdered at Gaza and Alexandria.

At Heliopolis in Syria, Constantine had closed and destroyed temples of the gods, not with the intent of persecuting the pagans, but for the sake of public morality since sacred prostitution was practiced there. It now seemed to be a good time for revenge. Fanatics massacred a deacon, dragged the Christian virgins from their convent, stripped them, and tossed them naked to the sport of the rabble, and then, cutting them to pieces, tossed their remains to pigs.[85] At a later date, St. Ambrose was to remind Theodosius in a celebrated letter of the fact that Jews and pagans burned many Christian basilicas during Julian's persecution.[86]

Julian's attempt to rebuild the temple at Jerusalem failed because of the earthquakes which devastated Palestine. Ammianus writes that flames were seen coming from the ground and burning the workmen and their scaffolding. This same incident is mentioned by St. Ambrose in his letter to Theodosius just mentioned.[87]

The cult which the Christians offered to the martyrs, especially in the East, assumed grandiose proportions. Julian reproached them for filling everything with sepulchers, and he praised those cities that burned the tombs of the Galileans. Finally, on February 12, 363, he published an edict prohibiting the celebration of funerals of any kind during the day.[88] Funeral processions should take place only in the evening or at night, so as not to contaminate the eyes of the living, since the purity of the day is consecrated to the gods of Olympus and to chaste works.

At Rome, in March, 363, where Julian had given permission for the replacing of the altar of Victory in front of the senate, the temple of Apollo on the Palatine was destroyed by fire. The Sibylline books only narrowly escaped a similar fate. It was a wretched augury for the Roman expedition against the Persians which was just getting under way. On June 26, about seventy miles north of Ctesiphon, the capital of Persia, at a spot twenty miles southeast of the modern city of Baghdad, Julian was pierced in the side by a lance hurled by an unidentified assailant during the course of a sudden assault by a band of Persians. He died the following night, at the age of thirty-two, after losing a great quantity of blood.[89]

Julian's biographers today do not so much blame or praise his tragic destiny as show respect for his sincere and noble, though misguided, soul. But it was otherwise in the summer of 363 when news of his death spread throughout the empire. The Christians give vent to unrestrained manifestations of joy, and in the cities of the East there were some revolts, popular uprisings, and even at times savage acts of revenge.

At Rome the senate decreed his apotheosis. Many of the pagans took his death as a warning. In his commentary on the prophet Habacuc, written in 392, St. Jerome recalls the fact that he was a student at Rome at the time of Julian's death, and that he heard a pagan remark in jest: "And the Christians claim that their God is patient!"[90]

St. Ambrose's ancient biographers make no mention of the

young man during these eventful years, but the fact that he lived for twenty-five years at Rome during these sharp and bitter struggles explains his own firmness as a bishop while carrying out his mission in the Church and in the State.

D(ominus) N(oster) FL(avius) CL(audius)
IVLIANVS P(ius) F(elix) AVG(ustus)

Bronze coin: Bust with crown, cloak, and breastplate.
See Cohen, *Monnaies*, VI, p. 368, no. 73.

SECVRITAS REIPV(licae): Apis bull with two stars

Julian the Apostate was born at Constantinople towards the end of 331. He was proclaimed Augustus at Paris in 360, and died June 26, 363, in Persia after an unsuccessful attempt to capture Ctesiphon.

III

Sirmium

o

Election of Valentinian: his character, his religious policy. Ambrose enters upon an administrative career and goes to Sirmium. The administration of justice. The tax structure. The social castes. Church and State in the fourth century. The peace of Constantine. The Christians: lights and shadows. The accession of Liberius.

The unexpected death of the Emperor Julian at so early an age caught both the army and his ministers by surprise. They were not prepared to pick a successor but there was no time for delay. The army was in the heart of Persia, far from its bases, and surrounded on all sides by enemies. Both the generals that had come from Gaul and those from the East agreed upon offering the purple to Salutius, a pagan philosopher, one of Julian's former friends. But Salutius, pleading his age and poor health, refused the offer. Then, perhaps through a compromise between the officers of the East and the West, Flavius Jovianus, an energetic Christian soldier in his thirties, born in Pannonia, was chosen instead. Jovian continued with the retreat which Julian had already begun. Accepting the humiliating terms of the truce offered by the Persians, he crossed the desert during the summer, and in October, 363, finally arrived at Antioch. He immediately abolished the anti-Christian laws of Julian, aiming, apparently, at a return to the policy of tolerance of Constantine the Great. The situation itself suggested such a policy. The pagan Themistius, a famous orator down to the time of Theodosius, declared in his speech for the assumption of the consulate by Jovian on January 1, 364, that, since God has placed a religious feeling in the hearts of all men, everyone should be permitted to worship Him as he thinks best, without violating that freedom of conscience which God has Himself given to men.[1]

A law of January 11, 364, restored to the Christians their right to teach in the schools.[2]

But on the morning of February 17, 364, even before he reached Constantinople, Jovian was found dead in his room at Dadastana (a town not far from the modern Ankara).[3] His death was perhaps due to the fumes of a charcoal brazier which had been placed near his bed. The army continued on its march, and at Nicea (the modern Iznik in Turkey) the military and civil leaders decided to nominate as emperor Flavius Valentinianus, a tribune of the imperial guard. The choice was partly the fruit of a compromise between Christians and pagans, and Valentinian always remained in the middle of the road, refusing to take a position against either party.[4] A pagan of Pannonian stock, he had been converted to Christianity before Julian's disastrous campaign in the East. A pagan historian, Zosimus, tells us that one day when Valentinian was accompanying Julian into a pagan temple at Antioch, Maximus of Ephesus sprinkled him with lustral water. Angered at this, he tore away the part of his cloak that had been touched by the water. For this impetuous act, the emperor dismissed him from his post and sent him into exile.[5] Modern critics discount this episode as being without foundation; and Valentinian's religious policy, which may be seen in his enactments preserved in the Theodosian Code, would seem to support them. It should, however, be noted that Ambrose seems to allude to the incident in his discourse on the death of Valentinian II where he states that his father because of his love for the faith had refused military service and the honors of the tribunate.[6]

Valentinian I was an absolute monarch, cruel at times, and since he had become accustomed to the rough discipline of the camps, he could not endure the softness of Roman society. He believed that authority should be upheld by severity.[7] His fits of rage carried him at times almost to the point of madness. On one occasion, at a hunting party, a page loosed a Spartan hound ahead of time since the dog in its eagerness had snapped at him. As a punishment, Valentinian had the boy beaten to death with clubs and buried on the same day. On another occasion, an armorer presented him with a beautifully embellished breastplate. Instead of giving the man the reward he expected, the emperor had him slain since the armor was a bit lighter than he had specified. A certain Africanus, an energetic lawyer, after administering one province, aspired to govern another. When the master of the cavalry, Theodosius, supported this request with the emperor, Valentinian rudely replied: "Go, count, and change his head for him since he wants a change in his province," and through this sentence, as Ammianus notes, an eloquent man perished simply because he was trying to improve his position like many others. The emperor kept two cruel she-bears, which he called Goldflake and Innocence, in cages near his bedroom. Their savage disposition was maintained by their attendants so that the emperor could enjoy the way they dispatched condemned criminals.

These tales are told by Ammianus Marcellinus, a contemporary historian with a reputation for seriousness and impartiality.[8] But recent studies have shown that his pages dealing with Valentinian are extremely biased.[9] He describes incidents that were simply impossible, and does little more than express the hatred of the Roman senators for an emperor who had dared to allow torture to be used on them when they were brought to trial. But if Valentinian was often rough and violent, he knew how to defend valiantly the frontiers of the empire. He was greatly interested in the general welfare of the state, and was not without a measure of culture. He knew Greek, and to pass the time he busied himself with painting and sculpture, and with some success. St. Ambrose does not speak ill of him, but rather in a sermon delivered after his death describes him as being already "in heaven," where he meets his second son slain by his enemies in the very flower of his age.[10]

One month after his proclamation as Augustus, Valentinian, at the earnest request of his soldiers, who were being urged on by the pagan party, chose a colleague in the person of his brother Valens. The latter was proclaimed Augustus on March 28, 364. The opposition would really have preferred a person outside the family. The pagan faction in disgust began a separatist movement which culminated in the revolt of Procopius in the East. He had been one of Julian's generals, but his revolt only lasted from September, 365, until May, 366.

In the summer of 364, in a castle near Nish in Serbia, the two brothers proceeded to make a division of the empire. Valentinian yielded to his brother the rich prefecture of the East, which extended from the lower Danube to the confines of Persia and took in Egypt as well. He retained for himself Italy, Illyricum, Gaul, Britain, Spain, and Africa. Later, at Sirmium they set about dividing and redoubling the administrative offices. Two courts and two consistories were thus established. After appointing new generals and new magistrates, the two brothers embraced and departed from each other. Valentinian went to Milan where he remained for a whole year. Valens went to Constantinople.

At this juncture, Ambrose enters upon his administrative career. The reorganization of the empire by Valentinian brought about many changes of position within the imperial bureaucracy. While in residence at his palace in Milan, probably in May, 365, Valentinian nominated Volcacius Rufinus as the new prefect of the *praefectura praetorio Italiae Illyrici et Africae* with its headquarters at Sirmium. Paulinus, the first biographer of the saint, tells us that Ambrose, having completed his studies at Rome, left the city to take up his duties as a lawyer in the prefecture of the praetorium.[11] Since the records show that he left Rome and only later came to Milan, it must be concluded that he went to Sirmium where Probus was then stationed, and which was at the time the capital of the prefecture comprising Italy, Illyricum, and Africa. He was accompanied to his new post by his brother Satyrus. During this same year, 365, Symmachus left Rome for Regium as the *corrector* of Lucania and Calabria, and Albinus for Constantina as *consularis* of Numidia.

Sirmium (the modern Stremska Mitrovica in Yugoslavia) was at this time a great city. Important roads linked it with Milan and Rome to the west and south by way of Aquileia, with Thessalonica and Constantinople in the east, and with the Danube, the Roman frontier, and the cities on the Rhine to the north. Situated as it was on the banks of the Save not far from its confluence with the Danube, it was not only the chief city in Illyricum, as the nearby Belgrade is for Yugoslavia today, but it was also the meeting place of the East and West. During these years the prefect at Sirmium had jurisdiction over almost all of the Danubian basin as well as over Italy and a large part of North Africa. His tribunal received and passed sentence on appeals made from the decisions of provincial governors.

A position as a lawyer at the prefecture was a modest one to which even provincials of curial rank could aspire. But for young men of the nobility it was the first step in a career that could bring great wealth. For Ambrose it proved to be a providential experience since it put him in daily contact with the working class and their various problems and needs, far from the leisured and decadent atmosphere of Rome.

St. Jerome and Ammianus Marcellinus both speak ill of the lawyers of the fourth century. When the former was a student at Rome, he frequently visited the courts and listened to the arguments of the most celebrated lawyers, but he was scandalized at seeing how they frequently broke off from the matter at hand to hurl insults at their colleagues.[12] Ammianus, in his turn, sketches various types of legal opportunists. There were those who sold the cases of the weak to military officials or influential people at court, and in this way obtained wealth and honors for themselves. Others sniffed the seeds of possible discord and parked on the porches of widows and orphans, and wherever they saw the possibility of some dispute between friends or relatives they stirred up implacable hatreds. If you pretended that you deliberately killed your mother, you could find lawyers who would promise you many ways of escaping punishment since they knew that you were rich. Finally, there were those who had quit their literary studies too soon and went about in constant search of food and dinners, and who were, moreover, so stupid that they could not remember ever having possessed a single book. As a consequence, when they were in a group of educated people, if they heard the names of authors, they thought that mention was being made of some strange fish or other food.[13]

One of the many serious evils in the system of government at this time was the wretched administration of justice. The same officials possessed administrative and judicial powers. The governor of a province was the judge of first instance in all civil and penal cases in his province. The vicar of a diocese and the prefect of the praetorium were judges for appeals, the latter for those of the whole prefecture.

Although the laws were in themselves good enough, an ordinary subject could not find a remedy against the wrongs inflicted by officials. These were both administrators and judges, and they could be bribed.

In his correspondence, Symmachus includes letters addressed to friends giving them directions on how to judge this or that case so that the sentence will be in his favor.[14] Ammianus relates the case of a government employee in Mesopotamia who was falsely accused of owing money to the public treasury. Because the powerful judges were interested in obtaining a conviction, and he did not have the money to pay the alleged debts, he admitted his obligations in writing. Then collecting a good many military secrets, he made an agreement with the Persian commander on the opposite side of the Tigris river. When the day for payment drew near and he saw that the count of the imperial largesses (minister of finance) was more and more inclined to favor his adversaries, he fled in desperation with his wife, children, and other relatives to the Persians. This incident occurred in the last months of the reign of Constantius II.[15] In his *Confessions*, St. Augustine tells us that Alypius "had been an assessor to the count of the Italian bounties. At that time there was a most influential senator to whom many were indebted for favors they had received, and many also stood in terror of him. This man wanted to obtain something forbidden by the laws through his usual influence. Alypius opposed it. He was promised a bribe, but he despised it with all his heart. Threats were made, which he trampled under foot. In the meantime, all were admiring such a rare spirit which did not wish to have such a man for his friend or fear him as his enemy, though it was very well known that he had innumerable means of doing good or harm to others. The judge for whom Alypius was acting as an assessor, although he was himself opposed to the request, did not openly refuse it, but handed the matter over to Alypius, saying that he was not permitted to handle it himself. And if he had, Alypius would have withdrawn from his service."[16]

In a similar fashion we see St. Ambrose when he was bishop congratulating Titianus, whom he calls his "little son," on the departure of Rufinus, the master of the offices, to another position, since Titianus would now no longer have reason to fear the suit in which he was then embroiled.[17]

The outcome of such disputes, however, frequently was disastrous. Toward the year 368, a former state official and three of his assistants, in a perfectly legal accusation, brought a charge against the count of Italy. The latter was ordered by the judge to answer the charge according to the laws, but the count complained about the accusation to Valentinian as if it were a personal offense. The emperor then ordered Diodorus and his three assistants to be put to death. According to Ammianus Marcellinus, the Christians still venerated their memory and called the place where they were buried at Milan "the Square of the Innocents."[18]

In his funeral oration for Satyrus, St. Ambrose tells us that his brother had been greatly admired at the tribunal of the praetorian prefecture. And the saint's first biographer states practically the same of Ambrose himself without mentioning any particulars. In 367, perhaps in May or June, Sextus Petronius Probus was named prefect at Sirmium. This noble Roman had been proconsul in Africa in 358 at the age of twenty-three. After serving as prefect of Italy at Sirmium, he was appointed prefect of Gaul in 380, and in 383 he was again made prefect of Italy. Despite the generous encomia lavished upon him by Ausonius and Claudianus, it is quite possible that the numerous high positions which he held in the government were not so much due to his administrative talents as to the influence which he possessed. The only way he could preserve his enormous wealth was by purchasing positions of authority. And these posts also provided him with means of further gain. Ammianus humbly confesses that it was not for him to decide whether or not Probus had secured his possessions justly or not in almost all the provinces.[19] He was, at least in name, a Christian, and, at the age of sixty, when he was on the point of death, he received baptism. Many nobles in the provinces governed by Probus lost everything. Others were constrained either to emigrate or to commit suicide because of his malfeasance.

When Probus arrived as prefect at Sirmium in 367, he found there the two brothers Ambrose and Satyrus. They also pertained to the Christian nobility of Rome, and he certainly helped them in their careers. Paulinus expressly states that Probus made Ambrose a member of his council.[20] Later, likely about the year 370, Ambrose was named *consularis,* or governor, of the province of Aemilia-Liguria; and he left Sirmium for Milan.[21] Satyrus also received an appointment as a provincial governor but we do not know where.

Because of their family connections and their father's former rank, the two brothers, as we have already observed, were destined to become high officials in the state. It was only natural that after the completion of their studies and some years of experience in lower positions they should attain the office of governor.

At this late date it is impossible to determine what their special responsibilities must have been under Probus, but it is certain that they must have had numerous occasions to become acquainted with the many griefs and hardships experienced by the provincials.

During his five years at Sirmium the future bishop obtained an intimate knowledge of the ills that afflicted the body politic. The most serious problem was that of taxation. The collection of taxes was so pitiless that it eventually brought about the almost complete destruction of the middle class and small owners. One of the difficulties was that Rome never had a regular budget. As a consequence, whenever it was confronted with some new need, it had to have recourse to special taxes. In the trying decades of the third century, these special demands took on the character of organized looting that seriously disrupted the flow of commerce. Instead of taxes in money, the emperors of the third century revived the more primitive system of collecting taxes in kind. This took the form of repeated collections of foodstuffs for the army, the city of Rome, and for state officials. Raw materials and manufactured goods were collected in a similar fashion. These contributions, which were emergency measures at the beginning, gradually evolved into a regular tax over and above what was regularly assessed. It was, moreover, difficult to foresee the future needs of the state. Depending upon the circumstances of a particular time, the *annonae*, as these special assessments were called, could be greater or lesser. They thus retained to a certain extent the appearance of emergency measures. The emperor annually fixed the amount for payment during the current year, but no one could foresee what he would have to pay the following year. Under Diocletian the system was simplified but rendered more inequitable. Everyone who was cultivating a piece of land had to declare how much he was farming and how many men and animals he was employing; and he was assessed accordingly. Since the tiller of the soil came to form a single unit with the land, he became bound to it and lost his freedom of movement. Artisans and shopkeepers, in addition to the payment of a uniform tax, had to hand over to the state a certain quantity of goods at a special price. Merchants in the cities, in addition to excise taxes, had to pay every five years the traditional crown gold, and on the occasion of the nomination of an emperor or some other great public event, they had to contribute other gifts as a token of their good will and congratulations. Some of the taxes were collected directly by the state. Among these were those on inheritances, manumissions, auctions, and imports. But most were collected by the cities and paid into the treasury of the province. From the time of Hadrian the richest members of a community were made responsible for these collections. In the third century the pressure of the state on the municipal bourgeoisie steadily increased. The *curiales*, that is, the members of the municipal senates, ended up as being unpaid hereditary employees of the state, obliged to act as tax collectors and to make up out of their own resources the arrears of the other members of the community. To prevent them from shirking their duties they were kept under the watchful eyes of bands of public officials.

Constantine was able to provide some relief for the economic problems of his day by stabilizing the currency. But this was of a short duration. The unjust and oppressive taxes and the ever increasing dishonesty and violence of the members of the imperial administration made a sane economy impossible. Since it was impossible to rebel, a wave of hopeless resignation spread over the whole empire.

If a farmer succeeded in bettering his property and adding to it, he knew that he would be raised to the rank of a *curialis*, and this meant further oppression, slavery, and ultimate ruin. Prudence advised against making fruitless efforts of improvement. Desperate means were sometimes used to improve one's condition: a peasant would try to enter the army or take up brigandage, a soldier would desert, a *curialis* would become a public official, a soldier, or a tenant, but it would all be in vain.[22]

The best way to eke out an existence was to attach oneself to some great landowner. Such a one was powerful enough to resist the demands of the imperial agents and to carry on like an independent prince.

Even in St. Ambrose we can read how laborers in order to support themselves had recourse to armed robbery.[23]

In such circumstances it is easy to see how a caste system should have arisen. Social position and profession were handed down from father to son. State employees enjoyed exemption from taxes and from mandatory services required of other individuals, and at the end of their career they received titles of honor, but their sons had to continue their work. Employees in the state industries, whether in the mints, or in the cloth mills, or elsewhere, were bound to the shops for life. Craftsmen of different trades were banded together into corporations, and they had to marry women engaged in the same type of work. In the cities such unions were official and obligatory. There were corporations of bakers, masons, coachmen, carpenters, blacksmiths, woodcutters (who provided the firewood to heat the baths), gladiators, mimes, musicians, and actors. The latter were practically slaves to the amusement for the people. Not only were actors and jockeys forbidden to give up their trade but they could not even leave their city. The soldiers, who were with difficulty recruited from the lower strata of society, had to serve for twenty years or more. They could marry, but by law their sons belonged to the army. If they tried to flee, they were pursued by the laws, as were those of the other categories as well.

From this it should be apparent why the strength of a Roman army from the middle of the fourth century on was in proportion to the number of barbarians serving in it. The fate of the farmers has already been mentioned, but it is further indicated by the following constitution of Theodosius: "A tiller of the soil may not go where he wants but must remain in the service of his patron, and no one can take him into his own service with impunity since the first patron has the right to recover the fugitive." The reason for this is that "everyone should endure his own fate."[24]

These various factors also explain the decline in population. Legitimate marriages now imposed burdens which were so impossible that many preferred temporary unions with slaves. Even though St. Ambrose considered it his special duty to exhort individuals to the practice of virginity rather than to enter into the married state, it is rather symptomatic of the times that he exhorts his people not to despise marriage and not to degrade themselves by illegitimate unions with slaves.[25] The decline in population is well indicated by references in the letters of both Symmachus and St. Jerome to thousands of acres of once fertile land that had returned to woods or deserts.[26] Nevertheless, it cannot be denied that, even during these years of decline, life on the great estates and in the large cities could be gay and brilliant and that the great lords continued to surround themselves with all sorts of luxuries. But the young official at Sirmium was too intelligent not to understand the sad realities. He was not one to be wrapped up in his own personal problems, and he must have given considerable thought to means of improving the system of government.

Ambrose's years at Sirmium, even apart from his activity on the council of the prefect, also offered him the opportunity of becoming intimately acquainted with the religious situation, specifically with the attitude of the civil authorities toward paganism and Christianity.

Men could still remember the last great persecution of the Church.[27] In the winter of 302-303, when Galerius went with Diocletian to Nicomedia, he convinced his senior of the need to suppress the new religion. In the third century, the Church had already acquired a considerable amount of strength and prestige. As one modern historian has observed, "oppression, compulsion, persecution were the mottoes of the State; love, compassion, consolation were the maxims of the Church. The Church, unique in this respect among the other religious communities, not only administered spiritual relief but promised and gave practical help in the miseries of actual life, while the State oppressed and persecuted the helper."[28]

Scholars differ widely in their evaluation of Diocletian and his accomplishments. Some have spoken highly of his moral principles and of the substantial goodness of his reforms. Others have maintained that these latter provide "the plainest proof of Diocletian's utter incapacity to invent anything new."[29] Despite the numerous possibilities at hand for a reorganization of the state, he simply took "the old beaten track which led directly to ruin and slavery."[30]

In such a case, then, just as in the first persecution under Nero the Christians served as a scapegoat for the burning of Rome, so in the last persecution under Diocletian they would have been used to distract the people from the emperor's notoriously unsuccessful financial reforms and to restore his lost favor with the general public. A remote preparation for the persecution, moreover, had been made by the anti-Christian propaganda of the philosophers Porphyry and Hierocles, and there was the added irritant of certain Christian sects such as the Montanists and Marcionites which maintained that military service was essentially wrong. But whatever were its causes, the first edict of this persecution, which was to be the longest and most severe in the history of Rome, was posted at Nicomedia on February 24, 303. The wife of Diocletian, Prisca, and his daughter, Valeria, abjured their faith, but countless others, including great dignitaries at court, refused to comply with the emperor's order.

On May 1, 305, beneath a statue of Zeus on a small hill near Nicomedia, Diocletian took off his crown and purple cloak and placed them on Galerius. He then retired to cultivate cabbages in the splendid gardens of his palace at Salona on the Adriatic coast. But the persecution continued, and it continued with varying degrees of intensity until April 30, 311, when Galerius, again at Nicomedia, published the edict of toleration which marked its end.

The right of Christians to exist as such and to possess property had been already publicly recognized by Alexander Severus almost a century earlier, but there was always the old Roman religion at hand to instigate new persecutions in the name of tradition. Moreover, there was a new religious movement in the empire that had gained ever increasing importance during the third century. This was a kind of all-embracing, abstract theism that worshiped a *summus Deus*, or "supreme God," a deity that appealed alike to the better minds of the Roman ruling class, to Neoplatonic philosophers, and to the devotees of the Eastern religions, a great many of whom could be found in the army and even among the emperors.[31] At one time this syncretistic theism seemed to be the most formidable antagonist of the God of the Christians. Naturally speaking, the fact that Christ and not Mithra became the God of all these worshipers was due in no small part to Constantine.

The night before the decisive battle with Maxentius at the

Milvian bridge on October 27, 312, "Constantine was warned in his sleep that he should have the shields of his soldiers marked with the heavenly sign before beginning the battle. He did as he was commanded and had the shields marked with an 'X' crossed from top to bottom by an 'I' bent over at the top representing the name of Christ."[32] These words of Lactantius have been endlessly discussed, and scholars have come up with the most diverse conclusions. However, it is now generally agreed that Constantine yielded to a religious impulse, though some maintain that this was of a merely superstitious and pathological order and others that it was genuinely supernatural. Here as elsewhere the decision depends pretty much upon one's point of view, whether it be from heaven or from earth.[33]

Political and military considerations would rather have argued against such a move. The Christians, especially in the West, were a small minority. Even in the cities, where they were most numerous, they did not constitute a twentieth of the population. Nevertheless the external manifestations of Constantine's adherence to the new faith multiplied after his victory. When he entered Rome on October 29, 312, he accepted from the senate a statue representing his imperial divinity, but he wanted a cross to be put in its hand. He remained at Rome until January 1, 313. Then he went to Milan for the wedding of his sister Flavia Julia Constantia and Licinius. It was in February, 313, that the two Augusti reached the decisions that came to be known as the Edict of Milan. A formal edict proclaiming tolerance and religious peace was probably never issued as such. The name has simply been given to the measures which they took by mutual agreement at Milan to stop the persecution, and to remedy its wrongs by revoking the confiscations of the preceding years and restoring to the Church the right to possess property that she had already enjoyed before the outbreak of the persecution in 303.[34]

The terms of this agreement are known from letters of Constantine written in February, April, and October, 313, and from the famous rescript of Licinius published at Nicomedia on June 13, 313. On the morrow of the most furious persecution, Christianity was not only tolerated but it enjoyed equal rights with the official pagan religion. Constantine, moreover, freed the Catholic clergy from the obligations of public office and service. Such exemptions had already been granted to other professions, including doctors, athletes, and professors, since their work itself contributed to the common good. Another indication of Constantine's devotion to Christianity may be seen in the monogram "X" engraved on his helmet in a coin from the mint of Pavia issued in 315. Rivalry between Licinius and Constantine gave rise to the persecution of Licinius in the East in 320. After defeating Licinius in 324, Constantine became the sole ruler of the empire and published laws in favor of the Church in the East, which had suffered so much more than that of the West. All the faithful who were still enslaved or banished were freed; the churches regained their lost patrimonies; and the relatives of the martyrs, or, if these were lacking, their respective churches, received the goods that had been confiscated from those who had suffered for the faith. In 318, Constantine compared episcopal jurisdiction with that of magistrates, and, in 333, he gave civil cognizance to the sentences pronounced by bishops. Many of his other decrees also give evidence of Christian influence. Thus he revoked Augustus's laws against celibacy; he made various provisions for public morality, among which were those which condemned concubinage and gave protection to those who were weak, to the innocent, and to prisoners and slaves. However, he was no persecutor of paganism. No temples were destroyed or closed simply because they were pagan. Seeming exceptions to this general rule, such as we find at Heliopolis and Alexandria, are to be explained by the scandalous character of the cults practiced there. Though he tolerated pagan institutions, it was obvious that he personally favored those of the new religion.[35] At Constantina in Africa he donated the land for, and paid for the construction of, a Christian basilica. He had another sumptuous basilica erected at Nicomedia in Asia Minor and placed in it the trophies of his victory over Licinius as a dedicatory offering to the Savior. He also raised up a great basilica at Antioch, two at Jerusalem (the Martyrion on the site of the Crucifixion and the Anastasis over the Holy Sepulcher), one at Bethlehem, and others at Naples, Capua, Ostia, and Albano. At Constantinople, in addition to many smaller churches, he constructed two basilicas, one of the Apostles and the other of Irene, or Peace. For the churches in his capital city, he had fifty precious manuscripts of the scriptures copied out. Rome also owes many churches to Constantine: the small basilica of Sts. Peter and Marcellinus on the Via Labicana, the basilica of St. Lawrence on the Via Tiburtina, the basilica of St. Agnes on the Via Nomentana, and the basilica of the Holy Cross. He donated the old palace of the Laterani, formerly used as an imperial residence, to the Roman pontiff, either Pope Miltiades or Pope St. Silvester, and built alongside it the basilica of the Savior. Finally, he erected basilicas over the tomb of St. Peter on the Vatican hill and over that of St. Paul on the Ostian Way. Something should also be said about their elaborate gold trappings. For example, in addition to endowing the churches with altars, chalices, patens, and lamps of various kinds, he placed gold crosses, each weighing one hundred and ten pounds, over the tombs of Sts. Peter and Paul. He also provided endowments for the churches in lands and mobile properties. The Lateran basilica thus received an annual income of 5,390 gold coins. Since each of these at the time of Constantine weighed 4.55 grams, the income was the equivalent of at least 31,000 dollars. From the same sources the baptistery of the basilica received annual revenues of 10,054 gold coins, or some 70,000 dollars. The annual income of St. Paul's basilica from its properties amounted to 4,070 gold coins.

It is no wonder, then, that a rich philosopher and enthusiast for paganism like Vettius Agorius Praetextatus, who was prefect of Rome in 367 and praetorian prefect of Italy in 384, could say with a smile to Pope Damasus: "Make me bishop of Rome and I will at once become a Christian!"[36]

The favors which Constantine lavished on the Church did not, however, remove all traces of paganism from his own personal life. Though he was extremely generous with the Church, he did not become an actual member of it through baptism until on the point of death. Worse still, as has already been noted, because of his despotic and fickle temperament he made numerous mistakes in letting himself be influenced by a faction of Arian bishops. The servility of these bishops and the confusion they created through their personal rivalries provided numerous occasions for the head of the state to intervene in matters that were of a purely ecclesiastical character. Such intervention under Constantine was still something of an exception, but under Constantius II the abuse came to be regarded as a constitutional prerogative with disastrous results for the unity of the Church.

With a stubbornness worthy of a better cause Constantius profoundly disturbed the normal operations of the Church. In addition to his constant meddling with, and tyranny over, the affairs of the Church was his intolerance of paganism. In this he received the support of a number of fanatics such as the converted Sicilian senator, Firmicus Maternus, who between the years 346-350 wrote a violent attack on paganism, exhorting the emperors Constantine II and Constans to extirpate it completely: "Greater authority must be used so that wretched men may be brought over completely to a sound frame of mind so that after they have been cured no trace of the former pestilence may remain. . . . Most pious emperors remove without fear the ornaments of the temples. Let the fire of your mints or the flames of your refineries melt down these gods, and transfer all their revenues to your own use and control."[37] During these years temples in Syria, Egypt, Phrygia, and Cappadocia were, as a matter of fact, pulled down. In his legislation, Constantius left no doubt as to his own will in the matter: there are strict provisions for the abolition of pagan worship and the closing of the temples. In many large areas of the empire these provisions remained a dead letter, but in others, especially where Christians were in charge of the administration, as in a number of Eastern provinces, the temples were actually closed. Julian's brief attempt to restore paganism has already been mentioned, but even though he failed in this the pagan reaction did not end with him.

When Ambrose began his political career, relations between Church and State were dominated by the religious policy of Valentinian I, which was one of non-intervention. According to his decrees, no religion approved by antiquity was to be regarded as illegal though, as his predecessors had done before him, he condemned both magic and astrology. The pagan Ammianus Marcellinus praises this emperor, who had been raised by the Christians to the throne after the death of Julian, for his religious tolerance.[38]

In Pannonia, Ambrose discovered that the country regions were for the most part pagan, and strongly attached to their traditional deities, just as they were in Italy. On the other hand, there were powerful groups of Christians in the cities, and they were becoming the majority. The attitude of the pagan aristocracy and the more cultured strata of society was on the whole one of hostility. Their antipathies were fostered by the writings of such individuals as Julian the Apostate and the rhetorician Eunapius of Sardis. In the anti-Christian polemic of these pagan apologists, Christianity was described as a kind of barbarism, a disease of the intellect, a hatred of light and life, and a mixture of various gloomy practices such as the worship of the martyrs, which seemed to them to be something indecent and disgusting. With brilliant irony in his *Against the Galileans*, Julian highlights the failure of certain Christians and even bishops to live up to their evangelical calling. When he was at Sirmium, Ambrose must have frequently heard expressions of contempt for the Christians coming from the high officials with whom he associated. For the pagans of the fourth century, the followers of Christ were a stupid lot lacking both feeling and intelligence.[39]

At Sirmium, however, there was also a flourishing Christian church, but during these years under the rule of an Arian bishop, Germinius. Unfortunate as this was, it did not mean the apostasy of the ordinary Christian. As Hilary of Poitiers notes in a work written in 365, "Under the priests of anti-Christ the Christians do not perish since they judge the faith of their bishops from their words. They hear that Jesus Christ is God, and they believe what is said. . . . The ears of the people are thus purer than the hearts of their bishops."[40]

In the year 356, Martin, a young layman of Savaria (today, Szombathely in Hungary) began an anti-Arian campaign. His zeal, however, brought down upon him the wrath of the Arian bishop of the city, and he was beaten and expelled.[41]

Even more spectacular was an unfortunate incident which occurred at Sirmium in 366, and which must certainly have come to Ambrose's attention. Three stalwarts of the city, Heraclian, Firmian, and Aurelian were thrown into prison for their opposition to Arianism. On January 13, 366, they were publicly questioned by the bishop in the church at Sirmium in the presence of the clergy and magistrates of the city and those of the public who cared to attend. When Heraclian defended his faith, the bishop, Germinius, became angry: "Was it perhaps Eusebius [of Vercelli] and Hilary [of Poitiers] that put these ideas into your head?" he asked. When Heraclian replied, Germinius was only further incensed and ordered the defendant to be struck on the mouth. The dispute then continued. Heraclian quoted Isaias, and Germinius St. Paul, both with little understanding. They then argued the divinity of the Holy Spirit without reaching any accord. The clergy and people fanatically demanded that the three should be put to death, but Germinius, having recovered his temper, opposed any such radical measure: "No, no, my brothers! They do not know what they are saying. If bishops have fallen into error, how much more simple fellows like these here before us."[42]

From the working class with which he must have come into contact as an advocate at Sirmium Ambrose could have learned some edifying lessons. Though the middle class was disappearing at this time, the lower class of free workers, who were replacing slave laborers, was increasing. Even if governmental regulations made such a life difficult, it was not entirely impossible. Work had acquired a new dignity. The laziness and sloth of both the very wealthy and of the unemployed mobs in the city found their clearest condemnation in the example of Christ and His apostles. For several centuries Christianity had been fighting the pagan contempt for manual labor and for the small merchant or salaried employee.[43] In the third century Tertullian had openly maintained that the least Christian worker knew more of the nature and perfections of God than Plato.[44] At the end of the fourth century, St. John Chrysostom described the poor shop of the Christian worker, who was both healthier and happier than the rich man at his leisure.[45] In their faith and in their prayer the Christians found the calm necessary for any undertaking. Labor was regarded as something ennobling even when it was obligatory and oppressive as it was in the corporations of the fourth century. In an epitaph of 341, a Christian woman is described as having been a "worker," almost as if this were a matter for boasting.[46]

In such surroundings, Christianity could give an excellent account of itself. Ambrose could see the good moral influence that the large numbers of Christians exercised in Sirmium, but here, as elsewhere, there were also sorry contrasts. Alongside the heroism of the ascetics and the sacrifices of the virgins there was the poor example too often given by the higher clergy, especially among the Arians.

Two letters of St. Jerome, one written to a young patrician woman Eustochium in 384, and another to Nepotian written in

394, can give some idea of these evils, even though Jerome obviously exaggerates. According to him, clerics, monks, nuns, and Christians living in the world are all only Christians in name. For one who was still outside the Church, like Ambrose at Rome and Sirmium, the Christian communities to which he was being invited by his family traditions were not without their defects. And, as a matter of fact, the Church, though holy in its origins and in its ends, is made up of real men, men as they are and not necessarily as they should be. During these years of serious moral decline, those who were being converted in ever increasing numbers were not always guided by the highest motives. They frequently brought with them into the Church their pagan way of life and thus contributed to lowering the intellectual and spiritual tone of the communities. St. Jerome aptly summarizes the situation by saying that the Church had become greater in power and wealth after the age of the martyrs, but weaker and poorer in virtue.[47]

A noble Christian woman, Fabiola, for example, after separating from her dissolute husband, entered into a second marriage while her first husband was still alive.[48] Sabinian, a deacon who had fled from Italy to escape the vengeance of an angry husband, renewed his exploits in Palestine.[49] A prominent Christian woman struck an old woman in St. Peter's basilica so hard in the face that she bled. She had been distributing alms to the poor in the church and became angry when the unfortunate beggar returned for a second coin.[50]

Though such incidents were certainly the exception, a reading of St. Jerome, even allowing for his usual polemic, leaves one with the impression that there were considerable disorders among the Christians of the fourth century. Thus he writes: "I cannot bring myself to speak of the many virgins who daily fall and are lost to the bosom of the Church, their mother. . . . The very clergy, who ought to inspire matrons with respect by their teaching and authority, kiss them on the forehead, and putting forth their hands (so that, if you knew no better, you might suppose them in the act of blessing), take wages for their visits. They, meanwhile, seeing that priests cannot do without them, are lifted up into pride; and, having experienced both, they prefer the license of widowhood to the restraints of marriage, calling themselves chaste livers and nuns. After an immoderate supper they retire to rest to dream of the apostles. . . . There are others—I speak of those of my own order—who seek the priesthood and the diaconate simply that they may be able to see women with less restraint. Such men think of nothing but their dress; they use perfumes freely, and see that there are no creases in their leather shoes. Their curled hair shows traces of the tongs; their fingers glisten with rings; they walk on tiptoe across a damp road so as not to splash their feet. When you see men acting in this way, think of them rather as bridegrooms than as clergymen. Certain persons have devoted the whole of their energies and life to the single object of knowing the names, houses, and characters of married ladies."[51] And in another letter to Nepotian, he advises him: "Seek for no worldly gain under Christ's banner, lest having more than when you first became a cleric you hear men say to your shame, 'Their portion shall not profit them.' . . . It is a shame to have to admit that whereas pagan priests, actors, jockeys, and prostitutes can inherit property, clerics and monks may not do so legally. And this is a disability which was not enacted by persecutors but by Christian emperors. I do not complain of the law, but I grieve that we have deserved such a harsh statute. . . . It is a disgrace to you if the consul's lictors or soldiers keep watch before your door, and if the judge of the province has a better dinner with you than in his own palace. If you plead as an excuse your wish to intercede for the unhappy and the oppressed, I reply that a worldly judge will defer more to a clergyman who is self-denying than to one who is rich; he will pay more regard to your holiness than to your wealth."[52] Jerome also inveighs against the custom of unmarried ascetics of different sexes living together: "How comes this plague of the *agapetae* to be in the Church? Whence come these unwedded wives, these novel concubines, these prostitutes, as I will call them, though they cling to a single partner? One house holds them and one chamber. They often occupy the same bed, and yet they call us suspicious if we fancy anything amiss. A brother leaves his virgin sister; a virgin, slighting her unmarried brother, seeks a brother in a stranger. Both alike profess to have but one object, to find spiritual consolation from those not of their kin; but their real aim is to indulge in intercourse. It is on such that Solomon in the Book of Proverbs heaps his scorn. 'Can a man take fire in his bosom,' he says, 'and not burn his clothes?' "[53]

In the third century, St. Cyprian had already condemned this manner of living together as a source of scandal. In the letter which the bishops of the East wrote to the pope at Rome in 267-268 complaining about Paul of Samosata, one of their accusations was that he kept two young women in his house.[54] And, late in the fourth century, St. John Chrysostom wrote two works condemning such asceticism. But he was not excessively severe: though he was himself ready to believe in the virtue of these virgins who lived with men who were practicing celibacy, he was not able to make others believe it, and such an abuse caused both Jews and pagans to deride the Church.[55]

The few extant texts referring to the *agapetae* are not sufficient to make us believe that they were widespread throughout the Christian world, but it is reasonable to suspect that at Sirmium and at Rome Ambrose may have learned of scandals connected with them. Later, as bishop of Milan, he took energetic measures to preserve the integrity of his flock. We see him, for example, purifying the Christian worship of the martyrs from pagan intemperance.

While he was still at Sirmium, Ambrose must certainly have heard of the death of Pope Liberius. After his return from exile, this beleaguered pontiff had remained undisturbed at Rome. He had not taken part in the Council of Rimini in 359, where all the bishops of the West had finally surrendered to the Arian pretensions of Constantius, and he had to see to it, practically by himself, that the decisions and the creed of Nicea were restored to their earlier efficacy. In this he had the support of Hilary of Poitiers, who passed through Rome on his way back from exile about the year 360. In a decree, probably issued in 362, Liberius condemned the Council of Rimini and fixed the conditions for the return of the Arians to the Church. Some extremists reproached him for his indulgence, but his moderation was really a credit to him.

When Felix died, December 22, 365, his followers had the good sense not to persist in their schism. Consequently, because of the meekness of Liberius, a union between the two hostile parties was effected. Although the clergy of Felix and of Liberius were thus officially reconciled with each other, they continued to look upon each other with some suspicion. By at least some of his subjects, Liberius was accused of having been overly generous with the Felicians.

Liberius died on September 24, 366. The intransigent anti-Felicians gathered together in the Julian basilica in the Trastevere. Among them were seven priests and three deacons. They elected the deacon Ursinus as pope, and he was hurriedly consecrated that same day, Sunday, September 24, by the bishop of Tivoli. Meanwhile, the great majority of the faithful and of the clergy, including former followers of Felix, elected the deacon Damasus as pope in the basilica of Lucina. Damasus had himself been a Felician. Since it was getting late in the day, the following Sunday was set for his ordination and consecration. As the group was breaking up it learned of the election that had taken place in the Julian basilica. Excitement ran high and many rushed to the church in the Trastevere. The Ursinians put up such a stout resistance that in the ensuing brawl some were killed and others injured. The following Sunday, October 1, Damasus, in accordance with a long-established tradition, was consecrated by the bishop of Ostia in the Lateran basilica.[56] The prefect of Rome, Viventius, instead of trying to settle the dispute between the two parties went into the suburbs of the city until the tempers of the people should have boiled down. Later, at the request of Damasus and others, he decided to expel the leaders of the Ursinians from Rome.

But their followers continued to meet together. Their priests were therefore arrested. But these were soon released in a popular uprising by their friends, who then seized the basilica of Sicininus (later known as the Liberian basilica and St. Mary Major) and converted it into a kind of fortress. On October 26, the supporters of Pope Damasus, including even some priests, laid siege to the basilica. At least one hundred and thirty-seven people were slain in the fighting that ensued. After giving this figure, Ammianus Marcellinus goes on to say that it is quite natural that those who wish to become bishop of Rome should do everything in their power to achieve it: "For when they obtain it, they will be free from care since they will be enriched by the gifts of matrons, and they will ride seated in carriages wearing elegant garments, and they will serve such fine banquets that their entertainments will surpass the dinners provided by kings. These men could be truly happy if, despising the greatness of the city behind which they conceal their faults, they would live in the fashion of certain provincial bishops, whose great temperance in food and drink, poverty of apparel, and eyes fixed upon the earth, commend them to the Eternal Deity and to His true worshipers as pure and devout men."[57]

The following year the emperor Valentinian, thinking that by this time peace must have been restored, allowed Ursinus and his followers to return to Rome. On September 15, 367, Ursinus solemnly re-entered the city. Subsequent rioting, however, forced the new prefect, Praetextatus, to again send him into exile on November 16. The Liberian basilica was restored to Damasus. Detained in Gaul, Ursinus did not appear again upon the scene for many years.

In the palace of the governor at Sirmium, where the prefect was also a member of the Roman aristocracy, the tragic events at Rome were closely followed.

During the years which he spent at Sirmium, Ambrose may have occupied himself with religious as well as legal matters if the Latin translation of the Greek *War of the Jews* by Flavius Josephus is to be attributed to him. During the Middle Ages this work was ascribed to Hegesippus, which is merely an alternate form of the name Josephus.[58]

It was probably about the year 370 that Ambrose was named *consularis,* or governor, of Aemilia-Liguria. As he sent him off to his new position, Probus, the praetorian prefect, counseled him: "Go and conduct yourself not as a judge but as a bishop."[59]

IV
Milan

○

Roman Milan. Ausonius's description of the city. The people. The inscriptions. Christian Milan. The bishops of the city. Auxentius. Ambrose as governor.

In the Peutingerian map, the Roman city of *Mediolanum,* later to be known as Milan, is merely indicated by two towers. But because of its strategic position, it was bound to grow extensively.[1] The Roman *itineraria,* or early pilgrim guides, mention five roads radiating from Milan: the first toward Bergamo, Verona, Aquileia, and the Balkans; the second toward Como, Spluga, Chur, and the countries of the North; the third toward Lodi, Piacenza, Ravenna, and Rome; the fourth toward Pavia, Turin, and Genoa; and the fifth toward Novara, Vercelli, Ivrea, Aosta, and the Great and Small St. Bernards.

References to Milan in ancient writers are extremely rare. Cicero mentions a treaty made between Rome and the conquered city of Milan. Plutarch, to show that Caesar was not fastidious in his eating, notes that the great general was once entertained by Valerius Leo on his way through the city. When he was served asparagus seasoned with "ointment," that is, with butter, and not with the olive oil customary at Rome, he ate it without complaint, though his Roman friends showed their disgust with the fare.[2]

In the first century before Christ, the primitive Insubrian settlement had become a *municipium,* or free city, with its own laws, but later, perhaps in the age of the Antonines, it became known as a "colony." This was not due to an influx of colonists like the five thousand, including five hundred Greek immigrants, that came to Como during the rule of Caesar. It was given this title in the second century as a mark of honor, while still retaining its earlier constitution as a municipality. At the end of this same century, Milan became the most important city beyond the Po. In the middle of the third century Gallienus and Valerian besieged Milan, where Manlius Acilius Aureolus had been proclaimed emperor by his troops before they eventually slew him. Milan was also among the nine greatest cities of the empire to which the Roman senate in A.D. 235 sent special notices of the nomination of Marcus Aurelius Tacitus as emperor. When Diocletian in 286 took as his colleague Marcus Aurelius Maximianus, a son of a colonist in the environs of Sirmium, the latter chose Milan as his place of residence. Finally, in 293, with the definitive organization of the tetrarchy, Milan became the official seat for the Augustus of the West, just as Nicomedia, and later Constantinople, was the official residence of the Augustus of the East. Throughout the whole of the fourth century, Milan retained its privileged position as a capital, but in 404 this was transferred to Ravenna.[3]

Certainly among the most notable events in the history of imperial Milan was the meeting of Constantine and Licinius in February, 313, for the marriage of the latter to the former's sister. On this occasion the two Augusti brought to a final halt the last persecution of the Church and defined the terms of religious peace. Constantine later reunited the whole empire under his sole authority, but it was again divided after his death. Of his three sons, Constantius II lived for the longest time at Milan, and it was here that this emperor in 355 proclaimed his nephew Julian as Caesar. Valentinian I stayed with his court at Milan from November 1, 364, to near the end of November, 365, when he took up again his official residence at Trier. During the first years of his reign, Gratian also lived at Trier, but in March, 381, he transferred his court and the offices of the empire of the West back again to Milan.

Throughout the third and fourth centuries the empire was suffering from various invasions of barbarians. During the reign of Valerian (270-275), bands of Marcomanni had devastated the land about the city. Such incursions prompted Maximian to surround the city with a new circuit of walls.

The most complete description of imperial Milan comes from the pen of Ausonius, who passed through Milan in 379 on his return from Rome to Bordeaux. His epigram of eleven lines may be translated as follows: "At Milan everything is marvelous. It has an abundance of everything: countless beautiful homes, men of great eloquence, a light-hearted populace, a site enlarged by a double wall, a circus and a covered theater which are the delight of the citizens, temples, a royal palace, a splendid mint, famous baths dedicated to Hercules with their porticoes filled with marble statues, and walls surrounded by a moat. All of these objects rival one another in beauty and grandeur, and they do not suffer in comparison with those of Rome."[4]

In his description of Milan, Ausonius fails to mention an amphitheater, one of the most popular places of amusement in a typical Roman town.[5] But we know that such a structure must have existed from a reference to it in Paulinus's *Life of St. Ambrose*,[6] from an epitaph of the gladiator Urbicus,[7] from a street still known as the Via Arena, and, finally, from possible references to it in the writings of St. Ambrose himself.[8]

As with many other cities in antiquity, it is not easy to determine the population of Milan during the fourth century. The walls of the city were two and one half miles in circumference and embraced an area of approximately two hundred and seventy-five acres. Claudius Mamertinus, in an oration in honor of Maximian, mentions the large crowds that gathered to watch the passage of Diocletian and Maximian in a carriage through the streets of the city.[9] From such isolated data, A. De Marchi has come to the conclusion that there were probably about 130,000 people dwelling in the city at this time.[10]

Certain it is, however, that the establishment of the imperial court at Milan meant an influx of thousands. The posts in the imperial bureaucracy and army had to be staffed with men of many different categories. The relatively few Milanese inscriptions frequently mention the corporations of the *fabri* and of the *centonarii.* The former were employed in the construction of buildings and the latter made the awnings which were soaked in vinegar and water to put out fires. They were thus a kind of "fire department." Their corporation was divided into twelve centuries, which were in turn divided into decuries.

The metalworkers, or those employed in the treasury, were enrolled in a third corporation, which was also divided into twelve centuries. The size of these corporations would seem to indicate the flourishing state of the laboring classes during the fourth century in Milan. But there is epigraphical evidence for other types of activity as well. There is still extant the epitaph of a businessman who had interests on both sides of the Alps, and who was at the same time the patron of the boatmen of Como. Another merchant from Apulia dealt in military cloaks, and another from Ravenna was a wholesaler of shoes. Publius Julius Macedon traded in cloth and skins. There was also a merchant from Metz who specialized in cloth for the army. Then there is the epitaph of a distinguished citizen who made his fortune as a banker. These various activities would lead us to believe that Milan was a center of foreign as well as local trade. Among the inscriptions are references also to *sagarii,* or *castrensiarii,* the fabricators of military cloaks. This seems to indicate that Milan was an important textile center at an early date, as it later was during the Middle Ages and still is even in our own day.

Another inscription refers to a corporation of muleteers of the Porta Vercellina and Jovia. Justus, a shoemaker of the *gens Atilia,* in addition to his name has left a picture of his worktable on his epitaph. Under the arch of the East gate may still be seen the dyer or tailor of the family of the Novellii cutting a piece of cloth, the emblem of his trade. Other examples of the same sort may be found in other epitaphs preserved in the Archeological Museum at Milan. On the tomb of his freedman, a patron has written: "His poorest works equalled the best of other artisans, and no one could equal what he himself did well." Such esteem for manual labor indicates a society in which work was no longer despised as it had been in ancient Rome but regarded rather as a source of wealth and honor.

The inscriptions also support St. Ambrose in what he will have to say as a bishop about the passion of his Milanese for horse races and theatrical productions.

A young man who died at the age of twenty-eight complains of his premature death on his tombstone and reminds the passer-by of his great enthusiasm for horses. On a stone in the Ambrosian library may still be seen a portrait of the actor Pilades as he lifts his mask and, as it is said, receives the applause of the *cives Mediolanenses* in the theater which stood near the church of St. Victor. Urbicus, a promising young gladiator who died at Milan when he was twenty-two, is represented in his armor with his dog beside him. On his epitaph he refers to his victories in the amphitheater. This was dedicated to him by his fond wife who had lived with him for seven years.

Other voices from ancient Milan may be found in the lament of a mother for her son who died at twenty-four, whom she calls an *animula iucundissima,* or "most delightful little soul"; in the delightful idyl of two children carved on a stone slab with a puppy as their playmate, in the gratitude of two students expressed on the tomb of their former teacher; in the bequest of twenty-four thousand sesterces of the pious and generous Albucia Magiana for three religious corporations; and finally, in the will of the devoted freedwoman Mirsile who left four hundred sesterces so that each year the tomb of her patron might be decorated with roses.[11]

Milan was also famous for its schools. Virgil left Mantua to complete his studies in this city. In the early second century, Pliny the Younger asked a boy at Como if he were a student. "Yes," was the answer he received. "And where?" "At Milan." "But why not here?" And then his father answered for the lad: "Because there are no suitable teachers here."[12] For the fourth century, we have a number of pages in the *Confessions* of St. Augustine describing his own career as a professor of rhetoric in the city.

Though Ausonius was nominally a Christian, his works are almost completely pagan in character, as is evident particularly in the obscene nuptial canto which he made up from lines drawn from Virgil. His reference to temples in his description of Milan should, as a consequence, be understood of pagan rather than of Christian structures. In the Archeological Museum there are some thirty marble statues of pagan deities. More than a third of the extant votive inscriptions are dedicated to Jupiter. There are six dedicated to the *Matronae*, divinities of Celtic origin worshiped in Northern Italy before the advent of the Romans.[13] Of the remaining inscriptions, three are dedicated to Hercules, two to Mercury, and one to Minerva. Among the Milanese inscriptions referring to priestly offices, there is one of a pontiff who was at the same time an employee of the city, another of a pontiff who was also a decurion, another of a flamen of Titus, another of a flamen of Trajan, another of a priest for the worship of Augustus and Rome, another of a priest for the youth of Milan, and still others of the same general nature. Six inscriptions refer to the cult of Cybele, the Great Idaean Mother. Albucia Magiana left a sum of money to the dendrophori, the cannophori, and the Martenses. The first two of these three sacred colleges took part in the processions in honor of Cybele on March 15th and 22nd.

There was at least one Mithraeum in imperial Milan, as there was in all of the cities of the Late Empire where troops were stationed. Evidence for this is found in the inscription of Publius Acilius Pisonianus. He had been a *pater patratus,* that is, a high dignitary in the cult of Mithra, and he states that at his own expense he had reconstructed a Mithraeum and a Mithraic grotto that had been destroyed by fire on land purchased at public expense.

A damaged inscription refers to a certain Gaius Gallio Atticus who in a solemn rite had sought the divine will by casting lots. As bishop, St. Ambrose warned his flock about the malice of such practices.[14]

A number of inscriptions from Milan furnish us with some information with respect to the religious attitudes and aspirations of the people whom St. Ambrose was to rule as governor. Here as elsewhere in the Roman world, the pagans of the fourth century were syncretistic. They worshiped not only the native Celtic gods and those introduced by the Romans but also Eastern deities such as Mithra and Cybele. The wife of the gladiator Urbicus, who died at the age of twenty-two, takes pride in the fact that he had fought thirteen times in the arena, and in the last two lines of his epitaph she recommends his Manes, or, as we would say, his departed soul, to the piety of the passers-by. In another inscription a dying girl consoles her father, who stands by her bed, with the thought that her misfortune has been decreed by fate. Another epitaph records the cry of sorrow which a mother directs to her son, a soldier of the Second Legion, who died far from home at the age of twenty-seven, and who perforce was left unburied by his companions: "Alas! you have deceived me, leaving me alone!"[15]

Some further notion of the pagan attitude towards death may be derived from the papyri of Egypt. Here as at Milan men were confronted with the sorrow of a death without any real hope for the future. Thus we read in a letter of a certain Hephaistion of the third century: "Since the gods have had no compassion on me, I will have none for them."[16] Eudaimonis, the mother of Apollonius, a recently deceased councilman, practically despairs at her loss, though she was naturally pious: "I have not taken a bath, and I have not worshiped the gods."[17]

Christians, on the other hand, did not exaggerate their grief and their misfortunes. In a letter of the fourth century, a Christian woman even in the midst of great suffering calls God good. While the prayers of the pagans were centered almost exclusively upon the goods of the present life, Calonike, a Christian, asks her mother, even though she is far away, to pray for her salvation, since "there is no one with me, neither brother, nor sister, nor friend; no one, that is, but God alone."[18] Timius informs his wife Sophia of the grave straits into which he has fallen, but he also tells her of his calm trust since "God will take care of us."[19]

From the first half of the fourth century comes the collection of letters addressed to the Egyptian monk Paphnutius. They contain numerous requests of individuals who hoped that through his prayers they might overcome some difficulty, especially of a spiritual nature. But even before the discovery of the papyri, there was known the request which the sinful woman Thais addressed to him that she might be forgiven her sins. Similarly, another woman sent Basil of Caesarea a list of her sins so that through his prayers they might be forgiven.

This is the kind of world that Ambrose must have also found at Milan. Although the Church of Milan could boast of a few martyrs during the last persecution, the history of the Church itself prior to the coming of St. Ambrose consists of little more than a list of bishops.[20] Mirocles is the first bishop of Milan about whom we know anything more than the name. With fifteen other Italian bishops and three bishops from Gaul, he took part in the council held under Pope Miltiades on Friday, October 2, 313, in the Lateran palace at Rome.[21] Before these nineteen prelates appeared Caecilian, the bishop of Carthage, and Donatus, his rival. The latter claimed that Caecilian should not be regarded as a bishop since he had been ordained by one who had been accused of being a *traditor* during the last persecution, that is, by one who had handed over *(tradidisse)* the sacred books to the police. This dispute marks the origin of the Donatist schism, which for more than a century was to torment the Church of North Africa. The bishops voted unanimously in favor of Caecilian, but the matter was not ended since the Donatists were able to persuade Constantine that they should be heard again at a new council to be held at Arles. At this council, which met for the first time on August 1, 314, Mirocles, the bishop of Milan, was also present.

The ancient episcopal catalog of Milan lists Mirocles as the sixth occupant of the see. From this it has been deduced, after corrections were made in the figures given in the list, that the Church of Milan had its origins about the year 206. Others, however, with more probability, have set the date back to the second half of the second century without attempting to be more precise. Whatever may have been the exact time of its origin, it is interesting to note that the formation of the Church at Milan more or less corresponds with the transformation of the ancient municipality into the Colonia Antoniniana, or Aelia, or Aurelia Augusta Mediolanum, which took place at the end of the second, or the beginning of the third century. Both of these events indicate the growing importance of the city.

Among the more prominent successors of Mirocles was St. Protasius. He is mentioned by St. Athanasius and took part in the Council of Sardica in the fall of 343.

St. Eustorgius succeeded Protasius. He is called a *confessor* by St. Ambrose, quite possibly because he had suffered for the faith during the persecution of Diocletian before becoming bishop.

During the episcopate of Eustorgius, two councils were held at Milan, in 345 and again in 347-348, to condemn Photinus, the heretical bishop of Sirmium.

Dionysius succeeded Eustorgius. He has already been mentioned in connection with the Council of Milan of 355.

The violence which Valens, the Arian bishop of Mursa (Osijek in Yugoslavia), used on Dionysius during the first session of the council angered the crowd which filled the church. Since the emperor deemed it wise to transfer the conciliar meetings from the church to the halls of the imperial palace, it seems likely that the Christians made up a considerable portion of the city's populace. Athanasius, who is one of the chief sources for these events, tells us that Dionysius, Lucifer of Cagliari, and Eusebius of Vercelli were all accompanied on their painful way into exile by the admiration and regrets of their respective subjects. In later years, St. Ambrose as bishop was to recall frequently, and with emotion, his predecessor Dionysius, who, after many years of banishment, asked God for the favor of dying far from his see so that he would not have to witness on his return the confusion into which his flock had been thrown by the misrule of the Arians.

Dionysius actually did die in exile, and the court influenced by the Arian bishops Ursacius and Valens chose as his successor Auxentius. The latter was an ambitious schemer from the East who did not even know Latin, the language of his new flock.

Auxentius was already notorious for his activities in Egypt some years before.[22] He had there been a collaborator of Gregory of Cappadocia, whom the Arian faction had installed as bishop of Alexandria in 339. St. Ambrose tells us that Auxentius occupied the see at Milan "with arms and soldiers."[23] St. Hilary of Poitiers in his attack on Constantius of the spring of 360 reproaches this Arian bishop with having "terrified with his madness the pious people of that city by entering the church with soldiers and tearing the priests away from the altar."[24]

In the summer of 359, Auxentius set out for the Council of Rimini where more than four hundred bishops of the Western provinces were assembling. The great majority of these were orthodox. Some eighty Arian bishops, as a consequence, withdrew from the assembly and held meetings of their own. Among the leaders of this dissident group was Auxentius. Matters dragged on at great length. In October they were concluded with the capitulation of almost all the orthodox. The last months of the reign of Constantius II were thus marked with the seeming collapse of the Catholic position. In all the major cities of the East the episcopal sees were occupied by Arians while the legitimate bishops were in exile. Nevertheless the ordinary Christians continued to adore Christ and offer to Him their prayers as the true Son of God.

After Julian declared that the exiled bishops could return to their sees, Athanasius was able to take up his residence again in Alexandria, Hilary at Poitiers in Gaul, and Eusebius at Vercelli in Italy. But Hilary was also concerned about the state of the Church in Milan. In a synod assembled at Paris toward the end of 360, he had Auxentius, Ursacius, Valens, and other Arian leaders condemned. But, unfortunately, the weight of this condemnation was not sufficient to bring about the flight of Auxentius from Milan. In the final months of 364, Hilary and Eusebius came to Milan to insist with Valentinian I that he should banish Auxentius. The emperor wanted to avoid any kind of outbreak in the city. He did, however, permit a meeting of ten bishops in the presence of two officials of his court. Auxentius was persuaded to sign an almost perfectly orthodox profession of faith. But this was not enough to satisfy Hilary. When he protested, Valentinian ordered him to leave Milan at once. Early in 365, Hilary published his work *Against the Arians and Against Auxentius of Milan,* in which he inveighs against those servants of Christ who find their strength in the protection of princes and take pride in the fact that they are loved by the world. He even goes so far as to call Auxentius a "devil."

From this scathing work we know that the Christians of Milan still maintained the true faith, though at the same time there were many who in their desire for peace and because of their attachment to their old churches were willing to meet with the heretics: "You do wrong in allowing yourselves to be beguiled by your love for the walls. You do wrong in venerating the Church of God in covered buildings. You do wrong in excusing yourselves under the pretext of making peace. Even the Antichrist could set up his dwelling in those places. The mountains, forests, prisons, ravines seem to me to be a safer place of refuge."[25]

The great bishop of Gaul died, probably in 367, without the consolation of seeing orthodoxy re-established at Milan.

Auxentius was again condemned in a Roman council attended by ninety-two bishops which Pope Damasus had summoned, probably in the fall of 371.[26] A Milanese deacon, Sabinus, carried the synodal letter of this council to Alexandria in Egypt.[27] But this condemnation, as the others before it, was also little more than a dead letter. During these last years of Auxentius, Philastrius came to Milan to take care of the Catholics there. He later became bishop of Brescia.

Auxentius was still ruling undisturbed at Milan when Ambrose, now thirty-five years old, came to the city to assume his position as governor of the province.

It was not necessary for a public official to be particularly outstanding to receive such a promotion. Then, just as now, the bureaucracy was a kind of caste, and promotions within the system could be easily foreseen. Among the few things which Ammianus Marcellinus can find to say in favor of Constantius II was the fact that he scrupulously examined the qualifications of those who were to be advanced: "Under him no one who was to hold a high position was appointed to a post in the palace suddenly or untried, but a man who after ten years was to be marshal of the court, or head treasurer, or to fill any similar post, was thoroughly known."[28] The same system continued during the reign of Valentinian.

The chief function of a provincial governor during the second half of the fourth century was to mete out justice. Lawyers were thus quite logically often chosen for such a post. In some provinces the governor was called a "consular" *(consularis)*, in others a "corrector" *(corrector)*, and in still others a "president" *(praeses)*, but their authority was substantially the same.[29] At this particular time the province of Liguria comprised Bergamo, Brescia, Como, Lodi, Milan, Novara, Pavia, Vercelli, and Turin, while the province of Aemilia included Bologna, Faenza, Forlì, Imola, Modena, Parma, Piacenza, and Reggio.

Since from the time of Diocletian the civil authority was carefully distinguished from the military, the administration of justice pertained to the governor of the province, whether he was *praeses, corrector,* or *consularis.* The collection of taxes in the various provinces was assigned to the members of the municipal curiae and other agents who were under the direction of the counts of the largesses, or, as we would describe them, the ministers of finance. When Ambrose was made governor of the united provinces of Liguria and Aemilia, he received the title of *consularis,* and as such became a member of the Roman senate. During these years the emperor, Valentinian I, had his regular residence at Trier, where the central offices of the government were located. From this northern city he conducted his campaigns against the Alemanni, using for this purpose the services of Theodosius, an excellent Spanish general and the father of the future emperor.

As governor, Ambrose received the title of *clarissimus,* given to those in the third rank of the civil hierarchy. In his new position he was responsible for public order in the extensive area about the valley of the Po. Most of his time was spent in the courts since he was judge of first instance in all trials, whether they were of a civil or criminal character. Since he could not delegate his jurisdiction he had frequently to travel about to the different cities to hear cases. A further duty was the supervision and maintenance of public buildings and of the stations maintained for the postal service. He had also to supervise the large numbers of civil servants in the provinces, and twice a year he had to make a report of his administration to the prefect of the praetorium. The latter had the authority to punish provincial governors for neglect of duty. In certain matters, however, a governor could have direct recourse to the emperor.

Though the dates are not exactly known, Ambrose seems to have been *consularis* from 370 to the fall of 374, when he was elected bishop.

The years which Ambrose spent as a provincial governor prepared him still more intimately for rule within the Church by furnishing him with countless contacts with the people in the various vicissitudes of their daily lives. Since Milan was one of the imperial capitals even when the emperor was not in actual residence, there was a great deal of activity in the city. This meant that conditions there were not quite as miserable as they were in other provinces. The wealth of the ruling class, on the other hand, may have made the contrast between the wealth of the few and the poverty of the masses more evident here than elsewhere. As bishop, Ambrose rarely recalled his career as governor, and when he did it was only in a passing manner. This was the time when he had "given himself to the world."[30]

More particular are his references to juridical problems and the duties of a judge. He cites God's condemnation of Cain as an example for judges to follow "so that they may learn to be patient and magnanimous and not be carried off by thoughtless zeal for vengeance and through a lack of sufficient reflection punish the innocent."[31] Moreover, "a judge should not act according to his own desires but should hold fast to what is contained in the laws. Imagine a civil judge. Can he go against the text of the imperial rescript? Can he go beyond the limits set by the emperor? How much more, then, should we observe the tenor of the divine commands!"[32]

Pity is not necessarily always right: "If a judge moved by the prayers of the children of a highwayman, or softened by the tears of his wife, believes that he should pardon one who is still intent on stealing, will he not be handing the innocent over to destruction when he frees one who is plotting the destruction of many?"[33]

He notes that there is nothing very surprising in the way that Eve was deceived by the serpent: "One who wishes to get the better of another usually deceives him. . . . A witness who adds something of his own to his description of what has occurred often vitiates the whole of his evidence with the lie."[34]

On the other hand, his condemnation of usury may have reference to his own juridical activity as a bishop.[35]

Valentinian I promulgated laws against the Manichees and also against astrology and nocturnal sacrifices, but he put no restrictions on the other traditional pagan rites.[36] In 370, he re-established the juridical status of the Church as it had been under Constantius, who had exempted the clergy from the extraordinary *munera,* or civic duties, and from membership in the local curiae. But to check the substitution of a clerical for a curial status, which could be a means of freeing oneself from weighty obligations, Valentinian decreed that a decurion, that is a member of one of the curiae, if he wished to receive holy orders, should leave his possessions to the curia to which he belonged or to a relative who assumed his office. In a constitution addressed to Pope Damasus, he forbade clerics and monks to enter the homes of widows and virgins in order to persuade them to make their wills out in their favor. He thus deprived them of the right of inheritance. Cardinal Baronius was of the opinion that this law had been inspired by Pope Damasus to check the avarice of the Roman clergy. Without going this far, St. Ambrose in his refutation of Symmachus, which we shall discuss later, while he deplores the restrictions of the laws with respect to ecclesiastics as compared with others engaged in the most disgraceful professions, does not grieve over the matter since he would rather have his clergy rich in graces than in money.[37] And, as we have already seen, this was an opinion which he shared with St. Jerome.

After ruling the Church to great advantage at Verona for some ten years, St. Zeno died there, probably in 372.[38] About this same time, in 370-371, St. Martin was consecrated bishop of Tours.[39]

Among the edicts issued by Valentinian was one exempting Christians in military service from the duty of guarding pagan temples. Similarly, actors and actresses who received baptism when in danger of death were no longer required to return to their profession if they regained their health. A Christian influence may also have been operative in his laws prohibiting infanticide under penalty of death and requiring parents to rear their children. In general, Valentinian strove to be impartial in religious affairs, and St. Ambrose expressly notes in a letter to Valentinian II that his father had decided that bishops, and not the emperor, were the proper judges of their own colleagues.[40]

In the year 370, at the end of a campaign led by Theodosius, the father of the future emperor, against the Alemanni, a large colony of these barbarians were settled in the Po valley. Though the emperor thus made them tributaries to the empire, he at the same time issued a decree prohibiting marriage between Romans and barbarians under penalty of death.[41] Obviously the foreigners were regarded as being essentially inferior to the Romans and only worthy of being subject to the latter.

During these same years there were a number of uprisings

in Rome which led to the burning of palaces and public baths. In 369 and 370, the prefect of the annona, Maximinus, repressed these outbreaks with great severity. The cruelty he employed against the Roman nobility was even criminal.

A number of high officials conspired to frustrate the excellent directives of Valentinian I with respect to economic and fiscal reforms. Worst of all these was Romanus, the count of Africa from 364 to 373. His greed was so excessive that it caused the revolt of Firmus, which was to plague the province for twelve years.

The condition of the laborers in the fields became even worse. A law of July, 371, extended also to Illyricum the obligation of the colonists to remain on the land they worked. The consequence of this was that farmers were being gradually reduced to the position of slaves. Attempts to escape from the land by flight were barred by decrees forbidding them to be enrolled in the public curiae, to accept public office, or even to enlist in the army.

A law of 365 obliged the *defensor civitatis*, or "city attorney," to defend the lower classes from the impositions of those who were more powerful. From this time on, this official came to be known as the *defensor plebis*, or "defender of the people."

In the East, however, even during these years the struggle with Arianism was still continuing. Valens, the emperor in the Eastern provinces, was fanatically opposed to Nicea. On the death of Eudoxius, bishop of Constantinople, in 370, Valens nominated Demophilus as his successor. Demophilus was the despicable Arian bishop of Beroea to whom Constantius II had entrusted the custody of Pope Liberius, from whom he finally extorted the condemnation of Athanasius. Many opposed the nomination, but Valens acted quickly to head them off. Eighty priests were placed in a boat, and when it was out at sea the sailors set it on fire. During these same months, the old bishop Athanasius learned to his joy that Basil (who was forty years old at the time) had been nominated bishop of Caesarea in

Cappadocia (the modern Kayseri in Turkey), and he saw in the new bishop, already renowned for his holiness and culture, the new champion of orthodoxy.

On the death of Athanasius in 373, however, new outrages were perpetrated in Egypt. The governor was anxious to appoint as his successor the leader of the Arian faction. Police invaded the churches at Alexandria; consecrated virgins were insulted and dragged naked through the streets; in one church a scoundrel dressed as a woman was lifted up on the altar; another sat upon the episcopal throne and parodied the homilies of Athanasius.

From the very beginning of his episcopate, Basil believed that the Church of Rome should be concerned with the trials of the churches in the East. On his own initiative he wrote to the bishops of Illyricum, Italy, and Gaul. In 372, Sabinus, originally a deacon of the Church of Milan who later moved to Rome (probably as a refugee after his expulsion by Auxentius or, possibly, as a representative at Rome of the Catholic community at Milan), arrived at Caesarea bearing a copy of the synodal letter of the Council of Rome held in the fall of 371.

Basil's fame became known even in Italy. His words and good deeds even made an impression upon the Arians. Although the emperor Valens knew that he was anti-Arian, he gave him property on which to erect his hospitals. When his son fell sick, Valens yielded to the pleas of his wife and had the bishop come to his court.

But despite all this, Valens continued to persecute the Catholics, and Basil had to exercise great prudence. In the winter of 371-372, the emperor passed through Caesarea and on the feast of the Epiphany assisted at Mass in the cathedral. At the offertory he also came to the altar to present his gifts. This could have afforded Basil the opportunity of reminding him of the eighty priests he had burned to death in the ship off Constantinople and of the Catholics of Antioch whom he had thrown into, and drowned in, the Orontes, but, instead, Basil prudently accepted the proffered gifts in the hope that the emperor would eventually have a change of heart.[42]

Such, then, were the conditions of the empire during the years in which Ambrose was exercising the office of governor in the vast regions of the Po valley.

CONSTANTIVS P(ius) F(elix) AVG(ustus)

Silver coin: Crowned bust with cloak and breastplate.
See Cohen, *Monnaies*, VI, p. 227, no. 17.

Constantius II was born at Sirmium August 7, 317. Acclaimed Augustus on August 9, 337, he died at Mopsucrene November 3, 361.

Episcopal Election

○

The dispute over the successor to Auxentius. The governor's intervention. His election. His renunciation of his property. Discretion and silence. Theological formation. His occupations as bishop.

When the Arian bishop Auxentius died in the fall of 374, many even outside of Milan believed that the time had come for vigorous action against the Arians. Up to his death in 373, Athanasius had continued to insist that Auxentius was one of the Arian leaders that had to be removed. As we have already seen, the Catholics of Milan were of the same mind, and in this they had the support of Hilary of Poitiers, Evagrius, a priest of Antioch who was for some time at Vercelli,[1] Philastrius, the bishop of Brescia, and most likely Pope Damasus as well. The Catholic opposition to Arianism under Pope Liberius had steadily increased under his successor, and there were now some of the orthodox clergy of Milan residing in Rome. As was observed in the last chapter, the synodal decree of the Council of Rome of the year 371 was carried to Athanasius in Egypt by the Milanese deacon Sabinus.[2] When Auxentius disappeared from the scene, Athanasius, Hilary, Eusebius of Vercelli, and Lucifer of Cagliari were already dead. The surviving heads of the more influential sees in the West were extremely anxious that a Catholic bishop should be placed in charge of the Church in the imperial city of Milan. Ambrose must certainly have been aware of these hopes from his various contacts with the people. Then too he had maintained a frequent correspondence with his sister Marcellina in Rome. Because of her social position and her life of dedicated virginity, she could easily have known the mind of the pope with regard to the see of Milan.

In the election of the successor to Auxentius, the prescriptions of the fourth canon of Nicea of 325, and perhaps also those of the eighth canon of Arles of 314, should have been followed. The first sanctioned the traditional custom of having a bishop elected by the faithful of the church which he was to rule together with its clergy. It further provided that the bishop-elect should be consecrated by the bishops of the neighboring sees in the presence of all the bishops of the province. In any case, there should always be at least three bishops present for the consecration. The eighth canon of Arles provided for the same minimum, but urged the presence of seven bishops when this was possible. In the fourth century, though the people and local clergy still had a voice in the selection of a new bishop, the major responsibility was in the hands of the bishops of the province. At Milan, after almost twenty years of Arian rule, the clergy must have been preponderantly Arian. But there must also have been a strong Catholic party made up of the surviving followers of Dionysius. They had been supported by the activity of Hilary of Poitiers and Philastrius of Brescia and they were now no longer hindered by the assistance which the state had given to the Arians. As we have already seen, Valentinian I on principle refused to take part in religious disputes.

As a consequence to all this, there was bound to be a furious struggle between the two rival parties when the time came for the election of a successor to Auxentius. The Catholics had on their side the bishops of the surrounding sees, while the Arians had the support of the majority of the local clergy, from the ranks of whom it seems to have been traditional for the future bishop to be chosen. Our most ancient source for the events at Milan in 374 is the historian Rufinus of Aquileia. In 403, when he was in some city in northern Italy, he wrote the following: "At that time Ambrose possessed the fasces in the province (that is, he was governor). Foreseeing grave disturbances, and even the destruction of the city (if the struggle over the succession should get out of hand), he entered the church to see if he could calm the people."[3] Paulinus, who wrote some twenty years after Rufinus, also mentions the violent uproar in the church. As governor, Ambrose was responsible for public order. He spoke in the church because he had to intervene.[4]

The forty-year-old governor was short in stature with a narrow but refined face. His beard and black mustache were in marked contrast with the white delicacy of his features. His large and expressive eyes were made even more striking by a slight dissymmetry, his right eye being a little lower than his left. His tranquil bearing betrayed the Roman aristocrat with a capacity for ruling.[5] All were well disposed toward him. The Catholics regarded him as one of their own. They knew that there had been a martyr in his family and that his sister was a consecrated virgin in Rome. These were ties that guaranteed his sympathy for the Church of Rome, the champion of persecuted orthodoxy. On the other hand, the Arians had no special objections to him. In religious matters he had followed the directives of the emperor and had shown himself kind to both factions.

We have no record of what Ambrose must have said to the crowd of disputants within the church. But whatever it was, it is quite certain that before entering the church he did not imagine that he would come out elected as bishop. In certain cities such as Rome, Constantinople, Antioch, and Alexandria, an episcopal see during the fourth century was not only a position of responsibility but also a source of wealth and honor. The fierce struggles to obtain the succession to Pope Liberius at Rome, Demophilus at Constantinople, and Meletius at Antioch were, as a consequence, not completely based on questions of dogma. But in all probability, the patrimony of the Church at Milan was not enough to arouse the ambition of a Roman senator, and the son of one who had been a high official in the praetorian prefecture.[6] Because of his high family connections and his relative youth, Ambrose's future prospects in the civil hierarchy were quite auspicious. In addition to this, there were some negative considerations in the responsibilities assumed by a bishop. It was an absolute rule, at least in the West, that a priest, and still more a bishop, should be celibate; and if a married man were elected bishop, he could no longer cohabit with his wife.[7] It is certain that Ambrose was at this time unmarried. But even though he was already forty, it cannot be said that he did not think of a family of his own.[8]

According to Paulinus, as Ambrose was addressing the people (probably from the apse where the bishops of the neighboring sees were seated), "the voice of a child *(vox infantis)* is said to have been heard crying out among the people 'Ambrose bishop!' "[9] Since the people had assembled for the election of a bishop and not to assist at a liturgical function, it seems quite unlikely that a woman could have brought an infant into the church at such a turbulent time. The voice thus seems to have been that of a young boy.

The cry was a pledge of peace and concord. The nomination of the governor for bishop from such an unexpected source delighted all on a number of counts, not least of which was the feeling in each of the two factions that the opposition had not carried the day.

Such an unexpected election of a layman to the episcopate was not entirely without precedent. On the death of Pope Anterus in 236, Fabian, who had come to Rome from the country with others of the faithful for the election of a new bishop, was himself elected pope. It is reported that a dove settled upon his head, miraculously pointing him out to the people, who all cried out: "He is worthy!" At Antioch, in 319, Philogonius, a lawyer esteemed by all for his charity was elected and consecrated bishop despite the fact that he was married and had a family. In 362, Eusebius, who was not only a layman but not even baptized, was elected bishop of Caesarea. In 381, the old senator Nectarius, a simple catechumen, was elected bishop of Constantinople. Again, in 410, a wealthy lord, Synesius, was elected bishop of Ptolemais and metropolitan of the Pentapolis in Cyrenaica. He hesitated to accept the honor for at least six months. In 411 he finally consented to be baptized and consecrated bishop by Theophilus, the patriarch of Alexandria, on the condition that he did not have to renounce either his wife or his Platonic ideas on the preexistence of souls. Though he took his episcopal office seriously, he never became perfectly orthodox, possibly due to the fact that he died not too long after his election.

All of these elections were made in opposition to the second canon of Nicea of 325, and still more to the tenth canon of the Council of Sardica of 343. These canons were based upon the principle laid down by St. Paul in his First Epistle to Timothy that no one was to be elected bishop who had only been a Christian for a short time.[10] These canons also condemned the abuse of choosing a layman as bishop because he was wealthy, or a lawyer, or held public office. To be eligible for the post, a candidate should have been a lector in the church and later a deacon or priest. Complaints about abuses in the choice of bishops may be found in the writings of St. Gregory of Nazianzus and St. Jerome. In a letter written between 395 and 401, the latter deplores the fact that one who is today a catechumen becomes a bishop tomorrow, and one who is today a producer of plays becomes tomorrow a consecrator of virgins.[11]

The bishops of the province who assembled in the basilica

at Milan did not hesitate to accept the nomination of Ambrose, whom they saw could bring peace to the Church. They would certainly have preferred not to act against the prescriptions of Nicea and Sardica, but they had to admit that this was the exception that proved the soundness of the general rule.

The problem now was to persuade Ambrose to give up his position as governor so that he might be ordained and then consecrated bishop. Since he enjoyed the rank of a "*clarissimus*," there was no law, theoretically at least, which would prevent him from giving up his post as *consularis* and receiving holy orders. But practically he was a functionary of the emperor, and there was the further fact that Valentinian had personally intervened to secure Auxentius in his see despite the various condemnations of Church councils. And it was Auxentius whom Ambrose would succeed.

Moreover, how long would the people and clergy be loyal to him if he were consecrated? To what extent could he depend upon their help? Would he be able to establish lasting peace within the Church? Later, in speaking of Dionysius, Ambrose would recall how that bishop had asked God that he might die in exile so that he would not have to return and see the harm that had been done to the clergy and the faithful by the maladministration of the Arians.[12]

But even apart from these difficulties, the young Roman aristocrat realized that he had here to decide about the future of his whole life. Deep within himself he knew that it was really Christ who was inviting him as He had one day long ago called the two fishermen Simon and Andrew as they were mending their nets in a far off province: "Come, follow me, and I will make you fishers of men." And they had proved to be worthy of the call, for they "immediately left their nets and their father, and followed him."[13]

At Rome, Sirmium, and Milan, Ambrose had gained a knowledge of paganism and of what the Church, which had suffered so much from the Arians and bad Catholics, should be. He had come to appreciate the good that had been effected through the words of Christ, and the beauty of a life lived according to the evangelical counsels, as he had seen it in his saintly sister Marcellina. In the general decadence of the empire there was an obvious need for moral reform.

The perfection of his later life can only be explained in terms of a sincere conversion to the service of God. He became the bishop that he was because of his generous response to a supernatural call. He knew also that in serving the Church he would continue to serve the State but on a higher and more efficacious level. The rest is history.

In the lives of the saints, flight to escape an ecclesiastical dignity is almost traditional. In 248, St. Cyprian was besieged in his house at Carthage by a crowd that was attempting to persuade him to be consecrated bishop. At Rome, in 251, Pope Cornelius had to be constrained by force to receive the episcopate. In June, 371, St. Martin fled from his monastery at Tours, but the people found his place of hiding and carried him back to his consecration. One Sunday in the spring of 391, the thirty-seven-year-old Augustine happened to be at Hippo. Despite his tears of protest, he was ordained a priest because the people so desired.

St. Ambrose would also be able to say of himself: "How I objected to my ordination!"[14] His biographer, Paulinus, has recorded some of his attempts to escape the honor. He first put the people's enthusiasm to a test by a show of cruelty, making use of torture in examining witnesses, contrary to his ordinary way of acting. He tried to tarnish his reputation by openly inviting prostitutes to his house. But neither of these attempts were successful in discouraging his admirers. Twice he tried to flee, first by pretending that he wished to retire to the tranquil life of a philosopher, and then by actually leaving the city. But it was to no avail. He lost his way during the night and in the morning found himself again at the gates of the city. He finally withdrew to the suburban estate of a noble, Leontius.[15] These various expedients, however, did enable him to defer his decision. He wanted to be sure of the emperor's approval, especially since he knew perfectly well the fits of anger to which Valentinian was subject. A report of what had happened had already been sent to the court at Trier, either by the bishops who had come together for the election or by some official of the administration.[16]

Later, in writing to Valentinian II, Ambrose expressly stated that "my people requested that they might have me as their bishop from your father, and he, yielding to this request, replied that if I were chosen and consecrated bishop there would be peace."[17] Valentinian was highly superstitious, and this doubtlessly influenced his decision. After he had been chosen emperor by the army, he was summarily summoned to Nicea to receive his proclamation as Augustus. But since he arrived on February 24th of a leap year, he hid himself for a whole day so as not to begin his rule on what was considered to be an unlucky day.[18] According to Rufinus of Aquileia, the emperor saw in this unexpected accord between the Arians and Catholics a special intervention of providence, and gave orders that the people of Milan should have as their bishop the man of their choice.[19] The vicar of the Italian dioceses, a high imperial functionary, who also had his headquarters at Milan, received these orders from Trier and published an edict threatening anyone hiding Ambrose with arrest and confiscation of his property. In his letter to the vicar, the emperor expressed his joy that one whom he had sent as governor was now sought as bishop.[20] This in itself was quite in harmony with his general religious policy—he did not want to interfere in ecclesiastical matters by imposing his own will upon the churches. Ambrose was later reproached with the manner of his election: he had been treated with special favor and elected out of purely human motives.[21] As a matter of fact, the choice made by the people had been definitely confirmed by the bishops present for the election. The delay in waiting for the approval of the head of the state was no more than an act of prudence and sign of deference. It also forestalled any possible changes of mind on the part of either the prince or the people.

When the imperial rescript of consent was received at Milan about a month after his election, Ambrose asked to be baptized by a Catholic bishop.[22] He received this sacrament of regeneration on Sunday, November 30, 374, and then, passing through various stages of the ecclesiastical hierarchy, he was consecrated bishop on the following Sunday, December 7.[23]

During the weeks spent in preparation for baptism and holy orders, Ambrose was assisted by the priest Simplicianus. He later regarded this edifying priest, who may have been a native of either Rome or Milan, as his "father."[24] Though an ancient tradition maintains that it was Limenius, the bishop of Vercelli, who actually baptized and consecrated St. Ambrose, there is no real certitude about the matter.[25]

Almost immediately after his consecration, the new bishop of Milan set the pattern for his future administration with a significant gesture: he handed over his wealth to the Church.

As has already been observed, a senatorial family such as that of the Ambrosii must have possessed a considerable fortune. From the travels of Satyrus we know that the family possessed properties in Africa, and perhaps also in Sicily, in addition to the house at Rome. From a formal statement of Paulinus we also know that at the time of his ordination Ambrose gave up all of his possessions, both mobile and immobile, to the Church or to the poor.[26] As a matter of elementary prudence, however, he reserved the income from his estates for his sister Marcellina.[27] This was also the time when his brother Satyrus resigned his position as a provincial governor and came to Milan. There he relieved Ambrose of temporal cares by taking into his own hands the management of the episcopal palace.[28]

As we shall see further on, Satyrus was to show himself no less generous with his possessions than his brother had been.

He died a few years later after refusing to make a will, despite the promptings of both Ambrose and Marcellina, so that they could the more easily dispose of his property for the benefit of the poor. Ambrose's own renunciation of his wealth was far more efficacious by its example with the people than any number of lofty discourses could possibly have been. Having accepted the honor offered him by the people of Milan, he had decided to be a Christian at heart and also a guide for others. Christ had told His disciples that they should leave all to follow Him. And this is what they had done. In following the more perfect way, Ambrose could speak with authority on the dangers of an attachment to wealth: " 'Woe to you rich! for you are now having your comfort.' With these words the Lord condemns not all of those who have wealth but those who do not use it well."[29] In commenting on the famous saying of Jesus that it is easier for a camel to pass through the eye of a needle than for a rich man to enter into the kingdom of heaven, he pauses to say: "What strong words!"[30] And with respect to the command of Christ to His disciples not to procure for themselves gold or silver or money or two tunics or shoes or staff, St. Ambrose will say to his clergy: "The Lord said this to His disciples because He was trimming, as if with a pruning knife, the avarice that grows in the hearts of men. . . . Contempt of riches is something that even among the saints is found only with difficulty."[31]

One hostile to St. Ambrose could have objected that the bishop, even though he had given his lands and villas to the Church of Milan, could enjoy the revenues from them either as the ruler of the see or as the brother of Marcellina. But his austere life was a sufficient refutation of any such accusation. Paulinus tells us that Ambrose spent many hours of the night in prayer, study, and writing, and that he fasted every day with the exception of Saturdays, Sundays, and the more solemn feasts of the martyrs. On such days he sat down to table for both lunch and dinner. On other days he dined but once, and that in the evening.[32] Possidius, the biographer of St. Augustine, has preserved for us some advice that Ambrose had given: "Never seek to find a wife for anybody; do not encourage anyone to enter military service; do not accept invitations to dine out when you are in your own city."[33]

Ambrose himself, if we may judge from the famous fifth-century mosaic, had the appearance of one who ate but little. His face, if it is not emaciated, is certainly lean. But his own austerity in the matter of food did not prevent him from inviting others to a well-supplied table worthy of his own position and of the city in which he lived. Our source of information on this score, however, is Sulpicius Severus, a noble from the environs of Bordeaux who after the death of his wife had become a monk at Tours. In the first book of his *Dialogues*, published only six or seven years after the death of St. Ambrose, Sulpicius relates that a certain high-ranking Vincent, the prefect of Gaul, when he passed through Tours frequently asked St. Martin to invite him to dinner. To support his request, he cited the example of St. Ambrose, who was said to have given dinners for consuls and prefects quite frequently.[34] But Martin of Tours was not at all like the bishop of Milan and refused to extend an invitation. The most serious difficulty with the account is that Vincent was not prefect of Gaul until after the death of St. Martin. At best it shows that not long after the death of St. Ambrose there was a rumor to the effect that he had frequently given great dinners for public officials, and this, of course, would not have been in itself very unusual.

Ambrose's renunciation of his possessions was also an indication of his orthodoxy if we take into account the scandal caused by very many Arian bishops in their ceaseless search for wealthier sees. So it was that, "naked and free," as Paulinus observes, the ex-consular Ambrose took up his episcopal duties.[35]

It was customary in the fourth century for a recently elected bishop to inform his colleagues in the episcopate of his election, at the same time declaring his orthodoxy and expressing sentiments of fraternal communion. The recipients would then send a letter in reply. Of the many that must have been addressed to St. Ambrose at this time, only one has been preserved, that of St. Basil. This bishop of Caesarea (in modern Turkey), whom we have already mentioned before, thanks God for having chosen as a guardian of His flock "a man of an imperial city, experienced in governing, eminent for his wisdom, noble by birth, and known throughout the world for the splendor of his wealth and the strength of his eloquence. And now this man, despising the power and the empty riches of this world, begins to rule an illustrious church in the true faith of Christ." He then encourages the new bishop in the following terms: "Take courage, man of God. . . . Fight the good fight, cure your people if they have suffered some harm from the Arian madness. Follow in the footsteps of the ancient Fathers!"[36]

In his letter, Basil invites Ambrose to write to him frequently, but no trace of such a correspondence is found. A partial explanation for this may be that at the beginning of his episcopacy he had to exercise great prudence. His first reference to the Arians in his sermons was probably made in February, 378, and even this was quite moderate. His first task was to reunite the clergy and the faithful. At the beginning of the sixth century, Severus of Antioch cites the example of Ambrose, who received the clergy ordained by Auxentius, in support of his own contention that the Church should accept the Antiochian dissidents.[37] There is no reason for rejecting this evidence which reveals Ambrose's attitude toward the former Arians in his first years as bishop.

One of Ambrose's earliest instructions to his clergy seems to be preserved in the preface to his treatise *On the Duties of Ecclesiastics*. It has all the appearance of a talk given to his priests very early in his rule. That they had been at odds with each other may be inferred from his praise of silence and discretion. He begins with an apology: "I do not think that I shall appear to be arrogant if in the midst of my children I yield to my desire to teach. . . . We can no longer escape the office of instruction which the obligations of the priesthood have laid upon us. . . . There is only one true Master who has not had to learn what He has taught others. Men, on the other hand, learn before they teach, and receive from Him what they hand on to others. But not even this has been my lot. For I was carried away from the judgment seat and the trappings of office to the priesthood, and began to teach you what I had not myself learned. I must therefore both learn and teach at the same time since I have not had time before to learn. But what should we learn before all else except to be silent so that we may be able to speak? . . . I know that very many speak because they do not know how to keep silent. Seldom is anyone silent, even when speaking does him no good. He, then, is wise who knows how to keep silent. . . . The saints of the Lord, therefore, who knew that the voice of man is often the herald of sin and that man's speech is the beginning of human error, loved to keep silent. . . . Let there be a door to your mouth so that it may be shut when necessary; and let it be carefully barred, so that no one arouses your voice to anger and you repay abuse with abuse. . . . Even when we are angry, since it is an affection of our nature and not under our control, let us not utter anything evil with our lips lest we commit a fault. . . . Our enemy tests our weapons and brandishes his spears. . . . He at times places before us the possibility of revenge as a kind of bait. . . . If, then, anyone feels his adversary to be near, he ought to be the more careful about what he says lest he yield to his enemy; but many do not see him. . . . If you return abuse for abuse, men will say: 'Both have given offense.' And thus both are condemned and neither one acquitted. He is therefore anxious to irritate me so that I may speak and act as he does. But it is the duty of a just man to hide his feelings and say nothing, to preserve the fruit of a good conscience, to trust himself rather to the judgment of good men than to the insolence of one who is accusing him, and to be content with the seriousness of his own intent. . . . One whose conscience is clear should not be troubled by false words, nor should he make more of another's accusation than of the witness of his own heart. He will thus also preserve his humility. But if he is unwilling to humble himself, he will say to himself: 'Does this man so despise me and speak such things against me in my very presence as if I could not open up my mouth against him? Why should I not also say things which can afflict him?' . . . Even if a slave should speak ill against him, the just man remains silent; even if a weak man calumniates him, the just man remains silent; even if a poor man accuses him, the just man remains silent. These are the weapons of the just; they conquer by yielding, just as those who are skilled in hurling javelins are accustomed to conquer when they retreat, and while giving ground strike with more telling blows those who pursue them."[38]

Certain individuals find it hard to get along with others even in normal circumstances. St. Ambrose knew perfectly well how harmful such quarrels among the faithful are to the mission of the Church. As a consequence, his advice to his clergy on this weakness of human nature was all the more necessary when we remember that among them were found the former followers of Auxentius and those who had supported Dionysius.

As we shall see later in more detail, Augustine stayed at Milan from the summer of 384 to May, 387. Even then, as we know from Augustine, "When Ambrose was not surrounded by people, which was only a fraction of the time, he either refreshed his body with light but necessary fare or his mind with reading. When he read, he scanned the pages with his eyes and searched their meaning with his heart, but his voice and tongue were silent. Often when we were present, for no one was forbidden to enter, nor was it his custom to have anyone's entrance announced, we saw him thus silently reading to himself, and never otherwise; and sitting long in silence (for who would dare to be a burden to one so intent?) we would depart. And we surmised that during the little time that he had at his disposal to refresh his mind he retired from the confusion of others' affairs, being unwilling to be distracted by anything else. And he was perhaps on his guard lest, if the author whom he was reading set down something rather difficult and one who heard him reading interrupted him with questions, he would have less time for this work and would turn over fewer pages than he wished; although the fact that he wished to preserve his voice, which easily became hoarse, could have been a good reason for his reading to himself."[39]

In 384, in his reply to the request of Symmachus, St. Ambrose himself developed the idea that no one is too old to learn.[40] Early in his episcopate he felt keenly the need he had to perfect his own religious training. Coming from the family which he did, he was not entirely without a spiritual background; but, in order to be able to speak with authority as a bishop at a time of such heated and subtle theological disputes, he had need of far greater learning than what he had attained in his early years at Rome.

He showed a surprising amount of concern to procure new books. In the first months of 381, probably in March, he was busy editing his three books *De Spiritu Sancto*, which he was writing for the emperor Gratian. For this work he made use of the sermons delivered in 380 by Gregory of Nazianzus in Constantinople, that is, works that could have been published only a few months earlier.[41]

Ambrose was obviously convinced that the truths of the faith must be adequately expressed if they are to have a practical effect on the lives of those to whom they are presented. Serious study occupied much of his time, and chief among his intellectual interests was an understanding of scripture.

In a letter written early in March, 379, to Constantius, a bishop whom he had recently consecrated, Ambrose begins a long series of exhortations on the reading of Sacred Scripture:

"The divine Scripture is a sea . . . , into which many streams flow. There are sweet and clear-flowing waters, and snowy fountains leaping up into life everlasting. There are good words like honeycomb and fair sayings which water the souls of those who hear them with a kind of spiritual refreshment and soften them with the sweetness of the moral laws. . . . You have a source from which you may drink once, and again, and always. . . . Fill therefore the bosom of your mind; so that your land may grow moist and be watered with its own fountains. . . . The Scriptures say: 'If the clouds are filled, rain will fall upon the earth.' "[42] And elsewhere he declares: "We should meditate and reflect at length upon the heavenly words of Scripture with our whole heart and mind, so that the spiritual nourishment of that food should penetrate into all the sinews of our soul. . . . Just as lambs grow fat with an abundance of milk, and just as well-fed sheep gleam with fat, so the prayer of the faithful nourished with this food of the apostles grows rich."[43] And again he notes: "An athlete who has not been trained in the palaestra does not dare to enter the contest. Let us therefore anoint the sinews of our mind with the oil of our reading. Day and night let us exercise ourselves in the palaestra of the heavenly Scriptures, and let the food of the spirit strengthen the limbs of our souls."[44]

Such were his instructions to others on the reading of the Bible, the fruit of which he had experienced in his own soul as is manifest from his constant use of scripture in all his works.

From a study of the Bible, Ambrose turned to the works of Christian authors. And here it is interesting to note that, though he was a Roman by birth and extremely practical in temperament, he devoted himself almost exclusively to the writings of the Greeks. He seems to have read little or nothing of the Christian writers of Africa, and still less of the other Latin authors of the West. This was not due to the fact that he was reluctant to use works which were perhaps already familiar to his clergy but to the undeniable superiority of the Greeks both in dogmatic exposition and biblical exegesis. Ambrose's excellent knowledge of Greek enabled him to read with ease the works of the Jewish authors Philo and Flavius Josephus, and the Christians such as Origen, Basil, Hippolytus of Rome, Eusebius of Caesarea, Didymus the Blind, and Athanasius.[45] In his commentaries he usually follows Philo and Origen, though he rarely mentions them by name. He uses Philo so freely that the Alexandrian's text can at times be reconstructed from his own. But this heavy borrowing did not lead him into error. His keen sense of orthodoxy enabled him to correct the excessively Jewish interpretations of Philo and the extreme allegorical interpretations of Origen.

Ambrose's extensive reading and profound meditation on these works were largely undertaken as a help to his own preaching, one of the most pressing duties of a bishop. As we shall see later, almost all of his numerous works were first delivered in sermons to his people or instructions to his clergy. As a rule he edited his discourses in the quiet and silence of the night since during the day, as St. Augustine observed, he was too often hindered "by a crowd of men with business to discuss whom he assisted in their troubles."[46] He usually wrote his works with his own hand so as not to be a burden to others and, as he remarked in a letter to Sabinus of Piacenza, so that he could perfect the expression of his thoughts as though he were quietly scanning with his eyes the words already spoken.[47]

In the fourth century, a bishop of Milan had many tasks to keep him occupied. He regularly assisted at the prayers of the faithful in the church. He had the principal role in the daily celebration of the Eucharist. He had to see that the catechumens were properly instructed for baptism; and he had to correct, assist, and console the penitents. At certain times of the year, during Lent for example, it was practically impossible for him to leave the city even for a short space of time.

The great charity of the Church is one of the ways in which it shows its superiority to every other religion. As has already been mentioned, Julian understood the apologetic value of works of charity and tried to inspire the pagan priests of the empire with that spirit of merciful compassion, kindness, and regard for the poor and lowly which he saw in the Church.

The early Church had a care not only for the poor, but also for the ascetics, virgins, and widows who had to be supported by the alms of the faithful. From a letter of Pope Cornelius, we know that the Church at Rome alone during the mid-third century supported some fifteen hundred widows and impoverished individuals.[48] These suffering members of the Mystical Body were regarded as an honor to the Church. Their needs were attended to by deacons who inquired about their wants and inscribed their names in the records of the Church. Ammianus Marcellinus makes mention of the poor Christians at Rome in his description of Lampadius, who became prefect of Rome in 366. On one occasion, when he was praetor, "being unable to endure the importunity of the people who often asked that many things should be given to individuals unworthy of them [such as mimes, actors, and charioteers], he summoned some of the poor from the Vatican and presented them with valuable gifts to show his own generosity and his contempt of the mob."[49]

At Milan as at Rome, the care of the poor was a major concern of the Church, and though there were deacons assigned to this task, the primary responsibility still pertained to the bishop, and frequently he had to intervene. St. Ambrose has left some pertinent instructions in this regard: "It is obvious that there should be a limit to our liberality so that our gifts are not bestowed in vain. Moderation should be used, especially by priests, so that they dispense their alms for justice's sake and not for empty show. More demands are made of them than of any others. Strong men come to them for no other reason than that they are tramps. They want to empty the coffers of the poor and deprive them of their means of support. Not content with a little, they keep asking for more. They point to their poor clothes as a claim for assistance, and lying about their age they ask for larger sums of money. If one trusts them too readily, he soon exhausts the fund set aside for the sustenance of the poor. Let there be a method in our giving so that the poor may not depart empty handed and the livelihood of the poor become the spoil of the dishonest. Many claim that they are in debt. The truth should be sought out. Some say that they have been robbed. Let the injuries they have received or knowledge of their persons prove it so that they may be the more readily assisted. Provisions must be made for those who have been expelled from the Church if they lack food. Thus one who employs moderation in giving is stingy towards none and generous towards all. For we should not lend our ears alone to the voices of those asking for help but we should use our eyes as well to look into their needs. Weakness cries louder to a good almsgiver than the voice of the poor. The cries of importunate beggars will extort more from us, but there should not always be room for impudence. He must be seen who does not see you. He must be sought out who blushes to be seen. Even the one shut up in prison should have recourse to you. Let him who is weighed down with sickness cry unto your mind since he cannot reach your ears. The more the people see your labors, the more they will love you. The more many priests whom I have known have given, the more they have received. For when anyone sees a good almoner, he gives him something to dispense to the poor since he knows that his compassion will not be in vain. For all want their gifts to assist the poor. And if they see one giving alms too generously or too sparingly they are alike distressed, for such a one either wastes the fruits of another's toil by needless gifts or keeps them in his own purse."[50]

These were instructions which he gave on various occasions to his clergy and which he published about the year 389. They were obviously drawn from his own experiences in dealing with the poor. But at times his exhortation to charity could be less calculating. On one occasion, for example, he declares: "Do not ask what each one deserves. Compassion is accustomed not to weigh one's merits but to assist one's needs, not to examine the justice of a case but to assist the poor. For it is written: 'Blessed is he that understandeth concerning the needy and the poor!' Who is it that understands? The one who has compassion on him, who sees in him a sharer in his own nature, who knows that the Lord has made both the rich and the poor. . . . Therefore, if you can assist another, do not put it off saying, 'I shall give tomorrow,' lest you lose the opportunity to practice charity. It can happen that while you are delaying he might die."[51]

A bishop during the fourth century was the natural protector of the weak, the condemned, and the oppressed. His help was all the more needed because of the sad conditions of public life. But it is also understandable that Ambrose had to advise prudence in the efforts of his clergy to rescue the weak or the condemned "so that greater evils are not brought about than those which they desire to remedy."[52]

As far as he was himself concerned, Ambrose did not hesitate to intervene on numerous occasions. Other bishops, especially in the East, exercised the same prerogative. St. Gregory of Nazianzus, for example, asked magistrates to reduce excessive taxes. St. Basil protested against the splitting up of a province which would have burdened the people with even heavier taxes. On another occasion he defended a widow whom an official was trying to marry against her will. In this he was strongly backed by his people who finally persuaded the magistrate not to use force to attain his goal.[53] Obviously, with Ambrose, as with other bishops, such interventions were not always undertaken without some danger of offense.

Another grave responsibility of a bishop was the administration of justice. The decline of the civil courts along with the traditional custom of Christians' bringing their disputes before the bishop rather than before a pagan judge brought into being the *episcopalis audientia*, that is, an authentic episcopal court.

Two laws of Constantine had already given a plaintiff the right of having recourse to a bishop even if the process had already been begun in a civil court, and the civil judge was further obliged to execute the sentence of the ecclesiastical tribunal.

Toward the end of the fourth century, the judicial functions of a bishop had become excessively burdensome. Possidius tells us that St. Augustine was occupied with settling cases during all his mornings and at times during the afternoon as well.[54] St. Ambrose gave as a rule for his clergy in these matters the one which he himself followed: Never refuse to intervene when there is a possibility of doing good, especially when the interests of God or of the Church are at stake; but when it is merely a question of money between the disputants, a bishop or priest may properly stand aside and engage himself in more profitable enterprises: "It is not the duty of a priest to intervene in money matters. In such cases it is frequently impossible for the loser not to be offended since he believes that he has been defeated through the efforts of the one who has interceded. A priest, therefore, should injure no one and be eager to assist all. To do this, however, belongs to God alone. . . . It is foolish to incur enmity because of disputes over money. On the other hand, grievous toils must be borne for the salvation of another. To run a risk in such a cause is praiseworthy."[55]

In thus spending his time, his possessions, and above all himself, Ambrose played the part of the shepherd of God's flock.

VI
The Virgins

o

Immorality in the ancient world. Divorce. Tepidity within the Church. The monastic reaction. Ambrose's encouragement of virginity. Objections. The new status of women. The calm balance of the bishop.

In our admiration for the achievements of the Romans, we may at times forget some of the serious defects of their ancient civilization. The splendors of Rome even during the Augustan Age could not entirely conceal symptoms of decay—the thirst for gold, the excessive luxury of the rich in contrast with the misery of the poor, the lack of public education, and the lavishness of the games which only flattered the indolence of the people and stirred up their cruel and morbid instincts. And among these evils must, of course, be mentioned the gradual dissolution of marriage ties.[1]

Roman laws punished adultery but tolerated concubinage and prostitution, and there were even women of noble families who had their names inscribed on the lists of public women kept by the aediles. The various attempts to "restore" the primitive Roman morality were practically all unsuccessful. Modesty and morality were probably never so greatly flaunted as when the emperor became their champion. Augustus's failure to amend the ways of his daughter Julia, whom he eventually had to banish, is a case in point. In the heat of argument, Ambrose goes too far when he questions the good intentions of the emperors in their attempts to encourage marriage, but his words nonetheless reflect grave disorders in the pagan world: "Those who worshiped the adulteries and evil deeds of their gods fixed penalties on celibacy and widowhood. As imitators of their crimes they punished zeal for virtue, and under the pretext of seeking an increase in population they actually did away with a concern for chastity."[2]

At the end of the first century and the beginning of the second, both Martial and Juvenal wrote harshly of the foibles and immorality of Roman women, but such charges are characteristic of satire in almost any age.[3] Certain it is, however, that divorce, which was unheard of in primitive Rome, became common toward the close of the Republic. Sulla, for example, took as his fifth wife Valeria, the young sister of Hortensius, who had herself already been divorced. After the death of his first wife, Pompey married three different times, the first two of these subsequent marriages ending in a divorce. Though he was considered a paragon of virtue, Cato Uticensis did not hesitate to remarry his wife Marcia who between the two marriages to Cato had been married to Hortensius and had added his wealth to her own. After living for thirty years with his wife Terentia, Cicero divorced her and refurbished his finances by marrying his rich and youthful ward Publilia. Terentia in turn married Sallust and later Messalla Corvinus. Seneca on one occasion noted that many famous women counted the years not by the names of the consuls but by those of their husbands.[4]

Technically, in Roman law an adulterer was a married man who had sexual relations with a married woman who was not his wife.[5] Ambrose also uses the term in such a precise sense.[6]

During the fourth century, slavery, as well as the circus, theater, and amphitheater were still flourishing institutions. Though a general decline in commerce had set in, trade in luxury goods with the Orient had been established.[7] On occasion

Ambrose deemed it necessary to speak out against feminine fashions and immorality.[8]

By ruling out divorce, Christ raised woman up again to her pristine dignity. St. Paul exhorted husbands to love their wives as Christ had loved the Church, sacrificing His life for it.[9] All Christians, whether slave or free, whether men or women, are to be one in Christ.[10] This was so true that in the third century Pope Calixtus declared that a secret marriage between a Christian woman and a slave should be regarded as legitimate even though such a union was forbidden by the laws of the state. Hippolytus deplored this decision of the pope as one favoring concubinage and abortions, but nonetheless as Calixtus had realized, the principle had to be saved.[11]

The influx of converts into the Church during the fourth century, when it came into favor with the State, created a new problem. Too many of these new Christians brought along with them their old pagan ways of thinking. This lowering of the moral tone of the Christian community was in turn counteracted by the rise of monasticism. The origins of this movement are difficult to trace, especially since "in history there are almost never any absolute beginnings." It has been said, with some degree of certainty, that "monasticism was born in Egypt during the second half of the third century."[12] It took its start with the anchorites such as St. Anthony and Paul of Thebes, if the latter may be regarded as an historical figure. An anchorite lived in the desert, usually near the Nile, and even when other anchorites came to the same area, they lived in separate quarters and were not subject to any common rule. About the year 320, Pachomius established the first monastery at Tabennisi in the Thebaid, some three hundred and sixty miles south of the modern city of Cairo. This marked the beginning of the cenobitic, or "common," life for monks. Those living in the community were subject to a definite, written rule. They applied themselves to manual labor and the study of scripture. In 340, Maria, the sister of Pachomius founded the first convent for women at Atribi in Upper Egypt. This form of monastic life was perfected and animated with a new spirit by St. Basil of Caesarea in the second half of the fourth century. But even before this, reports of the heroic virtues of the monks of the East had spread to the churches of the West. This was owing in a special way to Athanasius's stay at Trier in 335, and at Rome from 340 to 345.

As we have already observed, Athanasius's stay in Rome marked the beginning of monasticism in that city when a group of young women began to meet in the house of Marcella on the Aventine. For both men and women at Rome, monasticism at this time meant the renouncement of marriage, a greater austerity in one's way of life, fasts, and meetings for the sake of mutual edification, but they continued to live with their own families.

Eusebius of Vercelli had also become acquainted with Athanasius at Rome, and after his election as bishop in 345 he gathered a number of his clergy about him and began to live a monastic life with them under a common rule. According to Sulpicius Severus, about the year 357 St. Martin established a monastery, in this instance a simple cell, also at Milan.[13] Driven from there by Auxentius, he went to Gaul and settled at Ligugé, where he lived as a hermit. After his election as bishop of Tours in 371 or 372, he founded a kind of monastic community at Marmoutiers.

We also know of a group of virgins who seem to have led a common life at Aemona (Laibach) on the borders of Pannonia as early as 375. In 380 the Council of Saragossa forbade clerics to become monks out of a spirit of false pride.

Even during the preceding centuries there had been "encratites," that is, men who practiced celibacy and women who, for a supernatural motive, preserved their virginity; but they were now organized in a special type of life, and the practice of asceticism assumed proportions never known before. Numerous works were written in praise of the virtues of the monks.

About the year 357, Athanasius composed his *Life of St. Anthony*, which was soon translated from the Greek into Latin. This biography was the first in a long series, ranging from panegyrics with a historical foundation to novels of pure fantasy with marvels on every page. These works had a great influence even among the educated. The ascetic who conquered his passions, who practically freed himself from the physical necessity of eating, drinking, and sleeping, who wrestled strenuously with the evil spirits, became the hero of the age. It was no longer the martyr as during the time of the persecutions but the ascetic who conquered himself that was set up as a model for imitation.

And God did sustain them. Snakes fled at the very approach of Anthony; he cast out devils and worked countless miracles. In his life written by Athanasius, the devils already have a prominent part. He saw the walls of his cell open up and the demons pour in in the form of lions, bears, leopards, bulls, asps, and scorpions with a frightful din of hissing, shouting, roaring, and bellowing. They even inflicted such blows on his body that he could no longer stand on his feet.

The enthusiasm aroused by such narratives combined with the dire hardships of civil life provided a strong impetus to monasticism. But the monks also had fierce adversaries among the Christians, and even worse ones among the pagans. In 377, Valens, the emperor of the East, published a law against monks who aimed at concealing their sloth under a cloak of piety.[14] Seven years later, in 370, he ordered the governor of Egypt to break up the monasteries and enroll the monks in the army. According to Orosius a great many of those who refused to comply with the order were beaten to death.[15] Libanius ridiculed the monks for "eating more than elephants,"[16] and Eunapius declared that "they live like pigs."[17] In Rome, toward the end of 384, the crowd that attended the funeral of Blaesilla, who had died at the age of twenty, angrily shouted that she had starved herself to death. On the other hand, St. John Chrysostom invited his hearers at Antioch to go a little distance outside the city and visit the monks. There they would see a paradise on earth and angels clothed in the garments of men.[18]

Despite the general interest in monasticism at this time, St. Ambrose speaks very little of the monks and their miracles and heroic struggles. He certainly must have known of St. Anthony, but he never mentions him. On the other hand, he was an ardent champion of virginity.

Even though they may have been quite few in number, there were certainly consecrated virgins in the Christian community at Milan, and Ambrose must have taken an interest in them from the very beginning of his episcopacy. The writings of St. Paul, who had treated of virginity at some length, and the example of his own sister Marcellina inspired his discourses on this theme. During the year 377, he edited these various sermons and exhortations in the three books *Concerning Virgins (De virginibus)* and the single book *Concerning Widows (De viduis)*. These were therefore published before he had completed three years as bishop.[19]

His *De viduis* seems to have been aimed at dissuading a particular woman with grown children from entering a second marriage. He refutes the various pretexts alleged in such instances and then comes to the real reasons for such a step. Here he shows admirable prudence. A second marriage, or even more, is perfectly licit, though he does not himself favor such a decision. A woman must consider her own situation and abilities. As bishop he is giving advice to those who are sane and sober. Otherwise he would be wasting his breath. Further, he warns them to be on their guard against wolves in sheep's clothing who would senselessly impose on others the practice of heroic virtue of which they are themselves utterly incapable.

St. Ambrose later published other works on this same theme. In 378 he defended himself against the criticisms which had been made of his *De virginibus*. This was published under the title *Concerning Virginity (De virginitate)*. In 392, he delivered another discourse *On the Education of a Virgin (De institutione virginis).* The occasion for this was the veiling of Ambrosia, the niece of Eusebius, a great friend of his and bishop of Bologna. Finally, at Florence in the spring of 394, he delivered his *Exhortation to Virginity (Exhortatio virginitatis)* for the feast of the dedication of the basilica that had been built by the rich widow Juliana. Mention here might also be made of the sermon on a fallen virgin and her seducer *(De lapsu virginis consecratae* or *De lapsu Susannae).* This scathing address is always published with the writings of St. Ambrose, but it was probably composed by his contemporary Nicetas, bishop of Remesiana (in modern Serbia).[20]

St. Ambrose's teaching on virginity, as he himself declares, is derived from the Gospels and from the Epistles of St. Paul. Virginity is something that transcends nature, a virtue that descended from heaven with the Word of God. Virginity among the Jews was an exception. Because he was a virgin Elias was carried off in a fiery chariot. Among the pagans it had no real existence since the virginity of the Vestal virgins was for a period of years and not forever. It is, in fact, a specifically Christian virtue: "You have heard how great is the reward of virginity. A kingdom is gained by it, a heavenly kingdom marked by the life of angels. There is nothing fairer than that which I commend to you, that you should be angels among men, bound by no marriage tie. Those who do not take wives for themselves in marriage are like angels upon the earth. They do not feel the tribulation of the flesh; they know no servitude; they are preserved from the contagion of worldly thoughts; and they wholly attend to divine things."[21] At times Ambrose had recourse to less sublime arguments, even ridiculing the foibles of those who used cosmetics: "What truer witness, woman, is there of your lack of beauty than that you fear to be seen as you are? If you are beautiful, why do you hide your beauty? If you are not, why do you pretend that you are, not even having the satisfaction of a good conscience?"[22] He also mentions the trouble of finding a husband and the trials of married life: "How miserable is she who to find a husband is put up as it were for sale, so that the one who offers the highest price obtains her. Slaves are sold on better terms, for they often choose their masters; if a virgin chooses a husband it is an offence, but if she is not chosen it is an insult. And, though she is fair and beautiful, she both fears and wishes to be seen. She wishes to be seen so that she may fetch a better price; she fears lest the very fact of her being seen should not be fitting. What fears and suspicions she experiences as to how her suitors will turn out! She is afraid that a poor man may trick her, or a rich one spurn her, or a handsome one laugh at her, or a noble one despise her."[23] Despite the fact that Ambrose, carried away by his own rhetoric, speaks unfeelingly of the pains of childbirth, this was not owing to the fact that he failed to appreciate the sanctity of motherhood but because he wanted to prove at almost any cost the excellence of virginity. Elsewhere he records the many sacrifices made by mothers for their children and reminds his hearers that they should show their gratitude by their filial piety.[24]

But his best arguments for a life of virginity are drawn from higher motives: the Son of God by choosing a virgin for His mother has proclaimed the excellence of virginity.

Christ lives only in a chaste body. This is so well known that the pagan persecutors who condemned Christian women to suffer offenses to their virtue believed that they were inflicting the most humiliating punishment they could upon them. In a virgin, Christ finds His favorite dwelling, and He repays her with His love: "How then is Christ held? Not by the ties of injury, not by knotted cords, but by the bonds of charity. He is restrained by the reins of the mind, and clasped by the affection of the soul."[25] It is through her own purity, through her renunciation of every human love, that a virgin arrives at this mystical union. Consequently, a virgin, when she foregoes marriage does not renounce love. She finds for herself a greater and more mysterious love than merely human love, but one that is no less real and transforming. The miracle of love is that it transports those who are in love into another world. Though they live and speak as other mortals, they are different from others. Because of their preoccupation with each other, it seems that love transports them out beyond the limits of the material world to make them partakers in that which is absolute and eternal. This ideal concept of love which Ambrose had found in Plato, as we find it again today in Morgan, he interpreted in a Christian sense so that it might lend itself to the moral regeneration of women and of society in general.[26]

The finest aspirations of women find in Christ, their spouse, their noblest and deepest satisfaction. A mystical marriage with Christ is an ideal and at the same time the reward of a virgin's vocation, and it is worth the efforts required to achieve it: "Parents speak against her, but are willing to be overcome. They resist at first because they are afraid to believe. . . . They flatter you with choice pleasures to see if they can soften you with these different delights. You are being tried, O virgin, by such coaxing. These anxious entreaties of your parents are your first battles. Conquer your affection for your parents first, O maiden. If you conquer your home, you conquer the world. . . .

"I remember a girl once noble in the world but now more noble in the sight of God who, when she was being urged by her parents and other relatives to marry against her will, fled to the sacred altar. Where could a virgin have better fled than to that place where the sacrifice of virginity is offered? Nor was even that the limit of her boldness. She, an oblation of chastity, was standing at the altar of God, now placing the right hand of the priest upon her head, asking for his prayers, and now impatient at the just delay, placing her head beneath the altar. 'Can any better veil,' she said, 'cover me than the altar which consecrates the veils themselves? Such a bridal veil is most suitable because on it Christ, the Head of all, is daily consecrated. What are you doing, my relatives? Why do you still trouble me, seeking my marriage? I have long since taken care of that. Are you offering me a spouse? I have found one who is better. Make the most that you can of his wealth, of his nobility. Extol his power. Yet I have Him with whom no one can compare himself, rich in the world, powerful in empire, noble in heaven. If you have found such a one for me, I do not reject the choice. If you have not, you do me no kindness, my relatives, but an injury.' While the others remained silent, one broke out abruptly: 'If your father were alive, would he allow you to remain unmarried?' To this she replied with more devotion and a more restrained piety: 'And perhaps he has died so that no one might be able to prevent me.' This answer with respect to her father proved to be for him a prophecy, as was shown by his own speedy death. So the others, each of them fearing the same for himself, began to assist and not to hinder her as before."[27]

In these words Ambrose formulated the doctrine of the inviolability of a vocation.

His teaching on virginity had its roots in the teaching of Christ and of St. Paul, but St. Ambrose must have realized that the emphasis and fervor with which he preached it was something new. If the arguments he used were without precedents in tradition, there were models to whom he could point for imitation. First of all, there was the Virgin Mary, and then the Christian martyrs, Agnes, Thecla, and Soteris. When speaking of Mary, he lists the virtues which are to be found in the perfect virgin. And among these, for the virgin, the essential virtue is that of chastity. The ancients were little enough concerned with this virtue and even less with modesty. The license of the theaters was notorious, and on several occasions the Roman emperors had found it necessary to issue decrees prohibiting mixed bathing in the public baths.[28]

The Christian ideal of virginity did much to elevate the dignity of women. Just as charity was the typical virtue of the first century and obedience that of the sixteenth, so modesty and chastity were the typical virtues of a Christian in the fourth century.[29] And assuredly the preaching and writing of St. Ambrose played an important part in the development of this ideal. The indirect results of this preaching were manifold: a greater realization of the conflict between matter and spirit, of the value of sacrifice, especially that of the pleasures of sense. The natural sense of modesty in woman was thus elevated and obtained a new dignity and charm.

The young women at Milan who consecrated themselves to God in a life of virginity continued to live in their own homes, but at Bologna they lived together and "increased to the number of twenty."[30] How many dedicated virgins were there at Milan? two hundred? twenty? or only three or four? In two different discourses Ambrose expresses his sorrow that whereas young women came to Milan from Piacenza, Bologna, and even Mauritania to consecrate themselves to the Lord, he had not persuaded any of the Milanese to do the same: "If I preach here and persuade elsewhere, I should preach elsewhere so that I might persuade here!"[31] "They say, 'You teach virginity and persuade many.' Would that I were convicted of this! Would that the effect of such a crime could be proved! . . . Would that you carried your point with examples rather than attacked me with your words!"[32] Even today in otherwise fervent areas, vocations are frequently scarce. The same may have been true at Milan. But it certainly would be an exaggeration to believe that there were no vocations. The bishop knew of young women who were forbidden by their mothers to leave the house lest they go to hear him preach. It was only natural that his enthusiasm for a life of virginity should have met with opposition. Even in recent times he has been criticized for his contention that vocations to a life of virginity would increase rather than decrease the general population.[33] But as a matter of fact, the position which he defended is not at all naïve: "Is there anyone who has sought a wife who has not found one? . . . If anyone believes that the human race will decline in numbers because of the consecration of virgins, he should reflect upon the fact that where there are few virgins there are even fewer people, and where there is an earnest zeal for virginity, there also are more people. Ask how many virgins are consecrated at Alexandria, in the whole of the East, in Africa. Fewer are born here than are consecrated there. . . . If anyone should protest on this account, let him also forbid wives to live chastely since they would have more children if they were incontinent. When their husbands are away, let none of them remain faithful lest there be a loss of offspring."[34] In other words, Ambrose insists that a large number of vocations to a life of virginity is a sign of a fervent religious spirit, which is in itself an important factor in population.

To another objection, that by his continual exhortations to virginity he was condemning marriage, Ambrose replied: "Someone will say, 'You, therefore, discourage marriage?' No, I encourage it and condemn those who are accustomed to discourage it, so much so that I frequently speak of the marriages of Sarah, Rebecca, Rachel, and other women of old as instances of singular virtue. . . . I do not then discourage marriage, but I count the advantages of holy virginity. The latter is a service of a few only, the former of all. Nor could there be any virginity unless there were marriages from which virgins are born. I am comparing good things with good things, so that what is better may be seen more clearly."[35]

Ambrose comments on the teaching of Christ that it is not permitted to send away one's wife in order to marry another in the following terms: "Do not, therefore, send away your wife, lest you deny that God is the author of your union. For if you should endure and correct the habits of others, much more should you those of your wife. . . . It would be cruel if you would banish the mother while keeping the children, adding to the insult done to love the injury done to maternal devotion. It would be cruel if on account of the mother you should at the same time drive out the children, since the children should rather be a motive for forgiveness of the mother. How dangerous it is if you offer the tender age of a young woman to error! How wicked it is if you abandon her in her old age whom you enjoyed in her youth! . . . You think you may divorce your wife because you are not forbidden by human law, but you are by the divine."[36]

The virgins and the widows who consecrated themselves to Christ, who lived in prayer and penance and in the exercise of charity, became a living apology of the bishop's work, a proof of the fruitfulness of the Gospel teachings. This is the reason for the generous praise which St. Ambrose bestowed upon women. St. Jerome, on the other hand, in his zeal for virginity, while still remaining orthodox, became so extravagant that he at times offended his readers. When bidding women to remain silent and subject, St. Paul had given as his reason: "For Adam was first formed; then Eve. And Adam was not seduced; but the woman being seduced, was in the transgression. Yet she shall be saved through childbearing; if she continue in faith, and love, and sanctification, with sobriety."[37] Tertullian exaggerated this injunction of St. Paul in the following fashion: "You, O woman, are the gate of the devil, you reached your hand out to that tree of damnation, you were the first to rebel against the law of God, you persuaded him whom the devil did not dare attack to do evil, you shattered with your fickleness man, the image of God. Because of the death which you merited, the Son of God also had to die."[38]

Certain Gnostic movements went so far as to regard marriage as a work of the devil, and this aberration was encouraged by the spread of romantic tales which became fashionable from the second century on. Christian novels also sprang up modeled on the pagan romances and circulated under the names of the Acts of Peter, of Andrew, of John, and of Thomas. This apocryphal, and frequently heterodox, literature also dealt with such bizarre themes as the heroism of a young couple who separated on the evening of their marriage, or decided to live together as brother and sister. Sayings such as the following are attributed to Christ in the Gospel of the Egyptians: "I have come to abolish the works of woman."[39] In the Acts of Thomas the daughter of the king of Andropolis and her husband are exhorted to continence on the evening of their wedding in words condemning marriage.[40] It is thus not surprising that the canons of the Council of Gangra in Asia Minor show that the situation towards the middle of the fourth century was deplorable. Many women abandoned their husbands, others cut off their hair and dressed like men. Priests who kept their wives whom they had married before ordination, as was permitted by the Church discipline, were exposed to the contempt of the faithful. As a consequence, the council had to condemn those who despised marriage just as in an earlier century an apostolic canon condemned bishops, priests, and laymen who, out of contempt, abstained from marriage, meat, and wine.[41]

St. Ambrose, on the other hand, in exalting virginity, exalts also woman. He even defends her from the accusation of being the cause of the fall: "Indeed, we cannot deny that woman erred. But why should you be surprised if the weaker sex erred and fell since the stronger also fell? The woman had an excuse for her sin, but the man did not. She, as Scripture says, was deceived by the wisest of all creatures, a serpent; but you were deceived by a woman. In other words, a nobler creature deceived her, but a lesser creature deceived you. You were deceived by a woman, but she was deceived by an angel, even though an evil one. If you were not able to resist one less than yourself, how could she have resisted one superior to herself? Your sin absolves her. . . . But you, O man, say that a woman is a temptation to a man. This is true. And if she is fair, she is even more so. . . . But it is no fault of a woman to be what she was born."[42]

This balance is found in all of Ambrose's writings. The energy and enthusiasm which he showed in his advocacy of virginity is understandable in the context of his time. As bishop of Milan he was anxious to serve both the Church and State by doing what he could to raise the ideals and moral standards of his people. His moderation is noticeable even in details. He agreed with St. Jerome that a consecrated virgin should not use cosmetics or go about in fancy clothes, but he did not go so far as the latter as to forbid her to bathe.[43] And in this he was quite in accord with accepted customs. In the middle of the fourth century a canon of the Council of Laodicea forbade laymen and ecclesiastics to frequent the baths when women were using them, but it did not forbid bathing as such.[44] Such establishments were all the more necessary in that soap was unknown at the time and running water was a rarity in private homes.

Since Milan was a splendid imperial city with large public baths, some of these were probably reserved for women. St. Ambrose, as a consequence, did not have the occasion to inveigh against certain abuses condemned at Carthage by St. Cyprian.[45]

His teaching on virginity was highly efficacious. His insistence upon the virtue of modesty gave a new spirit and a new dignity to women. Purely human love thus also acquired a nobility of character which antiquity had never known.

In reading St. Ambrose's writings on virginity, however, we should remember that these were originally conferences given as a rule not to virgins but to the faithful in general. This explains their frankness of expression. He borrows some of his illustrations from the popular novels about the saints already mentioned. Today we would perhaps find the story of the soldier who went into a brothel to find a condemned Christian girl a bit out of place in a sermon. Instead of finding the girl for whom he was looking, he discovered a soldier dressed as a woman and exclaimed: "What is this? A girl entered here, and a man is seen instead. . . . I heard that Christ changed water into wine, but I did not believe it. He has now begun to change a person's sex. Let us get out of here while we still are what we were."[46]

Finally, in these sermons, and in the others which he preached from the very beginning of his episcopacy, may be noted his attacks upon the pagan cults—the "mysteries," the "sacred Phrygian ceremonies" (of the Mother of the Gods, Magna Idaea), the "orgies of Liber," and the worship of Vesta, which, as we shall see, afforded the occasion for a famous intervention on the part of the bishop.[47]

With respect, however, to the older deities of the Greek and Roman pantheon, St. Ambrose was fond of ridiculing them. He retold, for example, the old story of the tyrant of Syracuse who entered the temple of Jupiter and carried away the gold cloak of the god and substituted for it one of wool because gold is cold in winter and too heavy in summer. The same tyrant had the gold beard of Aesculapius shorn since it was not right that the son, Aesculapius, should wear a beard, when the father, Apollo, was beardless. The antipagan polemic of St. Ambrose, however, is calm in comparison with that of Firmicus Maternus, who, in his attack upon paganism which was written about the year 350, advised the emperors: "Remove, most sacred emperors, remove without fear the ornaments of the temples. Let the fires of the mint or the flames of the mines melt down these gods. Take all their gifts for your own use and control."[48]

St. Ambrose's attitude towards the pagans was quite different than that of this fiery Sicilian and more in harmony with the Gospels. When he was commenting upon the rebuke given by Christ to His two apostles, the Sons of Thunder, who wanted to bring down fire from heaven to consume the Samaritans who had refused hospitality to their Master,[49] St. Ambrose spent some time in explaining how patience is far more useful, how weakness should be endured and not crushed, and how virtue does not seek for revenge: "God calls those whom He wishes and He makes one pious as He wishes."[50] In his different works on grace St. Augustine will cite this saying of Ambrose at least five times.[51]

D(ominus) N(oster) VALENTINIANVS
P(ius) F(elix) AVG(ustus)

Silver coin: Crowned bust with cloak and breastplate.
See Cohen, *Monnaies*, VI, p. 397, no. 11.

VIRTVS EXERCITVS SISC(ia) P(rima)

Another portrait of Valentinian I in military garb and wearing a laurel wreath. On the obverse side he is seen holding the Labarum in his right hand, while his left rests upon his shield.

Valentinian I was born at Cibalae in Pannonia in 321. He was proclaimed Augustus in 364, and died at Brigetio on November 13, 375.

VII

The Death of Satyrus

o

Valentinian I against the Quadi and the Sarmatians. His death. Valens. The revolt of Procopius. The conspiracy of Theodore. The Huns. Visigoths and Ostrogoths. The rebellion of the Goths. The defeat at Hadrianople. The death of Satyrus. The gold of the Church used to ransom prisoners.

Valentinian I died at the age of fifty-five on November 17, 375, while engaged in a campaign against the barbarian Quadi and Sarmatians. At the time of his death he was staying in a military camp at Brigetio (now Szöny in Hungary). He had given orders for the construction of a fortified camp in the lands of the Quadi on the other side of the Danube (in what is now northern Austria) as if these were already subject to the Romans. When Gabinius, the king of the Quadi, mildly remonstrated, Marcellianus, the Roman general, pretended to assent to the request that no further steps should be taken. He invited the king with his retinue to a banquet, but as Gabinius was departing, Marcellianus had him slain, as Ammianus observes, "in impious violation of the sacred duties of hospitality."[1] The Quadi then formed an alliance with their neighbors, the Sarmatians, and crossing the Danube in a surprise move devastated the Roman territories in Pannonia, burning the towns and cities and taking their inhabitants as booty. In the course of their plundering, they almost captured the princess Flavia Maxima Constantia. This twelve-year-old daughter of Constantius II was passing through the country on her way to Trier to marry Gratian. Ammianus declares that she would have been taken prisoner while stopping to dine at a public villa called Pristensis if the governor of the province had not fortunately been present. Placing her in a state carriage, he took her in all haste to Sirmium twenty miles farther on.[2] Theodosius, the duke of Moesia and future emperor, succeeded in checking the Sarmatians. In the spring of 375, Valentinian I personally intervened. He passed the summer at Carnuntum on the Danube (now Altenburg, near Vienna), reorganizing the boundaries of the provinces and making preparations for a punitive campaign across the river. The Roman officials who had not been able to protect the territories ravaged by the barbarians were terrified at the prospects of the imperial inquest, but Valentinian did nothing. Though he habitually punished simple soldiers with severity, he treated their leaders with every consideration. Even Probus, prefect of Sirmium, despite his hated and tyrannical rule, was not brought to account.

In the late autumn the emperor sent ahead Merobaudes, a Christian general of Frankish origin, and count Sebastian, who had formerly been one of the best generals in Julian's army. They burned and destroyed the towns of the Quadi. Valentinian then advanced towards Aquincum (on the Danube nineteen miles north of Budapest). He also invaded the territories held by the barbarians and had all those he captured strangled without distinction of age. After putting the homes of the barbarians to flames, he returned without losses to Savaria (Szombathely), and then marched on to Brigetio (Szöny, on the Danube, opposite Komorn). Ammianus states that many prodigies that occurred during these days foretold the proximate demise of Valentinian: blazing comets were seen, heralds of the downfall of men of high position; lightning set on fire the palace, the senate, and the forum at Sirmium; an owl settled on the top of the imperial bath at Savaria and filled the air with baleful tones, nor could it be driven away by rocks or arrows. The night before he died, Valentinian himself saw his absent wife sitting with disheveled hair and dressed in mourning garments. The following day when he tried to mount his horse it reared up. In a fit of rage he ordered the hand of the groom, who had tried to assist him mount, struck off. Luckily, however, Cerealis, the tribune in charge of the stable, at the risk of his own life, put off the execution of the order.[3] A few hours later that same day, November 17, 375, ambassadors of the Quadi appeared asking for peace, seeking pardon for the past, and promising to provide men for the imperial armies. After being admitted to the imperial presence, they offered their excuses, supporting them with an oath and declaring that the hostile acts committed against the Romans had been the work of foreign brigands living near the river, adding moreover that these had been angered by the erection of the Roman fort across the Danube. In a fit of anger, Valentinian began to rail at them "in noisy and abusive language" for their ingratitude. He gradually calmed down, but an attack of apoplexy left him speechless and unable to breathe. He was carried to his room where a surgeon, who finally arrived after a frantic search, attempted to bleed him, but his efforts to save him proved fruitless. A few hours later the emperor was dead.[3]

Valentinian had had a son, Gratian, born at Sirmium May 23, 359, of Severa Marina. Then, about the year 369, he had divorced Marina to marry a Sicilian, Justina, the widow of Magnentius.[4] Justina bore him four children, Valentinian, Justa, Grata, and Galla. When his father died at Bregetio, Gratian was at Trier, while Justina with her children was at Murocincta, a hundred miles from where the emperor had died, and Valens his brother at Antioch. On August 24, 367, Valentinian had already proclaimed Gratian Augustus at Ambiani (the modern

Amiens in France), and in 374, to guarantee the succession by uniting his own family with that of Constantine, he had joined his fifteen-year-old son in marriage to the twelve-year-old Flavia Maxima Constantia, the posthumous daughter of Constantius II, and an Arian.

In November, 375, shortly after the death of Valentinian, Merobaudes a Frank, and Aequitius a Pannonian, both Christian generals devoted to the dynasty, had Valentinian's other son, the four-year-old Valentinian II proclaimed Augustus by the troops of Pannonia.[5] Gratian, the sixteen-year-old Augustus at Trier, received at the same time the news of his father's death and the nomination of his half-brother as his colleague in the empire. His reactions to this news, favorable or otherwise, is a matter about which historians have labored without reaching definite conclusions. At any rate, Gratian was now the Augustus for Gaul, Spain, and Britain, and acting as regent for his brother in Illyricum, Italy, and Africa, while Valens continued to rule in the East. This latter was a boorish and grotesque character, and his religious policy proved to be a succession of failures. Notwithstanding his otherwise able administration and his concern for reducing taxes, he nullified all his good intentions by giving a free hand to the rapacity of his officials.[6] His provinces in the East were still troubled by the countless Arian dissensions. There were schisms in the churches, and different bishops contending for the same sees. Valens, who remained an Arian as long as he lived, believed that his best course was to support the moderate Arians, who subscribed to the creed of Rimini. His wife, Albia Domnica, was also an ardent Arian, and the influence of Eudoxius, the Arian bishop of Constantinople, was likewise felt at court.

Nevertheless, during the early years of his reign, Valens was not able to take a very active interest in Arianism. In September, 365, Procopius, a friend and relative of the deceased Julian, rebelled, gained control of Constantinople, and had himself proclaimed emperor by two legions that happened to be passing through the capital. Despite the help of three thousand Goths who came to his support, Procopius was conquered and slain on May 27, 366.

In his desire for revenge, Valens waged war upon the Visigoths for three years because of the aid they had given to Procopius. In 367, before setting out on this campaign, Valens had himself baptized by Eudoxius. Two years later, in 369, the first phase of the Gothic war was concluded with a treaty of peace between Valens and Athanaric, and the emperor returned to Constantinople.

The conflicts that arose between the Arians and Catholics with the succession of Eudoxius to the see at Constantinople gave Valens the opportunity to intervene and begin his persecutions. According to St. Gregory of Nazianzus, "orders were given to the impious generals not to set out against the Persians, or to subdue the Scythians, or to repel other barbarians, but to turn the churches into slaughterhouses, to profane the altars, to stain them with human blood, and to violate the chastity of virgins."[7]

The alleged conspiracy of Theodore was discovered in 372. At a theurgic seance held perhaps at Antioch it was said that Valens would be succeeded by one whose name began with ΘΕΟΔ. A high functionary of the court, Theodore, was thus immediately marked out as the next emperor.[8]

As a matter of fact, Valens more than once had heard that his life was threatened. When he learned of the "conspiracy" of Theodore, he began an even more cruel persecution of the anti-Arians, and for two years there was a veritable reign of terror. The prisons no longer sufficed to hold the crowds that were arrested. Trials continued day and night, and were so summary that many learned of their condemnation even before they knew that they had been accused. From all sides, high dignitaries, rich lords, scholars, and those known to be interested in magic were brought in chains to Antioch.

Valens was particularly rabid in his hostility to occult practices and their devotees. It cannot be said that he persecuted individuals possessed of a high degree of culture for the simple reason that there were not many of the kind during the fourth century. Scholars and intellectuals were condemned and whole libraries were burned solely because they were connected in some way with the art of divination. One of the victims of this repression was the philosopher Maximus, Julian's instructor as a youth. Many of the wealthy lost their lives or purchased them at the price of all their possessions because of the greed of Valens and his assistants. According to Ammianus, the fear was so universal "that we crept about as if we were in the Cimmerian darknesses."[9] Bassianus, for example, because he had wished to discover from soothsayers whether his wife would give birth to a boy or to a girl, was despoiled of all his goods even though he was a high official; and he was only saved from execution through the intercession of his relatives.

Meanwhile, a much more serious storm was rising up against the empire in the East. About 375, after crossing the Volga, the cavalry of the Huns was seen on the shores of the Caspian Sea. This race, perhaps of Mongol origin, was composed of nomadic tribes from Central Asia who about the middle of the fourth century subjected and united with themselves the Alani, Iranian nomads who lived in the lands between the Aral Sea and the Ural river.

The Huns comprised a horde made up of many different tribes. Each tribe was made up of a number of clans, each clan of several camps, and each camp of five or six tents which provided shelter for five or six families under a single head, the one who owned the most livestock. When these inhabitants of the steppes were organized into a well-knit horde by an intelligent and bold khan, they soon set up empires which lasted till the death of their leader.

The more stable agricultural peoples were inevitably swept away by the mass of nomads. No defense could be set up against them. They flowed over into more civilized areas like a torrent rushing down from the mountains into the plains. Nothing could contain them. The same phenomenon occurred in the fifth century under Attila, in the twelfth under Genghis Khan, and in the fourteenth under Tamerlane. Ammianus describes at length the savage customs of these Huns. They furrowed the cheeks of boys with a knife so that the scars might check the growth of their beards. Their limbs were solid and well set, their necks large, and they were themselves tall, though somewhat stooped. They did not use fire to prepare their food but fed themselves on herbs and the flesh of any kind of animal, which they warmed a little by holding it between their thighs and the backs of their horses. According to this same author, one might take them for two-legged beasts rather than for human beings. They had neither houses nor huts, and from infancy they accustomed themselves to endure cold, thirst, and hunger. Once they had donned a garment, they never changed it till it fell to pieces. They lived as if they were fixed to their horses, eating, drinking, buying and selling while on horseback. With no fixed place of abode, they knew nothing about farming but wandered about with their carts on which they lived and where their wives wove the cloth for their rough clothes, gave birth to their children, and nursed them until they reached the age of puberty.[10]

About the year 370, the Huns, their numbers increased by the conquered Alani, launched an attack on the empire of the Goths. These were divided into two groups, one of which, known from the fifth century as the Visigoths, or "Wise Goths," had for some time had dealings with the Roman empire. Constantine, in fact, had accepted them as allies on the north bank of the Danube. In the third century, during the time of anarchy caused by the wars between the various Roman generals, they had taken captives from Cappadocia and had thus come in contact with Christianity. Under Constantius II the majority of the Christian Visigoths became Arians. Ulfilas, a reader in his church, translated the Scriptures into Gothic, a Germanic language.[11] About the year 332, when he was some twenty years old, he had lived for a time in Asia Minor, where he learned both Greek and Latin. He later returned to his own people across the Danube. In 341, he was sent as an ambassador to Constantius. At this time Eusebius of Nicomedia was sponsoring an Arian council at Antioch. He took advantage of this occasion to consecrate Ulfilas as bishop of the Christian communities among the Goths. Their church thus became Arian, and Ulfilas remained as its head until his death about the year 382. In 367 Valens waged war upon these Goths for the assistance they had given to the rebel Procopius. Their king, Athanaric, detesting both Christianity and the Roman empire, frequently persecuted both Arians and Catholics.

The other group of Goths, the Ostrogoths, or "Shining Goths," were also known as Greuthungi from the name of their principal tribe. About the middle of the fourth century under their king Ermenarich they had been organized into a powerful empire in the Ukraine, bounded by the Finns on the northeast, by the Slavs on the northwest, by the Tyras (Dniester) river and the Visigoths on the west, by the Aeruli of the Maeotis (the Sea of Azof) on the southeast, and by the Tanais (Don) river and the recently arrived Alani on the east.

Ermenarich faced with the savage violence of the Huns seems to have committed suicide about the year 375. His son Videric was taken to the West by his guardians and the entire kingdom of the Ostrogoths became a prey to the Huns. Athanaric, for his part, took refuge in the Transylvanian Alps and Carpathian Mountains with a number of Visigothic tribes. Other Goths, on the other hand, under the leadership of Fritigern and Alaviv asked to be taken into the empire on the other side of the Danube. It was perhaps on this occasion that Fritigern became a Christian. He was joined by many of the Visigoths who had been under Athanaric and also by many of the Greuthungi.

In the summer of 376, about fifty thousand men accompanied by women, slaves, and children, after a long and exhausting march, arrived at the Danube and asked permission of the Roman authorities to cross the river. Eunapius sets the figure at two hundred thousand men, but this seems to be exaggerated.[12] Valens received the embassy of the Goths at Antioch and could not refuse the request. There was also the added advantage that if these barbarians were admitted into the empire they could provide new contingents of soldiers. After long negotiations, the emperor gave his consent, but on rather harsh conditions: the Goths would have to surrender their weapons and hand over their children as hostages to be distributed in different cities throughout the empire.

The Goths would have accepted even these terms peacefully enough if the Roman officials charged with their execution had not proved to be so cruel and stupid. The barbarians gave up their arms, but then proceeded to buy them up again from the very Romans to whom they had been surrendered. No price seemed to be excessive, and they went so far as to sell their wives and children to regain their weapons.

The task of transporting these vast numbers of refugees was entrusted to two corrupt and incompetent generals, Lupicinus, Count of Thrace, and Maximus, Duke of Moesia, and it was their rapacity that was responsible for the woes caused by the emigration.

The people were eventually ferried across the river on boats and rafts, but a new problem arose immediately—the question of provisions. Lupicinus and Maximus were foolish enough to attempt to exploit the hunger of the barbarians. Instead of distributing them in different provinces, they kept them packed together near the Danube. The winter of 376-377 was a terrible one for the Goths. They had to pay exorbitant prices for the worst possible food. The Romans went so far as to exchange dogs for an equal number of slaves. When the Goths ran out of gold and slaves they were forced to sell their sons and daughters, thinking it better that they should at least live as slaves than to die of hunger.

The hatred sown by such cruelty soon became apparent. Seeking revenge, the Goths became wild and ruthless. Alarmed by the numerous signs of an imminent revolt, Lupicinus ordered Fritigern to lead the Goths toward Marcianople (Reka Devnya in modern Bulgaria). He invited Fritigern, Alaviv, and other leaders of the Goths to a banquet. They came with an escort of soldiers. In the meantime the ordinary Goths were kept far from the walls of the city, which they had vainly sought permission to enter in order to secure something to eat. Within the city a quarrel broke out between the soldiers who had accompanied Fritigern and the other Gothic leaders and the Roman troops stationed there. Lupicinus ordered the Goths waiting for their chiefs outside the palace to be slain. Within the palace, the Gothic chieftains sensed the danger and asked permission to go out and check the tumult outside. They then seized their weapons and forced their way through the throngs of palace attendants. Once clear, they fled on horseback to their own people.

Nine miles from the city, there was a conflict between the Goths and the Roman legions, which turned out to be a triumph for the former. Lupicinus barely escaped to the city. The Goths then donned the weapons abandoned by the Romans and poured out over the provinces. The crimes of Lupicinus and Maximus were soon expiated by the destruction of farms, the burning of villages, and the enslavement of the provincials. The Goths, crossing the Balkans, attempted a siege of Hadrianople (Edirne in Turkey), but since they lacked the technique of taking a walled city, they abandoned their assault and spread out to plunder Thrace throughout the summer of 377. The swarms of Goths were daily increased by liberated slaves, who had either been sold or had sold themselves into servitude for the bread that they hoped to obtain from the Romans. Many provincials no longer able to support the burden of the taxes also joined the marauding bands. These were welcome recruits since they could provide information on stores of provisions that had been concealed by the Romans. Men, women, and children were sought out and massacred as the Goths tried to avenge the wrongs they themselves had incurred.

In April, 378, Valens left Antioch for Constantinople, where he arrived on May 30. He had work to do: the conflagration which had started in Moesia had already spread to Macedonia and was threatening to go still farther. This same year from February to August, Gratian, the Augustus of the West, was busy stemming an invasion of the Alemanni Lentienses from the Alps that had been triggered by the Gothic successes in the Danubian basin.

The Lentienses living in the deep valleys of the Rhine had entered into a treaty with Valentinian four years earlier at Moguntiacum (Mainz). When Gratian withdrew several military contingents from the Rhaetian frontier to send them to the assistance of Valens in Thrace, the Lentienses prepared themselves for a mass emigration. Gratian then recalled the troops marching towards the East and with his combined forces gained a brilliant victory over the Lentienses at Argentaria (Horbourg near Colmar). With this victory, the line formed by the Rhine was secured for a quarter of a century. Having thus settled affairs in Gaul and Germany, Gratian left for Thrace, halting at Castra Arboris Felicis (near Bregenz) and Lauriacum (Lorch); but at Sirmium he learned that he was too late. Valens, restless and envious of the success of Gratian on the Rhine, had been unwilling to wait for reinforcements from the West. Spurning also Gratian's advice to be prudent, he decided to risk a definitive encounter without the assistance of his colleague.

In the imperial camp near Hadrianople, a supreme council of war was held. A Christian priest brought a proposal of peace from Fritigern. This may have been simply a trick of the barbarian leader to delay the battle until the arrival of

Gothic reinforcements under Alatheus and Saphrax. These overtures, however, were rejected by the Romans.

The battle took place on August 9, 378. Valens, leaving the imperial standards and the military treasury at Hadrianople, had advanced to meet the barbarian encampment formed by the circle of their numerous wagons some miles north of the city.[13] After his forces had been hastily drawn up for battle, Valens allowed himself to be tricked again into negotiating with Fritigern who was waiting for the arrival of the cavalry of Saphrax. In the meantime, the Romans, worn out by a forced march of some nine miles and tormented with thirst, were exposed to the scorching rays of the sun on a plain that had been burned by the barbarians.

Several squadrons of Roman archers wearied with waiting finally began an attack on their own initiative, but then the Goths were reinforced by the cavalry of Alatheus and Saphrax sweeping down from the mountains. Though it is impossible to trace the exact course of the battle, it seems that the charge of the Gothic cavalry on their flank disorganized the Romans. The imperial cavalry pushed ahead, but the infantry was caught between the enemy horse and the massed wagons of the Goths. Since they had no means of escape, the slaughter was terrible. More than twenty thousand Roman soldiers perished on the field. Some, however, managed to escape through the general carnage. Overcome with terror, Valens sought refuge in two regiments of the Palatine guard. It was reported that at evening he was carried wounded to a hut which the Goths then set on fire, not realizing that the emperor was in it. As a matter of fact, nothing more is known about him, nor was his body ever found.

Many generals, thirty-five tribunes, and two-thirds of the Roman army perished in the disaster. The victory of the cavalry over the infantry at the battle of Hadrianople proved, moreover, to be a significant event in military history. In a sense it marked the end of the art of war, which was not to be reborn until the fifteenth century with the perfecting of the Swiss infantry.

Since they were unable to storm the city of Hadrianople, the barbarians descended on the Bosphorus. Under the walls of Constantinople they were defeated by bands of Saracens in the pay of the empire. According to Ammianus, one of the long-haired and almost naked Arabs "uttering weird and hoarse cries rushed into the midst of the Gothic army and with a drawn dagger killed a man and with his lips sucked the blood pouring forth from his throat."[14]

After their defeat, the Goths dispersed to sack all the region lying between the Black Sea and the Adriatic. The provincials suffered horribly. Many were slain, many others were robbed of everything they had or were enslaved. Churches were converted into barns for horses, and there was the usual rape of women and girls. The general desolation was augmented by the want of provisions and the prevalence of disease. Many fled to Italy.

The plight of the people in the Danubian basin that resulted from the barbarian invasions was closely followed by St. Ambrose at Milan. We shall speak later of his journey to Sirmium in 376 which augmented his fears. In the early months of 378 he delivered his two discourses on the death of his brother Satyrus. The regrets which he expressed in these sermons are only intelligible in the light of the painful events that have just been summarized.

Until his appointment as governor of the province of Aemilia-Liguria, Ambrose had lived in close conjunction with his brother for many years, at Trier, Rome, and Sirmium, but his new position brought about their separation.

Practically all the information which we have on Satyrus comes to us from the two eulogies preached by his brother after his death. In addressing his brother, St. Ambrose notes the striking similarity that existed between them: "We seemed, I know not by what spiritual stamp or bodily likeness, to be one in the other. Who saw you and did not think that he had seen me? How often have I saluted those who, because they had previously saluted you, said that they had been already saluted by me? How many said something to you, and then declared that they had said it to me? What a pleasure and delight did I not frequently receive in seeing that we had been mistaken for each other! What an agreeable error, what a pleasant slip, what an innocent deceit, what a pleasant trick! For I had nothing to fear in your words or deeds, and I rejoiced when they were attributed to me."[15] The two shared their work, studies, and amusements. They were so inseparable that if one went out alone, those who knew them thought that the other was ill.

Even taking into account the rhetorical tone of the funeral orations, what Ambrose had to say about his brother was so true that it would have seemed impossible to keep them apart for long, and, as a matter of fact, their separation was relatively brief.

When Ambrose was *consularis* at Milan, Satyrus was filling a similar position elsewhere, though in what province is unknown. As governor he so won the good will of the provincials that, as Ambrose observed, the people looked upon him as a father rather than as a judge.

After the consecration of his brother as bishop in December, 374, Satyrus decided to sacrifice his own career so that he might assist him. He renounced his position, went to Milan, and took over the management of the episcopal palace, thus freeing Ambrose from the worrisome details of its administration. This also helped the bishop in his dealings with his clergy, who were still at odds with each other and were only gradually brought back together in the bond of unity that had existed before the coming of Auxentius.

Satyrus was also of assistance to his brother in directing the construction of church buildings, but unfortunately this could not last for long.

As we have already seen, the Ambrosii owned vast estates in Africa. A certain Prosper, living in Africa and possibly an agent for Ambrose, refused to pay some large sums which he owed after he learned that Ambrose had been elected bishop. He may have thought that a bishop would cancel the debts or, at least, that he was a creditor about whom he need have no further fears. But Satyrus was of another mind and did not think that the matter should be settled through default. If his brother did not need the money, it could be put to good use by the Church of Milan.

Since it would have been difficult to settle the matter at such a distance, Satyrus decided to go to Africa and see what he could do there. Ambrose suggested sending someone else since he did not want to expose his brother to the dangers and fatigue of the journey, but he failed to convince Satyrus, who set out from Milan, probably in the fall of 377.[16]

After he was already on his way, Satyrus received a letter from Ambrose asking him to return and insisting that he should not undertake such a lengthy voyage, but he continued his course. In Africa he found Prosper and was able to settle the matter in question. Before setting out again for Milan, he met Quintus Aurelius Symmachus, at that time the proconsul of Africa. In Symmachus's correspondence there is a letter addressed to his brother Celsinus Titianus and entrusted to Satyrus. It was probably at this time that it was written.

During the return voyage, either because of the bad weather (during the winter sailing was perilous and frequently suspended until spring) or because the ship was old, it had to be abandoned. According to Ambrose, Satyrus was such a strong swimmer that he could even make his way against the sea in a storm, but on this occasion he felt the need of supernatural assistance. Though he was not himself as yet baptized, there were on board ship some Christians who were carrying the Eucharist with them. In the fourth century, especially in some provinces of the East, the custom of reserving the consecrated host with oneself or in one's home was still widespread. Before diving into the sea, Satyrus asked the Christians for a particle, placed it in a handkerchief and tied it about his neck. Saved from the waters, his first thought was to find a church where he could give thanks to God since he felt that there was no duty so pressing as that of gratitude. He decided at once to receive baptism, but only from a Catholic bishop. He asked the bishop of the place where he had come ashore if he were in communion with the Catholic bishops, that is, with the Church of Rome. When he learned that he was not, he refused to receive baptism at his hands. The site of this encounter was probably Sardinia, which was still suffering from the Luciferian schism. Lucifer of Cagliari, as we have already seen, was one of the champions of orthodoxy at the Council of Milan in 355. But when he returned from exile, he refused to pardon "those who had fallen" at Rimini, and ended up by cutting himself off from communion with Rome.[17] Lucifer died about the year 370, but the schism he had begun continued in a desultory fashion for another twenty years. Satyrus refused baptism at the hands of the Luciferian bishop since he believed that the Church is the Body of Christ, and that one who would rend this Body would not profit by the passion of Christ since he did not have the faith that he should have. In these thoughts which St. Ambrose attributes to his brother, there is a whole treatise on the Church: to sin against the unity of the Church is to sin against Christ Himself. Satyrus therefore continued his voyage. Arriving at an orthodox church, he was baptized as he so earnestly desired, and he preserved thereafter the grace conferred.

It was perhaps during the course of his return from Africa that Satyrus visited Sicily. From a letter of King Theodoric from the beginning of the sixth century and from another of Pope Gregory the Great from the end of this same century, we know that the Church of Milan owned such extensive estates in Sicily that they could support the bishop of Milan and his clergy at Genoa after they had been driven out of their see by the Lombards.[18] It seems quite obvious that these were once owned by the Ambrosii.

On his way back to Milan Satyrus fell grievously ill, perhaps in Sicily, as the result of the fatigues of the voyage and shipwreck in the midst of winter. When after a long illness he finally recovered his health, he was able to return to Milan. But there, despite the care taken by Ambrose and Marcellina, his illness reoccurred, and this time he failed to recover. He died in February, 378. St. Ambrose experienced great sorrow at the loss of this brother who had been his constant companion, his comfort and support.

In the funeral oration which he delivered for Satyrus, St. Ambrose describes the last kiss which he placed on his brother's lips and how he closed his eyes in death. The body was then washed, as was the custom, and anointed with oils and perfumes. After it had been placed on a bier, it was placed on the shoulders of the members of the bishop's household and carried into the church. Ambrose himself helped to carry the sad burden. After the body had been exposed for several days, either in the episcopal palace or in the church, the funeral was celebrated. Then, as now, the principal part of the funeral service was the Holy Sacrifice of the Mass. When the time came for the sermon, St. Ambrose could see the eyes of those who crowded the church, especially those of the poor, filled with tears. He began as follows: "We have brought here, dearly beloved, my sacrifice, a sacrifice undefiled, a sacrifice pleasing to God, my lord and brother Satyrus. . . . I have no reason to complain, but rather to give thanks to God, for I have always desired that if any troubles should befall me or the Church that they should come upon me and upon my house. I therefore give thanks to God that in this time of common fear, when the advances of the barbarians are causing dread to all, my own personal sorrow has surpassed the common woe, and what I feared would happen to all has been turned upon me."

The bishop is consoled by the sorrow of his people. Satyrus will live on in his memory, but then he is again overcome by sadness: "And now, dear brother, where shall I go, or where shall I turn? The ox seeks for its fellow, and feels that it has lost something of itself, and with its frequent lowing shows its tender longing, if by some chance the ox which had helped it draw the plow has died. And shall I not, my brother, long for you? Or can I ever forget you with whom I always bore the yoke of this life?"

He recalls the last circumstances of Satyrus's life, his voyage to Africa, his shipwreck, baptism, and death. At one point he expresses his grave fears for the future: "For you, my brother, have been snatched away, not from us, but from impending perils. You have not lost your life, but you have been freed from the fear of threatening trials. So great was the compassion of your saintly mind that if you knew the danger in which Italy stands at the approach of the enemy, you would greatly grieve and lament that our safety depends upon the barrier of the Alps and that the defense of chastity is found in the barricades that have been made of fallen trees. With what sadness would you mourn that those dear to you are separated from a cruel and lustful enemy that spares neither chastity nor lives by such slight means."

The improvised defenses here referred to by St. Ambrose were those which had been erected in the passes of the Alps to check an invasion of the Lentienses Alemanni into Raetia, encouraged in that winter of 377-378 by the influx of Goths into the Danubian basin.

The bishop goes on to praise the great virtues of his brother, and then speaks of Christian hope: "So then my tears will cease to flow. We must heed the saving remedies at our disposal for there should be a difference between those who believe and those who do not. Let them therefore weep who have no hope of the resurrection, from which they are deprived not by a sentence of God but by their unbelief. There should be a difference between the servants of Christ and the worshipers of idols. Let these latter weep for those whom they believe to have forever perished. Let all their days be filled with tears. Let them have no rest from sadness who think there is no rest for those who have died. But let the advent of death wipe away all tears from us for whom death is not the end of all but of this life, since it restores us to a better state."[19]

Ambrose consoles his sister present in the church, greets his brother for the last time, gives him a final kiss and asks God to accept the sacrifice of Satyrus's death as one of the first fruits of the sacrifice of his own priestly life.

Satyrus was buried immediately to the left of the sepulcher of the martyr Victor, and Ambrose composed for him his still extant epitaph.[20] Seven days after the funeral, he delivered another discourse on his brother's death. But this time it was not to grieve at his departure but to instruct the faithful on the meaning of a Christian death. It is wholly philosophical in tone. Death should not be mourned since it is common to all men and frees us from the painful vicissitudes of the present life and opens to us the promises of the resurrection. During the course of his talk, Ambrose takes advantage of the opportunity to deplore and condemn the excessive manifestations of grief on the part of women, their shouting and their tearing of their hair and clothes. In comparison with the first discourse, which is vibrant and moving, this second seems somewhat cold. His arguments are monotonous and at times even childish. Nevertheless some of his observations are surprisingly ingenious and betray his earlier rhetorical training.

Since Ambrose twice mentions in his funeral oration that their patrimony had not been divided, it is probable that he did not complete the donation of his real estate to the Church of Milan until after the death of his brother. Despite the urgings of his brother and sister, Satyrus had refused to make a will. Instead, he gave his brother and sister full liberty to dispose of his property as they thought best. Ambrose then surrendered everything to the Church, including what had belonged to Satyrus, reserving however revenues from these estates for the support of Marcellina.

In Ambrose's eulogy of his brother, the faithful of Milan must have recognized a portrait of the bishop himself: it was that of a soul exquisitely Christian.

But Satyrus had died when the misfortunes for the people of the empire were just beginning. In the summer of this same year occurred the disaster at Hadrianople with the subsequent pillage of the provinces.

In a commentary on the life of Noah which he perhaps published in the fall of this same year, 378, St. Ambrose expresses the shame he felt at surviving his sons. It grieved him to live in a time when those who were most dear to him were afflicted with so many misfortunes and when the churches themselves were tossed about by so many storms.

It was possibly in November that he showed even greater affliction when expounding a verse from St. Luke on the Passion: "The Huns have attacked the Alani, the Alani the Goths, the Goths the Taifali and the Sarmatians, and the Goths driven back have in their turn assailed us in Illyricum, and the end is not yet in sight. Famine and pestilence are threatening both men and beasts. . . . These plagues have come upon us because we are at the end of time."[21]

Despite this, Ambrose was not crushed. He believed that Gratian would be a new David, a new Samson. But he also reflected on how he might be of some assistance himself in the general disaster. He suddenly thought of collecting a sum of money to ransom the captives of the Goths. For this holy purpose he even broke up the gold and silver vessels of his churches and had the pieces melted into bars to pay for those in the hands of the barbarians.[22] Later, in his struggle with the Arian faction in 385-386, this act of charity was brought up as an accusation against him.

In a page of his *De officiis,* Ambrose makes an admirable defense of his activity: "Who is so hard, cruel, and iron-hearted that he is not pleased that a man should be redeemed from death, that a woman should be saved from the lust of the barbarians which is worse than death. . . . The Lord sent the Apostles forth without gold, and they founded the churches without gold. The Church does not have gold to be stored up but to be laid out and spent for those in need. . . . Is it not much better that priests should melt it down to support the poor if other supplies are lacking than that a sacrilegious enemy should defile and carry it off? Would not the Lord Himself say, 'Why did you allow so many needy people to die of hunger? You had gold; you should have fed them. Why were so many captives offered for sale and not purchased, but were instead slain by the enemy? It would have been better for you to preserve living vessels rather than those made of metal.' No answer could be given to such questions. What if you were to say: 'I feared that the temple of the Lord would be unadorned.' He would answer: 'What is sacred has no need of gold; nor do those things which are not purchased with gold take delight in gold.' "[23]

Charity is the truest token of Christianity. St. Ambrose could well say: "The Church loses nothing when charity is gained."[24]

Detail from the left side of the sarcophagus under the pulpit in the basilica of St. Ambrose.

The infant Jesus is lying in the manger between an ox and an ass. "The presence of these two animals became so common in sculptures representing this scene that up until now no exceptions are known. St. Joseph is missing and the Virgin Mother may also be missing. On the cover of the famous sarcophagus at Milan even the shepherds are missing: but never the two animals" (G. Wilpert). St. Ambrose devotes a whole page in one of his commentaries on the meaning of the animals at the crib of Christ. See his *Exp. evang. sec. Lucam* 2.42.

VIII
Anti-Arianism

o

Ambrose's discretion. The succession of Germinius at Sirmium. Meeting of Gratian and Ambrose. The Council of Rome of 378. First works against the Arians. Theodosius. Refuge of the court of Sirmium at Milan. Confiscation of a basilica. Edict of Theodosius in 380. Illness of Theodosius and his baptism. Councils of Constantinople and of Aquileia in 381, of Rome in 382.

Having been elected bishop as the result of a compromise between the opposing factions of orthodox followers of Nicea and Arians, Ambrose had to spend his first years as bishop in reconciling his clergy and people among themselves. Of a delicate constitution and frequently ill, he naturally felt the need of affection. His sensitive temperament led him to seek for cooperation rather than conflict wherever possible, whether it was a question of reconciling the demands of nature and of grace, of body and soul, of Church and State, or of earth and heaven.

These contrary demands flow necessarily from the essential dualism found in man and in the world, and, according to one's point of view, Christianity balances them off in an admirable fashion (as for Newman) or accentuates them (as for

Pascal). And Ambrose, just as he showed an almost womanly tenderness with respect to his brother and sister, so also he was extremely sensitive to the ties of friendship and to the goodwill of his people.

His years as governor had taught Ambrose the different moods of people in the world, the best way to win their sympathy, the necessary tact to avoid offense even when wishing to assist them. Though nothing extraordinary, such knowledge was highly useful for one who, after receiving baptism and holy orders, was not to play the role of a monk in the deserts of Chalcis but to rule a large community in an imperial city.

Ambrose without doubt was deeply set on orthodoxy, but during the first years of his reign he had to practice prudence in his dealings with the Arians, who had become firmly entrenched in Milan during the eighteen years that Auxentius had occupied the see. On the very first page of the book which he published in 377, the *De virginibus,* when he had not yet completed his third year as bishop, Ambrose acknowledges the fact that some will be surprised that one who does not as yet know how to speak should dare to write and publish books for others. But at times one can express himself more perfectly with a pen than with his voice, and then, citing a proverb from one of Cicero's letters, he notes that a page does not blush.[1]

Prior to this he had published nothing; he had kept his peace and recommended silence, but nonetheless he had been extremely busy. In 376, as a matter of fact, after the death of Germinius, the bishop of Sirmium, when there was the question of electing a new bishop for the capital of Illyricum and territories on the Danube, Ambrose left Milan and traveled more than five hundred and fifty miles to guarantee by his own personal intervention the election of a Catholic bishop to that highly important see. Ambrose was particularly concerned with this election since as bishop of Milan he was also metropolitan of the provinces of Venetia and Histria, which bordered on those under the jurisdiction of the bishop of Sirmium.

As we have already seen, Ambrose had lived for five years among the officials of the Illyrian prefecture, and many of his former friends and associates must have still been living in the provincial capital.

At this time the Arians in Sirmium were enjoying the patronage of Justina, the widow of Valentinian I, who was living there with her children. She attempted to stir up the people against Ambrose, but he fearlessly entered the basilica and ascended the dias reserved for the bishops. One of the Arian virgins, bolder than the rest, went up to him, seized him by his robe, and attempted to drag him towards the area reserved for the women so that he might be beaten and driven out of the church. Ambrose rebuked her, saying: "Although I am unworthy of the great honor of the episcopacy *(sacerdotium)*, it is not fitting that you or one of your profession should lay hands on any bishop. You should therefore fear the judgment of God lest some evil befall you." Events proved the truth of the bishop's prediction. The woman died soon after, and Ambrose repaid the insult that had been offered to his person by mercifully accompanying the woman to her grave. The incident frightened the Arians and facilitated the election of Anemius, a Catholic bishop, to the see of Sirmium.[2]

It is quite possible that during his stay at Sirmium, Ambrose met Justina. Even if she was an Arian and supported the opposing faction, she was still the mother of an Augustus, Valentinian II, who was then five years old. Later, Ambrose would have to endure much from her at Milan. In 376 the widow of Valentinian I was about thirty-five years old and in the flower of that beauty for which she became so famous. In his history of the Church, Socrates tells us that Justina, since she was an orphan, had lived at different times with Severa, the first wife of Valentinian. Marveling at the great beauty of the girl, Severa sang her praises to her husband. This had such an effect on the emperor that he issued an edict which permitted a man to take two wives. He then, while keeping as his wife Severa, the mother of Gratian, took as his consort Justina.[3] We do not know, however, if this tale was current at the time when Ambrose was in Sirmium for the election of Anemius.

During the first months of Gratian's rule in the West a policy of liberty and indulgence seems to have been followed in contrast to the rude and imperious methods employed by his father. In such a tolerant atmosphere, Julian Valens was able to stir up interest in Arianism at Milan.[4] He had been a priest at Poetovio (Ptuj in Yugoslavia), whom the Arians of that city had put forward as a candidate for the episcopacy, but who was then expelled by the predominantly Catholic community. At Milan, Julian Valens met Ursinus, the exiled rival of Pope Damasus. They may have been able to organize a dissident community, but we have no direct information on this score. In the summer of 376, or perhaps of 377, the youthful emperor paid an official visit to Rome.[5] It is highly probable that on the occasion of this passage through Milan he was visited by St. Ambrose. If so, it was perhaps their first meeting.

In the final months of 378, probably toward the end of September on the occasion of the anniversary of Pope Damasus's election, a meeting of bishops was held at Rome. St. Ambrose seems to have taken part in it.[6] The synodal letter, *Et hoc gloriae,* which Pope Damasus and the assembled bishops sent to Gratian at the conclusion of the council expressly states that the signatories had come together "from every part of Italy," that is, not merely from the provinces attached to the city such as Tuscia, Picenum, and others extending down to Sicily. There are thus good reasons for believing that Ambrose also was present. Further, the synodal letter in form and content, according to one who has studied the style of St. Ambrose for years, betrays the hand of the bishop of Milan.[7]

The letter discusses the case of a Jewish convert to Christianity by the name of Isaac. Prompted perhaps by the followers of Ursinus, he had lodged a criminal charge against Pope Damasus. The case which was tried before the prefect of Rome was brought to the attention of Gratian, and he absolved the pontiff. To clarify the issue, Damasus wanted the assembled bishops to examine the whole affair. The synodal letter reminds Gratian of the fact that his father had acted prudently in providing by law that only bishops are competent to judge bishops, but if this policy of non-intervention were to be interpreted too literally by the state, it would have some regrettable consequences. The bishop of Parma, for example, had been deposed by a council of bishops but he continued to remain in office. The same happened at Puteoli. The prefect of the praetorium of Italy or the vicar of Milan or of Rome should see to it that the conciliar decisions are enforced. Moreover, with respect to the bishop of Rome, because of his position, it is inconceivable that he should be brought before the prefect. Only the emperor should pass judgment on him if he should be accused.

Gratian's answer to the letter of the bishops, *Ordinariorum sententias,* seems also to have been outlined by Ambrose.[8] He assents almost entirely to the requests made of him. Every bishop condemned by a council of Catholic bishops not submitting to such a decision and refusing to leave his see should be obliged to do so by the prefect of the praetorium of Gaul or of Italy. A bishop unwilling to answer to a summons before other bishops acting as his judges should be conducted to Rome under the care of the civil authorities. If there is a question of more distant regions (beyond the confines of the suburban provinces) the case should be deferred to the bishop of the metropolis, that is, of the capital city of the province. As for the request that the bishop of Rome should be subject only to the tribunal of the emperor, Gratian's answer is limited to a declaration that accusations against a bishop from individuals with little to commend them ought not to be heard too readily (by civil judges, as is understood). Was this a refusal? It seems better to explain the deliberate omission of a definitive answer as a scruple on Gratian's part: he could not even imagine that he, not yet twenty years of age, would be able to pass sentence on one who was himself a judge of bishops, and who was as a rule an old man. Damasus, for example, would have been almost eighty years old at this time. Such a scruple must have been suggested to Gratian by an ecclesiastic, almost certainly the bishop of Milan.[9]

In these same final months of 378, St. Ambrose presented the emperor with the first two books of his treatise *De fide, On the Faith.* He had written it rapidly but well at the request of Gratian, whom he had met, probably at Sirmium, after the Council of Rome.

Up until this time the nineteen-year-old prince had not been subjected to any clerical influence. He had grown up at the court of Trier in the shadow, it is true, of a Catholic father but one who was not particularly religious and who was on principle averse to doctrinal disputes. He had been educated by Ausonius, an enigmatic figure whose numerous works fail to reveal whether he was a Christian or not.

Why did Gratian in 378 ask Ambrose to prepare for him a simple exposition of the dogma of Nicea rather than some other bishop? Perhaps because at Sirmium everyone remembered Ambrose's resolute intervention in 376 for the election of a Nicean bishop in the capital of Illyricum.

At any rate, the first two books of the *De fide* mark the beginning of Ambrose's open struggle with Arianism. Six contentions of the Arians are refuted in a rapid though rather superficial fashion. Ambrose did not write against one or other Arian movement, but against the whole of Arianism in general. According to him, Arians are not men but beasts. Their heresy collects the poison of all others. They should not even be called Christians. They are like the Jews but worse than the Jews. They are like the pagans, but worse than pagans—worse, in fact, than the devils.

Turning to Gratian, he showers him with expressions of loyalty and adulation, and encourages him with eager optimism to fight the barbarians. In the summer of 378, as has been seen, Valens had been killed and hordes of Goths were devastating the Danubian regions. Faith, Ambrose writes, will give victory to Gratian more readily than the vain superstitions of the pagans or the sacrileges of the Arians, since the chastisement of the invasion had been provoked by heresy: "Failure to be faithful to God has brought about a loss of fidelity to the empire. I do not wish to recall the murders, the tortures, the exiles suffered by confessors of the faith nor the sees of faithful bishops that have become the reward of Arian traitors. Have we not heard that from Thrace to Dacia Ripensis, to Moesia, to Valeria Pannonica, the horror of sacrilegious heresy has spread like that of the barbarian invasion?"[10]

Ambrose saw the frightful array of Gog predicted by Ezechiel in these Gothic hordes. This Gog, who comes from the extreme north, is the mass of Goths over whom victory was promised by the prophet: "Enough, yes, more than enough, Almighty God, have we now atoned for the deaths of confessors, the banishment of priests, and the guilt of such great wickedness. It is sufficiently clear that they who have broken the faith cannot be safe. Turn again, O Lord, and set up the banners of Your faith. No military eagles, no flight of birds, here lead the van of our army, but Your Name, Lord Jesus, and Your worship. This is no land of unbelievers, but the land whose custom it is to send forth confessors—Italy, Italy that has frequently been tempted, but never drawn away. . . . Show forth now a plain sign of Your majesty, that he who believes You to be the true Lord of Hosts may . . . win the prize of victory for his faith."[11] From the end of 378 comes also the homily which will later form the first part of the tenth book of his commentary on St. Luke. His outlook is still more pessimistic; famine and pestilence are added to the Gothic devastation: *"We are at the end of the world."* But he does not lose confidence: in place of the ineffective Saul (Valens) a young David (Gratian) is advancing. Through his mouth Christ proclaims His mysteries. There is also a Samson (Theodosius) wise and energetic. These leaders will triumph over the barbarians and heresy.

Still in the fall of 378, after the Gothic invasion, Gratian published an edict of toleration for both Catholics and Arians, but excluding the Manichaeans.[12] He also decided to recall all the ecclesiastics exiled during the persecution of Valens. He told the Arian bishops, Palladius of Ratiaria (modern Arcer in Bulgaria) and Secundianus of Singidunum (modern Belgrade), who asked not to be deposed without a hearing, that he would summon a new council as they desired.

After learning of the defeat at Hadrianople, and faced with the barbarian invasion of the Balkans, Gratian had to appoint a strong collaborator to remedy the disaster. He made an intelligent choice. On January 19, 379, he presented Theodosius to the soldiers as his colleague.[13] Theodosius was a Spaniard, born January 11, 347, at Cauca near Segovia. His father, Count Theodosius, had been one of the best generals in the army of Valentinian I and had rendered outstanding service to the empire in Britain, Germany, and particularly in Africa by crushing the revolt of Firmus. Later, during the first months of Gratian's rule (that is, at the beginning of the year 376) the emperor had him decapitated at Carthage. We do not know why his ministers had him sign such an order. Theodosius's son resigned his post as duke of Moesia after his father's execution and retired to private life, living for two years on his estates at Cauca in the Sierra de Guadarrama.[14]

Immediately after the death of Valens, Gratian recalled him to court. In the last months of 378, Theodosius destroyed the bands of the Sarmatians that had returned to invade Pannonia in a brief but successful campaign. Because of his excellent military background obtained under his father in many different regions of the empire, Theodosius was eminently suited to wear the purple. People admired the simple majesty of his person and looked upon him as another Trajan, the *optimus princeps*. The official panegyrists such as Themistius and Claudian claimed that there was a blood relationship between the two great Spaniards, but the silence of Pacatus makes this rather doubtful. Older historians such as Seeck represent him as a flabby individual, lazy and irresolute, and incapable of providing a solution to the grave problems that disturbed the complicated structure of the empire. As a matter of fact, although he was timid, choleric, and afflicted with poor health, Theodosius did solve a number of them. Among these problems were those rising from the Goths and Persians. He re-established and maintained order in the provinces and effectively cooperated in settling the religious controversies. If he did not deserve the title of "Great" for all his actions, he certainly deserved it for his fluid and clear-sighted policy.

After making him Augustus, Gratian placed him in charge of the two Illyrian dioceses of Dacia and Macedonia, and of the East. He set up his headquarters at Thessalonica (modern Saloniki in northern Greece), and gradually succeeded in suppressing the bands of Goths scattered about in search of plunder.

In the autumn of 378 or the following winter, Justina and her children and retinue must have left Sirmium and taken refuge in Milan, since Illyricum was no longer safe. Numerous other refugees must also have come to the city at this same time from the provinces along the Danube. The immediate result of this Arian immigration was new trouble for the Church at Milan. The Arians, certainly prompted by the empress, seized a basilica. Ambrose probably appealed to Gratian, but the latter was too concerned with preserving the peace to intervene. There were already troubles enough, and he was not anxious to stir up any more. He ordered the vicar of Italy to close the basilica at Milan now occupied by the Arians but claimed by the Catholics.

Perhaps the letter which Ambrose wrote to Constantius, a bishop probably of Claterna, near Imola, in the province of Flaminia, can be dated early in March of 379. It deals with pastoral problems. Constantius was a bishop recently elected, perhaps through Ambrose's influence, since he calls him his son. He tells him that his preaching should be simple and clear. He exhorts him to the practice of Christian virtue. He should be strictly honest and upright even in the absence of witnesses: "What difference does it make if we are enclosed within walls and shielded by darkness and without accomplices? We are always under the eye of a judge whom no one can deceive. . . . The riches of this world should serve to save the soul and not to destroy it. You, O bishop, should be a model to all!"[15] He then recommends him to show kindness to the heretics coming from Illyricum so that they might be converted, and prudence in shielding his flock from their errors. He begs him to visit frequently the neighboring church of Imola where a bishop was to be elected. He, himself, could not attend to this since he was too busy because of the approach of Lent, and he could not travel so far.

After restoring order in the Balkans and entrusting the East to Theodosius, perhaps in June, 379, Gratian started out on his return from Sirmium to Trier, passing through Venetia and Liguria. It is most likely that it was at this time that he wrote with his own hand and sent to Ambrose a brief letter expressing his confidence in, and esteem for, the latter: "I am very anxious that he whom I remember when he is absent and whom I have in mind should also be physically present. Hasten therefore, O devout priest of God, to come to me so that you may teach me already holding to the true faith. . . ." He further asks the bishop to add to his treatise on the faith written to oppose the Arians an exposition of the orthodox teaching on the Holy Spirit.[16] The decree of tolerance, published at Sirmium by Gratian in the fall of 378, had given rise to new disturbances at Antioch, where the Macedonians denied the divinity of the Holy Spirit and had again isolated themselves from the followers of Nicea.[17]

Ambrose was naturally flattered at receiving a personal note from the Augustus of the West. Such a token of favor was not a common occurrence. At this period even a Christian emperor was considered as being something more than human, and the pompous ceremonial of Diocletian was still in force. In his reply to the emperor, he noted: "You have written the whole letter with your own hand so that your writing itself may testify to your faith and piety."[18] But he was not at all intrigued with the thought of becoming a court prelate in the imperial palace. The Arian bishops had already discredited this profession. Further, if he had accepted the invitation, he would have had to abandon his church, and he was convinced that he could best serve the interests of the kingdom of God by staying at his own post.

Ambrose's letter to Gratian on this occasion is carefully worded. He tells the emperor that he will hasten to come to him as he has been requested, that he has thought constantly of him during the preceding weeks, that he has followed every step of his journey with his prayers, not only publicly in the church as was his duty as a bishop, but also in private because of the regard which he has for one who has secured peace for the Church and silenced the wicked. He also tells him that he is writing the treatise on the Holy Spirit, but it will take a little time to complete.

The outcome of this letter was the emperor's lifting the sequestration of the church claimed by the Arians at Milan and its restoral to those holding the Nicean creed, that is, to Ambrose.[19]

A law of Gratian issued at Aquileia on July 5, 379, limited the privileges formerly enjoyed by wandering clerics engaged in trade, dispensing, however, the clergy from taxes on small transactions.[20] At the end of July, the emperor was at Milan, where he probably remained a few weeks.

It was perhaps as the result of a meeting with St. Ambrose that Gratian decided to publish at Milan, on August 3, 379, the edict *Omnes vetitae,* abrogating the decrees of tolerance issued at Sirmium.[21] Heresy must be abolished. This change of policy is highly significant, but it would be wrong to accuse Ambrose of meddling in politics or Gratian of childish submission. The situation in August, 379, was quite different from that of the year before. The Gothic invasion had been checked. With Theodosius in the East, the young emperor had no further fears from that quarter. Moreover, his colleague was a convinced Catholic. Even from the purely political point of view, religious unity would be definitely advantageous. In his *De fide,* Ambrose had already maintained that heresy was a weak defense against the barbarians and that invasions occur in those areas inhabited by heretics. And, as a matter of fact, all of the orthodox episcopal sees were at this time centers of stability and the support of sound Roman traditions. The interests of the empire coincided with those of orthodoxy and the former governor did not believe that he was acting as a spiritual guide in pointing this out to the prince: the loyal collaboration of a bishop did not diminish the prestige of the Church and did not threaten the autonomy of the civil power. Ambrose, moreover, did not ask Gratian to compel the heretics to abjure; he only wished to deprive them of the liberty which they had to harm and disturb the Church.

Modern historians have not been the first to accuse the bishop of having forced the hand of the young prince. Ambrose himself felt it necessary to forestall jealousy within the court circle and attributed the new policy favoring orthodoxy to Gratian.

Theodosius, the Augustus of the East, spent the winter of 379-380 at Thessalonica. There, on February 28, 380, he published a famous edict ordering the people to subscribe to his own religion, that is, the religion which "the Apostle Peter once taught the Romans and which is now professed by Pope Damasus and Peter, the bishop of Alexandria."[22] These two names guaranteed Theodosius's own orthodoxy to which he was eager to bring the dissident churches of the East.

Although he avoided using the term *consubstantial* defined at Nicea, Theodosius proved his faith in Nicea by insisting that all should believe in the divinity of the Father, Son, and Holy Spirit, three persons with one identical majesty. Those who do not hold the same beliefs as Pope Damasus and Peter of Alexandria should be regarded as heretics: "Those who follow this norm can be called Catholic Christians. We regard the others as mad and diseased in mind. As heretics they will be held to be infamous, and in addition to the divine sanctions, they must expect to be also punished by us."[23] This edict, which had the immediate effect of law, manifests Theodosius's determination to end the everlasting dissensions in the East between Arians and anti-Arians; and his motives were largely political.

Gratian's edict of 378 had brought about the return of the orthodox bishops to their sees, but there was still no peace. At Antioch, the spiritual capital of the East, the orthodox bishop Meletius found in his city the schismatic communities of the Arian Dorotheus, the Apollinarist Vitalis, and the Nicean Paulinus. Paulinus, although he was supported by Rome and by Alexandria, had few adherents, but he did not on this account come to an agreement with Meletius. There were thus in a single city four different communities, all Christian, and all at odds with each other.

At Constantinople the followers of Nicea tried to elect an orthodox bishop to oppose the Arian Demophilus. They brought in Gregory of Nazianzus whom Basil had consecrated a few years earlier as bishop of Sasima. But Gregory had never gone there. Coming to the capital from his monastery at Seleucia in Isauria, Gregory performed prodigies of zeal, but during the Easter vigil the Arians entered his little church and routed the faithful with a shower of rocks. At the same time an Egyptian adventurer named Maximus with the backing of Peter of Alexandria was attempting to supplant both Demophilus and Gregory as bishop of Constantinople.

In the last weeks of March, 380, the Augustus of the West, Gratian, left Trier, and took the road for Italy and Illyricum.[24] The reason for this journey is not known. It is probable that Gratian was present for the Easter services, April 12, in the cathedral at Milan. At any rate, he certainly met Ambrose at this time. The fruit of this meeting was the law of April 24, 380, later completed by two others of May 8, 381, according to which Christian actresses and the daughters of Christian actors were by special favor allowed to give up their profession, but if they should become sinners, they were to be compelled to take up their former occupation.[25]

To understand the force of these laws, we must recall what we have seen earlier with respect to the caste system which had been introduced into the social and economic life of the Late Empire. We should also take into account the immorality of the theater which made such a career incompatible with one's duties as a Christian. There can be no question about St. Ambrose's part in the promulgation of these edicts. Gratian, like Theodosius, was now a definite supporter of orthodoxy, and he had definitively abandoned his father's policy of nonintervention.

In the summer of 380, Gratian sent reinforcements to the Danubian frontier. At the beginning of September he was at Sirmium with Theodosius. There they decided that the Eastern provinces of Illyricum should be returned to the Augustus of the West. The pressure of the Goths in these areas was always burdensome. It was perhaps at this meeting that the two Augusti agreed upon a strategic retreat in Pannonia and Thrace. Or it may have been that a serious illness of Theodosius during the autumn months obliged Gratian to undertake negotiations with the Goths and Vandals by himself and to grant them permission to settle on the Roman side of the Danube in Pannonia.

In October, 380, Gratian returned to Trier and remained there until the end of February, 381.

Theodosius, gravely sick and in danger of death, summoned Acholius, bishop of Thessalonica, assured himself of the bishop's orthodoxy and was baptized.[26] He later recovered and on November 24, 380, entered triumphantly into Constantinople. The following day the Arians were deprived of their churches, which were then turned over to the Catholics. Demophilus was banished and Gregory of Nazianzus solemnly enthroned in the basilica of the Apostles. Plans were then made for a great council to be held the following year to settle the many vexing problems that confronted the Church.

On January 10, 381, Theodosius published a new anti-Arian edict for the East: he forbade all those who did not accept the faith of Nicea to assemble; he also ordered the churches to be restored to the Catholics.[27]

On January 11, 381, the old Gothic king Athanaric entered Constantinople to render his submission and was received with royal gifts by Theodosius. But he unfortunately died during these days of celebration and was buried by order of Theodosius with a solemn funeral. The pacification of the Goths was gradually achieved. They were recognized as allies, received lands to cultivate, and enjoyed a certain amount of autonomy but under the rule of the emperor. They were even exempted from taxes. In return, they had to provide contingents of soldiers with their own leaders for the imperial army. Thus order was restored to the Danubian provinces of the East.

In March, 381, Gratian returned to Milan, and Ambrose presented him with his three books *De Spiritu Sancto*, as he had already presented him towards the end of 380 with the last three books of his *De fide*, which completed the earlier two of November, 378. These new books *On the Faith* were composed of sermons preached by Ambrose a short time before. Since he had been sharply attacked by the Arians, he was compelled to keep up his own polemical writings. Palladius had answered with a treatise of his own.[28]

The bishop now attacked the Arian sophistries with more energy and in a more orderly fashion. The Arians frequently erred because they interpreted the scriptures too literally: "It is the spirit which vivifies," the bishop insists. He then justifies the use of the term ὁμοούσιος "consubstantial," which had been consecrated by the Council of Nicea. He calls to mind the martyrs who had suffered for the Nicean Creed and describes the heretical intrigues at the Council of Rimini in 359. He also maintains that a scriptural text, if it is to be understood properly, cannot be torn from the context which gives it its meaning.

In the last book of his *De fide* he again exalts Christ and His reign. He is subject to the Father, but with a voluntary and exemplary subjection that belongs solely to His humanity, and which springs from His love for His father. He is omniscient: "Do not the Arians constantly say that all knowledge cannot exist in Christ? For He, they say, stated that He knew not the day nor the hour. . . . If we ask why He was unwilling to state the time, we shall find that it was not owing to ignorance but to wisdom. For it was not to our advantage to know, so that we, being ignorant of the actual time of future judgment, may ever be, as it were, on our guard, . . . lest the day of the Lord should come upon us in the midst of our wickedness. For it is better for us to fear rather than to know the future, as it is written: 'Be not high-minded but fear.' . . . For the adulterer cannot cease from his desire of committing adultery unless he daily fears the prospect of punishment, nor can the highwayman forsake his hiding place in the woods unless he knows that he is constantly threatened by punishment. The majority of men are incited to evil by the thought of impunity, but they are checked by fear."[29]

As we have already seen, Ambrose assails the Arians in the strongest terms. They are demons, snakes, madmen, counterfeiters, worse than the devil in their pride, and worthy of execration. The earnestness of the bishop indicates the strength of the Arian reaction against him and his efforts to restore orthodoxy.

While these three books *De fide* are a collection of sermons, the three books *De Spiritu Sancto*, like the first two of the *De fide*, were written to be read. This treatise is notable for its clarity in expounding the Catholic doctrine on the third person of the Blessed Trinity. In order to praise Gratian, Ambrose recalls the troubles for the Church under Constantius II. He mentions again the basilica that had been seized at Milan by the Arians, and that had finally been restored to the Catholics. He insists that conversion from heresy is a guarantee even of political security. At the end of this work, with powerful arguments, he again demonstrates the unity, equality, and divinity of the three persons of the Trinity.

When he wrote these books, Ambrose followed very closely the similar works of Didymus and Basil. He made no pretext of originality. Caught in the numerous duties of his office, the bishop of Milan did not have a great deal of time for theological speculation and, moreover, he was not particularly gifted in this regard. Nevertheless, modern theologians have pointed out the clarity of these writings. They are much more convincing than his models, even if for the sake of clarity much of the profundity of the Greek originals has been sacrificed.

These books, however, were severely criticized by St. Jerome. The latter had been asked by Pope Damasus to translate the work of Didymus the Blind on the Holy Spirit. In 386-387, after the death of Damasus and his own departure from Rome for Jerusalem, Jerome published this translation. In his preface to it, he makes a sharp attack on the work of St. Ambrose: "I preferred to translate the work of another rather than be like a crow (as some have been) and trick myself out in the disguise of others. A short time ago I read the books of a certain individual on the Holy Spirit, and, as the comic poet has put it, I have seen an ugly Latin copy of an excellent Greek original. It is not well argued. There is nothing substantial about it, no pretense of style that could charm a reluctant reader. The whole is soft and weak, although neat and pretty and tricked out with bright passages gathered from all sides. . . . Certainly, anyone who reads Didymus will know from whom the Latins have stolen, and will despise the streams when their source is tapped."[30]

Since Ambrose must have known the motives which prompted such a manifestation of prejudice and bad temper, motives which are unknown to us, he could not have been as surprised as we are at reading this.

Coming to Milan in March, 381, Gratian entered into a firm and lasting friendship with its bishop. Ambrose was anxious to break down the last Arian resistance in the West and persuaded Gratian to convoke a small council of orthodox bishops from Italy and Illyricum upon whom he could depend. They assembled at Aquileia in September, 381.

In the meantime another meeting was held from May to July, 381, for the bishops of the East at Constantinople.[31] The one hundred and fifty bishops that attended the council were largely concerned with the problems of particular bishops. Gregory of Nazianzus was unanimously recognized as the legitimate bishop of the capital city. Towards the end of May, Meletius, bishop of Antioch, who was present at the council, passed to his reward. The debates which took place among the bishops over the appointment of his successor were somewhat more than lively. At Antioch there was already another bishop, Paulinus, but he had few followers and had been irregularly consecrated by a Westerner, Lucifer of Cagliari, in 362. Despite this obvious handicap, Gregory of Nazianzus, in his desire for peace, insisted that he be recognized as the legitimate bishop. The other bishops at the council, however, would not even hear of it. Later, in describing the opposition which he experienced at this council, St. Gregory said that "one who had been perfected in the fear of God and the exercise of the ministry would not even have spoken to the young bishops talking nonsense and leaping up like wasps into the face of their adversary."[32] Later, a number of Egyptian bishops and Acholius of Thessalonica arrived at the council. The former openly showed their distrust of Gregory by abstaining from appearing at the sacred functions over which he presided since they held that his election had been invalid. Acholius, moreover, had received instructions from Pope Damasus that were sharply opposed to Gregory. The latter, who had already on other occasions threatened to return home, became so exasperated that he could no longer be kept in the city. He addressed a moving farewell to the faithful of Constantinople, who for almost three years had been inspired by his words and charity, and returned to Nazianzus in Cappadocia.

The council elected as his successor Nectarius, an old, still unbaptized senator. Before returning to their respective sees, the assembled bishops voted upon and approved four canons, the third of which was to have particularly serious consequences: the bishop of Constantinople has a primacy of honor after that of the bishop of Rome since Constantinople is the new Rome.

The canon, which was passed to check interference on the part of the powerful bishop of Alexandria, actually turned out to be the affirmation of an independence that lead to schism. St. Gregory had already inveighed against the vain ambitions of the city. By means of this canon, the civic and political preeminence of Constantinople was made the basis for a claim of precedence over the other churches, whereas the bishop of Rome had never brought forward Rome's position in the world as the reason for his primacy.

The council came to an end on July 9. On July 30, Theodosius sanctioned its decisions with an edict and again ordered the churches held by heretics to be handed over to Catholics.[33] At

Antioch a native priest named Flavian was elected bishop. According to the second canon of the council that had just recently ended, the bishops of other civil dioceses, of Egypt for example, or the West, could not interfere in matters concerning churches outside their own civil dioceses. To their displeasure at the election of Flavian, the Easterners simply answered: "Too bad for you!"

Thirty-six bishops were present at the council of bishops summoned by Gratian at Aquileia.[34] The sees of twenty-four of these are known. Two were from Africa, six from Gaul, three from Illyricum, thirteen from Upper Italy. Of these latter, Ambrose was from Milan, Valerian from Aquileia, Eusebius from Bologna, Limenius from Vercelli, Sabinus from Piacenza, Abundantius from Trent, Philastrius from Brescia, Maximus from Aemona (Ljubljana), Bassianus from Lodi, Heliodorus from Altinum, Exsuperantius from Tortona, Diogenes from Genoa, and Eventius from Pavia.

This combination of bishops was wisely chosen by Ambrose. The two Arian bishops, Palladius of Ratiaria and Secundianus of Singidunum, were ordered to appear. The former made an appeal to the emperor at Sirmium to rescind the order, but his efforts proved fruitless. After various preliminary discussions, the plenary session of the council was finally held in a hall in the basilica at Aquileia on Friday, September 3, 381. The meeting, which lasted from six in the morning until about one in the afternoon, was presided over by Valerian. Ambrose knew how to bring matters to a point. There were no theological debates about doctrines which presumably had the support of all. Instead, there was a regular trial. The former civil judge, drawing on his long experience in the courts, acted as both public prosecutor and chief justice. The two Arian bishops, Palladius and Secundianus, were deposed and excommunicated. No action could be taken against Julian Valens since he had stayed at Milan to strut about during the bishop's absence. Since the carrying out of the decisions of the council depended upon the emperor, he was asked to issue a decree of banishment for Valens. In the synodal letter *Benedictus* drawn up by Ambrose, the principles for regulating the relations between Church and State are set forth with great clarity. They are opposed to the disastrous tradition of excessive interference in religious matters on the part of the emperors.

The Church calls on the secular arm, that is, it asks the State to carry out the decisions reached by ecclesiastical authorities, but it vindicates its own spiritual freedom with respect to the State. In this particular instance, the bishops ask Gratian to remove the heretics Palladius and Secundianus from their sees, but they reserve to themselves the right to see to the election of their successors.

"It is the duty of the State," Ambrose writes, "to give to the Church that material assistance which she demands. It is also to the interest of the State to do so, and Christ our Lord will reward it for this assistance."[35]

In a synodal letter, the Council of Aquileia also asked Gratian to stop by his authority the intrigues and meetings of the followers of Ursinus at Rome.[36] The emperor granted the request. He dispersed the troublemakers, deposed the heretical bishops, and banished them from their sees. In all this, St. Ambrose had received the previous approval of Pope Damasus. In fact, he was so considerate of the latter that Palladius in the violent book which he wrote against him accused Ambrose of being a slave and client of the bishop of Rome.[37]

In the last official document of the council, the letter *Quamlibet*, addressed to Gratian, Valentinian, and Theodosius, the bishops expressed their joy at seeing the restoration of the unity of faith in the empire of the West. Ambrose could rest content that his long struggle with heresy had been crowned with victory. But such was not the case. The bishops assembled at Aquileia were perfectly aware of the schisms that split the churches of Antioch and Alexandria. In their final letter, the *Quamlibet*, they suggested that the emperors should give orders for a council to meet at Alexandria to settle the rival claims for the two sees.

The East, which had given rise to Christianity and to monasticism, always exercised a strong influence on the West. This was particularly true with respect to St. Ambrose, whose reading helped him to be at home in the world of Basil and Athanasius. And, in his attack on Arianism, he must have instinctively turned towards the East since it was there that the heresy had had its origin and where it was still active.

Confusion, however, was caused at Aquileia during the council by the appearance of Maximus, who had attempted with the assistance of the Egyptians to supplant Gregory of Nazianzus in the see of Constantinople. He had been disavowed by Theodosius and the council at Constantinople, but when he presented himself before the fathers of Aquileia they were taken in by his claims and accepted him as the legitimate bishop.

After the dissolution of the council, Ambrose continued to busy himself in his own name and that of the other bishops with the claims of Maximus and Paulinus of Antioch. He took the matter up with Theodosius in the letter *Sanctum.* Hoodwinked by Maximus, he went so far as to say that Nectarius and Flavian were intruders, and to support this he repeated some rather absurd gossip. He also expressed his regrets that he had not been invited to take part in the discussions. He did not claim "a right of examination, but there should nonetheless have been a common agreement of wills."[38] He then asked Theodosius to convoke an ecumenical council at Rome.

But in this particular matter the bishops of the East were better informed and more accurate in their decision than those at Aquileia. There was no reason to reopen the debate. We do not have Theodosius's reply to Ambrose, but it was obviously unfavorable since Ambrose in a new letter, the *Fidei,* apologizes in a tone of calm dignity but repeats his claim that a general council at Rome would not be absurd.[39]

If Ambrose's failure to accept a decision made in the East

with full knowledge of the circumstances is in itself regrettable, his general attitude was sound in that it pointed out the danger of a separation of the churches modeled after that of the divisions in the empire.[40] The Church is one as Christ is one. The union among the churches should be above anything else. The bishops of the West had a right to know the decisions of the councils held in the East. That the East had specifically excluded the West from a council like that held at Constantinople was a wrong which the bishop of Milan regarded as a personal affront, and he had reason to complain.

Theodosius then sent an embassy to Rome to announce the election of Nectarius to the pope.

The Arians, even though they were defeated and deposed, continued to stir up troubles for Ambrose. Jealous of the fact that he had won over the affection of the prince, they first aroused the enmity of influential persons at court against him. It is perhaps in the beginning of 382 that the bishop was confronted by the two Arian *cubicularii* at Milan. These two members of the imperial court raised an objection about the Incarnation. They wanted to know what the bishop would say about the doctrine of Apollinaris of Laodicea who, to defend the impeccability of Christ against Arius, had denied the freedom and intelligence of His human nature. This was a heresy which did not concern the West. Nevertheless Ambrose made an appointment with the two courtiers for the following day in the Portian basilica. When the time came, however, they failed to appear. While the bishop and the people were waiting for them, they had gone for a ride in a carriage outside the city to show their contempt. Their excursion had a disastrous end. Both were hurled from the carriage and killed, as it later became known.[41]

Even though the *cubicularii* failed to show up for the discourse, Ambrose delivered the sermon which he had prepared to the congregation that had assembled in the church. In it he gave an exact account of the Church's teaching on the human nature of Christ, which contradicted that held by Apollinaris. He later published this discourse and added to it a long appendix on the Trinity which he dedicated to Gratian.[42] The latter had in the meantime sent him a new Arian objection, coming certainly from Palladius, the deposed bishop. This was in itself a proof of the fact that Palladius could still catch the ear of the emperor.

The Council of Rome, which Ambrose had suggested to Theodosius, was summoned by a letter of Gratian in the summer of 382. Among the bishops present were, in addition to Pope Damasus, Ambrose, Valerian of Aquileia, Britton of Trier, Anemius of Sirmium, and Acholius of Thessalonica. Although the Eastern bishops were invited to attend, none showed up with the exception of Paulinus of Antioch and his protector Epiphanius of Salamis.

We have very little information on this council. Nectarius was recognized as the legitimate bishop of Constantinople, but Flavian was not acknowledged bishop of Antioch since the bishops of the West still continued to support Paulinus. On the occasion of this council St. Jerome also returned to Rome. About the year 377 he was forced to leave the desert of Chalcis since even the monks were divided by the disputes of the rival parties in the neighboring city of Antioch. After leaving the desert, Jerome stayed for a couple of years in Antioch where he lined himself up with the small group that favored Paulinus. There, at the earnest insistence of this party, he consented to be ordained a priest on the condition that he could retain his freedom and not be encumbered with pastoral cares. About the year 379 he went to Constantinople to continue his scriptural studies under the direction of Gregory of Nazianzus.[43] He had begun these earlier by attending the lectures of the elderly Apollinaris of Laodicea in the churches of Antioch.

At Constantinople, Jerome became one of the most ardent and enthusiastic supporters of Gregory. He was attracted to him by his asceticism, his austerities, his love not only for learning but for a fine phrase, even though they both appreciated the vanity of this type of beauty. They were, moreover, of a similar temperament, very sensitive, inclined to irony and sarcasm, and at the same time extremely tender. Jerome must have passionately followed the heated arguments of the council of 381 which brought about the abdication of his teacher and his return to Cappadocia. Since this left him something of an orphan in the capital, Jerome gladly accepted the invitation which Epiphanius and Paulinus must have extended to him to be their interpreter at the Council of Rome towards the end of the summer of 382. Epiphanius, now at least seventy years old, was received as a guest in the house of Paula, a noble Roman woman who had been left a widow at the age of twenty-two and who, despite her five children, had consecrated herself to the ascetic life on the advice of Marcella. Later, Paula and her young daughters were to play a prominent role in Jerome's life. We do not know what part Jerome took in the council. Damasus at this time was almost eighty, and he had come to know Jerome through his letters. The pope now took him as his secretary and assistant. Ambrose must have seen Jerome at this time in Rome, but there does not seem to have been any intimacy between the two. The bishop of Milan belonged to the old Roman aristocracy, whereas Jerome, even when he would enter into the homes of patricians as a spiritual director, would always be regarded as something of an intruder, if not as an actual employee.

In his biography of St. Ambrose, Paulinus mentions a miracle that occurred at Rome after his consecration as bishop. This could have taken place on the occasion of his first visit to the city in 377. More likely, however, it should be referred to his second stay in the city for the council of 382. By this time the fame of the sanctity of the bishop of Milan would have been more widespread in his native city.

According to Paulinus, Ambrose was invited to the home of

a noble Roman woman (a *clarissima*) in the Trastevere. Since Marcella was most likely in Milan during these years, he was in all probability a guest, just as Epiphanius was, in the home of Paula. One day when Ambrose was celebrating Mass in this house, the owner of a bathing establishment who was confined to her bed by paralysis had herself carried to the room so that she might touch his vestments. When she kissed them, she immediately regained her health and began to walk.[44]

The Athanasian Creed was probably composed towards the end of 382. It is a kind of simple catechism aimed at instructing even the less educated on the essential dogmas of the Trinity and Incarnation. The insistent repetitions of the articles of this creed seem to embody the hymn of victory which Ambrose raised after ten long years of exhausting struggle against Arianism.[45]

D(ominus) N(oster) GRATIANVS
P(ius) F(elix) AVG(ustus)

Bronze coin: Bust with crowned helmet, cloak and breastplate. See Cohen, *Monnaies*, VI, p. 436, no. 54.

Gratian was born at Sirmium in 359. He became Augustus on August 24, 367, and was slain at Lyons on August 25, 383.

IX
Political Action

Priscillian at Milan. Measures taken by Gratian against paganism. Death of Acholius at Thessalonica. The essay on Abraham. The usurpation of Maximus. The death of Gratian. St. Ambrose's first mission to the court at Trier.

Ambrose's vigorous action naturally brushed against many interests and susceptibilities. Justina, the widow of Valentinian I, kept a watch on him from her imperial palace at Milan. All the hopes of the last Arian adventurers were converged in her, although her influence was still weak since her son, the Augustus, was only ten years old. Gratian's ministers saw that his friendship with the bishop meant a lessening of their own traditional power. Paulinus narrates that one day Ambrose went to the master of the offices, Macedonius, to intercede for one who had been accused, but the door was shut in his face. The bishop let the minister know that he, too, would one day seek refuge in the Church and would find the doors closed.[1] The hostility of the government officials to Ambrose may also be seen in their treatment of the Priscillianists.

Priscillian was an educated Spaniard of noble birth who, about the year 370, began to propagate some strange theories around Merida and Cordova. These were received with great enthusiasm by the upper classes, and especially by the women who flocked about him.[2] On what was perhaps an orthodox ascetical foundation, he tried to reform Spanish Catholicism through the introduction of strange and disturbing practices such as the use of noncanonical writings; nocturnal meetings in secret places; prolonged fastings, even on Sundays; the custom of praying naked; an interest in astrology; and the habit of not consuming the host at the communion of the Mass but carrying it home. Such strange activities brought upon him accusations of Manichaeism, immorality, and magic. Three bishops of the Iberian peninsula, Hyginus of Cordova, Idatius of Merida, Ithacius of Sossuba (Ossonoba in Portugal), rose up to oppose the propaganda of Priscillian. Unfortunately, in their zeal against the false asceticism of Priscillian, they made use of means hardly less condemnable. This was particularly true of Ithacius, a stout, worldly, and shameless prelate, who cut a very sad figure in this affair. There were other bishops, however, who supported the Priscillianists. A council held at Saragossa in October, 380, condemned some of the ideas attributed to Priscillian and his disciples, but without naming individuals. Priscillian was ordained bishop of Avila shortly afterwards. In the meantime, in 381, Idatius and Ithacius obtained a decree of banishment from Gratian for the "false bishops and Manichaeans." Priscillian was forced to retire to Aquitania.[3] Here he was enthusiastically received and gained many new proselytes, among whom were Eucrocia and Procula, the widow and daughter of the orator, Delphidius of Bordeaux, who is mentioned by Ausonius, Ammianus, and Jerome. But the bishop of Bordeaux banished Priscillian and his followers from the city. They then went to Rome. Pope Damasus refused to receive the appeal which Priscillian and his followers made to him. They therefore went to Milan. Sulpicius Severus tells us that Ambrose also was suspicious of them. On the other hand, Priscillian succeeded, perhaps by bribery, in acquiring the favor of Macedonius, the master of the offices of the court at Milan.[4] Despite Ambrose's objections, Gratian's decree against "false bishops and Manichaeans" was revoked. Priscillian then returned to Spain. Ithacius, threatened with a trial before the proconsul for having calumniated Priscillian and his followers, barely escaped to Trier, where he succeeded in winning over the bishop Britton and the prefect of the praetorium. The latter suggested handling the dispute in his own court. But the proceedings were broken off through the intervention again of Macedonius. This was another proof that Ambrose, despite his friendship with the emperor, did not dominate him. At times others were more influential with him than the bishop.

After his return from the Council of Rome in the fall of 382, Ambrose met Gratian at Milan on his return from a military expedition along the Danube.[5] Under the obvious inspiration of the bishop, the emperor made two grave moves against paganism. The altar of Victory was removed from the senate chamber at Rome; the priestly colleges, including the Vestal Virgins, were deprived of their exemptions and immunities, and their revenues were confiscated.[6] Such measures were bound to exasperate the pagans, but Gratian was perhaps unaware of the political consequences of his acts, or at least he gave no thought to means which would enable him to meet the opposition.

Quintus Aurelius Symmachus, the *princeps senatus* and a famous orator, then came to Milan as a representative of the Roman senate to ask the emperor to rescind these measures.[7] Pope Damasus, on the other hand, sent a group of Christian senators to Ambrose with a counter-petition.[8] His intervention proved to be so effective that Symmachus and the other Roman delegates were not even received. Some months later, in 383, after the death of his first wife Constantia when she was only twenty years of age, Gratian married a second time. His first wife had been an Arian, but his second, Laeta, was an orthodox Christian.

On May 21, 383, Gratian promulgated a law against those

who apostatized from Christianity and returned to paganism.[9] This was similar to two laws issued by Theodosius during this same year.

Ambrose's serenity and confidence during these months are manifest in his writings since he knew that he could now count on the full support of Gratian in his plans for the restoration and advancement of religion.[10] In the winter of 382-383 the bishop Acholius died, and the clergy of Thessalonica wrote a letter to the bishop of Milan to inform him that when Acholius died he had designated Anysius as his successor.

Ambrose's reply is filled with both sadness and joy.[11] He speaks of his great friendship with the deceased. He recalls the fact that once when he was himself sick Acholius had come to his bedside in Milan, had embraced him, and wept for him. Acholius, who had been reared in a monastery in Achaea, had been sought by the Thessalonians as their bishop because of his virtues. After his election he had frequently traveled to councils in the West. And now, having departed for heaven, he has left his mantle to Anysius as Elias had once left his to Eliseus.

In addition to this letter to the clergy of Thessalonica, Ambrose wrote another to Anysius, and in it we find another enthusiastic eulogy of the dead bishop.

His small work on Abraham, which consists of two sermons which he had preached and an essay, is perhaps also to be dated in the Lent of 383. The treatise is a commentary on some chapters of Genesis. Two sermons, which comprise the first part of the work, were preached to catechumens who were preparing for baptism. The advice which he gives on the choice of a wife is interesting, especially since Possidius, in his life of St. Augustine, says, as we have already seen, that Ambrose made it a point of principle not to undertake to get a wife for anybody.[12] But here, in his instruction to the catechumens, he states: "With a saint you will be a saint and with one who is perverse you will be perverse. If this is true in general, how much more so it will be in marriage, where there is but one flesh and one spirit. How can there be a union of charity if there is divergence of faith? Beware, therefore, O Christian, of giving your daughter as a wife to a Gentile or to a Jew. Beware of taking as a wife a Gentile or a Jew or a stranger, that is, a heretic, or anyone not of the faith. The foundation of conjugal fidelity is a love of chastity. If your wife adores idols whose adulteries are known to all, if she denies Christ who is the teacher and rewarder of the virtue of chastity, how can she love this virtue? It is not enough that she should be a Christian unless you have both been initiated to the sacrament of baptism. You should rise together at night for prayer, and you should entreat God with your joined petitions. . . . Learn then what should be sought in a wife: Abraham did not seek gold nor silver nor land, but the favor of a good character." The bishop himself may have even smiled when he said: "Perhaps when you, my daughters, who are looking for the grace of Christ, when you hear these things, may say: 'Why do you forbid us, O bishop, to have what Rebecca received as a gift and yet you encourage us to be like Rebecca?' But I answer: 'Rebecca did not have those rings and earrings which are such a frequent source of dispute within the Church.' "[13]

The second book of the *De Abraham* is a rather abstruse dissertation containing discussions on etymologies and many Greek quotations. In it, Ambrose attacks Plato, Aristotle, the Pythagorians, and the Stoics. He becomes almost fanatical in denying any good in pagan philosophers: either what they say is bad, or, if there is something good they have to say, it has been derived from the scriptures.

Ambrose, however, did not want the proscription of paganism to degenerate into a persecution of the pagans. A person in high position and a supporter of the old religion had offended Gratian by telling him that he was unworthy of his father, perhaps because he was not as indulgent towards the pagans. He was condemned to death for treason. Ambrose, in the spirit of Christian charity, and to avoid the regrettable consequences which would be attributed to the zeal of the Catholics decided to intercede.[14]

He went to the palace, but the officials then told him that it was impossible to see the prince since he was busy hunting in the park, his favorite pastime. Ambrose's insistence was to no avail, and the time for execution was rapidly approaching. The bishop knew that Gratian's ministers were reluctant to cause him any trouble. He did not lose heart but found a side gate and was able to confront the emperor. Gratian at first appeared a bit irritated by this importunity. But he then gave in and granted the favor requested by the bishop. A number of facts lend credence to this narrative of Sozomen: there were influential pagans at court, and the bishop was not afraid to pass over formalities. The prince, moreover, was at the time busy with the chase.

Gratian, as a matter of fact, was a bit mad about this sport. Although he was intelligent, cultured, sober, and virtuous, he was still something of a boy at twenty-four.[15] The pagans Eunapius and Ammianus say that he was ignorant of men and of the world, and even the Catholic Rufinus recognized his political limitations, his youthful thoughtlessness. At a time that demanded an iron hand, the empire of the West was governed by a sports enthusiast. Among the many sports which Gratian passionately followed, he preferred the chase and wasted whole days in slaughtering wild beasts with bow and arrows in his great parks. It is foolish to blame Ambrose for the fact that this Christian prince was not equal to his responsibilities, and gratuitous to assert that the bishop took advantage of Gratian's limitations and inexperience. He later proved to be equally bold with, and influential over, Theodosius.

Another cause of the catastrophe of 383 was Gratian's enthusiasm for the barbarians. It was not particularly strange that this young prince surrounded himself with a dense crowd of huge blond Alani. More than three centuries earlier Augustus had set the style. It was quite reasonable to entrust the protection of one's own person to foreigners. A bit stranger, however, was the fact that the prince dressed at times like the Alani. But here also it should be remembered that in the fourth century the so-called "barbarians" represented what was best in the Roman army, and that most of the generals preferred to retain their own Germanic names and not to change them as had been done in earlier times. Moreover, it had become the style to dress like the barbarians at the end of the fourth century. This was so true that authorities deemed it necessary to pass laws forbidding such an unbecoming custom.

Still stronger resentment must have been aroused in those who favored the older Roman ideals at seeing the prince's policy of absorbing the Germanic races and his attempts to assimilate and incorporate into Roman territory the Lentienses, Vandals, Goths and Alani. But there was already a tradition to this effect. Unfortunately, Gratian did no more than imitate what other, and greater rulers had done before him. The practice of accepting groups of barbarians into the empire and leaving them complete freedom in law, customs, and language, that is, abandoning the idea of Romanizing them, was to have disastrous consequences. At any rate, it is interesting to note that in following this course Gratian must have been influenced by his Frankish generals, Merobaudes and Arbogast. Such a policy was certainly opposed to the deepest convictions of Ambrose. The bishop in this matter had the same narrow outlook as that of even some recent historians who are scandalized to read in Orosius and in his teacher, St. Augustine, that the barbarian invasions into the Roman world were not so very much different from the Roman invasions of Africa, the East, and of Gaul. That such an argument was unintelligible to Ambrose is reasonable enough: he came from the Roman aristocracy. The scandal taken by more modern historians is less comprehensible.[16] Other critics not less informed have long since accepted the ideas of St. Augustine. They maintain it was not solely the barbarians that brought about the destruction of the Roman empire and that "the antiquated idea that ancient civilization was destroyed by the barbarian invasions . . . cannot be resuscitated."[17]

The emperor was thus opposed by Arian, pagan, and nationalistic forces. But it was one of the common rebellions that marked the history of three centuries of Roman imperial despotism that eventually caused his downfall. The revolt had its origins among the troops in Britain. Even granting that its immediate occasion was in the disgust and indignation which filled the legionaries at the sight of a Roman prince who even gave up the dress and habits of his own country, it is necessary to remember that fourteen years earlier, in 369, a similar revolt had broken out in Britain under the leadership of a certain Valentine who had been relegated to the island for political reasons. At that time the revolution seems to have been based on the desire to affirm the right of autonomy for Britain, and it demanded all the energy of the father of the emperor Theodosius to quell the rebellion. In 383, the legions stationed in Britain hailed as their emperor the Spanish general Magnus Maximus. He may have been personally opposed to Gratian for having raised another Spaniard, Theodosius, to such a high position. Later Maximus declared that he was forced by the troops to take the purple. He crossed the English channel from Richborough and marched on Paris. At the first news of the revolt, Gratian left Verona and headed for Gaul. When the opposing forces met, Gratian did not attack at once, but this delay favored the usurper. Gratian was not popular in Gaul. For one thing, he had left his residence at Trier for long periods of time and had eventually carried the court to Milan. The contest was less a battle than a desertion. Gratian, thinking that he would be able to resist the rebellious forces and begin negotiations for peace if he were protected by the Alps and the walls of Milan, fled from the field; but at Lyons, perhaps even against the orders of Maximus, he was treasonably murdered by the count Andragathius. Socrates and Sozomen write that Gratian on his arrival at Lyons was immediately informed that Laeta, whom he had recently married, was waiting for him on the other bank of the Rhone. The emperor hastened to cross the river to meet her. A coach surrounded by a guard near the bank was waiting for him. He ran up, intent upon embracing his wife. Instead he was met by Andragathius coming out of the coach. The latter, hurling himself at the young emperor, slew him with his dagger.[18]

Gratian thus died on August 25, 383, at the age of twenty-five without issue. The bishop of Milan in his commentary on Psalm LXI, which, however, was not written before 387, has a long digression on the death of Gratian and speaks out strongly against his treacherous assassins.

Many influential men in his service fell with Gratian. Paulinus especially notes that the master of the offices, Macedonius, was slain at this time while vainly seeking refuge in a church.

The new ruler of Gaul had no reason to fear the other Augustus of the West, the twelve-year-old Valentinian II, who remained in the imperial palace at Milan with his mother Justina. Theodosius, on the other hand, preoccupied as he was with Persia where the new king, Sapor III, could be a source of trouble, had to overlook the tragedy in the West. There is no need to imagine any connivance on the part of the Augustus of the East with Maximus, his fellow countryman and former comrade in arms, to do away with the sons of Valentinian, especially since we have no evidence in this regard. Maximus must have first thought of securing the possession of Gaul and then offering peace to the court at Milan. At Milan, however, it was feared that Maximus would not stop at the Alps. Count Bauto, as a preliminary precaution, sent troops to fortify the Alpine passes while he began to negotiate with the Huns and the Alani so that they would march against the Alemanni who were allied to Maximus.

Bauto, a Frankish general and probably also a pagan, had already been the master of soldiers *(magister militum)* under Gratian and now, under Valentinian II, he became a kind of "protector" to the emperor, the first of a series of "patricians," including Stilicho, Aetius, Richomer, and Odoacer.

Maximus's proposals for peace were received at Milan with relief, but then it was soon realized that if Valentinian II went to Trier a court and a government could no longer be sustained at Milan, and the young prince would thus lose that bit of sovereignty he still possessed.

On the other hand, the authorities at Milan could not reject Maximus's request and in this way provide him with an excuse for an attack, especially since with the few troops at their disposal they had also to defend the Alps from the Alemanni pouring into Raetia. Someone had to be found who could intervene with Maximus. Such a negotiation would give Theodosius time to decide if he should step in. At this juncture the Arian Justina entrusted her son to Ambrose. The bishop embraced the lad and assumed his defense.

Ambrose was commissioned to negotiate with Maximus at Trier as imperial legate of the court at Milan. It was unprecedented for a bishop to be entrusted with such a high political mission. A year later Ambrose would say that he had simply undertaken the defense of a widow and an orphan. But, as a matter of fact, the Arian Justina and her pagan minister Bauto had not chosen the bishop by accident. It was well known that Maximus represented himself as a champion of orthodoxy and had been baptized shortly before he was hailed as emperor. Just as his orthodoxy secured for him the support of the bishops, so it could provide him with a new excuse for interfering in the government of Italy controlled by pagans and Arians.

Ambrose must certainly have understood why this delicate task was entrusted to him. Nevertheless, he accepted the responsibility. He had already experienced the advantages of personal contacts between ecclesiastical and civil authorities. Moreover, he knew that by assisting Valentinian, he would acquire a fund of sympathy and gratitude which would counteract the baneful influence of the Arians upon the empress.

In September or October, 383, the bishop left Milan. He was accompanied by many other dignitaries. Their swift carriages left the shore of Lake Como, climbed up to Chiavenna through the valley of the Liro and crossed Mount Spluga at a height of over twelve thousand feet. At this time there probably was already snow in the pass. They then descended through the valley of the Häusser to Chur and the Rhine, which they then followed to Mainz. Here they met an embassy from Trier traveling in the opposite direction. Count Victor had been sent by Maximus to negotiate with the authorities in Milan. He wanted Valentinian to come and live at Trier like a son near his father. Without trouble Maximus would thus have obtained the actual sovereignty of the entire West which Gratian had already held in his own name and that of his younger brother. Such a proposition had probably been foreseen by both Ambrose and Justina, and it was of such a type as to make the outcome of the bishop's mission highly problematical even before his arrival at Trier. Still, Ambrose also knew that Marcellinus, the brother of Maximus, was being held at Milan as a "guest." The bishop, therefore, continued his journey and came to Trier. There he was admitted into the presence of the emperor in a public audience of the consistory.

Ambrose was anxious not to create any difficulties. He did not claim that he should be received in a private audience as would have befitted his rank. As a true diplomat, he measured his words carefully. He had come to treat of peace and was disposed to make any concession. As for the request that Valentinian should move to Trier, Ambrose declared that he could give no answer since he had no instructions on this point. But then, how could a woman and a boy cross the Alps in winter? Maximus was not convinced. He decided to wait for the return of Victor. In the meantime, Ambrose was also asked to regard himself as a "guest" at Trier. On his return, Count Victor reported that the court at Milan was eager for peace with Maximus, but that it could not, at least for the present, move to Trier. Ambrose also must have declared that Maximus's request would have been fulfilled at a more suitable season. The bishop could now depart. On its return journey, his party ran across a second embassy from the court of Milan at Valence, near the confluence of the Isère with the Rhone. This second embassy had been sent to negotiate with Maximus on the basis of the terms that had been carried to Milan by Victor. A definite agreement was reached. The historian Rufinus writes that the court of Milan pretended to receive with joy the peace which Maximus, also pretending, offered with joy.[19] Maximus was recognized as the legitimate Augustus for Britain, Gaul and Spain, while Valentinian retained Italy, Africa, and Illyricum. Theodosius after some hesitation also recognized Maximus, and, officially at least, it seems that a perfect harmony was established among the three governors, so much so, in fact, that at Alexandria and in other areas ruled by Theodosius, statues were raised in honor of Maximus and his portrait was even stamped on the coins of Constantinople.

Bauto was thus able, with the help of contingents of Huns and Alani, to provide for the defense of the Alps and Danube against the invasions of the Alemanni and the Juthungi.

Ambrose, probably passing through the Mont Cenis and the valley of the Dora Riparia, descended to Turin and arrived in Milan, perhaps in January, 384. Even in the face of the complete absence of any mention in the sources for his life, biographers have every reason to imagine the enthusiastic reception given to Ambrose by the people of Milan and their expressions of sincere gratitude. This mission of their bishop had been a great event for the people, and its results seemed good. No less festive a reception, even if perhaps less sincere, must have been shown Ambrose in the imperial palace. The child Augustus and his mother must have hailed him as their savior. As a matter of fact, not many months later Maximus would accuse Ambrose of having played a trick on him, of having prevented his gaining an easy and decisive victory.

Ambrose must also have thanked God since his success indicated a triumph for the faith. As a minister of that Church which the State only a few decades before had recognized only as a public peril to be rooted out, he had assumed a diplomatic role in the interests of the State. As its agent he had secured peace for the State. Great demands were made on the bishop, who had to show himself before a man in whom he saw the murderer of the twenty-four-year-old emperor, who had been as dear to him as a son. This man of the Church had feared that the heart-rending death of Gratian would mean the collapse of that slow work of Christianizing the empire for which as bishop he had toiled and suffered for some ten years. He regarded his political activities as a pastoral duty. There was need to preserve the work begun while waiting for the opportunity to bring it to perfection.

Anti-Paganism

o

Paganism in the fourth century. Roman religion. The feasts. Oriental cults and their spread. Attis and Cybele. Isis. Mithra. Syncretism. Neoplatonism. The life of Apollonius of Tyana. The second embassy of Symmachus. The victorious intervention of St. Ambrose.

A general survey of Ambrose's public life will show that he followed a definite course of action. His first efforts were directed towards re-educating his subjects in Christian asceticism. In 381 at the Council of Aquileia, he began his active campaign against Arianism, and this eventually removed the schism from the Church and strengthened it interiorly. The third stage of his activity was taken up with his struggle against paganism.

In the first half of the fourth century the Christians in the West were probably still a minority. At Milan, however, as may be concluded from Ambrose's sermons, the majority of the people in the second half of the fourth century were Christians. When he became bishop in 374 there were at least three basilicas, or churches, at Milan large enough for meetings of the faithful.[1] One of these was called the *vetus*, that is, the "old" basilica. Another was called the *nova*, or "new" basilica. It was also known as the *maior*, or "larger" basilica, in comparison with the other. The Basilica Maior was located in the square in front of the present cathedral of Milan, and at one time was one of the largest churches in the West. Its very size would indicate that the old cathedral had no longer been large enough to hold the many new Christians. When he was bishop, St. Ambrose built two other churches; the Basilica Apostolorum, which is today called San Nazaro, located on the Via Romana, and the Basilica Ambrosiana, which is still called by this name even though it was completely rebuilt between the eighth and twelfth centuries. An indication of the size of these basilicas may be seen in the comparison which St. Ambrose made between a church and the sea. The faithful entering through many vestibules are like the waves of the ocean, and their singing is like the crash of the billows.[2]

But at Milan, just as at Rome, the Church was opposed by the more wealthy and influential classes. The educated pagans still remained attached "to their traditions," and they clung to them all the more tenaciously in that they must have unconsciously felt that their cause was now lost.

The duel that took place between Symmachus and St. Ambrose in the summer of 384 over the altar of Victory has come to be regarded as symbolic of the conflict between paganism and the new religion, and the victory of Ambrose as the forecast of the eventual victory of Christianity.

As we have already seen, the bishop of Milan had to leave the city during the summer of 382 to take part in the Council of Rome. On this occasion he had the opportunity of seeing once again the spectacle of official Roman paganism, and of reflecting upon the retention of cult ceremonies and public support for institutions which did not contribute to the public welfare.

As we have also seen in the last chapter, Gratian, in the fall of 382, took vigorous measures against paganism.[3] The extensive revenues of the priestly colleges at Rome were appropriated by the State, and the funds were used for public works and, in particular, to raise the salaries of those engaged in public hauling. Even if St. Ambrose disavowed any direct involvement in the passing of these laws, he must have exerted some influence upon their author. Their passage produced a sudden reaction on the part of the Roman aristocracy, and Symmachus was sent to Milan to make an official protest. St. Ambrose, however, succeeded in preventing the legation from even being received.

In the summer and fall of 383 matters took a turn for the worse. Gratian was murdered and the bishop now found himself almost as a stranger or enemy at the court of Milan, where other opposing influences were now in control. Bauto, the supreme commander of the military forces of Valentinian II, was a pagan. At Rome, in 384, the pagan Symmachus was named prefect of the city and the pagan Praetextatus prefect of the praetorium.

A powerful anti-Christian reaction was being projected which aimed at abolishing the last measures taken by Gratian under the inspiration of Ambrose.

What was paganism at this time? The praise given to it by the pagans and the condemnation of it by the Christians make it difficult to decide.

The ancient religion of Rome was now quite dead and had been so for some time, but the official forms still survived. The religion of Rome had originally been a rather simple worship by the farmers of Latium of numerous but rather undistinct deities. This cult had during the course of the centuries been greatly enlarged by imports from Etruria, Greece, and the East. But it never satisfied either the intelligence or the hearts of men searching for a metaphysic which would explain the world and a morality which would make this world endurable.

The famous frescoes of the Etruscans come almost entirely from their tombs. And they represent the world of the dead. Like the Semites, the Etruscans believed that the souls of the dead descended into the earth. A substantial part of Roman religion was also concerned with the worship of the dead, the *manes*. In the atrium of every Roman house there was a family altar and carefully guarded portraits of the dead. In the second century of the Empire, however, Juvenal noted a certain skepticism at Rome, saying that no one believed any longer in the *manes* nor in the lower world with its bark of Charon and frogs in the Stygian swamp.[4]

Little enough reverence was shown for Jupiter. Suetonius tells us that when Vespasian was on the point of dying the thought of his proximate apotheosis came to him, and he said with a smile, "I feel that I am about to become a god."[5]

In the fourth century, Firmicus Maternus, whose violent exhortations to the Christian emperors to abolish paganism have already been noted, was not concerned with attacking the ancient religion of Rome. The objects of his hostility were the mystery religions that had come to Rome from the East. This indicates that while the latter were still alive and dangerous the former did not even need to be refuted.

But the official forms continued in existence. The ancient religion was endowed with immense wealth, both tangible and artistic. In addition to grants from the State, the generosity of private individuals provided huge revenues for the temples. The numerous priestly dignitaries also enjoyed stipends from the State. Constantine exempted the priests and flamens of the African municipalities from the payment of certain taxes. Constantius II still left jurisdiction to the college of pontiffs at Rome in matters of burial. And Julian the Apostate made an earnest attempt to revive official paganism.

Valentinian I had given a ruling to the effect that priests in the provinces were exempt from curule duties and enjoyed the privileges and honors reserved to counts. Honors, exemptions from burdens and monetary rewards all contributed to keeping the ancient ceremonies of the traditional Roman calendar on their feet.[6] Thus, for example, March 17 was the feast of the *Liberalia*, when boys of Rome donned for the first time the *toga virilis.* Two days later was the feast of the purification of weapons, the *Quinquatrus,* when the Salian priests performed their sacred dance. The twenty-fifth of April was the feast of the *Robigalia,* one of many celebrated that month. In May, on the feast of the *Vestalia,* the Vestal virgins went through the motions of doing for the city what the mother of a family did for her house in guarding the hearth and the domestic economy. In July the feast of the *Neptunalia* was celebrated to drive away drought. In December on the feast of the *Saturnalia,* people exchanged lighted tapers and dolls baked out of dough. In February, the last month of the religious calendar, were celebrated the *Lupercalia.* The high point of this feast was reached when the naked Luperci, armed with whips made from the skins of sacrificed goats, ran through the city striking women who offered themselves to the blows to obtain fertility. And in addition to these feasts there were many others of greater or less importance.

A third century papyrus discovered in the excavations at Dura Europus, a Roman fortress built on the bank of the Euphrates, shows that the military forces stationed there still observed in the third century these ancient feasts of the Roman religious calendar.[7] In the fifth century at Rome Pope Gelasius again had to urge the civil authorities to prohibit the *Lupercalia.*[8]

All of these feasts culminated in expensive and often cruel and obscene shows in the circus and theaters. This proves that these religious festivals did not favor true piety. An incident that occurred in 383 may be profitably recalled, especially since St. Ambrose also refers to it. The harvest in Egypt, Africa, Spain, and Italy had been poor. There was a threat of famine at Rome, and extraordinary measures were at once taken to expel all the foreigners from the city. St. Ambrose expressed his indignation of this in the following terms: "Beasts do not drive out beasts, yet man shuts out man. Wild beasts and animals consider the food which the earth yields to be common to all.

They all give assistance to those like themselves; and man, who ought to think nothing human foreign to himself, fights against his own. . . . From that extensive city were expelled those who had already passed most of their life in it. They went forth in tears with their children, whose exile they bewailed; and they grieved over the broken bonds of union, the severed ties of relationship."[9]

Ammianus tells us that on this occasion, "Those who practiced the liberal arts (very few in number) were summarily thrust out of the city while the genuine attendants upon actresses of the mines, and those who for the time pretended to be such, were kept with us, while three thousand dancing girls, without even being questioned, remained here with their choruses, and an equal number of dancing masters."[10]

And yet during the fourth century there was an increased interest in religion at Rome and, in general, throughout the empire, despite the decline of the older cults. There were many reasons for this. Among these was the almost universal poverty of the masses, the decline of learning, and the ever increasing burdens of the State. As a consequence the people sought help from the Oriental cults that came to Rome from Anatolia, Iran, Syria, and Egypt. These seem frequently to have been a strange combination of mortification and sensuality, of asceticism and voluptuousness. After long centuries of expansion and contact with each other, in the third and fourth century the gods of these Eastern religions had become the subjects of quite similar myths. The Thracian Dionysus, the Egyptian Osiris, the Syrian Adonis, and the Iranian Mithra are all gods who suffer, die and rise again. In the Augustan Age their cults were already widely diffused, but the period of their greatest development was during the third century. This was in part due to the syncretism of the princesses of the Syrian dynasty of the Severi. According to one historian of the religion of this period, "the mysteries spread through the empire following the merchant vessels which poured the wares of the East onto the scales of the West, and accompanied the marching legionaries to the boundaries of the empire on the Danube and the Rhine. In the cities and in the fields slaves and servant girls sought solace for their fate in their devotion to their ancestral gods whose missionaries they had become.

"But these racial ties, if they explain the diffusion of the mysteries among the lower classes, do not explain why they were also accepted by the more educated and were able to satisfy those interested in philosophy. The real reason is to be found in the fact that these mysteries, tied in with astrology, could be interpreted according to the physical science of the time, which regarded the universe as being animated by an immanent principle of life. This principle was identified with the sky and its manifestations, especially the sun, which set the pattern of the rhythm of the seasons in the world and the pulsation of all life whether vegetable, animal, or human."[11]

The mysteries exercised a powerful attraction since they promised to their faithful freedom from sorrow and death, making them in some way sharers in the very nature of God. Moreover, the splendors of the feasts, the languor produced by the music of the East, the nervous tension induced by macerations of the flesh, the excitement of the dances, and the complicated, exotic liturgies all helped to arouse religious enthusiasm and to create a feeling of brotherhood among the adepts. Moreover, during the fourth century there was an increased concern for the fate of the individual after death, which can be partially attributed to the slow penetration in the second and third centuries of Christian ideas into areas hostile to Christianity.[12] Pliny the Elder, a natural historian who died on the shores of the Bay of Naples during the eruption of Vesuvius on August 24, 79 A.D., attributed the concept of an afterlife to human vanity, but in the age of St. Ambrose no pagan would have written in such a fashion.[13] All spoke of the hereafter, of an eternal life which was not now regarded as being passed under the earth in company with the dwellers of the lower world but high in heaven, from which the spark of life, the soul, had descended. From Tertullian we know that the followers of Mithra believed in an afterlife in heaven and in the resurrection of the dead.[14] The most ancient of the Eastern mysteries at Rome was that of the "Great Mother of the Gods." The Latin name, *Mater Deum Magna Idaea,* was taken from the name of Mount Ida in Phrygia in Asia Minor. She was a symbol of the fertility of the earth and had as her companion, spouse, or lover, Attis, who died in the fall to rise again in the spring just like the earth's vegetation. Special honors were given to Attis from the fifteenth to the twenty-seventh of March. In the first century these gained official recognition in the empire.

Initiation into the mysteries of Attis and Cybele was through the taurobolium. The name itself was derived from the fact that the bull slain during the ceremony was struck from a distance by a spear. Its blood flowed down through holes in the pavement upon the one to be initiated, who stood naked in a pit below. From this pit the initiate then came forth covered with blood but "reborn for eternity" *(in aeternum renatus)*. The rites of the taurobolium could also be vicariously applied for the salvation of other individuals, including the emperors, and even for cities. At times it was repeated since it was believed that its efficacy did not last more than twenty years.

Despite all the gore of the ceremony, it had a redemptive meaning. For the primitive right of mutilation through which the initiate, by imitating Attis, united himself with the great mother Cybele, there was substituted a real hierogamy. The initiates formed confraternities composed of Galli, that is, mutilated priests of the goddess, and dendrophori and cannophori, who carried the reeds and the pine that represented Attis in the processions that took place during the ceremonies in March. After a fast which lasted from the fifteenth to the twenty-second of March, on the night of the twenty-third they celebrated the vigil of the burial of Attis. At this time the Galli scourged themselves to blood and mutilated themselves. Finally a light was shown and a priest invited the initiates "to have confidence in the god who had reached salvation since through him they also would be freed from pain." Then, on March 25, there was a procession with lamps and torches and cries celebrating the resurrection of the god Attis, who was carried about with Cybele in a four-horse chariot.

On the Vatican hill at Rome there was a great center for these mysteries known as the Phrygianum. The hill itself perhaps is named for the prophecies (*vaticinia*) which the archigallus pronounced after the taurobolia. Inscriptions at Milan refer to the worship of the Idaean Mother Cybele, and to her servants, the cannophori and the dendrophori mentioned above.

The mysteries connected with the Idaean Mother were the most loathsome of all. Wild dancing, weird music, and intoxicating drinks created an atmosphere of unbridled license. "I do not know," St. Augustine tells us, "what happens in the mysteries of the Great Mother, but I know well the persons who conduct them."[15]

The second phase of this invasion of Oriental cults was marked by the introduction of the mysteries of Isis from Egypt. Caligula, Domitian, and Caracalla all built temples to Isis at Rome. She also was a fertility goddess, a goddess of a hundred names who in the fall wept for her divine spouse Osiris, whom she then found and raised from the dead. Great festivals were held in her honor in the spring and fall of the year. Her rites were celebrated in great detail. The goddess was washed, clothed, and adorned. Women, particularly those of easy virtue, like the friends of Tibullus and Propertius, had a great devotion to Isis. Apuleius in his famous novel, *The Golden Ass*, describes the emotions experienced by Lucius when he was brought before the image of the goddess, his joy in pausing to contemplate her, and his tears when he had to leave. Among the cult objects of Isis carried in the processions were, however, some which even the pagan Apuleius thought it better not to name.[16]

The cult of Mithra reached Rome much later than that of Cybele, Isis, Serapis, Astarte, and Bellona, but it acquired more followers than all the other mystery religions. Mithraic monuments are to be found everywhere—from the coasts of the Black Sea to northern Britain and the boundaries of the Sahara.

The legend connected with this cult represents Mithra as the god of light who is born of the sky and is the source of vegetation. He challenges the Sun and then mounts his chariot with him. He gives water to men, which he causes to spring forth from a rock to irrigate the plains, and achieves a glorious victory over an untamed bull, which he captures, throws to the earth and slays. Despite the treacherous onslaughts of the demons, all goods come to nature and to men from this sacrifice.

The worshipers of Mithra were always grouped together in small congregations. As a consequence, the caves and subterranean rooms *(mithraea)* where his liturgy was celebrated were rather small. In a great city like Rome there were perhaps a hundred mithraea. Forty-five of these have thus far been discovered at Rome and seventeen at Ostia.[17] In addition to the priesthoods, there were seven successive grades of initiation.

At the beginning of the fifth century St. Jerome wrote to Laeta the following: "Did not your own kinsman Gracchus, whose name betrays his patrician origin, when he was prefect of the city a few years ago, overthrow, break down, and tear to pieces the grotto of Mithra and all the dreadful images in it? I mean those through which the worshipers were initiated as Raven, Bridegroom, Soldier, Lion, Perseus, Sun, Crab, and Father? Did he not, I repeat, destroy these and then, sending them before him as hostages, obtain for himself Christian baptism?"[18]

The banquet of Mithra with the Sun was commemorated in the Mithraic liturgy by the sacred meal in which the initiates participated, each with the mark of his particular grade. Singing had a great place at these meetings. The common worship consisted in prayers offered facing the sun at dawn, noon, and evening. The chief feast was celebrated on December 25. This was the birthday of the Unconquered Sun *(Sol Invictus)*, coming immediately after the winter solstice when the Sun, after reaching its lowest point on the horizon, is reborn, that is, begins to mount again into the sky.

There is an obvious parallel between the great spring festivals of Cybele-Attis, of Isis-Osiris, and the Christian Pasch, and also between the Mithraic feast of December and the celebration of Christmas. Are the pagan mysteries to be considered as a sacrilegious and diabolical parody of the Christian mysteries, or, on the other hand, did the Christian mysteries borrow elements from the pagan mysteries so as to more effectively combat them? This is not a new question, but it can be discussed today more calmly because of our greater knowledge of the facts, due largely to archaeological discoveries.

The worship of Mithra seems to have been serious and moral. Only men were admitted to the mysteries. Its complementary cult was that of the Great Idaean Mother into which women, in particular, were initiated. At Ostia their two temples were next to each other. In the third and fourth centuries, however, all of the mysteries, whether of Cybele, Mithra, Isis, Serapis, or Sabazius, were but different forms and special aspects of what was essentially one religion. Juvenal expressed his indignation that the waters of the Orontes in Syria flowed into the Tiber, and he ridiculed the Phrygian, Chaldean, and other Eastern charlatans who sold salvation for a goose or promised the magnificent legacy of a childless plutocrat to others.[19] A point was reached where the attraction of these mysteries was felt to be a danger even for Christians. St. Augustine recalls the impudence of a priest of the Great Mother who continually cried out, probably with the intent of gaining clients among the Christians: "But Attis is also a Christian."[20]

This helps to explain the decrees passed by Theodosius and Gratian against apostates from Christianity.

In the fourth century the Oriental religions had combined with the ancient religion of Rome to form a single unit. Vettius Agorius Praetextatus had been prefect of Rome in 364 and again in 367. In the year 384 he died at the age of fifty-four while holding the post of prefect of the praetorium. From an inscription dedicated to his memory, we know that he had been augur, pontiff of Vesta, priest of the Sun, quindecemvir, *curialis* of Hercules, initiate of Bacchus and of the divinities of Eleusis, hierophant, neocorus (that is, inspector of temples), one purified in the taurobolium (in the mysteries of Cybele), and "father of fathers" (in the mysteries of Mithra). On the inscription his wife, Achonia Fabia Paulina, gives thanks to her husband for having made her an associate in all these honors. She was a priestess of Cybele and Attis, an initiate through the blood of the bull, and so forth.[21] In the year 376 a senator Ulpius Egnatius Faventinus erected a monument to the Mater Idaea and Attis. On it he is called "father," sacred "herald" of the sun god invincible Mithra, chief of the servants of Bacchus, priest of Isis, and initiate through the bloody bath of the taurobolium.[22]

These initiations were also favored by the philosophy then in vogue, that is, Neoplatonism. The Neoplatonists claimed to be perpetuators of Plato's thought that had been enriched by the speculations of the Stoics and Philo. They were particularly interested in man and his destiny. Neoplatonism tended to be more of a religion than a philosophy, but it could not bring true peace of heart. It did, however, maintain the primacy of the spiritual life over that of the body and senses, and taught that true beauty is within and that it is found by re-entering into one's self, that mere knowledge is not sufficient for wisdom and salvation but that there is need of action, of giving oneself entirely to a personal ideal.

The great advocates of such a philosophy of life in the third century were Plotinus and Porphyry. Religious syncretism, too, was particularly active in this same century. The emperor Aurelian, for example, aimed at reuniting all the forces of Hellenism in the worship of *Sol Invictus,* to whom he erected a magnificent temple on the Quirinal in the year 274.

In the second half of the fourth century cultivated pagans were still interested in Neoplatonism, but somewhat less enthusiastically. Virius Nicomachus Flavianus, a cousin of Symmachus, who was governor of Sicily in 364, vicar of Africa in 367, prefect of the praetorium in 391-392, and one of the leaders of the pagan reaction at the time of Eugenius, translated the life of Apollonius of Tyana into Latin. It had been written originally in Greek by Philostratus at the beginning of the third century.

The work had been composed at the request of Julia Domna, the wife of Septimius Severus. It may be described as an historical romance very much like certain apocryphal acts of the apostles. Apollonius is the ideal Pythagorian. He is an abstemious vegetarian wonderworker who, dressed in linen, goes about in search of wisdom, first of all among the magi of Babylonia, then among the brahmans of India, and the gymnosophists of Ethiopia. He is initiated into the mysteries of Eleusis and has an interview with the shade of Achilles. He abhors barbaric sacrifices: his own worship consisting in worshiping the sun at dawn. He prayed as follows: "O ye gods, grant me whatever is due." The reason for this prayer was that "If I am among the number of worthy men, I shall obtain more than I have said: but if the gods rank me among the wicked, then they will send to me the opposite of what I ask; and I shall not blame the gods, because for my demerit I am judged worthy of evil."[23]

In this fictionalized biography Apollonius has no knowledge of Christians. But this is not too surprising since Philostratus deliberately omits reference to them. When he translated the work a century and a half later, Nicomachus Flavianus certainly intended it to be propaganda against the Christians.

At the very time when Ambrose was girding himself for battle, the forces opposed to Christianity were being nourished by a number of hostile writings. These included the second-century *True Word* of Celsus, which Origen had thoroughly refuted in the third, the fifteen books of Porphyry *Against the Christians*, and the writings of Julian the Apostate, which continued to have a harmful influence. In the work of Philostratus, Apollonius of Tyana is implicitly opposed to Christ.

The paganism of the common people was also hostile to Christianity. When he preached to his people, St. Augustine knew that they were still exposed to many hardships for their faith.[24] And this was in Africa, where Christianity had spread more rapidly and earlier than in Rome or Milan. When they met a Christian, pagans would at times scoff at him, treating him as a fool and saying that he had neither heart nor head. They mocked the crucified God of the Christians, denied the possibility of a resurrection, and ridiculed their alleged charity by pointing to the various divisions among the Christians.

In fine, the teaching of the Church ran up against the same difficulties as it does today. If God wishes only what is good, if He has created man for love, why does He send us so many trials and tribulations? The Creator does not seem to be greatly preoccupied with His creatures. How, moreover, is it possible for God to become man? Even more, why should He experience our miseries and suffer and die as a criminal? And if redemption is absolutely necessary for men, why was it put off for so many centuries? Why is its diffusion so slow in the world? Why does God permit that the majority of men remain outside of it? These are truly serious difficulties which Gregory of Nyssa heard from the people of his day, and which he sought to answer in a catechetical discourse which he delivered in 384. On the other hand, these are difficulties inherent in the Christian message and are thus common to every age, since without them, faith would not be selective, would not be that which it should be, that is, a laborious daily conquest: "The kingdom of heaven suffers violence, and the violent bear it away."[25]

This complex political and religious situation must be regarded as the basis upon which the bishop of Milan built. He believed that even from a natural and political point of view the empire had everything to gain by a direct suppression of institutions which had lost their reason for being. He was convinced that if the true religion cannot be imposed upon individuals, the State can and should favor its diffusion and make its practice possible.

And he lived for his religion; he had consecrated his entire life to Christ. He could not remain indifferent to the moral degradation in which so many were languishing, as if Christ had not come also for them. He, therefore, did not hesitate to act.

Gratian's laws of the year 382, which deprived paganism of its resources and confiscated the goods of the temples, struck a serious blow against those institutions which survived chiefly through grants and revenues contributed by the State. Through these laws, the State had been neatly separated from paganism and become laicized. The pagan aristocracy realized at once that the very life of the ancient religion was at stake, and they energetically set about rescuing it.

In 384, after the failure of the first legation of Symmachus to Gratian, the battle was renewed, and with greater likelihood of success. The high offices of the State in Italy were now in the hands of pagans. From the government of Valentinian II, an edict was obtained for the return of building materials taken by private individuals from public buildings, that is, by Christians from pagan temples.

Symmachus, the prefect of Rome, was accused of using torture even against clerics in carrying out this edict. He proved the falsity of this accusation, having the support of the testimony of Pope Damasus in this. In September, 384, after wisely preparing the way, Symmachus presented himself at the imperial consistory in Milan. There, before the Augustus Valentinian II and his ministers, he read his *relation*. The gods have avenged the measures taken by Gratian, who had been badly advised two years earlier. By this he obviously meant Ambrose and Damasus. There had been a much greater scarcity of crops than usual. In the name of the senate and of the city of Rome, Valentinian is entreated to return to the policy of his father who, although he had been a Christian, had not been intolerant. Moreover, we all adore the same Divinity, and not all come to God and to the truth by the same road. There is a question of endowed goods taken from the priestly colleges at Rome. Why should not the law that applies to the rest of the citizens be equally applicable to the priests and Vestals? Goods left to the temples represent the last will of the dying. The treasury, by seizing and impounding them, has been guilty of theft. They should be restored. Regard should also be had for tradition. Just as each infant that comes into the world is endowed with its own soul, so the divine intelligence has assigned different cults and different protectors to the different cities. Each race has its own destined genius. Let everyone worship and believe as he thinks best, but let him esteem the religion of his fatherland, respecting the rites and the piety that have made Rome great and powerful. In the course of his memorial he represents Rome pronouncing the following famous words: "Excellent princes, fathers of your country, respect my years to which pious rites have brought me. Let me use the ancestral ceremonies, for I do not repent of them. Let me live after my own fashion, for I am free. This worship subdued the world to my laws; these sacred rites repelled Hannibal from the walls, and the Gauls from the capitol. Have I been reserved for this, that in my old age I should be blamed?" Symmachus finally ends his plea with the following exhortation: "May there be a return to that religious policy which reserved the empire for your Highness's divine parent, and furnished that blessed prince with lawful heirs. That venerable father beholds from the starry height the tears of the priests, and considers himself censured by the violation of that custom which he willingly observed. Amend also for your divine brother that which he did by the counsel of others, cover over the deed which he knew not to be displeasing to the senate."[26]

To a modern reader this famous discourse may seem to be somewhat cold. But when it was delivered at Milan, even the Christians were moved by its appeal to patriotism and to the ancient glories of Rome. All who were present at the consistory, both pagans and nonpagans, seemed to hold that the requests made by Symmachus were reasonable, namely, that the altar of Victory should be set up again in the senate, and that their positions and government support should be restored to the priestly colleges at Rome.

But Ambrose was able to counter the proposals. The boy of thirteen who was now acting as emperor was the son of Christian parents. Although she was an Arian, Justina could not agree with the arguments of Symmachus, even if she had wished to annoy the bishop. It was imperative that Gratian's work should not be destroyed, especially since it was being continued with even greater energy by Theodosius, the Augustus of the East, who had come to Italy a few months before and who had probably seen Valentinian II at Milan in August.

The bishop, as a consequence, wrote at once a respectful but very firm letter. "Ambrose, bishop, to the most blessed prince and most Christian emperor Valentinian. Just as all men who live under Roman rule serve in the armies under you, the emperors and princes of the world, so too do you serve as soldiers of almighty God and of our holy faith. For there is no sureness of salvation unless everyone worships in truth the true God, that is, the God of the Christians, under whose sway are all things; for He alone is the true God, who is to be worshiped from the bottom of the heart; for 'the gods of the heathen,' as Scripture says, 'are devils.' . . . Since, then, most

Christian emperor, you owe to the true God faith and zeal, care and devotion for the true faith, I wonder how some have come to hope that you would feel it a duty to restore by your command altars to the heathen gods and furnish the funds necessary for profane sacrifices. For if you give them what has for a long time been claimed either by the imperial or by the city treasuries, it will seem that you are contributing something from your own funds rather than restoring what is theirs. They are complaining of their losses, who never spared our blood, who destroyed the very church buildings. And they, who by the last law of Julian denied us the common right of speaking and teaching, are asking you to grant them privileges. They are asking for those privileges through which even Christians have often been deceived. Through these privileges they have tried to trap some, partly through their lack of foresight and partly through their desire to escape the burden of public services. And since even under Christian princes not all are found to be brave, many have lapsed.

"If these privileges had not been abolished, I could prove that they should be removed by your authority; but since they have been forbidden and prohibited by many princes throughout nearly the whole world, and were abolished at Rome by Gratian, of august memory, the brother of your Clemency, out of regard for the true faith and were nullified by rescript, do not, I pray you, destroy what has been established in accordance with the faith, nor rescind your brother's precepts. In civil matters, if he established anything, no one thinks that it should be treated lightly, while a precept about religion is trodden under foot. Let no one take advantage of your youth. . . . I urge you to defer to the merits of illustrious men, but God must certainly be preferred to all. If we have to consult about military matters, the opinion of a man experienced in warfare should be sought, and his advice followed. Where it is a question of religion, think about God. No one is offended because God is preferred to him. . . . Let everyone bear it patiently if he cannot extort from the emperor that which would offend him if the emperor desired to extort it from him. . . .

"But if any, Christians in name, think that any such decree should be made, be not misled by mere words or deceived by empty names. Whoever advises this, and whoever decrees it, sacrifices. . . . This cannot be decreed without sacrilege, and I, therefore, beg you not to decree or order it nor to subscribe to any decrees of that sort. . . . It cannot be said that the senate has made this request, for a few of the heathen are making use of the common name. Nearly two years ago when the same attempt was being made, blessed Damasus, bishop of the Church at Rome, elected by the judgment of God, sent to me a memorial which the Christian senators in great numbers put forth, protesting that they had given no such authority, that they did not agree with such requests of the heathen, nor give consent to them; and they declared publicly and privately that they would not come to the senate if any such thing were decreed. . . . This memorial I sent to your Clemency's brother, and he decided from it that the senate had not given any instructions to the legates concerning the financial support of superstition. . . . But refer the matter to the father of your Piety, the emperor Theodosius, whom you are accustomed to consult in almost every case of greater moment. But nothing is greater than religion, nothing more sublime than faith. If it were a civil case, the opposing party would have a right to reply; it is a religious case, and I as bishop intervene. Let a copy of the memorial which has been sent be given to me, so that I may answer it more in detail, and then let your Clemency's father be consulted about the whole matter, and may he deign to give us a reply. Certainly if anything else is decreed, we bishops cannot suffer it without alarm and pretend not to take notice of it. You may come to the church, but you will either find no priest there or one who opposes you. How will you answer a priest who says to you, 'The church does not seek your gifts, because you have adorned the temples of the pagans with gifts. . . . The Lord Jesus refuses and rejects your service because you have served idols'? . . . What will you answer to these words? That you are a child that has fallen? But every age is perfect in Christ, every age is full of God. No childhood as admissible in faith, for even children have confessed Christ to their persecutors with fearless lips. What will you answer to your brother? . . . to your father? who with greater grief will say, 'You judged very ill of me, my son, when you supposed that I could have connived at the heathen. No one ever told me that there was an altar in the Roman senate house, I never believed that such great wickedness could have been committed that the pagans sacrificed in the common assembly of Christians and pagans. . . .' Since, therefore, you see, O emperor, that if you decree anything of this kind, injury will be done first to God and then to your father and brother, I entreat you to do that which you know will be profitable for your salvation before God."[27]

The bishop could speak so strongly because he knew that the court could not risk an open struggle with him. Maximus, the Augustus in Gaul, would have been overjoyed to see an opportunity of intervening open up to him. Ambrose's request for a copy of Symmachus's memorial was granted to him.

Symmachus's words were universally acclaimed: they were proper, dignified, noble, and to the point. The bishop of Milan also came from the Roman nobility. Better than the others he understood the force of the demands, but he had to say that there were others even stronger: "The illustrious prefect of the city has set forth three propositions in his memorial which he believes to be valid: that Rome, as he says, asks for her rites again, that pay be given to her priests and Vestal virgins, and that a general famine followed upon the withholding of the stipends due to the priests. . . . These sacred rites, he says, drove Hannibal from the walls and the Gauls from the capitol. And so, while the power of the sacred rites is proclaimed, their weakness is betrayed. . . . Why did the Romans allow themselves to be besieged, if the arms of their gods were fighting for them? . . . Let the Vestal virgins, he says, retain their privileges. . . . But how many virgins have been gained for them by these promised rewards? Barely seven virgins are chosen. This is the sum total gathered together by the fillets and chaplets for the head, the dye of the purple robes, the pomp of the litter surrounded by a company of attendants, the greatest privileges, immense profits, and a prescribed time of virginity. Let them lift up the eyes of their souls and bodies and see a people of modesty, a people of purity, an assembly of virginity. They have no fillets as ornaments for their heads, but a veil common in use but ennobled by chastity, . . . no delicious luxuries, but the practice of fasts, no privileges, no gains. . . .

"If a priest seeks the privilege of exemption from curule burdens, he has to give up his inheritance and all his property. If the pagans suffered this, how they would complain! . . .

"The Church has no possessions of her own except the faith. This furnishes her with her returns, her increase. The possessions of the Church are for the maintenance of the poor. Let them count up how many captives the temples have ransomed, what food they have contributed for the poor, what exiles they have supplied with the means of livelihood. . . .

"Let them imagine that the injuries done to their gods were avenged in the past year. Why have they not been noticed this present year? . . . The earth has rendered her produce with interest. . . . If the old rites pleased, why did Rome also take up foreign ones? . . . Whence is the pattern for Cybele washing her chariots in a stream counterfeiting the Almo? Whence were the Phrygian bards, and the deities of unjust Carthage always hateful to the Romans? . . . They ask to have the altar of Victory erected in the senate at Rome, where most of those who come together are Christians."[28]

The bishop therefore supported the neutrality of the State in religious matters and freedom of worship. In glowing terms he defends progress in human life and thought.

Symmachus's petition, despite the extensive sympathy it found at court, was rejected.

Some of the arguments which Ambrose used against Symmachus could have been turned against himself. He seems to be somewhat inconsistent in advocating the neutrality of the State in religious matters while at the same time appealing to the secular arm against heresy and paganism. He could have answered that neutrality was good as long as it served to separate the State from paganism. But this would have been a lawyer's trick. He was at the time engaged solely in polemics. Later he would have the opportunity to perfect his thought in this regard and further his activities.

The petitions of the Roman senate were renewed later under Theodosius, Valentinian, and Eugenius, but without significant results since the battle had been won once and for all. With the exception of the brief period during which Eugenius usurped control of the empire, the altar of Victory languished in an obscure corner of the curia and was never again restored to its original site.

The new faith required new altars, just as the relations among men were permeated with a new spirit which the harsh society of antiquity had never known. Christianity proved to be the ultimate victor over the ancient Roman religion, over Neoplatonism, and even over the mystery cults.

"The great religious struggle had to end with the victory of the more spiritual contestant, since the spirit is always victorious."[29]

THE IDEA

A bas-relief of the twelfth century in the Castello Sforzesco at Milan

This relief which belongs to the city art collection measures six feet, 10-11/16 inches by one foot, 4-11/16 inches. It was brought to the Castello Sforzesco in 1926 from the church of Santa Maria Beltrade after its closure. It represents the procession which took place on February 2 from the cathedral of St. Thecla to Santa Maria Beltrade. Two priests wearing chasubles are carrying a painting on which is represented the Madonna and Child. Beneath these figures is the word IDEA. The priests are followed by a crucifer wearing a cope and carrying a cross, by a deacon in a dalmatic carrying a missal, by the archbishop wearing a cope and miter and holding his crosier in his left hand while he blesses the people with his right, and finally by four priests. Three of these are carrying candles and the last one, with a long beard, supports himself with a cane. See S. Vigezze, *La scultura in Milano* (Milan, 1932), pp. 70-72. For the procession on February 2 with the IDEA, see Puricelli, *De Ss. Martyribus Nazario and Celso* (Milan, 1656), pp. 490 ff. This procession of the Madonna-Idea seems to have been a Christian continuation of the spring celebration in honor of Cybel, the great *Mater Idaea*. See also A. De Marchi, *Le antiche epigrafi di Milano* (Milan, 1917), pp. 255-264.

XI

The Conflict with the Court

○

St. Ambrose's second mission to Trier. The trial and execution of Priscillian. Death of Pope Damasus and departure of Jerome from Rome. Intrigues of Justina against St. Ambrose in 385. The demand for an Arian basilica. Holy Week of 386. Siege and truce. The discovery of the bodies of Protase and Gervase. The honors shown to relics.

In October or November, 384, Valentinian II asked St. Ambrose to again go to the court of Maximus at Trier.[1] Ambrose's twenty-fourth letter is a report to Valentinian on this second official mission. It was written before his return to Milan and is our only source for what has already been mentioned about his mission of the preceding year. The purpose of the new journey was to carry to the Augustus of Gaul a letter from the Augustus of Milan asking permission to remove the body of Gratian, who had been killed at Lyons in August, 383. Perhaps, also, there were other reasons for sending Ambrose, the champion of Catholic orthodoxy, a second time as imperial legate to Maximus. During the summer of 384, Theodosius had recognized Maximus as the legitimate Augustus of the prefecture of Gaul. The court at Milan would have to follow suit. What could Maximus give in exchange? He could at least promise not to cross the Alps. It was a wise move to send Ambrose on such business: it removed any pretext Maximus might have had to intervene in Italy as the champion of orthodoxy. On his arrival at Trier, Ambrose asked for a private audience on the basis of his episcopal dignity and his position as imperial legate.

The master of ceremonies, Gallicanus, consulted Maximus on this request, and then replied that he could only be received in the general audience of the consistory. Ambrose declared that such a treatment was an insult, but he did not on that account give up the pursuit of his mission.

He had hardly entered the consistory when Maximus, the Augustus, arose to give him the kiss of greeting. The other ministers motioned to Ambrose to mount the steps of the throne. But the bishop stayed in his place and asked instead: "Why do you wish to embrace one whom you do not know? If you had known me, you would not have received me here." Maximus made an effort at sarcasm: "It seems, my dear bishop, that you are a bit agitated."

But Ambrose did not lose his presence of mind. During his mission of the preceding year, he had become accustomed, it is true, to being received in the consistory, but then he was entreating for one who was weak, and an orphan. Now he was speaking for one who was equal to Maximus. "And thanks to whom has he become my equal?" "To the grace of God, who has preserved Valentinian on the throne that he gave him." Maximus began to rave. "Yes," he shouted, "you and Bauto tricked me. On the pretense of protecting a royal child, you strove to secure power, and you sent the barbarians against me." But even then the bishop did not keep silent. It was ridiculous for Maximus to claim that he had been prevented from invading Italy the preceding year because of the bishop's intervention. Further, Ambrose had tricked no one. If he had actually saved Valentinian and Justina, he had reasons to congratulate himself. To whom more than to orphans and widows should a bishop offer his protection?

Then he explained the official reason of this second embassy: Maximus should at least favor Gratian's brother with the body of the slain emperor. Ambrose again reproached Maximus, whom he now regarded as a tyrant, for having allowed the Juthungi to devastate Raetia and for having killed Gratian's generals.

Maximus listened on, possibly to learn the reasons why Ambrose should have recalled all the various points of dispute and in such a provocative fashion. Finally he grew weary and suspended the audience.

During these same weeks the trial of the Priscillianists was coming to a head at Trier.[2] The circumstances of this controversy have already been described. In the summer of 384, a council of bishops at Bordeaux had examined the question and had deposed the Priscillianist bishop Instantius. But when another Priscillianist made an appeal to the imperial tribunal, the process was transferred to Trier.

Maximus had been pleased by the appeal, since it gave him an opportunity to interfere in ecclesiastical disputes; and the eventual confiscation of the properties of the condemned would furnish him with the means he urgently needed for his military projects.

St. Martin did everything he could to entreat Ithacius to desist: he protested against the intervention of a lay judge in a question of Christian doctrine, and begged that no blood be shed. But the opposition persuaded Maximus to have the inquest carried through. Evodius, prefect of the praetorium, was commissioned for the task, and succeeded in having Priscillian condemned in the spring of 385 on charges of immorality and the practice of magic. Maximus pushed his show of orthodoxy to the point of having Priscillian murdered with six of his companions, among whom was the matron Eucrocia. This proved to be a *cas célèbre* since Priscillian was regarded as the "first victim" of the "secular arm."

During his stay at Trier, the process against the Priscillianists was being drawn up, but St. Ambrose refused to communicate with the bishops who presented themselves as accusers in religious matters before a secular tribunal.[3] Like St. Martin, he deplored such a procedure, because he believed that heretics should be converted and not slain.

Since such an attitude on the part of Ambrose indicated that he not only excommunicated the bishops but, at least implicitly, the emperor as well, Maximus ordered him to be expelled from the city: "When he saw that I would have nothing to do with those bishops who communicated with him or who were seeking the death of certain individuals, even though these were in error in the faith, he became angry and ordered me to depart without delay. I readily obeyed, though many believed that I would not succeed in escaping the plots laid against me. I set out, grieved only by the fact that I had learned that the old bishop Hyginus, who barely had a breath still in him, was being banished. When I went to the counts and asked that they should not permit an old man to be expelled without clothes and without a couch, I myself was sent out of the city."[4]

St. Ambrose's two missions to Trier, in 383 and 384, and his strong opposition to Symmachus's requests were matters of extraordinary importance. Even without desiring it, the bishop of Milan was attracting a great deal of attention. Despite his frail appearance and small size (he was only five feet four and three/sixteenths inches tall), his moral stature, especially among those who knew him only from reports, was growing to heroic, even biblical proportions. Ambrose, who ruled in a city that was a seat of government and where there was an emperor who at least partially owed his crown to him, represented the power of the Church more conspicuously than did the eighty-year-old Damasus, who could not, from Rome, intervene directly in the policies of the Augusti at Milan, Constantinople, and Trier. This was all the more true in that the aged pontiff had even to endure violent attacks from the followers of Ursinus and arraignments before the civil authorities. He is best known today for the fifty-nine epigrams which he composed to honor the martyrs. These poems, though they have been criticized both because of their form and content, were magnificently carved in stone by his calligrapher, Furius Dionysius Philocalus. During the Middle Ages they were eagerly read and transcribed by many generations of pilgrims.

But, as a matter of fact, more recent historians, even those who are not Catholics, are inclined to re-evaluate the importance of the pontificate of Pope Damasus, pointing out his quiet but tenacious activity, his scriptural undertakings, his restoration of the catacombs, his great gifts of organization, and his magnanimity.[5] Even we have attempted to show that on different occasions Ambrose was no more than the agent *(longa manus)* of the pope at Rome.

On December 11, 384, Damasus died. He was succeeded by Siricius, a former deacon of Pope Liberius. Jerome, who had been on intimate terms with Damasus during the preceding two years at Rome was a possible candidate for the office. Under Siricius he never enjoyed the same favor that he had under Damasus.[6]

Jerome's enemies took advantage of the turn of events to get their revenge. In 382 he had been enthusiastically received by the group about Marcella in her home on the Aventine. He was happy to impart to these women of the Roman aristocracy the lessons he had learned as a monk in the desert of Chalcis and in the schools of Antioch and Constantinople, where he had spent long and weary hours in the study of Sacred Scripture. There in the house of Marcella he found the widow Lea and Asella (who had consecrated herself to God from her earliest childhood) as well as Paula, the noble lady who, having lost her husband in 378 when she was thirty-one, had renounced the vanities and pleasures of the world to devote herself to prayer and works of charity.

In the spring of 384, Jerome wrote a letter to the sixteen-year-old Eustochium, the third of Paula's daughters. It created a storm of protest in Rome. Many, instead of admiring Jerome's wise counsels, his enthusiasm for the spiritual life, and his earnest exhortations to the practice of Christian perfection were appalled by his bitterly sarcastic remarks about worldly clerics, wandering monks, and foolish virgins. The death of Paula's second daughter, Blaesilla, in the summer of 384 was the source of further embarrassment to St. Jerome. She had been left a widow at the age of twenty after only seven months of marriage, and after a grave illness had decided to lead a life of fasting and austerity as Jerome had been advising her to do. In November, only three months after her "conversion," she died to the great anguish of her mother and sisters. Lea had also died only a short time before.

In his letters, Jerome has left a touching account of the anguish felt by Paula and Marcella at their loss, but he also had the poor taste to inveigh against their sorrow, which he thought was excessive.

The funeral of Blaesilla provided an occasion for those who were hostile to the monks at Rome to demand their expulsion.[7] Jerome himself became the object of further animosity because of his new editions of the Psalms and Gospels. At the suggestion of Pope Damasus and with the help of Greek texts, he had corrected and published a new Latin text of these works used in the Church. In general it may be said that he was jarring the sensibilities of too many people all at once. Even Marcella frowned at some of the violent sayings of her spiritual director and would have liked to put her finger on his mouth to silence him.[8]

Damasus's death made Jerome's further stay in Rome impossible. Many accused him of indiscretions, some of even worse defects, and one went so far as to spread calumnies about his relations with Paula, but these had to be publicly retracted. In August, 385, a crowd of friends and admirers bade him farewell at the harbor of Ostia as he left Rome for good. This departure can hardly have been voluntary. It seems that there must have been an inquest dealing with his activities at Rome.

No one took up his defence and he was asked to leave the city. Could the bishop of Milan have had a part in that "senate of Pharisees"? It is a well-known fact that Jerome's hostility to Ambrose only appears after the year 384. Before that he spoke of Ambrose with much favor.[9]

The year 385 also marked the beginning of a violent opposition to St. Ambrose on the part of many whom he had defeated in his struggles against heresy and paganism.[10]

The increasing power of the bishop caused particular distress in the imperial palace. Justina, the queen mother, was anxious to direct Valentinian as she thought fit and without the interference of others. Whether this desire was prompted by religious zeal or not cannot now be determined. What we do know about her is derived from the hostile observations of her adversary Ambrose. After the collapse of the pagan reaction, which had turned out to the bishop's entire advantage, she laid the grounds for a great offense against him with the assistance of the Gothic officers and the court officials.

Towards the end of 384, Mercurinus Auxentius, the Arian bishop of Durostorum (Silistra in Bulgaria) arrived at the Arian court at Milan and was welcomed as a guest. He had been deposed from his see the previous year by Theodosius. Since he had been a disciple of Ulfilas, he naturally felt a great deal of sympathy for the numerous Goths who formed the major portion of Valentinian's troops. A small Arian community was organized. It may be that Mercurinus took the surname of Auxentius at Milan as an indication of his desire to rehabilitate the memory of Ambrose's predecessor.

Ambrose in the meantime was keeping an eye on the coalition the empress was drawing up against him. To resist the threatened attack, he sought to unite the faithful even more solidly together. His preaching in December, 384, is surprising for the care shown to gain the goodwill also of the wealthy.[11] He tells his people that riches are not in themselves evil but the bad use which is made of them, that wealth, which is harmful to those who are bad, is a help to those who are good. He insists upon the duties of children towards their parents. Though he was always an ardent advocate of virginity, he extols in moving words a mother's sacrifice. He declares that one must have a regard for the needs of the poor and of the Church, but the first duty is to one's parents.

In 378, on her arrival at Milan, Justina had claimed a basilica for the use of the Arians. In order to appear impartial, Gratian ordered the church to be closed after Ambrose had refused the request, and it was only in the summer of 379 that the bishop was able to have it opened again.

On January 1, 385, the general Bauto was inaugurated as consul.[12] The emperor Valentinian was present for the ceremony. The official speech for the occasion was delivered by Augustine of Thagaste, a heretic, who a few months earlier had been appointed professor of rhetoric for the schools at Milan.

Now that the Arians again had a bishop, Ambrose was asked by the court early in 385 to hand over a basilica to them. The request was probably for the Portian basilica outside the walls of the city.[13] When he refused, he was ordered to appear before the imperial consistory. While the discussions were taking place within the palace and the bishop was setting forth his reasons for refusal, crowds of the faithful who had been informed of what was to happen, gathered about the gates. The soldiers of the guard were unable to disperse the agitated mob. The court had to yield and begged the bishop to quiet the uproar so that it would not develop into an open revolt.

Baffled on this score, the empress at once thought of a more prudent plan of attack. Since the whole imperial bureaucracy felt humiliated at being unable to force the hand of the bishop, and since the new Auxentius was madly set on obtaining a church and cathedral, the court moved to Aquileia. Here it remained from the end of August, 385, to at least December 11. This absence served to keep the bishop of Milan at a distance. The Arians were able to get along without a basilica since their meetings were not so large that they could not be held in one of the rooms of the imperial palace, but there was a question of principle: At court they were anxious to get rid of the "tyranny" of Ambrose which was upsetting the whole city.

Towards the end of 385, the court returned to Milan. There, on January 23, 386, a law was published permitting freedom of worship to those who professed the faith of Rimini, that is, to the Arians, and threatened with death anyone who dared to impugn this freedom of worship or the law itself. Those who professed the faith of Rimini had a right to meet. But the formulation of the text was in itself a cause of dissension: Benevolus, an official in the imperial chancellery, refused to cooperate in this act of apostasy. He would not listen to promises of promotion and was dismissed.[14]

Those in the palace expected Ambrose to be intimidated and that he would give up a church. But since they did not dare to seize one by force and did not want reports of an open conflict with the bishop to be carried beyond the Alps, they were disappointed. Ambrose was only the more set in his refusal. In February, 386, the imperial court was transferred to Pavia, and Ambrose brought together some of the bishops of the provinces dependent upon Milan to gain their approval of his line of action.

The weapons of a bishop are prayers and tears. But still he will only yield to force. They ask for the Portian basilica? The bishop will shut himself up in it with his flock. At this time a basilica comprised much more than the hall used for the church proper, namely various adjoining rooms and courts as well. Dalmatius, a notary of the court, came to Ambrose from Valentinian to suggest the erection of a commission which would settle the question of the basilica.[15] Ambrose and Auxentius would each have the right of nominating the same number to it. But Ambrose refused to have anything to do with the plan.

Dalmatius then suggested that he might leave the city so

as not to suffer any harm. A certain Euthymius even had a carriage waiting for him at a neighboring house.[16]

In March the court was again at Milan. Imperial troops were ordered to surround the basilicas and their adjoining buildings. Rather than a siege or occupation, this was a police measure taken to prevent disorders. The tension lasted for some weeks. Ambrose supported the people with his fiery eloquence, introduced antiphonal singing of the psalms, and taught the people simple but inspiring hymns, so that they would not become weary during the changes of their continuous watch.

The people crowded about their bishop with enthusiasm. The court was symbolic of all the oppression and restrictions they had experienced; and this show of open resistance only increased Ambrose's popularity, which he had earned by his complete dedication, unceasing toil, exemplary life, penances and mortifications, and the sacrifice which he had made of all his possessions. St. Augustine, who was in Milan at this time, states that his mother was the first present for the activities and watchings of these weeks.

Then Ambrose wrote a strong letter to Valentinian.[17] He began by trying to make him understand that a lad such as he was, hardly even a catechumen, should not be so carried away by the flattery of his courtiers as to forget the rights of a bishop. Then he tells him that he cannot comply with his request to come to the palace since he would have then to discuss the matter with one whom he did not know if he were a bishop or not, or from where he came. Did Valentinian want him to leave Milan? But where could he safely go? Was not the law of January aimed at removing from their churches bishops who did not accept the faith of Rimini under penalty of death? In matters of faith bishops should pass judgment on emperors and not the other way around. He could not go to the consistory to discuss this since that would be submitting the Church to the State; and laymen, even if they are emperors, are not competent judges in matters of faith. As for his leaving Milan, Valentinian should have no illusions. He has been told by the other bishops that if he left his church at such a time, it would be like handing it over to the heretics.

As the weeks passed the besiegers became more weary than the besieged. The latter could go to their homes each evening. The bishop, however, expected a new attack. He multiplied his exhortations. We have his preaching during these weeks in his two books *On Jacob,* or *On the Happiness of the Just,* and four homilies in his *Commentary on the Gospel of St. Luke.* Jacob is the model of the just man, happy despite the troubles caused him by Isaac, Esau, and Laban. Eleazar is another model since he was able to resist temptations, bribes, and threats of torture during the persecution of Antiochus. The Macchabees, whom Ambrose describes as young, strong, and faithful, are also to be imitated.

In commenting on the verse in St. Luke, "Behold I send you as lambs among wolves," Ambrose assails Auxentius in the following terms: "Are not heretics who plot against the flocks of Christ to be compared with these wolves? . . . You should not be surprised that they seem to have a human form. But if outwardly they seem to be men, inwardly they growl as wolves. . . . If anyone is influenced by outward show, let him ask about their fruits. You hear that a certain one is called a bishop, but you know his thefts. He is dressed like a sheep, but acts like a thief. Without he is a sheep, but within a wolf. There is no limit to his plundering. His limbs have been hardened as if by the cold of Scythian nights. His mouth is bloody. He goes about seeking whom he may devour. . . . He screams instead of preaching. He denies the author of his voice, and not confessing the Lord Jesus, the giver of eternal life, he mingles bestial sounds into his sacrilegious speech."[18]

Referring to the creed of the Council of Rimini in 359, he condemns the bishops who then lost the favor of God to secure that of the emperor. In his preaching he insists upon patience and moderation since Christians should not imitate the violence they deplore in others. He strives not to offend but rather to win the sympathy of all the different classes of the faithful. He teaches that an abundance of material goods is often an occasion for the development of vicious habits, but is still more often an incentive to virtue.

With the approach of Easter the struggle was renewed with greater intensity. On Friday, March 27, 386, high officials, counts of the imperial consistory, came to the bishop and demanded not now the Portian basilica but the large new basilica within the city's walls. Ambrose replied that a bishop could not hand over to them a temple of God.

On Saturday, March 28, the prefect of the praetorium came to the church where Ambrose was celebrating and asked him to give up at least the Portian basilica. The bishop then asked the people present what he should do. Before their universal protest the prefect withdrew, saying that he would refer the matter to the emperor.

The court then decided to occupy the Portian basilica by force. While Ambrose, on Sunday, March 29, was in the baptistery of the basilica explaining the creed to the *competentes,* that is, those who would receive baptism on the following Holy Saturday, he was told that officials of the court *(decani)* had entered the Portian basilica and were hanging the curtains that marked off the place for the emperor in the church.[19] With this gesture the civil authority actually seized and occupied the basilica. Rumor of what had happened brought the people running to the spot. Ambrose, however, remained at his post. When he had finished his explanation of the creed, he began the celebration of Mass.[20]

It was probably on this Sunday that he delivered his discourse *On the Handing Over of the Basilica,* or *Against Auxentius:* "Why then are you disturbed? I shall never willingly desert you, though if force is used, I cannot meet it. I shall be able to grieve, to weep, to groan. Against weapons, soldiers,

Goths, my tears are my arms, for these are a bishop's defence. . . . I cannot take anything away from the temple of God; nor can I give up what I have received to guard and not to give up. In doing this I am acting for the emperor's good, for it would neither be right for me to give it up, nor for him to receive it. . . . They asked whether He thought that the right of tribute should be given to Caesar; these want to give to Caesar the right of the Church. . . . We pay to Caesar what is Caesar's, and to God what is God's. Tribute is due to Caesar, we do not deny it. The Church belongs to God, therefore it ought not to be assigned to Caesar. For the temple of God cannot lawfully be Caesar's. That this is said with respect for the emperor cannot be denied. For what is more respectful than that the emperor should be called the son of the Church?"[21]

During the Mass, Ambrose prayed with tears that no blood might be shed because of the church. He also sent priests and deacons to free an Arian priest, Castulus, whom the people had attacked in the square. The merchants *(corpus mercatorum)* were punished for siding with the bishop by being ordered to pay an extraordinary tax of two hundred pounds of gold, to be handed over within three days. Some were even imprisoned. But there was no surrender. All this happened in the last days of Holy Week. At this time debtors and sinners were usually pardoned, but within the city there was now the clanking of chains and continued harassing of the orthodox Christians.

Influential citizens were threatened so that they might persuade the bishop to yield. The courts were suspended, and all the officials of the court were told to keep themselves ready at the palace for any eventuality.

On Tuesday of Holy Week, March 31, counts and tribunes again came to the old basilica where the bishop was staying and insisted that he give up the Portian basilica. The emperor wanted it, and it rightfully belonged to him. Ambrose replied that if they had asked him for his money or for his estates, he would not refuse to give them up, even though they belonged to the poor. But the things of God are not subject to an emperor. Inwardly, however, he was afraid that troops might seize the church by force, and he begged God not to allow him to survive the ruin of the city.

Among those who came from the court were Gothic tribunes. Ambrose asked them: "Has the Roman empire taken you into her service so that you might disturb the peace? If our country is destroyed, where will you go?"[22] At their request that he calm the people, he refused: only God can calm them.

They then withdrew, and Ambrose spent the remainder of the day in the old basilica. Only in the evening did he return to his palace to rest and to be ready if they should wish to carry him off.

On Wednesday, April 1, he saw, as soon as he left his house, that troops had surrounded the new basilica. From the cries of the crowd he then learned that soldiers were also ringing the old basilica. Nevertheless, he celebrated the sacred rites in the old basilica as he had on the preceding day. During the public reading of Scripture he was informed that a large crowd had gathered at the new basilica and the people were asking for a reader. Some of the soldiers had already told the emperor that they did not want to oppose the bishop. However, they were still willing to obey him if he, the emperor, would take part in the religious ceremonies together with the Catholics. Otherwise they would go off to Ambrose. Carrying out their threat, some began to enter the church. The women became frightened, and one even fled. The soldiers then shouted that they had come not to fight but to pray.

On Wednesday of Holy Week, then as now, there was a reading from the book of Job in the Milanese liturgy. Ambrose seized the opportunity to apply the lesson to the present situation: The temptations and persecutions which Job had to endure are now being renewed. The allusions to Justina are transparent: she is like Jesabel, like Herodias. Then he repeats his arguments against the emperor; "It is not right for me to hand over the basilica nor is it fitting for you, Emperor, to receive it. No right permits you to violate the house of a private citizen; do you think that the house of God should be taken away? It is said that an emperor may do anything he wishes since he is in charge of all. I answer: 'Do not deign to think, Emperor, that the empire has any right over those things which are divine.' "[23] While he was still preaching, individuals came to tell him that the royal curtains had been removed from the Portian basilica and that the crowd assembled there was asking for their bishop. Ambrose then began to preach again marveling at what had happened, and he sent priests to the other basilica.

An imperial notary came to protest: Why had the bishop acted against an order of the emperor? Why had he sent priests to the Portian basilica? If he wanted to play the tyrant, he should say so clearly. Ambrose defended himself: When he had learned that the basilica had been invaded by soldiers, he had limited himself to tears. He had not yielded to the pressure of those who urged him to go there in person, saying that it was impossible to give up the basilica, but that he should not fight for it. Also, when he learned that the imperial curtains had been removed, he had not gone there himself but had sent some of his priests. Is this tyranny? Moreover, there is a saying that many more emperors have sought the priesthood than priests have sought the empire. The prince against whom God has raised no adversaries should be on his guard that he does not himself become subject to a tyrant. Maximus does not say that Ambrose tyrannizes over Valentinian. But this same Maximus now complains that it was the embassy of Ambrose that prevented his invading Italy. In fine, priests have never acted as tyrants, although they have frequently been forced to endure them.

The troops were still surrounding the basilicas. At the Portian basilica, boys were amusing themselves by tearing up curtains, hung in anticipation of the emperor's arrival and then removed. All Wednesday of Holy Week passed in sadness; no solution seemed to be in sight. That evening Ambrose could not return home; the soldiers still surrounded the old basilica and would not let the people depart. He thus passed the night in a room or sacristy of the basilica reciting psalms.

The following day, Holy Thursday, April 2, after the solemn reading of the Book of Jonas, while Ambrose was explaining the teaching of the book on the forgiveness of sins and the conversion of sinners, he was interrupted by the applause of the congregation at the good news brought by the soldiers. The emperor had ordered them to lift the guard on the basilicas and to restore the fine paid by the merchants. The joy and enthusiasm of the faithful knew no bounds. It was the day on which the Lord had given himself for us in the Eucharist, the day on which in the church at Milan public penitents were accustomed to be absolved.[24]

In describing the various phases of this struggle to his sister Marcellina, Ambrose had no illusions that all was finished; he knew that the courtiers called him a tyrant, that Valentinian had told the counts in the palace: "If Ambrose ordered it, you would hand me over to him," that one of his ministers, Calligonus, spoke of beheading the bishop who condemned the emperor. To this Ambrose had replied: "May God permit you to do what you threaten. I shall suffer what a bishop should suffer, and you will do what servants are accustomed to do."

The Lord wished to reward the weary labors of his faithful servant, providing him with defenders more powerful than the opposing human forces. On June 17, 386, Ambrose had an excavation made in the cemetery near the Porta Vercellina in the area facing the gates of the cemeterial chapel of Sts. Nabor and Felix. There were found the bodies of the two martyrs, Protase and Gervase. St. Augustine, St. Gaudentius of Brescia, St. Paulinus of Nola, and his biographer Paulinus all say that Ambrose had received a revelation concerning them. But he, in writing to his sister Marcellina about the events, speaks only of an ardent premonition.

The evening of Thursday, June 18, the sacred relics were deposited in a neighboring chapel, the basilica of Fausta, where a vigil was kept through the whole night. The following day they were solemnly transferred to the newly completed Ambrosian basilica to consecrate it by their deposition. During the course of their journey, a man blind for many years recovered his sight on touching the clothes of the saints. Many other miracles occurred. Ambrose, in his letter to Marcellina, reports the enthusiasm of the people during those days. In the same letter he refers to the sermons he preached to the faithful so that they might thank the Lord with him for having given them such heavenly protectors.[25]

The "discovery" of these relics at Milan in 386 marks an important epoch in the history of the cult of the martyrs. In Latin the word relic *(reliquiae)* means "the remains of the deceased," but in the fourth century in the language of the Church the term assumed a specifically sacred meaning.[26]

Before this the ancient pagans had already venerated the remains of famous men and heroes.[27] In 469 B.C. the body of Theseus, after its place of burial had been revealed by a prodigy, was solemnly transferred to Athens.[28] At Rome the staff used by Romulus in taking auguries was on display, and the toga of the wife of Tarquin. Even in those early days there were charlatans who pretended to own the lyre of Paris, the bones of the sea monster to which Andromeda had been offered, and the shell from the egg of Leda.

Among the Christians, from the second century on, a similar concern was felt for preserving the remains of the martyrs. In itself this was but a natural expression of reverence and esteem. In the fourth century the cult of relics developed impressively. While at Rome the bodies of the martyrs continued to profit by the absolute inviolability given to tombs by Roman law, and the relics that were distributed were only substitutes (little pieces of cloth that had been touched to the bones or to the tomb),[29] the Greeks did not think it disrespectful to dismember the bodies, and from this rose the custom in the East of transferring and dividing the remains of the saints.

Among the most ancient translations was that carried out by Gallus, the brother of Julian the Apostate. About the year 351 he had the body of St. Babylas carried to a new church at Daphne, a suburb of Antioch, to sanctify this famous site of pagan pleasures.[30]

In 356 the remains of Sts. Timothy, Luke, and Andrew were solemnly brought to Constantinople. Many other translations took place under Theodosius. Then the practice spread of dismembering the bodies of the saints. Already in the fifth century Theodoret noted that many basilicas boasting that they possessed remains of a martyr frequently had nothing more than small particles of their bones.

In matters of discipline and worship, the Church of Milan followed as a rule the practices of Rome, but in some particulars it followed the customs of the Eastern churches instead.[31] An example of this Eastern influence may be seen in the "translation" at this period of the relics of martyrs.

After the great discovery of 386, Ambrose in 393 discovered at Bologna the bodies of the martyrs Vitalis and Agricola, and again at Milan in 395 the bodies of Sts. Nazarius and Celsus.

The enthusiasm for the cult of the martyrs occasionally gave rise to deplorable abuses. As early as 401, St. Augustine in a work entitled *De opere monachorum* publicly denounced those adventurers dressed like monks who were always on the move and sold relics of martyrs, if, indeed, they were martyrs.[32] Even before this, a law of Theodosius forbade the transferring of the bones of a martyr from one place to another, their division, or sale.[33]

The unexpected ending of the quarrel with the court in Holy Week, 386, was due not so much to the fickleness of the fifteen-year-old Augustus at Milan as to the fear of a war with Maximus, the Augustus at Trier. To gain the support of the bishops of Gaul and Spain, Maximus was posing as the champion of orthodoxy. On receiving news of the turmoils at Milan, he wrote a letter to Valentinian reproaching him for his hostile policy towards the Catholics, his violence against the churches, his blockading of bishops in basilicas.[34] It provided a good pretext for intervening in Italian affairs.

Ambrose may also have informed Theodosius of the Arian intrigues at Milan. The Augustus of the East during these months was in mourning. In 385 his six-year-old daughter Pulcheria had died, and a short time later his Spanish wife, Aelia Flaccilla.[35] Authoritative historians maintain the probability also of an intervention on the part of Theodosius.[36] The court yielded, but not simply because of the bishop.

The popular enthusiasm generated by the discovery of the two ancient martyrs was echoed far and wide. Relics, feasts, or churches in honor of Sts. Gervase and Protase were to be found at Ravenna, Brescia, and Rome; at Vienne and Rouen in Gaul; at Carmona in Spain; and even at Carthage in Africa.

In his *Confessions*, St. Augustine recalls the events that took place at Milan in the spring of 386 and declares that "when the pious people kept watch in the church, ready to die for their bishop," the Lord revealed to Ambrose the place where the two martyrs had been buried "to check the madness of a woman, but of a woman who was a queen."[37]

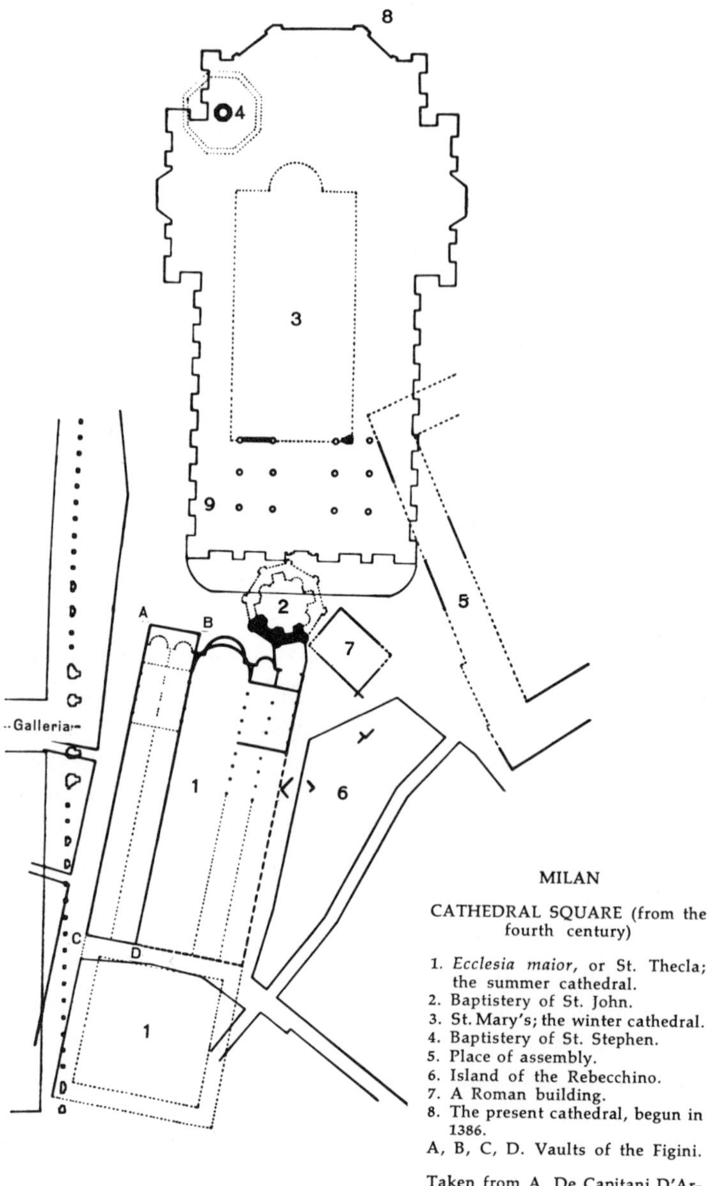

MILAN

CATHEDRAL SQUARE (from the fourth century)

1. *Ecclesia maior*, or St. Thecla; the summer cathedral.
2. Baptistery of St. John.
3. St. Mary's; the winter cathedral.
4. Baptistery of St. Stephen.
5. Place of assembly.
6. Island of the Rebecchino.
7. A Roman building.
8. The present cathedral, begun in 1386.

A, B, C, D. Vaults of the Figini.

Taken from A. De Capitani D'Arzago, *La chiesa maggiore di Milano* (Milan, 1952).

XII
His Preaching

o

The charm of his preaching. His exegesis. Allegorical interpretations. The Alexandrians. The Hexameron. Water, sea, sun, hail, birds, the crowing of the cock, and the beauty of man. God's repose. Instructions on the sacraments.

Marcellina was very fond of her brother, but she did not as a rule stay in the episcopal palace at Milan.[1] Of her own choice she lived on an estate in the country which could not have been many miles outside the walls of the city. Unfortunately, not a single letter from Marcellina to her brother has been preserved in St. Ambrose's correspondence.

With the approach of Holy Week, 386, it had been possible to foresee that the Arian friends of Justina would do all in their power to obtain a basilica in which to celebrate the solemn Easter liturgies. What delight was there in carrying out the magnificent rites in the hall of the palace? A church was needed and people to attend the services. This had also been a cause of concern to Marcellina. How would it all end? Her sleep was troubled, and she wrote frequently to Milan for news.[2] Much of the information which we have about those eventful days comes from a letter which Ambrose wrote to his sister on the evening the crisis ended, or the day after. He gives a rapid résumé of what happened between Friday, March 27, and the evening of the following Thursday, April 2, and ends with a reference to the "worm before the dawn,"[3] that is, to the insect which had gnawed at the ivy which had sheltered Jonas, causing it to wither. The reference was probably suggested by the reading of the Book of Jonas at the evening service of Holy Thursday.[4]

In his letter Ambrose tells his sister that the troubles seem to be ended for the moment, "but the emperor's words full of excitement foreshadow future and worse troubles. I am called a tyrant, and even more than a tyrant. For when the counts were entreating the emperor to go to the church, and said that they were doing this at the request of the soldiers, he answered: 'If Ambrose bade you, you would deliver me up to him in chains.' You can think what may be coming after these words. All shuddered when they heard them."[5] In his sermon against Auxentius, Ambrose had already declared; "They say that the people have been bewitched by the chanting of my hymns."[6] Fortunately we have in addition to his own writings further evidence for his charm in the memoirs of St. Augustine, who listened to him many times during the course of his stay of nearly three years (384-387) at Milan. Augustine at the age of thirty had come to Milan from Rome and Africa. He was not at the time a Catholic, much less devout. Everyone knew that he "barked" at the Catholic faith. Yet every Sunday he went to hear St. Ambrose.[7]

It is somewhat difficult for us to explain the precise charm of Ambrose's preaching. We have, indeed, the text of many of his sermons, but they were all reworked before publication. No one can claim to know the genius of Verdi or of Grieg who only has had their scores in his hands. If their music is to be appreciated, it must pour forth as a sparkling cascade of living sound. In general, if one reads but a few of the thousands of pages left by St. Ambrose, one gains the impression that the austere bishop before publishing his talks and sermons removed from them the lively particulars and spontaneous observations which must have characterized them, as we may conjecture from the stenographic report of his debate with Palladius at Aquileia in 381. It is like having a glass of champagne which has been standing too long, and which has lost its seething, sparkling bubbles. The majority of his sermons contain comments on passages from Sacred Scripture read in church. Confronted with the size of this collection, one wonders how the bishop found time to write so incessantly.

The answer is that the majority of these writings are simply reproductions of sermons and instructions.[8] This is so true that it can often be seen where one sermon ended and another began.

Ambrose looked upon preaching as one of the principal duties of a bishop. During the services on Sundays and feast days he never failed to address his people. During Lent he preached every day. In the course of his sermons he frequently turned to scripture since he looked upon it as a never-failing source of inspiration.

His intimate knowledge of the Bible enabled him to express his ideas in scriptural terms. Frequently his preaching was no more than a running commentary on the biblical text itself. He did not know Hebrew, but he had an excellent knowledge of Greek, and he liked to compare the text of the Greek Septuagint with other versions of the Old Testament. He also made use of the original Greek of the New Testament.

Despite his many sermons on the Gospel of St. Luke, the sum total of his works shows that he preferred to preach on the text of the Old Testament. The reason for this was that the Old Testament needed more explanation for his flock. It had been used by Christ himself, and its reading in the church created certain difficulties. Because of his hostility to paganism, Ambrose did not usually distinguish between the errors of the heathen and their accomplishments in the arts, in science, and in philosophy.[9] Since he believed that paganism was responsible for many evils in the world, he condemned it roundly. He had therefore to find in the scriptures all the natural wisdom that the pagans found in the writings of Pythagoras, Plato, and Aristotle.

Christianity cannot be blamed for this narrow-mindedness of the bishop of Milan since his attitude was typically Roman. Other great Christians of this time were much more liberal.

If we could believe Ambrose, Pythagoras imitated David in imposing a rule of silence upon his disciples. Socrates read and borrowed from the Bible. In Egypt, Plato had become acquainted with the writings of the Hebrews and had taken from them a number of his best ideas. Job and David are to be found in Sophocles. Aristotle and the Peripatetics spoke of happiness in the solemn tones of tragedy, but the Bible also speaks of it in simple and direct terms. The same is true of Cato and of the Stoics. All this provided so many other motives for studying and explaining scripture. And Ambrose applied himself to it with such persistence that the fame of his exegesis induced many to consult him, as we can see from his correspondence.

Ambrose's exegesis is primarily allegorical.[10] This was in keeping with the very old conviction that poets express not only beautiful fantasies, but also profound teachings on the nature of the world and the human soul behind the mask of fable and fiction. In the fifth century before Christ, Theagenes of Rhegium had already explained the battle of the gods in the Iliad allegorically, seeing wisdom in Athena, licentiousness in Ares, passion in Aphrodite, and so on.

Homer was thus explained in both a physical and a moral sense. The Stoics, in particular, made use of allegory to solve the difficulty created by immoral or ludicrous stories found in the myths: the gods and their occasionally scandalous activities are poetical interpretations of nature, of its laws, and its phenomena.

Allegorical exegesis thus became an integral part of Greek culture. When educated Jews in the Hellenistic Age came in contact with Greek philosophy, they were not able to restrain their admiration and envy. Were their scriptures, which God Himself had dictated, inferior to the wisdom of the Greeks? No, since allegory offered them a means of finding philosophy in the Bible and defending the unpleasant incidents narrated in scripture which were despised by the pagans.

The chief exponent of Jewish allegorical exegesis is Philo. According to him the literal sense of scripture is not to be rejected, but neither is it of itself sufficient: the letter of the scriptures is like the shadow of the body—the true reality and the true contents of scripture is that which stands behind the letter. When the letter of the biblical text appeared to him to be untenable, he gave it a purely mystical significance. Thus, for example, he spiritualized the story of the creation in six days.

In the New Testament we see that Christ regarded allegorical exegesis as perfectly legitimate, saying, for example, that the marvelous experience of the prophet Jonas would be verified also in Him. In his epistles, St. Paul makes continuous use of allegory; the first Adam was a type of Jesus Christ; the lot of the Israelites in the desert was of a typical character and was written for our instruction; the law of Moses was a shadow of the future reality whose body and true being are to be identified with the Christian economy; the Synagogue is the figure of the Church, and so forth. These figures had for St. Paul a spiritual significance which the literal sense did not at all diminish.

Later, in actual practice, the Fathers of the Church favored the allegorical interpretation of scripture for moral edification and apologetics. In the catechetical school of Alexandria, allegorical exegesis was organized into a definite system. Clement dedicates the whole of the fifth book of his *Miscellanies (Stromata)* to the justification of allegory: "All then, in a word, who have spoken of divine things, both barbarians and Greeks, have veiled the first principles of things, and delivered the truth in enigmas, and symbols, and allegories, and metaphors, and such like tropes. . . . And the Spirit says through Isaias the prophet, 'I will give thee treasures, hidden, dark,' but the treasures of God, and the riches which do not fail, and which are difficult to hunt out, are wisdom. Moreover, the poets, who learned theology from the prophets, philosophize about many things through suggestion. By these I mean Orpheus, Linus, Musaeus, Homer, Hesiod, and those who are wise in this sense."[11]

Origen went even further. Being forced to combat the exaggerated literalism of the Jews and certain Gnostic sects, he became convinced that there are certain pages in scripture which cannot be taken literally: "What man of sound mind could believe that there was a first, second, and third day, with morning and evening, when there was not yet a sun? Who could be so foolish as to think that God planted a garden like a gardener? And when it is said that God walked at midday in the Garden of Eden, and that Adam hid himself under a tree, no one believes that this is an actual history which was materially realized, but that it symbolizes mysteries. . . . There are countless passages where one who is not completely dull understands that many things have been described as if they really happened, but which were not materially verified as far as their literal sense is concerned."[12]

Even among the Latins there had been others before Ambrose who had used allegory in their interpretation of scripture. But he drew his inspiration from the Greeks. Although they are rarely cited, Philo and Origen are constantly being used by Ambrose in his exegesis.

And this is understandable. His commentaries have no pretensions to being scientific. They formed a part of his preaching. They provided him with a means of presenting the Bible to the faithful in a way which would move and edify them. He had, moreover, to combat the Arians who had become heretics through a too literal interpretation of scripture; the Manichees, who, finding the Old Testament insufficiently spiritual, rejected it as a work of the devil; and, finally, the pagans, who were fond of comparing the riches of classical literature with the books read in church.

In the scriptural text he distinguished a literal, a moral, and a spiritual, or mystical sense. The second assists us in regulating our conduct and the third instructs us about Christ and His kingdom. He believed that literal and spiritual explanations of scripture were necessary, but his primary interest was in the moral allegorical sense.

In allegory Ambrose found a solution for every moral problem in scripture, such as the drunkenness of Noah, the adultery of Abraham, the cursing of Job.

By means of an allegorical explanation every word of the sacred text becomes rich with instruction. At times his reasoning may be said to be somewhat subtle. The name "Isaac" means smile. Now a smile is a sign of joy. The source of joy is Christ. Isaac was, therefore, a figure of Christ. If Isaac is a figure of Christ, his wife, Rebecca, is a figure of the Church and of the soul. Consequently, the story of Isaac and Rebecca illustrates the relations between Christ and the Church, between the Lord and the soul.[13]

At times Ambrose's exegesis is also rather quaint. When speaking of the earthly paradise, he explains the temptation by the serpent in a literal sense. Then he corrects himself. He knew, as we also know from St. Augustine, that there were certain Catholics who followed Philo and interpreted Eve's conversation with the serpent in an allegorical sense. He, therefore, adds: "So that our sermon may not be a source of offense, let each one interpret this passage as he will. For there has been one before us who said that sin was committed by man through lust and sensuality, seeing in the appearance of the snake a symbol of pleasure, and understanding by the figure of the woman the sensuality of the mind and of the soul, which the Greeks call *αἴσθησιν*; he claims that according to the scriptural account the mind, which the Greeks call *νοῦς*, became a sinner after the senses had been deceived. In Greek, therefore, νοῦς is properly masculine, while αἴσθησις is feminine."[14]

This purely allegorical interpretation obviously goes too far.

The greatest of Ambrose's exegetical works is his *Hexameron,* a commentary on the scriptural description of the creation of the world in *six days.* It was largely inspired by works with the same title written by Origen, Basil, and Hippolytus. Modern scholars who have compared Ambrose's commentary with that of Basil (the other two are lost), have accused him of plagiarism. St. Jerome, on the other hand, who was able to study all four of these works, tells us that Ambrose has published a revision of Origen's *Hexameron,* following more closely, however, Hippolytus and Basil than Origen. This implies that Ambrose's commentary is more orthodox than Origen's. Nevertheless it is rather strange that despite the fidelity with which he follows Basil's order, and the use which he makes of Basil's words as if they were his own, Ambrose never even once mentions the Greek original. The explanation of such a procedure, which is not confined to the fourth century, may perhaps be found in the rhetorical character of the book: it is a collection of sermons, and a preacher is not as a rule expected to indicate his sources.

In the *Hexameron,* Ambrose is primarily interested in the literal sense of the sacred text. He gives a brilliant description of the various creatures mentioned in it. He discusses the heavens and the earth, the sea and the stars, and plants and animals. In addition to their outward appearances he describes their physical properties. The result of this was that his work soon gained the reputation of being a veritable "natural history," and the best of his time.[15]

Scientific knowledge as such appeared to St. Ambrose to be something vain and presumptuous. He held that the study of the so-called laws of nature without reference to scripture was false and contradictory. Natural objects, even after their creation, do not, as far as he is concerned, develop according to intrinsic laws, but simply because God has ordained it so in the scriptures. Further, the only real advantage to be obtained from the study of physical phenomena, whether it be the quality of the stars, of plants, or of animals, was, still according to Ambrose, the instruction and example which they provide for men either as individuals or as members of a natural or supernatural society. From his point of view, the world was cast in a single mold. God deliberately made the first creatures to be examples for others that were to follow. Man, the last object of creation, but one who forgets this fact through sin, should retrace his steps with the help of those creatures that have been more faithful to the divine command.

During the course of his exegesis, St. Ambrose treats of a great variety of topics. He refers to, or develops at some length, such matters as the following: the virtues and vices of those who are single and those who are married, political problems, the fact of creation, the errors of pantheism, of Platonic trialism, of Gnostic dualism, of eternally subsistent matter. He also discusses the Manichaean doctrine of good and evil, the reason for evil in the world, the permanence of species, free will, merit, astrology, the false gods of the heathen, original sin, the Trinity, especially with respect to the Word and the Holy Spirit, coeternal and cocreating with the Father, the unity of the Church, its triumph over persecutions and heresies, and, finally, its rites and customs.

The defects of the work should also be noted. One of its principal failings is its persistent Platonism which would place the essence of humanity in the soul alone. This is somewhat surprising in a work which contains such wonderful descriptions of the body and its functions. In his treatment of plants and animals, Ambrose makes many acute observations on such things as the sex of plants and their various properties, the permanence of natural species, the relation of one species to another, and the individual and social instincts of birds and fish. But he also includes a fair amount of dubious material and fantastic tales that were common to the science of his age. He thus believed that bees and vultures conceive without seed, that the Phoenix rises from its ashes, that the remora, a kind of fish, can stop a ship, that certain herbs will restore eyes to the blind, that water can be changed into salt, and similar curiosities of unnatural history.

In this he shared the common interest of his time in "marvels" *(mirabilia)*. His contemporary, Ammianus Marcellinus, maintained that geese flying over the Taurus mountains carry pebbles in their beaks so as not to attract eagles by their honking, that the pyramids of Egypt cast no shade, that silk grows on trees in China, and that pearls are produced from dew.[16]

The best parts of Ambrose's great work on the creation of the world are the third book, where he treats of plants; the fifth, where he discusses birds and fish; and the second section of the sixth, where he deals with the human body.

"The waters know how to come together, how to fear, and how to flee when God commands it. Let us imitate these waters and recognize one congregation of the Lord, one Church. There were once gathered here waters from every valley, every marsh, and every lake. The valley is heresy; the valley is paganism, because 'the Lord is God of the hills, but is not of the valleys. Hence it is that there is exultation in the Church, but among the heretics and pagans there is sadness and weeping. Hence it is said in Scripture: 'In the valley he set up tears.' The Catholic people have therefore congregated from every valley. There are not now many congregations, but there is one congregation, one Church. Here also it is said: 'Let waters be congregated from every valley,' and there was made a spiritual congregation, there was made one people. Out of heretics and pagans has the Church been filled.

"The valley is a theater, the valley is a circus where the horse 'useless to safety' runs, where there is base and vile contention, where there is the ignoble strife of litigants. From those, then, who used to follow the circus, faith has grown in the Church and the attendance is daily increasing.

"The marsh is self-indulgence, the marsh is intemperance, the marsh is incontinence. In it are found wallowing-places for lusts, the grunts of beasts, and the hiding places of passions. Whoever fall into it sink down and fail to emerge. Here men slip and waver as they walk. Here water fowl are muddied when they bathe. Above it are heard the mournful cries of doves. Here the slow turtle buries itself in the slime. From this comes the saying: 'A boar in the marsh, but a stag in at the springs.' Therefore from every marsh, where like frogs they sang their ancient complaint, have come together faith, purity of heart, and simplicity of mind."[17]

The bishop thus saw how his people had been transformed. Rescued from the mud of paganism, they were profiting by the purity and nobility of the Church. His description of the sea is justly famous:

"God therefore saw that the sea was good. Fair is the sight of this element when it foams with its surging white caps and rolling billows, or when it bedews the rocks with its snowy spray, or when it is ruffled by a milder breeze and is not tossed against the neighboring shore in violent waves, but manifests itself to one seeing it from afar in purple colors of calm tranquility. When it meets the shores in a fond embrace of peace, how gentle is the sound, how pleasing the splash of the water, how delightful the rhythmic beating of the waves! Still I think that the beauty of such a creation is not to be reckoned by the standard of our own eyes but in its totality, that is, by its harmonious conformity to the intention of its Creator.

"Good, then, is the sea. First, because it supplies the necessary moisture for the earth, secretly furnishing it as if with useful fluid through its veins. Good is the sea in that it is the resting place for rivers, the source of rain, a receptacle for the soil carried off by streams, and a carrier of merchandise. It links distant peoples together, defends us from the perils of warfare, and hedges the fury of the barbarians. It is a help in time of need, a refuge in danger, a delightful place for relaxation, and a source of health for those who are ill. It unites those who have been separated, cuts down the toil of travel, affords an escape to men in trouble, provides means for paying taxes, and is a source of livelihood when crops fail. Rain is brought from the sea to the earth since water is drawn up from it by the rays of the sun and its moisture borne along. The higher it rises, the colder it becomes because of the shadow of the clouds. And this is the source of rain, which not only tempers the dryness of the earth but fructifies the famished fields.

"Why should I mention the islands which often adorn the sea like jeweled necklaces? Men who flee there from the illicit pleasures of an intemperate world choose to lie hidden with a firm purpose of preserving continence and thus avoid the dubious troubles of this life. . . . And the islands voice their approval with their peaceful chorus of blessed waters and echo the hymns of blessed men. . . .[18]

"Hence it is that the sea is often rightly compared to a church which at the first approach of the people 'disgorges a tide' through all its vestibules. Then, as all the people unite in prayer, there is a sharp sound in the church like that of receding waves. The chanting of the psalms in turn by men, women, virgins, and children is like the pleasant crash of breaking waves. And why need I mention that water washes away sin while the saving breath of the Holy Spirit breathes over it?

"May the Lord help us to sail these waters in a fair bark and come safely to harbor. May He not allow us to experience temptations too great for us to bear so that we do not experience shipwreck in our faith. May He grant us profound peace, and if there is anything which may arouse the storms of this world against us, may we have as our watchful pilot our Lord Jesus Christ, to calm the storm with His word of command and to bring peace again to the sea."[19]

In the first four chapters of the fourth book of the *Hexameron*, which treat of the sun and the stars, may be found clear references to the worshipers of Mithra, of whom there were many even in Milan.

"In our reading of the Scripture, the sun, which before this did not exist, must now arise. We have already passed the first day without a sun; we have also gone over the second without a sun; and we have completed the third without a sun. On the fourth day God commands the luminaries of the heavens to be made, the sun, the moon, and the stars. The sun begins to take shape. Cleanse, O man, the eyes of your mind and the inward gaze of your soul, so that no mote of sin may dull the keenness of your mind and disturb the gaze of a pure heart. Cleanse your ear, so that you may receive the clear flow of Sacred Scripture in a pure vessel and let no contagion enter in. The sun with its great splendor forestalls the day, filling the world with its great light, warming it with its radiant heart. Beware, O man, lest you weigh only the greatness of the sun, so that its excessive brilliance does not blind the vision of your mind, as it does the eyes of one who looks directly at it. . . . Do not look upon it as a god, to which you see the other gifts of God preferred. Three days have passed, and no one has sought for the sun. Everywhere there has been an abundance of brilliant light. For the day, too, has its light which is itself the precursor of the sun. Do not therefore rashly trust yourself to the sun, though it is the eye of the world, the joy of the day, the beauty of the heavens, the charm of nature, and the most noticeable of creatures. But when you see it, think of its Author; when you admire it, give praise first to its Creator. If the sun which shares its being with other creatures is so pleasing, how much goodness is there to be found in that 'Sun of Justice'? If it is so swift that in its rapid course by day and night it passes over all things, how great is He who is always everywhere, and who fills all things with His majesty! If that which is bidden to come forth is wonderful, how much does He surpass our admiration of whom we read: 'Who commandeth the sun and it riseth not'? If the sun is great, which daily rises and falls according to the changes of the seasons, how great must He be, also, who, 'when he emptied himself' that we might be able to see Him 'was the true light that enlightens every man who cometh into this world'! . . . If it is a loss for a blind man not to behold the beauty of this sun, how much greater is the loss of the sinner who, despoiled of the gift of the True Light, endures the darkness of eternal night!"[20]

Ambrose's descriptions of the habits of animals are at times delightful.

"What tricks are played by the crab in its search for food! It is particularly fond of oysters and seeks to make a feast for itself from an oyster's flesh. But just as it is eager for food, so it is aware of the danger, for the hunt is as difficult as it is perilous. The difficulty comes from the fact that the food is shut up within a hard shell. . . . The danger lies in that the shell may close upon its claw. The crab, therefore, has resort to a trick and treacherously deceives its prey. Accordingly, since all things are attracted by pleasure, it looks for a time when the oyster, in a place sheltered from the winds and exposed to the rays of the sun, opens up its double doors and unbars the bolts of its shell so that its body may enjoy the pleasure of the open air. At this moment the crab stealthily slips in a pebble so that the oyster cannot close its shell. Having thus acquired an entrance, the crab inserts its claws without danger and feeds on the flesh within the shell."[21]

Birds "are a great incentive for arousing our devotion. For who having the common sensibilities of man would not blush to end the day without a recitation of the psalms since even the tiniest birds usher in the approach of day and night with their regular tribute of sweet song?"[22]

"How well the cranes carry out their anxious watching in the night without command and without compulsion! You may note the guards at their appointed places. And while the rest of the flock is asleep, others make the rounds and see if an attack is threatened from any quarter and with their constant vigilance provide complete protection. When he has completed his period of guard duty, a watcher arouses with a warning cry the one who is destined to take his place as sentry, and prepares himself for sleep. The new guard willingly accepts his lot. He does not, as is the custom with us, slowly and reluctantly renounce his sleep. . . . They also preserve order in their flights. By acting in turn as leader they alleviate their fatigue. At a fixed time, one takes a position ahead of the rest as if running before the standards. He later turns back and yields to a successor the task of leading the flock. What is nobler than this, that toil and honor are open to all, that power is not distributed among a few, but is by a kind of voluntary lot ascribed to all? This resembles the functions of the old republic and is a model for a free state. From the beginning men began to establish a political system based on nature by following the example set by birds. That there might be an equal participation in toil and honor, each individual in turn learned to share responsibilities, to divide up duties and commands. There was thus no one without an office, and no one without a task to perform. This was the fairest form of government. No one became accustomed to unbroken power; and no one was crushed by long submission. Advancement was without envy because of the order of the duties to be undertaken and the time set for them; and obedience was more bearable since it fell to the common lot of all. No one dared to oppress another when the latter in his term of office could show his scorn. Toil was not burdensome since it was relieved by the thought of a dignified office in the future. But when the lust for domination began to claim for itself undue powers, and when this same lust was unwilling to relinquish the powers it had assumed, when military service began no longer to be a common right but a kind of servitude, when men were more anxious to seize power than to follow the established order of attaining it, then the performance of tasks was regarded as a burden, and what was not voluntarily undertaken soon left room for negligence. How reluctantly men submit to assigned guard duty! How hard it is to get anyone to accept a perilous post in a camp that is imposed by a royal command!"[23]

"Let us now come to the turtle dove, which the law of God chose as a chaste gift. When the Lord was circumcised, a dove was offered, since it is written in the law that there should be presented 'a pair of turtle doves or two young pigeons.' For this is the true sacrifice of Christ: chastity of body and grace of spirit. Chastity is attributed to the turtle dove and grace to the pigeon. It is said that the turtle dove, when widowed by the loss of her mate, was 'weary of the bridal chamber' and even of the very mention of marriage, since 'her first love, turning traitor, cheated her through death.' He was thought to be unfaithful in that his love was not lasting, and cruel with respect to his charm since he caused more pain by his death than he had caused sweetness by his love. The turtle dove therefore rejects a second marriage and does not break the laws of chastity or her pledges to her beloved, reserving her love for him alone, cherishing for him alone the name of wife. Learn, O women, how great is the charm of widowhood, which even birds are said to observe.

"Who, then, has given laws to the turtle dove? If I search for a man, I shall not find him. No man has dared to propound laws with respect to widowhood since not even Paul dared to ordain that it should be preserved. Rather, he says: 'I desire therefore that the younger widows should marry, bear children, rule their households, and give no occasion to the adversary to speak evil.' And elsewhere: 'It is good for them if they so remain. But if they do not have the self-control, let them marry, for it is better to marry than to burn.' Paul wishes that the steadfastness of turtle doves should be found also among women. Also, he exhorts the younger widows to marry since our women can scarcely maintain the chastity of doves. Therefore it is God that has infused into the turtle doves this virtue of continence. He alone prescribes that which all must follow."[24]

Vultures are said "to conceive without male seed and to generate offspring without the union of the sexes. And their offspring are said to live to be a hundred, nor does 'the limit of a natural span of life await them.' What do those who are accustomed to ridicule our mysteries say of this when they hear that a virgin has brought forth a child—they who maintain that it is impossible for one who has had no intercourse with a man to have a child? Is it to be thought that what is possible for vultures is impossible in the Mother of God? A bird brings forth without the assistance of a mate, and no one denies it. But because Mary, a virgin, though betrothed to a man, brings forth, they question her chastity."[25]

"The crowing of the cock is also pleasant at night. And it is not only pleasant but also useful, since like a good servant it rouses the sleeper, warns one in trouble, and consoles the traveler by proclaiming in round tones the passing of night. When the cock crows, the robber leaves his place of ambush, the morning star arises and illuminates the sky. When the cock crows the fearful sailor is freed from sadness, the storms and tempests stirred up by gusts of wind at eventide subside. When the cock crows, the devout heart rises up to prayer and resumes the office of reading. Lastly, it was when the cock crowed that the 'rock of the Church' washed away the sin which he had committed by his denial before the crowing of the cock. At its crowing, hope returns to all, the sick are comforted, the pain of wounds is relieved, fevers become less raging, faith returns to the fallen, and Jesus looks down on those in trouble and corrects those in error. He looked upon Peter, and his sin at once departed. His denial was cancelled and his confession followed."[26]

These quotations have been taken from a sermon given the evening of a Holy Thursday. The sermon preceded the Eucharistic sacrifice and the solemn reconciliation of the penitents.

St. Ambrose's explanation of the origin of the world ends in the sixth book of the *Hexameron* with a study of the higher animals and particularly of man. After giving repeated proofs of the absolute superiority of the soul over the body, he goes on to describe the beauty of the human body and its various parts.

"How pleasant and fair is even the top of the head! How attractive are its locks of hair, how honored in the aged, how respected in priests, how terrible in warriors, how beautiful in the young, how becoming in women, how sweet in children!"[27] He then passes on to describe the forehead, eyebrows, eyes, ears, nose, mouth, teeth, and the marvels of the voice. "And what should I say of the kiss, the pledge of charity and love? Even doves kiss each other, but what is this in comparison with the charm of a kiss of a human being in which the note of friendliness and kindliness shine forth, and in which the faithful affection of perfect love is manifested? Hence it is that the Lord condemned the outrage perpetrated by His betrayer, saying: 'Judas, dost thou betray the Son of Man with a kiss?' "[28]

When he has finished discussing the different parts of the body, Ambrose brings his series of sermons and the entire work to a close with a few thoughts on God's repose: "But now there should be an end to our discourse, since the sixth day has been completed and the work of creation has ended. Man, who is the first of all living beings, the summation of all, and the delight of every earthly creature, has now been made. Surely we should pay our homage of silence, since God has rested from all His labors in the making of the world. He has found His rest in the depths of man; He has rested in his mind and will. He had made man capable of reason, an imitator of Himself, a striver after virtue, and one eager for heavenly favors. God rests in him as He has said: 'In whom shall I find repose except in him who is humble and peaceful and who trembles at My words?' I give thanks therefore to our Lord God who has wrought a work in which He might repose. He made the heavens; I do not read that He rested. He made the earth; I do not read that He rested. He made the sun, moon, and stars; I do not read that He rested there. But I do read that He made man and then found rest in one whose sins He might forgive."[29]

With these moving words Ambrose brings to an end his great work on the creation, the *Hexameron*. It is a mirror of his own soul—candid, sweet, rich, and yet strong and austere.

The allegorical interpretation of scripture accustomed Christians to find symbols everywhere, to seek for the spirit behind what is material, to see in the charming shapes of natural objects the symbol and vesture of thought. The genius of the Middle Ages is already felt in the exegetical works of St. Ambrose.

But Sacred Scripture and the Christian authors of the East were by no means Ambrose's only source of inspiration. He drew also from pagan writers. Many studies made in recent years have made it possible for us to assist at his arduous labors. He copied whole sentences from the works of Plotinus. But when he borrowed from this celebrated Neoplatonist of the third century, he carefully censored his original, removing every allusion to Hellenic myths or pagan cults or philosophical speculations that was irreconcilable with Christian teaching.[30] Here again we see the broad culture of the bishop of Milan, his eagerness to profit by every sound idea, no matter where he found it. In fact, we can almost see him smile as he makes slight changes in his pagan texts to remove references to the old gods, who by this time were for the pagans themselves little more than names.

Among all the works of the bishop of Milan, the six instructions which he gave to the neophytes for six days after their reception of baptism on Easter, perhaps in 390 or 391, deserve special mention. Every year the bishop gave similar instructions. This brief work begins with the words *De sacramentis*, "Concerning the Sacraments," which also serves as its title.[31]

It is a famous and precious work since it contains the oldest extant Latin text of the Canon of the Mass and the oldest text of the Latin liturgy for baptism. In this treatise he notes with regret that the people of Milan did not receive the sacraments as frequently as they should, and he speaks of the advantages to be derived from the washing of feet during the liturgy, a custom which he admits was not observed at Rome.

During the sixteenth century the *De sacramentis* was violently attacked by Protestants on the grounds that it was spurious. The real basis for the attack, however, was the fact that the work contains formulas practically identical with those of later councils with respect to the dogma of the Real Presence of Christ in the Eucharist. Today theologians and philologists are more and more inclined to recognize the work as coming from Ambrose's pen. But how are the undeniable differences from his other writings to be explained? As we have already noted several times, St. Ambrose, after preparing and delivering his sermons, corrected and edited them before publication. These six instructions, however, were taken down by a stenographer who was present when they were delivered and are thus preserved *just as they were given.* A few lines from these sermons will show how practical Ambrose was in his preaching. He frequently repeats himself, seeking above all to be as clear and accurate as possible: "Christ descended [into the river Jordan]; John, who was standing by, was baptizing; and, behold! the Holy Spirit descended in the shape of a dove *(quasi columba).* It was not a dove that descended, but the shape of a dove. Remember what I said: 'Christ took to Himself flesh, not the shape of flesh *(sicut carnem)* but the truth of flesh itself. Christ took to Himself true flesh.' The Holy Spirit, however, did not descend as a true dove *(in veritate columbae)* but He descended from heaven in the shape of a dove. John therefore saw and believed."[32] Ambrose also knew how to illustrate a point from his own experiences in daily life: "There are some individuals, at least I know one of them, who, when I told him: 'At your age you have an even greater obligation to be baptized,' replied: 'But why should I be baptized? I am without sin. Have I committed some sin?' . . . Christ had not yet opened his eyes, for there is no man without sin."[33]

In the sixth century, Cassiodorus, the former Roman senator, used the following comparison to explain the charm of Ambrose's words: They are like milk—bright, sweet, substantial.[34]

XIII
The Fairest Conquest

o

Life of Augustine before his arrival at Milan. His meeting with Ambrose. Monica. The refrigerium. The bishop's preaching and his silence. Augustine's conversion and baptism.

During the Easter Vigil on the night of April 24-25, 387, Ambrose had the great consolation of baptizing and anointing with chrism Augustine, a young African of thirty-two.

The bishop of Milan had given to the Lord all his earthly possessions, his wealth, palaces, public offices, and those who were dearest to him in his family. Every day of his life he spent for Christ in the service of the poor and of the truth. In return God gave him the gift of reading minds and winning over the hearts of others.

Augustine would also become a bishop, and would appear in the history of the Church as one who, because of his keen intellect, would dominate the course of succeeding generations and centuries, would explain the message of the Gospels in a way that would be definitive for those in search of the truth, and would himself become a Father of the Church. But he would always remember that it was the bishop of Milan who had shown him the way by his example, and who had brought him to faith and Christ.

Augustine's stay at Milan, from the fall of 384 to May, 387, and his conversion are especially important for the story of the life of the bishop of Milan, since his *Confessions* enable us to see Ambrose close at hand in the intimacy of his house, and to catch a glimpse of him that is not found in his own more formal works.

Augustine came from a modest bourgeois family of a small city in Numidia, Thagaste, the present Souk-Ahras, situated sixty-two miles southeast of Bona. His father was a *curialis*, or town councilman, and, though he possessed some means, they were not sufficient to send his son to school at Carthage. But Romanianus, a wealthy lord of Thagaste, came to the boy's assistance.

After completing his first years of schooling in his native town, Augustine studied grammar in the neighboring city of Madaura from the age of thirteen to sixteen. Since his father could not afford to send him on further, he had to interrupt his studies for a year. It was then that Romanianus came generously to his aid, and Augustine was able to go to Carthage, where he remained from 371 to 374.

Studies were not his only interest in the great African city. At Thagaste he had already proved to be somewhat wayward, and his mother felt it necessary to warn him secretly "not to fornicate and, above all, not to commit adultery."[1] At Carthage his conduct was even worse, but he finally reached a kind of compromise. When he was seventeen, he started living with a girl, and in 372, when he was eighteen, he became a father. This union, considering the customs of the times and the natural law, was a true and valid marriage, even though it had to be regarded as being illegal according to the civil laws because of the different social status of the two.

Through the generosity of Romanianus, Augustine was not

only able to pay for his schooling but also to maintain a family. He had left home as a catechumen and returned to it as a Manichee. Since his mother refused to receive him into her home, he accepted the hospitality of Romanianus.

He taught grammar for one year at Thagaste, and then, in 375, he moved to Carthage. Romanianus was the only one whom Augustine had told of his plans for moving, and it was this same benefactor who provided him with the necessary means. In the metropolis he conducted a school of eloquence for eight years, from 375 to 383.

But Augustine, now thirty years old, was not happy: he had not found peace. Friends of his, who were perhaps Manichees, persuaded him to try his fortunes at Rome. "I did not decide to go to Rome because my friends who advised this promised greater gain and honor in that city—although at the time these things did attract me; but instead, the chief, and practically only reason that took me there was that I heard that the youths pursued their studies there more quietly and were restrained by a stricter discipline, so that they could not rush boldly when they pleased into the class of one who was not their master unless he gave permission. On the contrary, at Carthage, the students enjoy unrestrained and shameful freedom. They break in impudently and like madmen disrupt the order set by the teacher for the greater profit of his students. With marvelous stupidity they commit many outrages that would be punished by the laws if custom did not protect them."[2]

Contrary to what he had always done before, Augustine did not mention this project to Romanianus, who later regarded Augustine's abrupt departure as nothing but a brainstorm. He continued to esteem him and assist him financially. On the eve of his departure, Augustine had to trick his mother, who suspected that he was leaving: "But why I left to go elsewhere, You, my God, only knew, nor did You reveal it either to me or to my mother who wept desperately at my departure and accompanied me to the coast. There she held me close so as to keep me back or to accompany me, but I deceived her, pretending that I had a friend whom I did not wish to leave until he could sail with a fair wind. . . . Yet when she refused to return without me, I succeeded with some difficulty in persuading her to spend the night in a chapel dedicated to the blessed Cyprian which was not far from our ship. During the night I stole away without her, while she remained to weep and pray."[3]

Towards the end of 383, when Ambrose was on his way to Trier on his first diplomatic mission, Augustine arrived at Rome. He was received as a guest in the home of a Manichee, which was not unusual since he was still attending the meetings of this sect. He fell gravely ill, perhaps as a consequence of the voyage. Recovering his health, he opened a school of rhetoric, but again with little success. "Then, without wasting time, I undertook to do that for which I had come to Rome, namely to teach rhetoric. I first gathered together in my lodgings some students, to whom, and through whom, I began to become known. Then I learned that things happened at Rome which I had not had to suffer in Africa. It was quite obvious to me that those riotous incursions of young rogues were not committed there. 'But,' as I was told, 'all at once many students conspire together so as not to pay their fees to their teacher. Breaking their given word and despising the obligations of justice out of their love of money, they go off to another. . . .' Consequently, when Milan sent a request to the prefect of the city at Rome, asking for a teacher of rhetoric for that city and providing the means of travel by public conveyance, I made application with the help of those men far gone in Manichaean follies (from whom my departure was to separate me, though neither they nor I knew it) so that I might be given an audition by the prefect of the time, Symmachus, and after being approved be sent to Milan. Thus I came to that city and to Ambrose the bishop, known throughout the world as one of the best of men."[4]

These lines were written by Augustine in 396-397, ten years after the events narrated, when the reputation of the bishop of

Milan had passed far out beyond the confines of his see, especially after his conflict with the emperor Theodosius and the latter's reconciliation with the Church on Christmas, 390.

Symmachus's choice of Augustine as a teacher of rhetoric at Milan fits in well with the events connected with the second legation of the senate to the court at Milan for the re-erection of the altar of Victory in the curia.

In a few important cities, professorial chairs were maintained by the state, but in others they had to be locally financed. A law of Gratian of May 23, 376, stipulated that the salaries of professors should be fixed and suitable: twenty-four "provisions" were allotted to teachers of rhetoric and twelve for teachers of Greek and Latin grammar. In the larger cities such as Trier, thirty "provisions" were allotted to teachers of rhetoric, twenty to teachers of Latin, and twelve to teachers of Greek.[5] It is probable that the magistrates of Milan who had to provide for the chair of rhetoric in their city discussed the matter with Symmachus in the summer of 384 when he was in Milan on his famous mission. Symmachus had been proconsul in Africa for some years. It was probably in the winter of 377-378 that he commissioned Satyrus, who had come to Africa to deal with Prosper, to carry a letter for him to his brother Titianus in Rome. Symmachus would certainly not have known Augustine when the latter at the age of twenty opened up his school of eloquence at Carthage. But he must have been quite readily disposed to accept the recommendations of Augustine's African friends and the Manichees in Rome. Julian's edict on teaching had been abrogated by Valentinian I in 364, and in 376 Gratian had dispensed the cities from the obligation of submitting for imperial approbation the names of grammarians and rhetors being appointed to the schools. The request of the Milanese decurions provided Symmachus with a good opportunity of getting even with his rival and relative, Ambrose, by sending an anticlerical to the university at Milan. Augustine was a Manichaean, and consequently would be much opposed by the

Catholics and well received by the pagans. Augustine himself later admitted that he "had barked many years not so much against the Catholic faith as against the fictions of carnal imaginations," and that he had been "rash and impious" in condemning what he should have investigated for himself.[6]

Augustine's nomination to the post at Milan is another indication, however slight, of the pagan reaction which began to take shape after the tragic death of Gratian, and which brought it about that in 384 practically all of the high offices in the State passed into the hands of pagans. When he reached Milan, Augustine could not avoid calling on the bishop as an act of courtesy. Ambrose, on his own account, would certainly have been interested in the new professor and would have heard of his attendance at the meetings of the Manichees at Rome and of his somewhat irregular family life, that he was living with a woman who was not his wife even though she was the mother of his twelve-year-old son. All of this was sufficient to make Ambrose believe that Symmachus had good reasons for recommending Augustine to the Milanese.

Augustine, in his turn, even though he was no longer an enthusiastic Manichee after his encounter with Faustus, had not yet found a substitute for Manichaean dualism and was not making any great efforts to find one. Manichaeanism had at least given him some peace of conscience in that it had enabled him to reconcile his high ideals with the actual baseness of his own way of life. As a consequence, when he first met Ambrose, there was very little in common between the two which would have formed the basis for a friendship, but much to keep them apart. Ambrose was in his fifties, a member of the Roman aristocracy, and for more than ten years he had been a bishop in a capital city. The African rhetor, on the other hand, was a provincial, a Berber by race, of slight means, a member of an obscure bourgeoise family of a distant country, and twenty years younger than the bishop. The two were in effect living in different worlds, and although he was a Christian and a bishop there was no reason for Ambrose having a special interest in Augustine. His friends, as may be seen from his correspondence, were important figures in the Church and State. No one at the time could foresee the future greatness of the young professor. He could possibly become another Ausonius, or publish some learned work, but that was all. Further, Ambrose was rather badly prejudiced against both philosophy and dialectics: "They [the Arians] find the strength of all their poisons in dialectical disputations, which, according to the opinion of philosophers, do not have the power to build but have only an interest in destruction. But God has not been pleased to save his people through dialectics: 'For the kingdom of God is in the simplicity of faith and not in the contention of words.' " Moreover, "do not they [the Arians again] draw all the attractiveness of their impiety from philosophy?"[7] Ambrose's reservations with regard to philosophy were so well known that a legend grew up during the Middle Ages that the bishop of Milan had added to the litanies the invocation: "From the dialectic of Aristotle, deliver us, O Lord!"[8] Finally, St. Ambrose was busy about a thousand tasks, the same tasks which Augustine would one day come to define with a sigh as his "luggage" *(sarcina)*, his heavy duties as a bishop.[9]

Keeping in mind these historical facts, we can read with greater understanding Augustine's account of his meeting with Ambrose: "And I came to Milan, to Ambrose the bishop, known throughout the world as one of the best of men, Your devout servant, whose eloquence at that time was busily distributing 'the fatness of Thy wheat,' and 'the gladness of Thy oil,' and 'the sober intoxication of Thy wine' to Your people. And I was unknowingly led to him by You, so that through him I might knowingly be led to You. That man of God received me in a fatherly fashion and welcomed my visit with episcopal dignity *(satis episcopaliter)*. And I then began to love him, first indeed not as a teacher of the truth, which I completely despaired of finding in Your Church, but as a man who was kind to me. I listened to him eagerly as he preached to the people, not with the intention that I should have had, but, as it were, to search out his eloquence, to see whether it agreed with his fame, or whether it flowed forth less or more abundantly than was reported. I was held in suspense, intent upon his words; but I was careless and scornful of the matter. And I was delighted with the sweetness of his discourse. . . . And as I opened up my heart to catch his eloquence, the truth that he spoke likewise entered in, but only gradually.[10]

"My mother had now come to me, strong in her piety, following me over land and sea, and she found me in grave danger because of my despair of discovering the truth. . . . But to You, the Fountain of Mercies, she poured forth more frequent prayers and tears that You might hasten your help and enlighten my darkness. And more eagerly than ever she ran to the church and hung upon the lips of Ambrose, as 'to a fountain of water springing up into everlasting life.' For she loved that man as an angel of God, because she had heard that I had been brought by him in the meantime to that doubtful state of mind that I was in, and she felt certain that I would pass from sickness to health. . . . She loved him dearly because of my salvation, and he loved her in turn because of her most religious way of life, shown not only by her good works, but also by the fervent spirit with which she visited the church; so that when he saw me he would often break out in her praise, congratulating me on having such a mother, and not realizing what a son she had in me, who was doubting about everything and did not believe at all that a way of life could be found."[11]

Probably Ambrose was not as ignorant about him as Augustine imagined. In fact, Ambrose's place in the *Confessions* would not be intelligible if his work were to be limited solely to his preaching in the church, in acquainting Augustine with Simplicianus, in giving him a book that Augustine did not read, and in baptizing him. Above all, Ambrose's friendship with Monica could not be understood: "And so, when my mother brought to the shrines of the martyrs meal, bread, and wine, as she had been accustomed to do in Africa, and was stopped by the sacristan, when she learned that this had been forbidden by the bishop, she submitted so reverently and obediently that I myself marveled that she was so easily changed into a critic of her old customs rather than become a despiser of his prohibition. For no love of wine lay hold of her spirit, nor did the love of wine stir up in her a hatred of the truth, as it does in many men and women who grow sick when they hear 'a hymn of sobriety,' like drunkards at watered wine. But when she had filled her basket with the usual food, intending only to taste it and to give the rest away, she never allowed herself more than one cup of wine watered down for her temperate taste, and taken as a pledge of honor. And if there were many tombs of the dead which seemed worthy of being honored in this fashion, she carried about with her the same cup, to be used everywhere, which was not only very weak with water but also by now quite warm; and she gave this in sips to those present since she was there seeking devotion and not pleasure. But when she learned that these practices were forbidden by the famous preacher and pious bishop even to those who acted soberly, lest any occasion of drunkenness might be given to those who loved to imbibe, and because these customs were very much like the pagan feasts in honor of the dead, she most willingly gave them up, and instead of a basket full of the fruits of the earth she learned to bring to the tombs of the martyrs a breast filled with purer petitions. . . . But still it seems to me, my Lord and God (and such is the feeling of my heart in this matter in Your sight), that my mother would not perhaps so easily have given up this custom of hers if it had been forbidden by another whom she did not love as much as Ambrose."[12]

We thus come to know by chance, from a passing reference to it in St. Augustine, that Ambrose had decided to prohibit the *refrigerium* at Milan before the year 385.[13] The custom of celebrating a festive reunion of relatives over, or near, the tombs of their dead had endured from time immemorial. Provisions were often made in wills to take care of the expenses for such banquets on the anniversary of one's birth. In addition to these private anniversaries, the pagan Romans were accustomed to remember their dead in a special manner during the month of February. On the twenty-second of this month, the whole family would go to eat and drink at the place of burial of their dear ones. This day was known as the *cara cognatio.* The original idea behind the feast was to bring refreshment and comfort to the dead. There were holes in the tombs through which wine and food could be passed to those within.

A ceremony that includes eating and drinking, since human nature is what it is, naturally tends to become an occasion for feasting. In Africa, this custom instead of *refrigerium,* or *parentalia,* was commonly called *laetitia,* that is, "joy," or "revelry." For some time after the persecutions the Church had to tolerate banquets at Christian tombs, but it sought to give them an appearance of charity and almsgiving for the poor. What was done for ordinary Christians who had died was done with much greater fervor at the tombs of the martyrs. Eating and drinking at the tomb of a martyr was an undertaking that could be the object of a vow, as may be seen from a number of the oldest graffiti in the Roman catacombs.[14] With the large increase of Christians in the fourth century, abuses in connection with the cult of the martyrs became intolerable. St. Paulinus of Nola tried to find some excuse for the crudity of the faithful who were convinced that they honored the martyr Felix at his tomb even with their tipsiness.[15] Since splendid basilicas rose over the tombs of the martyrs, it was there that people frequently went to celebrate a *refrigerium.* At times these could take on the appearance of a great banquet. When Pammachius provided a great dinner on the occasion of the death of his wife Paulina in 397, the five naves of the basilica of St. Peter at Rome were not large enough to contain all the friends and poor who came there to eat.[16] Even in Africa it was known that there were common sights in the Vatican basilica that were anything but edifying. St. Augustine sought to excuse the *vinolentiae quotidianae* found there by noting the large number of pilgrims to the site and the fact that the bishop's residence was at some distance from the basilica.[17] There were at least three Italian bishops of the fourth century who publicly denounced these customs as a shame: Zeno of Verona,[18] Ambrose of Milan, and Gaudentius of Brescia.[19] In a sermon delivered about the year 390, St. Ambrose says that those who go to drink at the tomb of a martyr with the notion that their drunkenness will be pleasing to him are stupid, since the martyrs prepared themselves for their heroic trials through fasting.[20] From Monica's experience we know that the bishop of Milan did not limit himself to pious exhortations. He had specifically ordered the sacristans of the basilicas and the caretakers of the cemeteries where the martyrs were buried not to permit anyone to enter with things to eat and drink. This prohibition can lead us to believe that sacred drunkenness was no less serious at Milan than it was in Africa, as we know from St. Augustine's description of it. When the bishop of Hippo took measures to abolish these abuses he had recourse to the example of bishops across the sea: "Nothing can be said by us more briefly nor more truly against those who object, 'Why now?' except that we should say, 'At least now!' "[21]

Turning again to Augustine's experiences at Milan, we see that his mother, intending to provide a fully legitimate marriage for her son, made the mistake of having him send back to Africa the woman with whom he had lived for fifteen years: "In the meantime my sins were multiplied, and that woman with whom I had been used to lie was torn from my side as though she were an impediment to my marriage, but my heart clung to her and was broken and wounded and bled. And she returned to Africa, vowing that she would know no other man, leaving me with the natural son I had from her. But I, unhappy, was no imitator of that woman, and restless of the delay, since it would be two years before I would obtain her whom I was seeking, because I was not a lover of marriage but a slave of lust, procured another woman, but not as a wife."[22]

In this departure of the woman with whom he had been living, and still more in her vow, may not some influence of the bishop's constant preaching on virginity and virtue be seen? Even Augustine was becoming more and more interested in the bishop and in his way of life: "I regarded Ambrose himself as a happy man according to the world, honored as he was by such authorities. Only the fact that he was unmarried seemed painful to me. But I had no means of knowing or even guessing what hopes he had, what struggles he had against the temptations that were associated with his high position, or what consolation he had in his adversities, and what savory joys his mouth hidden in his heart experienced from Your Bread. Nor did he know of the burnings in my soul, nor the danger I was in from the abyss. For I was unable to ask him what I wanted as I wanted, since throngs of busy people to whose weaknesses he was tending barred me from his ear and mouth. When he was not with them, and this was but a very little of the time, he either refreshed his body with necessary sustenance or his mind with reading. But when he read, he scanned the pages with his eyes and his heart searched out the sense, but his voice and tongue were silent. . . . Perhaps he was on his guard lest some listener following it with greater intent might ask him about some more obscure passage which he was reading, . . . although his real reason for reading to himself may have been to preserve his voice which easily grew hoarse. . . . But certainly there was no opportunity for me to learn from that sacred oracle of Yours, his breast, what I desired unless it was something that could be heard briefly.[23]

Ambrose kept silent, since to free Augustine from the fetters of sensual pleasures, which were his greatest difficulty, the grace of God was needed. Then too, the words of a bishop would have only chafed the wound. Still Augustine went to church every Sunday to hear him.

At Ambrose's preaching, the new professor at Milan must have blushed to realize that he had "barked" against the Catholic faith without really knowing it. "I was confounded, I was converted, I was overjoyed, my God, that the only Church, the body of Your only [Son], did not relish those childish trifles [of the Manichees]. . . . I often gladly heard Ambrose observing in his sermons to the people, as though he were most earnestly commending it as a rule: 'The letter killeth, but the spirit quickeneth.' "[24]

Later he met Simplicianus, the saintly priest who would facilitate for him the path of his return. In the Lent of 386, even Augustine was moved at seeing the struggle between the bishop and the court and the whole city upset with dismay: "The faithful flock stayed night and day in the church, ready to die with their bishop, Your servant. My mother, Your handmaid, was one of the leaders in these cares and vigils, living on prayers."[25] In June, however, there was general rejoicing at the discovery of the bodies of the two martyrs, Gervase and Protase. In July the same year, Augustine experienced the definitive crisis with the scene in the garden at Milan, the flood of tears, the child's voice: "Take and read!" and the transformation wrought by the words of St. Paul.[26] Augustine courageously broke with the habits that till then had entangled him; he also left the school, and at the end of August withdrew with his mother Monica, his fifteen-year-old son, Adeodatus, and a number of friends to the villa of Verecundus at Cassiciacum.[27]

From there he wrote Ambrose of his desire to receive baptism. And early in March, 387, he left the villa to take part in the instructions, examinations, and rites at Milan which during Lent prepared the catechumens for the sacrament. "We were baptized, and the anxiety of our past life fled from us. Nor during those days was I sated with wonderful sweetness as I meditated upon the depth of Your design for the salvation of the human race. How abundantly I wept at Your hymns and songs, being sharply moved by the voices of Your Church sweetly singing. Those voices flowed into my ears and truth streamed into my heart, so that the affections of piety welled up and my tears fell, and I was happy with them."[28]

In the month of May they left Milan. While they were waiting at Ostia to sail for Africa, Monica fell gravely ill and "on the ninth day of her sickness, and the fifty-sixth year of her life, and the thirty-third of mine, that pious and religious soul was freed from the body."[29] In August, 388, after a year of residence in Rome, Augustine returned to Africa. Those five years of absence had transformed him. He was another man.

Ambrose and Augustine were opposed to each other in age, social condition, temperament, and habits of life. But to say that Ambrose did not understand Augustine, and that he kept him at a distance would be to reveal one's ignorance of both of these great men. It has been held that in 386 Augustine was not converted to Christianity but to Neoplatonism. According to such an hypothesis, Ambrose would have had nothing to do with his conversion; Augustine's frequent reference to the bishop of Milan as to his father, his teacher, his master, and his sponsor would be nothing more than pious frauds perpetrated by an excessively humble soul, or, at best, pious imaginations. Such claims have been made and occasionally still are made by scholars of different countries.[30] But to such hypotheses it may be said: Augustine lived for seven years as a professor at Carthage where there were excellent Catholic bishops; he remained for two years at Rome during the reign of the great and venerated Pope Damasus. Who knows how many excellent sermons he could have heard at Carthage and at Rome? Yet it was neither at Rome nor at Carthage, but at Milan, after only two years of residence, that he decided to leave his professorial chair and prepare himself for baptism. His doubts had been resolved by the "most blessed bishop Ambrose."[31]

Ten years after his first meeting with the bishop of Milan, he reflected on the road he had taken and penned an autobiography that has become a classic: numerous pages are filled with a grateful remembrance of that bishop beyond the sea. Later, when he was seventy years old, he had the misfortune of seeing a pupil of his whom he had proposed for the bishopric of a town not far from Hippo accused of crimes of every sort: assault, theft, licentiousness. Augustine was desolate. He thought seriously of resigning his post.[32] Forty years had passed since his own conversion at Milan, and more than twenty since the death of Ambrose. Yet it was precisely during these months of profound discouragement that Augustine begged the deacon Paulinus to write the first biography of the bishop of Milan. On August 28, 430, Augustine himself died. Almost immediately, or at most only a very few years later, his life was written by another bishop, Possidius, who had lived with Augustine for some forty years. In the first pages of his book, Possidius recalls the events at Milan in 386-387 and notes that it was God who inspired St. Ambrose to speak about those very problems that tormented Augustine and in such a fashion as to free him from his doubts. Thus, "through Ambrose Augustine received both the teaching of salvation within the Catholic Church and the sacraments" which effect that salvation.[33]

In the eyes of Ambrose, however, the converted professor must have remained *unus multorum*, one of many. In 396, nine years after his departure from Milan, Augustine was to become a bishop in Africa, but Ambrose may have never heard of it.

When his mother was carried to her tomb at Ostia, Augustine was so crushed that he could not even weep. He attempted to bathe, but found in it no relief, only weariness instead. He slept a little. Waking up, he tells us: "As I was there in my bed, I remembered those true words of Your Ambrose. For You are,

God, Creator of all things,
and Ruler of the poles, clothing
the day with beautiful light
and night with pleasing sleep,

so that sleep may refresh our
wearied limbs for labor's toil
and ease our tired minds
and free us from anxious griefs.[34]

The recollection of this hymn relieved him of the burden of his sorrow. The tears came and flowed without stint.

In 429-430, when Augustine was old and wearied after so many years of arduous labors in defense of the Church and of the faith, he had to answer the accusation of Julian of Eclanum that he had himself invented original sin. Again he had a recourse to Ambrose: "My teacher in this matter is Ambrose, whose books I have not only read, but I have also heard him speak; and through him I received the waters of regeneration. I am far from being equal in my deserts to him, but I confess and maintain that in this matter I do not differ at all from my teacher."[35] Ambrose's influence on Augustine may be seen especially in his teaching on the sacraments, his interpretation of Scripture, and in his general principles of ecclesiology.[36] During those years of struggle for the freedom of the Church at Milan, Augustine came to recognize the meaning of Catholicism and what the Church is—not a wan group of ascetics separated from the actualities of life, but a great living tree, a faith which acts as a leaven against all the forces of evil in or outside of man, a well-ordered organism, a precise creed, a teaching, and a principle of authority. He had feverishly sought for the truth, and he found in Ambrose the only truth which could satisfy him, a truth lived in love. This is the reason why St. Augustine always cherished the remembrance of the fatherly bishop of Milan who had opened his eyes to the truth, had clothed him with the white baptismal garment, had washed his feet as Christ had washed those of His apostles, and who at his First Communion had placed in his hand the Eucharist and made him taste how sweet is the Lord, and how pleasant is His yoke.[37]

AEL(ia) FLACCILLA AVG(usta)

Bronze Coin. See Cohen VI, p. 464, no. 7.

Aelia Flaccilla, the daughter of Antonius, prefect of Gaul under Gratian, was born in Spain and married Theodosius before he became emperor. St. Ambrose referred to her as "a soul faithful to God"—*fidelis anima Deo (De obitu Theod. 40).* Theodoret wrote highly of her piety and charity *(Eccl. hist.* 5.19). Her funeral oration was delivered by St. Gregory of Nyssa.

XIV
The Penance of Theodosius

o

The misfortune of Domninus. The flight of the court from Aquileia. The war between Theodosius and Maximus. The anger of Theodosius. The return from Antioch. The question of Callinicum. The slaughter at Thessalonica. Ambrose's intervention. The reconciliation.

On January 1, 387, Valentinian II began his third consulship at Milan. Symmachus, along with others, was invited to come from Rome for the festivities. The court remained at Milan until the second half of May, when it moved to Aquileia. New and serious threats from the barbarians were rising up in Pannonia. Valentinian II and his counselors believed that they could more readily obtain aid from the Augustus at Trier than from the emperor at Constantinople, possibly because Theodosius had let it be known that he was not too happy with the Arian tendencies of the Milanese court. The new embassy from Aquileia under the leadership of the Syrian Domninus, who enjoyed the full confidence of Justina, was received at Trier with extraordinary cordiality. Maximus thought at the time that he could take advantage of Domninus's stupidity to transport his troops into Italy without too great a risk.

The latter was given a good contingent of troops and sent

back to Italy with the fullest assurances. But behind these troops the bulk of Maximus's army under his personal leadership could penetrate into Italy through the opened pass of Monginevro. Domninus, confident in the success of his diplomacy, was disillusioned when the reinforcements which he had brought with him also rebelled against Valentinian.[1]

In May, 387, Maximus was at Milan. Valentinian and his mother and the court did not even consider the possibility of resistance. In September, the young emperor, his mother Justina, his three sisters, and Probus, then prefect of the praetorium for the fourth time, embarked at Aquileia and set sail for Thessalonica. This populous imperial city formed a part of Illyricum, over which Theodosius seems to have extended his jurisdiction that same summer of 387.

Theodosius, when he was asked for help by Valentinian and Justina, decided that they should wait for him at Thessalonica. He hesitated to declare war on Maximus, who was claiming that he had occupied Italy to restore the faith of Nicea. Maximus had now broken the agreement he had made with Theodosius in the summer of 384. It would have been difficult for Theodosius to think of coming again to terms with him. But before deciding what he should do he was anxious to take up the matter with the youthful Augustus, Valentinian, who had fled to Thessalonica. A contributing factor to the discussions which took place in the imperial palace in that city was perhaps the beauty of Galla, the fifteen-year-old sister of Valentinian. Theodosius had been a widower for two years, and Justina's maternal wiles were able to bring about the marriage without much delay.

In this regard, the pagan historian Zosimus relates an incident that certainly could have happened but for which there is no further proof. At a session of his council, Theodosius suggested entering into negotiations with Maximus to obtain from him without armed intervention the restitution of the Italian provinces. While the senators stood in silence, Justina, who in this emergency had finally given up her Arianism, presented her daughter Galla to Theodosius. He declared that he would gladly marry her. Her mother gave her consent so that Theodosius might avenge the death of Gratian by declaring war on his murderer Maximus.[2]

In the meantime, Maximus, apparently without much resistance, had occupied the whole of Italy. Perhaps the story told by Ambrose of the treasure which a widow had placed in the church at Pavia should be referred to the few months of Maximus's reign in Italy. At the demand of one holding an imperial rescript, the treasure was handed over. When Ambrose learned what had happened, he told the bishop that he should recover the deposit and send it back to the widow.[3]

At Rome Maximus angered the Catholics of the city by his harsh treatment of those who had burned a synagog in the city.[4] But we have no direct reports on his relationship with the bishop of Milan.

As early as June 14, 388, Theodosius at Stobi in Illyricum had issued a decree against heretics, thus abrogating the law of Valentinian of January, 386, which was no longer actually being observed. Theodosius made a forced crossing of the Save at Siscia and defeated the troops of Maximus at Poetovio on the Drave.[5] The latter was slain by his own soldiers at Aquileia on August 28.

Valentinian II with his mother and his two other sisters embarked at Thessalonica with the intent of withdrawing some of Maximus's forces from Pannonia. His fleet secured a victory over that of Maximus in the waters off Sicily. After the victory, Valentinian sailed for Ostia. It was during these months of war that his mother, Justina, died.

At the beginning of October, Theodosius entered Milan as conqueror and sole master of the empire. His meeting with Ambrose marks the beginning of the final and most brilliant phase of the life of the bishop of Milan.

The Roman empire was now for the last time to be ruled

by a single prince. Theodosius, who had left his eleven-year-old son, Arcadius, at Constantinople as nominal lord of the East, now restored a part of his lost power to the seventeen-year-old Valentinian. He sent him as Augustus to Gaul, though his power seems to have been more apparent than real. Theodosius, at least for the time being, fixed his residence in the palace at Milan, where he remained from October, 388, to April, 391.

Ambrose must have known a number of things about Theodosius—his fight against the Arian heresy, his choleric disposition, and the courage and wisdom he had shown in the reorganization of the Eastern provinces after the Gothic disaster.

In January, 387, Theodosius had decided to ask for a special contribution on the occasion of the celebration of his tenth year as emperor. The condition of the Danubian provinces after the Gothic invasion and the military expenditures that had been made justified the tax, which was bound to weigh particularly heavily upon the wealthy cities of the East. At Alexandria there were meetings of protest in the theater. Worse occurred at Antioch. The discontent here turned into an open revolt.[6] The statues of Theodosius, his father, his first wife Flaccilla, and his two sons Arcadius and Honorius were torn from their pedestals, broken to pieces, and dragged through the streets during the last days of January.

Theodosius's anger was soon felt. A corps of archers reestablished order in the city. The madness of the people gave place to terror at the thought of the punishments to come. The rich fled from the city, and the bishop Flavian was sent to Constantinople to plead for those who remained. According to the Church historian Sozomen, Flavian asked the young men who sang at the imperial banquets to chant the psalms of supplication as they were at that time sung in the churches at Antioch.[7] When Theodosius heard these strange, haunting melodies, he was moved to tears: they even fell into the cup in his hand. Meanwhile, twenty-four days after the revolt, the imperial legates pronounced the sentence at Antioch: the circus, baths, and theaters were to be closed; the city itself should be deprived of its privileges; the free distribution of grain was to be abolished; and the guilty should be brought to trial.

From these crucial weeks there have come down to us a number of speeches of Libanius and some famous sermons of St. John Chrysostom, then a priest at Antioch, encouraging the citizens in their despair. The monks also came down from the mountains in swarms to persuade the officials to at least suspend execution of the death sentences.

On Holy Thursday, April 22, after a whole Lent spent in fear and trembling, the people received word from Flavian that the emperor had granted his pardon. On Easter morning in the great basilica that was crowded to the doors, Chrysostom reported the meeting of Theodosius with Flavian, and he invited the Antiochians to thank God and the emperor for the complete amnesty.

Even after his victory over the army of Maximus, Theodosius showed his longanimity. Through the intervention of Ambrose he remitted the sentences of many condemned to death or exile.[8]

Thus, seven years after his rather unsatisfactory correspondence in 381, the bishop of Milan had dealings again with Theodosius and met him personally for the first time. This meeting gained for him the immediate favor of the emperor.

In the fall of 388, Ambrose, while preaching on the story of the patriarch Joseph alluded to the recent political troubles, and in his exposition of the twentieth chapter of St. Luke, he was carried away by his enthusiasm: "Now is the acceptable time. The year is no longer frozen with the wintry frosts of dark treachery, nor while the ice is still about does the crude crust of blasphemy stay rigid under the dense clouds; but the earth, freed from the storms of sacrilege, is now bringing forth new fruits. It is truly fruitful. The storm of all dissensions has died down; all the heats of worldly desire and all the waves of trouble which the people of Italy, once through the fires of Jewish, and more recently Arian, cruelty, have experienced, are now tempered with a serene calm. The storm is passed, harmony is afloat, faith breathes again."[9]

By this time, Valentinian was a serious convert from Arianism, and there was reason to believe that through Theodosius the Church would reap a rich harvest. But Theodosius was not yet as docile a son of the Church as Ambrose would have liked him to be. The emperor, on his part, accustomed to the flattering attentions of the Oriental bishops, must at times have marveled at some of the deeds of the bishop of Milan. One day, when he was assisting at the celebration of the Eucharist, Theodosius took a place near the altar among the priests. Ambrose sent a deacon to let him know that he could not remain there, but that he should go down to his place among the faithful, among the laity, since the purple made him an emperor but not a priest.[10]

Theodosius had to confess that before he knew Ambrose he had not known what it was to be a bishop. Ambrose dedicated to him a treatise written in defense of King David: despite his serious sins of murder and adultery, that ancient king was still an example upon which one might properly reflect. What man has ever succeeded in living without sin? It should not be too surprising that even David fell. If there is anything at which we should be surprised, it is this: the sight of a powerful king raised above the laws who was able to submit himself to the correction of a prophet, whereas ordinary men, when they are rebuked by priests, as a rule do nothing but look around for excuses and try to conceal their faults. Because of his humble submission, David succeeded in disarming God's indignation.

Theodosius and St. Ambrose, however, had quite different ideas with regard to their respective powers. In December, 388, because of the riots at Callinicum, they came into radical conflict. Callinicum was an important military post on the Euphrates, near the modern ar-Raqqah in Syria. The Christians had burned the Jewish synagog in the city; and, in their turn some monks, angered by being disturbed during the course of their traditional procession on August 1, had destroyed a chapel of the Valentinian Gnostics, an heretical sect.

During these years, the wealth and proselytism of the Jews provoked almost everywhere outbreaks of anti-Semitism. Theodosius, who was anxious to preserve order in the empire, ordered the count of the East to find the culprits and compel the bishop of Callinicum to rebuild the synagog. Such punishment would discourage similar violence elsewhere.

St. Ambrose looked upon these orders as being an offense to the Church. He wrote to the emperor from Aquileia, where he was at the time presiding over the election of the new bishop Chromatius. In his letter he states that it is his duty to speak, since who would dare to tell the truth to the emperor if a bishop were afraid to do so?[11] It will be a disgrace if the Jews write on the front of their synagog: "This temple of impiety was built from the spoils of the Christians." In his letter, Ambrose employs every artifice and refinement of courtesy so as not to offend the emperor, but he does not on that account refrain from making a threat: the emperor should listen to him writing as he does in secret, if he does not wish to hear him in church.

Theodosius did not give in. Then the scene took place that Ambrose himself describes for Marcellina.[12]

When the emperor was present in the church in the midst of a crowd of people, the bishop undertook to explain the following verse from Jeremias: "Take with you a staff of walnut." He goes on to say that a bishop can at times give orders which are bitter like the rind of a walnut, but the fruit within is sweet. After many obvious allusions to the problem confronting the emperor, Ambrose turned directly to Theodosius and told him that he ought to honor the Church and each of its members.

Then, as he descended from the dais from which he had preached, the emperor said to him, "You were referring to us." Ambrose admitted as much. Then Theodosius declared, "The command that I gave for the synagog to be rebuilt by the bishop was indeed somewhat harsh, but it has been corrected. The monks commit a good many crimes." When one of the officials began to speak violently against the monks, Ambrose silenced him. He then asked the emperor for permission to celebrate the Mass without fear. The emperor sat down and nodded, but did not openly promise that he would not punish the Christians. Ambrose remained standing, and the emperor promised to emend his rescript. Ambrose then asked him explicitly not to bring the Christians to trial. The emperor yielded to the request and Ambrose ascended the altar which, he tells his sister, he would not have ascended unless he had received this promise.

Even the saints can make mistakes, since they also are men. Ambrose certainly asked too much of the emperor that day. His great love for the Church led him to regard as a victory the emperor's acquiescence to this excessive demand. Church historians can only deplore it, but those who find in this episode the origin of the deviations and the anti-Semitism of the Middle Ages exaggerate its importance.

In order to understand how Ambrose could have gone so far, and certainly not to defend his action, we must recall at least two things. The first of these was Theodosius's still imperfect attitude towards the Church.

In carrying out the condemnation of Arianism pronounced by the Council of Constantinople in 381, Theodosius had used forms that implied the continuation of Constantine's dangerous ecclesiastical policy: the last word in Church affairs even with respect to matters of faith and the orthodoxy of bishops belonged to the emperor. In the synodal decree *Fidei* of the Council of Aquileia of 381, Ambrose had already shown his bitter distress because of the profound differences that existed between his own concept of the relations between Church and State and those of the emperor. It was imperative that he assert the right of autonomy for the Church in its own sphere. It was well and good that a bishop should be judged and condemned for violations of the laws, but the civil authorities should take into account the fact that a bishop is not just another citizen, and should defer such a judgment to ecclesiastical authorities.

The second factor that had to be considered was the lamentable subjection at court of a long series of Arian bishops that had lowered the episcopal dignity, and the shameful treatment which the Church both in the East and in the West had suffered at the hands of Constantius II.

Ambrose had personally witnessed the troubles which the Church had incurred at Rome during the reign of Pope Liberius and their unfortunate outcome in the schism of Ursinus. Still more, at Milan, where he had succeeded to Auxentius, he had experienced the bitter fruits of Caesaropapism: ten years of toil had not been sufficient to eradicate it completely.

The Church in the West would never have known Arianism except for the unwarranted meddlings of the emperors. These had been the source of endless dissensions, wasted energies, and countless misfortunes for the Church.

In this matter of Callinicum, Ambrose must have seemed to Theodosius to be even less tolerant than the monks. It may well be that he gave in to prevent a crisis in the Western world where his authority was not yet fully solidified. It is also possible that the emperor felt that the bishop was deliberately making exhorbitant demands of him to counteract the excessive docility of other bishops, particularly in the East, towards the civil authority. Whatever the case may have been, a definite coolness between Theodosius and Ambrose seems to have developed in 389-390.

Theodosius probably had some reason for suspecting high ecclesiastics in general. Another unpleasant incident had occurred. Early in the summer of 388, when Theodosius was at war with Maximus, Theophilus, the bishop of Alexandria, thought he should do something to secure the favor of the victor, whoever this might turn out to be. The bishop of Alexandria was a power indeed. He ruled over a hundred bishops in the six metropolises of Egypt almost as if he were a pharaoh. He enjoyed commercial monopolies and unrivaled prestige in all the Nile valley and controlled enormous sums of money. Theophilus was, moreover, personally ambitious and without scruples, and he governed the churches of Egypt like an absolute monarch. But to carry on in such a grand manner he had to have the approval of the emperors. When civil war broke out, he was placed in something of a quandary. He wanted to present his congratulations to the ultimate victor as soon as possible. For this purpose he sent his priest Isidore to Italy with gifts and two letters, one for Theodosius, and the other for Maximus. Isidore was to have delivered to the ultimate victor the one addressed to him and to have destroyed the other. But he was so careless that he let himself be robbed of the compromising letters, which then became public domain.[13] This was an added reason for Theodosius's remaining aloof from lofty prelates in the Church, and for carefully distinguishing between their exalted offices and their persons, not always so exalted.

On June 13, 389, Theodosius with his son Honorius, now five years old, made his solemn entrance into Rome. He paid his respects to the senate and listened to the panegyric which the orator Latinius Drepanius Pacatus delivered in his honor. Pacatus extolled him as the conqueror of Maximus, the avenger of Gratian: "This god whom we see here in our midst has been given to us by Spain."[14] During the preceding months, Symmachus had delivered a panegyric in praise of Maximus. When Theodosius came to Rome, he took refuge in a church of the Novatians. The emperor stayed in the Eternal City for three months, and there he must have soon come into contact with the bishop of Rome, Pope Siricius. And, as a matter of fact, Theodosius's law prohibiting the stay of Manichees in Rome and depriving them of their civil rights dates from June 17, 389.[15]

Theodosius showed the greatest deference and regard for the great lords of the pagan nobility and visited them in their luxurious homes. He generously pardoned Symmachus. While still in the city, he received ambassadors from the King of Persia who possibly had been sent to complete negotiations about Armenia. Some years before, Sapor III had sent gifts of precious jewels, silk, and elephants to Theodosius. Or it may have been that these ambassadors had come to announce the death of Sapor III (388) and the accession of Bahram IV to the throne. The incident narrated by Paulinus about two noble Persians who stopped in Milan on their way to Rome may perhaps be associated with this embassy.[16] For a whole day, from six in the morning until nine in the evening, they were engaged in a conversation with the bishop through an interpreter. They left him in admiration, "and to show that they had come for no other reason than to get to know more perfectly this man whose fame had been reported to them, on the next day, bidding farewell to the emperor, they set out for Rome, wishing to know the power of the famous Probus. Having achieved this, they returned to their own country."

Some are of the opinion that the long conversations that Theodosius had with the Roman aristocrats put new vigor into the pagan party. Towards the end of 389, when Theodosius had already returned to Milan, a third Roman legation came asking him to abrogate Gratian's famous provisions of 382 for the abolition of pagan worship.[17] Ambrose again intervened, but Theodosius was vexed at this intrusion.

The pagan request was rejected, but not because of the bishop's advice. Theodosius had other reasons for such a refusal, the chief one being financial. In the treaty of peace with the Visigoths in 382, Theodosius had promised these barbarians exemption from taxes and considerable sums of money if they would defend the Danubian frontier. He did not know how, or simply he could not see how he could remedy the unfortunate economic situation which he had inherited from his predecessors except by increasing the already unbearable taxes. To re-establish a fund for the support of the pagan priests was simply impossible. Instead of granting this request, Theodosius was forced to place a further burden even upon the Catholic clergy.

A law of June 27, 390, obliged the *curiales* who wished to enter the clergy to give up all their goods to the curia.[18] Other measures that wrought hardship to the Church were also taken during this same year. It seems that they should be attributed to the determination of the emperor to counteract the interference of the bishop of Milan.

On June 21, 390, an edict was issued at Milan forbidding widows to serve as deaconesses in the Church before they had completed their sixtieth year: under the sanction of nullity, their wills were not to be made out in favor of the Church, clergy, or poor, but only for the benefit of their heirs.[19] On September 2, another law was passed which forbade monks to live in the cities: they should stay in the deserts or wildernesses as befitted their vocation.[20]

The prefect of Italy, Nicomachus Flavianus, was, during these same months, a pagan. Tatianus, the prefect of the East, was likewise a pagan. St. Ambrose had ample proof of the court's hostility. He knew that Theodosius had frequently been angered on learning that decisions made in the imperial consistory had been revealed to the bishop and had ordered the members of this body not to say anything to the bishop.

During these two years of 389 and 390, when he was deliberately excluded from the counsels of the court, Ambrose busied himself more than ever with his pastoral labors. It was during this time that he published his three greatest works: his commentary on Psalm 118, his treatise on the duties of ecclesiastics, and his commentary on the Gospel of St. Luke. This latter work was the object of an ill-tempered attack by St. Jerome. In 390 or 391, when Jerome published his Latin translation of Origen's homilies on St. Luke, he mentions in his preface, without naming him, a commentator on Luke whom he describes as "an ill-omened crow that caws and tricks itself out with the most brilliant colors of other birds while it is actually nothing but black itself." In his Apology which he wrote against Jerome, Rufinus cites this passage and notes that Jerome was here alluding to St. Ambrose.[21]

The forced abstention of the bishop of Milan from court affairs, however, was rudely interrupted by a notorious incident which marked the high point of his public activity.

In April or May of the year 390, a serious revolt broke out in Thessalonica, the capital city of Macedonia. The Teuton Butherich, who was in charge of the barbarian troops stationed there, imprisoned a jockey. The occasion for this act was an edict which had been published some months earlier by Theodosius threatening those guilty of unnatural vice with death. Despite the violent protests of the crowds that wanted to see the jockey again racing in the circus, Butherich refused to release him. A popular riot broke out; Butherich was stoned and his body dragged through the streets.

In a violent fit of rage, Theodosius ordered a fearful penalty. The people of Thessalonica were invited into the circus. While they were expecting the start of the races they were surrounded by soldiers who proceeded to massacre them.[22] During three hours of slaughter, thousands of defenseless men, women, and youths perished.[23]

A cry of horror went up throughout the whole Roman world. After giving his first order, when his anger had cooled down, Theodosius had sent a second command cancelling the first. But unfortunately this reached Thessalonica too late.

During these weeks the emperor was not at Milan, but nonetheless Ambrose, the bishop of the capital, had to speak out in the name of common humanity and of the Church. Theodosius would have to admit that he had committed a crime, repent, and accept the sanctions of the Church.

St. Ambrose left the city before Theodosius returned so that he would not be obliged to meet him. Instead, he wrote a confidential letter to the emperor. He did not dictate it as he usually did but wrote it with his own hand, so that the emperor would alone be cognizant of its contents. This letter, which was written in September, is extremely tactful and shows that the bishop was not interested in condemning but that he only wished for the sinner to be converted and live. By telling the emperor that he had seen him coming into the church *in a dream* and that he had not been able to celebrate the mysteries in his presence, Ambrose delicately informed him that he should regard himself as being excommunicated for his crime.

Ambrose tells Theodosius that it is impossible to come and see him, and that, on the other hand, it would be even worse if he remained silent; "I cannot deny, august emperor, that you are zealous for the faith. I do not doubt that you fear God, but you are of such an impetuous nature that you are at once turned to compassion if anyone placates you, and, on the other hand, you are so aroused that you can scarcely control yourself if anyone angers you. . . . I have preferred to draw your attention to this impetuosity secretly rather than perhaps irritate it by deeds in public. . . . At Thessalonica has occurred something which has no parallel in history. I was unable to prevent it; rather, I frequently told you how cruel it would be. Your attempt to revoke your order shows that you have realized the gravity of your deeds. It is something that I could not excuse. When the first news of it reached us, there was being held in the city a council of the bishops of Gaul. There was no one who did not groan; there was no one who took the matter lightly. Even if I, Ambrose, kept you in my communion, your crime would not have been forgiven. Rather, I would have been the object of public indignation if there had been no one to tell you that you had to be reconciled with our God."[24]

The bishop, who had been seriously ill, had used his sickness as an excuse for leaving the city: he went to some unknown place to regain his health. He knew that Theodosius was not yet ready to do what was required of him and the whole letter is a subtle plea for penance on the part of the emperor.

We do not know Theodosius's reactions to this letter. It was only published after the death of Theodosius, and perhaps also only after the death of the bishop, by his literary executors. In June, the emperor was at Milan; he then moved to Verona. From a law published in this latter city on August 18, 390, we may conclude that Theodosius was conscience-stricken: "No decree carrying a sentence of death should be carried out immediately, but only thirty days after its publication."[25] It may well be that the emperor by means of this law wished to show St. Ambrose that he was truly sorry for what had occurred.

Before the end of November, Theodosius was again at Milan. That he presented himself at the entrance of the church as if to challenge the bishop's authority and that he was then turned away is certainly legendary. Byzantine historians have described what St. Ambrose had written in his letter to the emperor about his dream as if it actually occurred. We only know that Theodosius sent his minister Rufinus *(magister officiorum)* to Ambrose to determine the manner of his reconciliation: the emperor recognized his mistake and was surrendering.

He came to the church to ask for his penance, leaving behind his royal insignia. He publicly expressed his sorrow for his sin and asked the pardon of the Church. As St. Ambrose formally attested, he, the emperor, was not ashamed to publicly request it. And St. Augustine wrote that the people wept to see the dignity of the emperor so humbled.

The reconciliation took place on Christmas, 390. Theodosius

was absolved and readmitted to the sacraments. With good reason an Italian historian has questioned Manzoni's statement about the conversion of Napoleon: a much higher dignity than that of Napoleon had already submitted to the shame of Golgotha.[26] For the first time in history a monarch publicly recognized the fact that he also was subject to the eternal laws of justice, and a bishop vindicated for himself the right of judging and absolving even kings.

Unfortunately, even some modern critics have seen in Theodosius's repentance only the excessive power of the Church and the weakness of an impotent prince or the "humiliation" of the imperial dignity.[27] As a matter of fact, that Christmas of the year 390 is a great date not only in the history of the Church but in the history of civilization as well.

St. Ambrose's courageous gesture is a symbol of the primacy that law and reason must have over brute force, a lesson that needs to be learned now perhaps more than ever before. That it was the Catholic Church in the person of one of her bishops that affirmed this principle, which alone makes life worth living, is to her great and lasting credit.

The Moralist

The theology of St. Ambrose. Christian ethics and the Ambrosian synthesis. Old words and their new meanings. Against avarice and lust. Marriage. Charity. Indicia. The fallen virgin. Pessimism and optimism.

In *The Golden Legend* of Jacobus de Voragine we are told "that St. Ambrose once being on his way to Rome, was received as a guest in a Tuscan villa, the home of a very wealthy man, and that he earnestly questioned his host about the state of his fortune. To this his host replied: 'My fortune, my lord, has always been blessed and happy. See the great wealth that I possess, and slaves and servants without number. All my desires have been fulfilled, and I have never suffered reverses, nor even displeasure.' When he heard this, St. Ambrose was overcome with astonishment and said to his traveling companions: 'Get up, get up! Let us get away from this place with all speed, for the Lord dwells not in this place.' "[1]

This story from one of the most popular writers of the Middle Ages shows the deep impress which the teaching of St. Ambrose had upon the medieval mind. On the other hand, St. Ambrose's "teaching" played no great part in the manuals of the nineteenth century. At the present time, however, we are beginning to re-evaluate his merits as a speculative theolo-

THE SILVER "CASKET" OF ST. NAZARIUS

This was used by St. Ambrose in his dedication of the new *Basilica Romana,* or *Basilica Apostolorum.* Relics of the saint contained in the silver box were placed beneath the high altar. The basilica later came to be known as that of St. Nazarus. The reliquary is shaped approximately like a cube, measuring 6-1/8, by 7-7/8, by 6-1/8 inches. The four sides and cover of the casket which are made of silver plates about 3/32 of an inch thick, have reliefs which were hammered into the metal from the rear and finished off in front with a chisel. Christ among the Apostles is represented upon the cover. The Virgin and the Magi, the judgment of Daniel, that of Solomon, and the three youths in the fiery furnace are represented on the four sides. Two rows of letters seem to be scratched on the bottom. These were first noted by Monsignor Enrico Villa. See P. L. Zovatto, "L'urnetta argentea di s. Ambrogio nell'ambito della rinascenza teodosiana," *Critica d'Arte* (Florence, 1956), XXI, pp. 2-11, where the graffiti on the bottom are also reproduced. The casket is now preserved in the treasury of the basilica of St. Nazarus on the Corso di Porta Romana at Milan. See Volbach-Hirmer, *Frühchristliche Kunst,* p. 65, nos. 110-115, where there are five large photographs of the box.

gian, even though it is true that the best of him is not to be found in his books. Although his writings were largely of an occasional character and the fruit of his preaching, they served to put the Christian world of the West in contact with that of the East, and had familiarized the West with the profound speculations of Eastern theologians. This was particularly true with respect to the doctrine of the Trinity.

In his exposition of the Incarnation, St. Ambrose stresses the true humanity of Christ and the role it plays in man's salvation. "The phrases which he uses to describe the two natures (human and divine) united in the one divine person of Christ were so happy that they were repeated at the councils of Ephesus (431) and Chalcedon (451)."[2] His explanation of the Redemption is not always consistent: he readily describes sin as a contract through which man sells himself to the devil; the latter, as a consequence, has rights over us which must be paid for by the blood of Christ. In the formulation of this theory, St. Ambrose follows Origen. It may well be that he had also read the indignant protest of St. Gregory of Nazianzus to such a concept. Elsewhere, however, he approaches the theory of substitution and satisfaction: Christ has satisfied God's justice in our stead; since He has been made one of us, He is one with us.

With a clarity and fullness that is new, Ambrose explains the doctrine of original sin. He points up the keen awareness which a Christian should have of the ruin wrought by sin and the need of grace. This train of thought was later deepened and developed by Augustine along the lines laid down by the bishop of Milan.

Just as sin unites a man with the devil almost as if in a single body, so grace, according to St. Ambrose, intimately unites the soul with God. He stresses the fact that the redemption of each soul is achieved by its personal union with Christ, and that this union can take place only in the Church, the virgin bride of Christ, the mother of countless children whom she has begotten through the sacraments.[3] This mysticism of St. Ambrose had a great influence on St. Augustine, and through him, upon the Christian piety of the West.

The doctrine of the Eucharist found in Ambrose one of its most important expounders: Christ is truly present in the Eucharist; the bread and wine are miraculously changed at the consecration so that they become something other than what they were before; this change is effected by the recitation of the words as instituted by Christ, that is, by divine words that have come from God. Ambrose also gives the oldest extant Latin text of these words in his treatise *On the Sacraments.*

Communion is the sign of the completed redemption. The purpose of the Mass is the offering which the Church makes of herself in union with Christ. It is also offered on behalf of the dead.

Penance as a sacrament is also the object of a lengthy exposition by St. Ambrose. He distinguishes between more serious faults, even those which are secret, for which there is need of a private confession to a priest followed by public penance, and the lighter daily failings which may be forgiven even without the intercession of the Church.

St. Ambrose also contributed greatly to devotion to Mary: the Madonna is the ideal virgin, the model and teacher of virginity; but she is also at the same time the Mother of God, the new Eve who begins a new history of the world. She is without stain of sin, the vanquisher of the devil, the symbol of the Church. Against the heretics he defended the virginity of Mary even *in partu,* that is, while giving birth.[4]

Ambrose's teaching on the primacy of the bishop of Rome is exceptionally clear. We have already seen his attitude toward the papacy in his description of the baptism of Satyrus: according to him, only those bishops are Catholic who are in communion with the Church of Rome. He was so emphatic on this point that Palladius, the bishop of Ratiaria deposed by the Council of Aquileia in 381, in a violent treatise accused him of making himself a slave to the bishop of Rome.[5]

At times it would seem that Ambrose, especially in his disputes with Theodosius, acted as if he represented the whole Church and not merely the see of Milan, and there is no questioning the fact that his personality was so strong that in certain crises he seems to have overshadowed the bishops of Rome. This has led even outstanding historians into the exaggeration of speaking of Ambrose as though he were the actual pope in the face of a number of bishops of Rome who by the same political circumstances had been reduced to a position of rather limited influence.

Some still speak of a rivalry between Milan and Rome. Support for this is supposed to be found in a certain coldness between the two, which many regard as quite undeniable. Other historians, however, are more reserved in their interpretation of the limited data available for deciding the question and admit neither the coldness nor the rivalry.

There can be no doubt as to the originality of St. Ambrose's concept of the relations between Church and State. We have already dealt with these when speaking of the struggle he had with the court of Justina and the vigorous action he took to see that Gratian carried out the conciliar decisions of Aquileia in 381.

The clear distinction between the two powers, their mutual autonomy, their necessary agreement in mixed matters, the subjection of the emperor to the Church when there is question of sin, the absolute supremacy of the moral law from which the civil authority is not exempt—all these are fruitful formulas foreshadowed in the works of St. Ambrose. Responsible historians are here unanimous in stating that the historical importance of Ambrose cannot be exaggerated. His thought strongly influenced Augustine, Gregory the Great, and the later popes of the Middle Ages.[6]

These are problems that are always with us since they are intimately involved in every civil society. They are never completely solved since the actual can never be conformed entirely to the ideal. They are difficult problems since their Christian solution opposes the inordinate desires arising from human ambition.

As a matter of fact, the Church achieves that which men allow it to achieve. It is to St. Ambrose's lasting credit that his keen intuition was able to point out the ideal which in time would become the teaching of the Church itself.

St. Ambrose was not led to a theoretical solution of these problems by a habit of speculation, for which he had neither the time nor the inclination, but by his pastoral interests. These same interests led him to attempt an exposition of Christian morality.

About the years 389-390, he published his treatise *On the Duties of Ecclesiastics*.[7] This is made up of a series of conferences to his young clergy. These were later put together to form a tract on Christian ethics which could be used instead of the great syntheses that had been made by pagan writers and philosophers.

The Christians did not as yet have a theoretical or practical exposition of moral problems in general. Ambrose attempted to fill the gap, and his work, although it is defective in its make-up, weak at times in argumentation, and lacking in unity and clarity, played an important role in the ecclesiastical traditions of the Middle Ages and marked an important date in the history of human thought.

The great number of manuscripts of this work that have come down from every century proves that it was widely read. Quotations from it show that it was an object of continuous study, even more, it must be confessed, than it was worth.

In composing his *De officiis,* Ambrose had before his eyes Cicero's work of the same name. And he followed its plan rather closely. In the first book, he points up the important distinction between the commandments and the counsels. He then discusses the morally good (the *honestum*) and the obligations which spring from the four cardinal virtues: wisdom, justice, temperance, and fortitude.

In the second book, he expounds the Christian concept of the supreme good in opposition to that of Cicero and other pagan philosophers. He also discusses the useful (the *utile*), which consists in goodness and piety, and is inseparable from the *honestum*, the morally good.

The third book is concerned with conflicts arising between the *honestum* and the *utile*. The major difficulties are resolved by appealing to the example of Christ our Lord, from which His followers can never prescind. This final book ends with a warm eulogy on friendship.

St. Ambrose not only takes the general plan of his work but also many ideas and whole phrases from Cicero, and in so doing he implicitly recognizes the permanent value of this work of the pagan moralist. It is rather distressing to note, however, that he feels no gratitude towards his model and holds him in slight esteem while borrowing extensively from him without any scruple. Instead, in a number of places, he rather paradoxically claims that, in plundering the works of Cicero and other pagan philosophers, Christians are doing no more than repossessing stolen property, since the pagans themselves had obtained their wisdom from the divinely inspired books of the Hebrews.[8] This was a conviction which he shared with earlier Christian writers and one which was probably derived from the Jews of Alexandria.

Nevertheless, St. Ambrose as a moralist has constructed something new since the Gospel upon which he builds his moral system is different from that upon which the pagans built theirs.[9] Though there were some exceptions, the pagans in general did not consider their obligations under a religious aspect, that is, as the expression of the will of God; for them, morality was something autonomous and, as a consequence, at least for ordinary mortals, something quite fragile.

In principle, though certainly not in practice, Cicero, the Roman aristocrat, did not recognize any obligations which he might have towards the plebeians, towards strangers, slaves, or women, but only towards himself and, by extension, towards the state, with which the aristocracy identified itself.

Christian morality, on the other hand, flows necessarily and logically from a faith in God. It is based on the teaching that God is the Father of all men and that He wishes to be loved in them. God is moreover the Giver of every good and particularly that of His Son, who died for man's salvation. He is also the Rewarder in the world to come, since the present life has meaning only in reference to it.

Ancient Stoicism furnished Ambrose with numerous concepts, divisions, and classifications. In accepting these, however, he transformed and animated them with a new spirit, defending them with new motives. Thus within the virtue of temperance, highly praised by the Stoics, he includes the Christian virtues of shame and modesty.

The Stoic ideal of conformity to nature as being the ultimate norm of morality is readily accepted and Christianized: nature for the Christian is the created image of God, and just as God cannot make anything which is not good, so evil is something contrary to nature.

And just as prudence for Ambrose also comprises piety towards God, so justice should be integrated with charity. This latter is not Cicero's beneficence which seeks the well-being only of those who act kindly towards us, or from whom such treatment is expected, but a much higher and much more active good: a virtue which invites us to do good to all, to go out in search of secret sorrows, to share poverty with the poor, to deprive ourselves so that others may not perish.

Like Cicero, St. Ambrose divides the virtue of fortitude into that which is domestic and that which is military. As a bishop primarily occupied with the care of souls, he touches only briefly on the latter. Nevertheless he shows his keen affection for his country, the Roman empire, even going so far as to confuse Christian fidelity with fidelity to Rome and permitting the practice of usury when it contributes to the harm of the barbarians. In contrast to the rigorism of Tertullian and Lactantius, who forbade Christians the use of arms, he admits that there is such a thing as a just war, though he would have preferred that such a war should be defensive rather than offensive. Still he believed that arms could be used to vindicate one's honor.

Both Aristotle and Horace had little regard for the *vulgus profanum*, people of a humble station in life. Those whom they esteemed, and in this Cicero was like them, were great-souled individuals. St. Ambrose, on the other hand, looked upon humility as a virtue, a kind of art: Christ died for the poor, for the common people, just as much as He did for those more favored, and He had advised His followers that they must become like little children if they wished to enter the kingdom of heaven. Aristotle brooked no interference in his personal affairs or suggestions as to what he should or should not do. He felt that his own knowledge was quite sufficient in such matters. The Christian, on the other hand, has learned to be docile. He knows his own weakness and his own ignorance. Morally he is always a beggar, and if he acts well, it is because he has received from the Lord both the will and the ability to do so.

For pagans in general, and not merely the pagan philosophers, poverty was a burden and almost a disgrace. In their eyes, one who like St. Ambrose gave away lands and homes was foolish. And yet, compassion and consideration for the weak and poor had been an essential part of Hebraic prophetism before it was taken up by Christianity.

We thus find in St. Ambrose's moral teaching a certain similarity to that of Cicero and the Stoics, but also striking innovations. The attempt to compare his work with that of Cicero and the Stoics is quite superficial. It is simply false to maintain that Christianity did no more than bring to completion an evolution that was already far advanced in pagan philosophical schools.

If the opposite were true, there is no means of explaining how it is that Christianity did not remain closed up in a school like the other systems of ethics but was instead spread far and wide throughout the world. Nevertheless it is still true that Christian moralists neither spurned nor rejected the patrimony of the past. By looking upon it as a treasure, and by holding on to what was best in it, they helped to mold our own Christian civilization.

The bishop of Milan was too intelligent to maintain that all Christians are saints and all pagans are scoundrels, that in actual practice Christianity is to paganism as light is to darkness. He had a keen realization of moral evil, and he strove with every means at his command to raise the moral tone of individuals and of society in general.

The world in which he lived was marred by flagrant inequalities. He defended the fundamental equality of men and their right to the goods of this world: "Philosophers have maintained that justice consists in looking upon common, that is, public goods, as being public, and upon private goods as something belonging to oneself. But not even this is a natural principle, for nature showers her gifts in common upon all. For God has so ordained that all things should be produced so that there should be common food for all, and that the earth should in a sense be the common possession of all. Common law is thus the product of nature, whereas private law has come from prescriptive use."[10] Even despite these words, which are frequently misunderstood, St. Ambrose was no more a socialist than Cicero, Seneca, or St. Basil of Caesarea. He was not condemning the social order of his day as something wrong, nor did he condemn outright the system of slavery that had been common from antiquity. He looked upon the emancipation of slaves as a work of Christian charity, but only when they had been properly prepared for their new status: "It is not nature that makes one a slave, but lack of wisdom; it is not manumission that makes one free, but education."[11]

St. Ambrose appeals to the status of men at the dawn of

history, not because he thought it possible to return to it, but because he wished to teach men the merely relative values of material goods and the grave obligations which men have of observing justice and charity. The Church in turn has always taught a certain detachment from the things of this world, and though she has favored just social reforms she had not advocated these at the expense of the legitimate rights of individuals. St. Ambrose impressed this also on the minds of his hearers by reminding them of the fact that God is concerned about men and their actions and that He at least, if no one else, will vindicate the weak that are trampled under foot. Further, though beasts may prey on one another, men should assist their fellow men. Obligations are the foundations of rights, and even a slave should enjoy the dignity of a man. These fundamental principles should help us to understand St. Ambrose's frequent attacks on avarice and those guilty of it, especially in his book on Naboth. And, as we have seen, before preaching in this manner, St. Ambrose had given an example of detachment by renouncing his own property before he became a bishop.

Paulinus in his biography of the saint tells us that he groaned at seeing the greediness of those in power, their love for money to the oppression of the poor.[12] On one particular occasion a usurious creditor would not allow his debtor to be buried until he had himself been paid. Ambrose ordered the body of the deceased to be carried into the usurer's house. Covered with confusion, the latter asked the bishop to spare him this shame. But Ambrose was resolute and the money-lender with his servants had to carry the dead man to his tomb.[13]

In his sermons Ambrose referred to many other incidents to illustrate his teaching. On one occasion he recalled a particularly distressing scene: a father grieving over the fact that he had not sold his sons to one who could at least have fed them.[14] He probably did not actually witness such an incident but rather read it in a homily of St. Basil.[15]

He raised his voice against the extravagant living of the

wealthy. When we recall how Symmachus spent vast sums on games to honor his son on his election to public office, we may well believe that St. Ambrose was not exaggerating when he described the homes and interests of the rich: they lived in huge palaces adorned with silver and gold, with rare marbles and mosaics; and their stables sheltered horses which they were training for the races. As for their tastes in food, "The sea does not suffice for their luxurious living. They must have special oyster beds so that they may know the age of each. And they build tanks for fish lest the sea fail to provide fish for their banquets."[16]

There were women who could not drink except from golden cups, nor sleep except on beds of silver, and whose fingers and necks were burdened with precious jewels. Though God is "a craftsman and painter of distinction," there are women who "erase that painting by smearing rouge upon their faces with their natural whiteness. The resulting picture is not one of beauty but of ugliness, of fraud rather than of simplicity. It is something passing that is spoiled by rain or perspiration. . . . Do not put aside the painting made by God to assume that of a prostitute."[17]

Ambrose also inveighs against the mania for the theater and the circus, where the populace of the city found nothing but incentives to laziness and vice.

Mention has already been made of Ambrose's earnest exhortations to a life of virginity and asceticism. Still, though he extolled continence, he did not condemn marriage, and he was anxious that married couples should lead a good life and be on their guard against certain abuses: "Men should learn to love their children. And this they may learn from the pious practice of crows who diligently accompany their offspring in flight, and, concerned lest they may possibly fail because of their weakness, they supply them with food and continue this office of feeding for a long time. On the other hand, the females of our species soon give up nursing even those whom they love or, if they are of the wealthier class, they disdain to nurse them at all. Those who are quite poor, on the other hand, expose their infants and cast them aside, and deny that they are theirs when discovered. Even the wealthy, in order that their inheritance may not be divided among many, kill their own offspring in the womb. With poisonous drugs they snuff out the fruit of the womb within this very organ, and thus life is taken away before it is given."[18]

St. Ambrose insists upon the mutual esteem and affection which husband and wife should have for one another: "If it happens that a husband should undertake a trip to a foreign land, no distance, no absence should weaken their mutual love. The same law binds the present and the absent; the same bond of nature preserves the rights of conjugal love between those who are far apart and those who are present to each other. The necks of both are joined together under the same blessed yoke even if one of them should find himself in some far off place, since they have received the yoke of grace, which is one of the spirit, not of the body. . . . Your husband endures your defects and your womanly fickleness, cannot you, O woman, endure your husband? Adam was deceived by Eve, and not Eve by Adam. It is right that he whom the woman induced to sin should assume the role of guide lest he fall again through feminine instability. But he is repugnant and uncouth! Yet once he pleased you. Should a husband be chosen at many different times? The ox and horse look for and love their mates, and if another is substituted in their place, they are unable to bear the yoke and feel that something is lacking to them. You repudiate your partner and think that a change should frequently be made. And if he fails you for a single day, you bring in a rival, and immediately without knowing the reason, yet consciously, you do violence to your sense of shame. . . . Adultery is a serious offense and a sin against nature. In the beginning God formed two creatures, Adam and Eve, that is, man and wife. He formed woman from man, that is, from Adam's rib. And He ordered them both to live in one body and in one spirit. Why do you separate the one body? Why do you divide the one spirit?"[19]

In commenting on St. Paul's advice to the Corinthians, "Art thou bound to a wife? Do not seek to be freed," St. Ambrose observes. "It is well said that 'You are bound,' since man and wife are bound together by a bond of love and are linked to each other by the bridle of affection."[20] On the other hand, when the pagans spoke of love or wrote about it in verse, they did not as a rule take as their theme the love of husband and wife. In this matter of conjugal morality, Ambrose is very practical, much more so in fact than some modern moralists. He insists upon temperance even in the use of marriage. He recalls the words of St. Paul on the advantages of temporary abstinence by mutual consent for advance in the spiritual life, openly teaching that temperance is necessary here as well as in eating and drinking, even going so far as to say that one who goes against the apostle's advice is a kind of adulterer.[21]

He condemns the revels of the rich in scorching terms, the orgies of the officials, the excessive luxury of the nobles. To make his audience appreciate more fully their degradation, he describes wretched soldiers who lose their wits in drink and women who carry on like bacchants.[22]

It was also his duty to correct. Besides pagans and Arians, there were lax Catholics in the city. Among their faults, as we have already seen when speaking of St. Monica at Milan, was the way they celebrated the feasts of the martyrs: "They carry their cups to the tombs of the martyrs and drink there till evening and think that they otherwise cannot be heard. O the folly of men, who think that drunkenness is a sacrifice, who think that drunkenness pleases those who learned to endure their suffering by fasting!"[23]

Ambrose also warned his clergy about "vagabonds." They should watch out for those individuals who were well and strong but who came to beg for food and lodging solely because they were "taking a trip." Another curious phenomenon of the time were the pilgrims (or *periodeutoi*) who, after obtaining letters of commendation from their bishop *(litterae formatae)* travelled about visiting the more important shrines while expecting hospitality of the local churches.[24] The councils of Elvira, Arles, and Sardica were all concerned with this problem. A canon of the Council of Nimes of the year 394 states that no one is obliged to offer hospitality to such individuals who revel in the alms of the churches.[25]

The bishop was also a father. If he showed great severity towards evildoers, he showed even greater kindness to the poor, the sinners, and to all those who had need of encouragement, advice, and consolation.

A certain bishop Marcellus had given his possessions to a widowed sister on condition that when she died she would leave them to the Church. Her brother Laetus, however, attacked the validity of the gift. The case was tried before the tribunal at Milan, but no decision was reached. It was then entrusted to Ambrose so that he might work out an equitable solution.

Ambrose, who had much experience with cases in court, was able to decide the matter to the satisfaction of all. He assigned the goods of Marcellus to Laetus on the condition that he provide his widowed sister with an annual income. This also pleased Marcellus, who was happy to see his relatives again at peace with each other. The only party that seems to have lost out was the Church, but St. Ambrose declared: "Nothing is taken away from the Church that is a gain for piety. For charity is not a loss for Christ, but a gain. . . . Do not fear that the Church has no share or part in your liberality. It has received even greater fruits from you. It has received the advantage of your learning. It has the service of your life. It has the profit of your ministeries."[26]

Sisinnius, one of Ambrose's friends, refused to keep his son any longer in his house, and still less his son's wife, whom he had married against his wishes. Though Ambrose, as we know from Possidius, would not on principle undertake to procure a wife for anybody, he took the side of the son in this particular instance and wrote as follows to his father: "I attribute it more to your own piety than to your love for us that you have forgiven at my request our son for having taken a wife without consulting you. . . . You have done well in recognizing yourself as a father. You were rightly indignant, and I am glad to admit the fault so that your fatherly indulgence may be more highly praised. The offense, moreover, was committed against you as a father since you should have chosen by your own judgment one who was to have the place of a daughter. For we obtain children either by nature or by choice; in the former instance there is the element of chance, in the latter that of judgment. . . . You have a right to be angry with your son in that he chose a wife for himself, but also a reason for forgiving him. You have acquired a daughter without the peril of making a choice yourself. If he has chosen a good one, he has obtained a grace; but if he has erred, you will make them better by welcoming them, and worse by rejecting them. Indeed it is a better plan for a girl to be given to one's son by his father; but there is a greater show of respect when she is brought by the son to his father, and when chosen by her husband is brought into the home of her father-in-law. The son fears that his choice may be displeasing, and the daughter-in-law that her attention may be the same. The father's right to choose her makes her proud and haughty; fear of offense humbles her; and shame keeps her in her place. If your son is perhaps offended, as commonly happens, he will not be able to blame his wife as if he were free from blame himself. Rather he will strive to show at once the good judgment which he had in his choice of a wife and her respect for him."[27]

Truly we see here how the bees placed their honey in the mouth of the lion.

A virgin of Verona by the name of Indicia was accused of

breaking her vow of chastity. She made an appeal to St. Ambrose, and he ardently defended her against what he thought was an unjust calumny.[28]

Since at this time Aquileia was not yet a metropolis, the bishops of the province Venetia-Histria, among whom was the bishop of Verona, were suffragans to the bishop of Milan. Indicia, condemned by her own bishop, used her right of appeal and took her case to Milan. Ambrose made a complete investigation of the matter. He summoned her accusers before his tribunal. He inquired into how the trial had been conducted by Syagrius, the bishop of Verona. He investigated the rumors which had spread the report that Indicia had not only violated her vow of chastity but had also killed her child. In his letter to Syagrius on his conduct of the investigation, he deplores the fact that at Verona they had wanted to submit the woman to a physical examination by obstetricians. He notes that physicians themselves are skeptical about the conclusions to be derived from such an examination. Nevertheless, he later hinted to his sister Marcellina that she might be willing to be a witness to such an examination if Syagrius should request it. Marcellina declined the invitation but said that she had never noticed any defects in Indicia's character, that she had lived chastely in the home of the Ambrosii at Rome after her brother had already left the city. After consulting other bishops on the matter, Ambrose finally decided that Indicia was innocent of the charges laid against her. He excommunicated her accusers, and in his letter to Syagrius he reproaches him from having been influenced by others and reminds him that bishops should rather establish than receive norms of conduct. He expresses the hope that the people of Verona will not be offended by his decision: as a rule they do not find fault with the measures taken by their metropolitan.

The authenticity of a discourse *On the Fall of a Consecrated Virgin (De lapsu virginis consecratae)*, which is found among the works of Ambrose, is rather doubtful. But even if the bishop who wrote it was not Ambrose, some of the thoughts expressed in the work are much like those of the bishop of Milan.[29]

A virgin of a noble family, after consecrating herself to God, committed a grave sin and then killed the child that had been born as the result of her fall. The author of this work defends the good name of other virgins and condemns in strongest terms the guilty parties. He recalls the day of the woman's solemn consecration, and in the end he reminds the woman of what she should do to redeem herself.

The difference between the punishment inflicted upon fallen virgins by pagans and by Christians is even here symbolic. During this same century, Symmachus asked the magistrates at Rome to inflict the ancient penalty of entombment while still alive upon a Vestal who had been unfaithful, whereas in these two instances we have a milder law at work.[30] Ambrose defends the Christian woman who has been accused, and the author of the *De lapsu virginis* invites the guilty woman to repentance.

Studius, a Christian magistrate, asked Ambrose if it were licit for him to condemn criminals to death. The bishop replied that he could rightly make use of the sword but he advised him to be lenient. If even the pagans think it praiseworthy to administer public office without shedding blood, how much more praiseworthy should it be for Christians? In any case, even if on the day when he condemns a person to death Studius does not necessarily have to abstain from receiving the sacraments, he would do well in voluntarily abstaining out of respect and reverence for sacred things.[31]

The sum total of St. Ambrose's works makes it quite clear that he was not a pessimist. St. Augustine, on the other hand, who confessed himself to be a "pupil" of the bishop of Milan, was greatly preoccupied with the problem of the mingling of good and evil in the world and even in the Church. And he seems to have been frightened by it all. Though St. Ambrose was also aware of this problem, he was not alarmed. "Your

Church does not say: 'I am well, and I do not need a physician,' but 'Heal me, O Lord, and I will be healed: save me, and I will be saved.' An image of Your Church is found in that woman who came from behind and touched the hem of Your garment saying within herself: 'If I will but touch his garment I will be saved.' The Church, therefore, confesses her wounds; she desires to be cured."[32]

At Milan, just as in Africa, when there were gladiatorial shows or contests in the circus, St. Ambrose must have frequently noticed that only a few came to listen to him. St. Augustine was disconsolate at seeing the church empty on such days, and he was horrified at the thought that many of those who were entranced by the obscene shows of the mimes were the same people whom he would later see in church on Christmas and Easter.[33] Such complaints are not found in St. Ambrose. It may be that he had a deeper appreciation of human weakness. It may also be that he knew that religion, like human affection, is something quite delicate, and that, as a consequence, only a few are capable of reaching its heights.

A great modern theologian who had read many times through the very extensive works of St. Augustine came to the conclusion that the African bishop leaves an impression of defeat and disillusionment: the activity of the Church upon earth according to him is more a work of salvage than one of progressive construction; it is a question of saving what can be saved from certain shipwreck; the world is like a sick man without means of recovery though his doctor continues to treat him as the disease spreads through his body.[34] Ambrose, on the other hand, is never so sad or gloomy: human realities, though tainted with evil, always remain good. They are "creations," that is, works of God who can draw good even out of evil: "Look down, O Lord, upon the weakness of the human race and see the wounds which You [by Your coming] have cured. No matter how great is Your regard for us, You will find still more reasons for compassion. Extend, we pray, Your healing hands; and cure what is ill, strengthen what is doubtful, and preserve in constant faith what is already sound."[35]

This represents not only the moral teaching of St. Ambrose but that of Christianity as well. We find in both a great understanding of men and of their weaknesses, a reasonable confidence in their potentialities, an ardent striving after the highest ideals, which for many are actually unattainable, in the conviction that the effort is not made in vain, an absolute confidence in the assistance of our Heavenly Father, a large sympathy for everything in the world of nature and of art, an interest in science and in faith, since the kingdom of God is at hand when God shall be all in all. This moral teaching is, in fine, that harmony of concepts, sentiments, and norms of conduct which Newman has called "the fullness of Catholicism."[36]

XVI
Music and Poetry

o

Innovations introduced by St. Ambrose in Church music and chant. His poetry. The hymn of morning. The hymn of evening. The martyrdom of St. Agnes. The prayer of the virgins. The inscriptions. Titles for pictures.

According to a tradition based on the *Confessions* of St. Augustine, St. Ambrose became a poet during the siege of the Milanese basilicas in 386. It should be remembered, however, that the *Confessions* were written at least ten years after those eventful days and that St. Augustine did not carefully distinguish what had been introduced at this time by St. Ambrose. Further, it is practically impossible to believe that there was no singing at all before this in the churches at Milan. There must have been at least some chanting of the psalms as there was elsewhere.

What St. Ambrose introduced at this time must consequently have been antiphonal singing: the singing was no longer limited to a single voice which the congregation answered from time to time, but a regular choir was formed and trained. This group could then sing more elaborate compositions or could join in with the people in singing antiphonally, one group alternating with the other.

The *holy nail* is enclosed in a crystal container and reserved in a niche high in the vault of the apse of the cathedral of Milan. Every year on May 3 it is brought down for public veneration. The picture is a copy of a copper engraving, sufficiently faithful, that is to be found on the frontispiece of G. V. Corno, *Il sacro chiodo, tesoro del Duomo di Milano* (Milan, 1647). The holy nail in the cathedral of Carpentras retains the shape of an ancient bit, two types of which may be seen below. See Ch. Rohault de Fleury, *Memoire sur les instruments de la passion de N.S.J.C.* (Paris, 1870), pp. 172 ff. It is not known when the nail in the cathedral of Milan was brought there. The earliest evidence for its presence in the old cathedral, St. Thecla, is in a document of 1389 which states that "one of the nails has been kept there from ancient times"—*in ipsa repositus ab antiquo unus ex clavis.* See A. Tamborini, *Un'insigne reliquia della passione nel Duomo di Milano* (Milan, 1933), p. 26. The contrivance of ropes and pulleys used for lifting the cloud which raises the canons on May 3, so that they can take down the reliquary, was made from a design of Leonardo da Vinci in 1489.

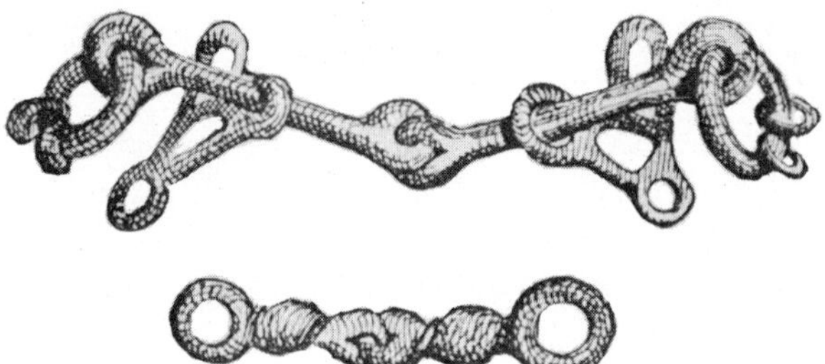

Music was actually something new in the Church in the fourth century. From the letter of Pliny to Trajan, written about the year 112 A.D., we know that the small bands of Christians who met together during the first centuries did sing some hymns, but the singing was probably quite simple and may have been little more than a mere recitative.[1] On the other hand, when the early *domus Ecclesiae*, or chapel in some private home, was replaced by the basilica which could hold large crowds of people coming together for the celebration of the Eucharist, it seemed proper to make use of more elaborate modes of music along with the other arts to enhance the splendor of the religious functions. The practice seems to have had its origins towards the middle of the fourth century in the churches at Antioch and in the Euphrates valley, that is, among those churches which used Syriac in their liturgy.

In a letter written in 375, St. Basil defends himself from the criticism of those who blamed him for having introduced antiphonal singing into his church at Caesarea. He notes that it is a custom which is now spread throughout the churches of Egypt, Palestine, Syria, and those along the Euphrates.[2] In the Church of Antioch music and chant were so far developed that, as we have already seen, bishop Flavian had the Antiochian melodies sung at the emperor's table when he went to Constantinople to intercede for the people with Theodosius. In 398, when St. John Chrysostom became bishop of Constantinople, he introduced the Antiochian melodies into his church.[3]

Just as Antioch was the center of diffusion for music in the East, so Milan became the leader in antiphonal singing in the West. According to both St. Augustine and Paulinus, it was St. Ambrose who introduced this type of singing.[4] Both declare that he introduced it during the weeks in the spring of 386 when the basilicas at Milan were being "besieged."

The older way of singing in church was rather austere: a reader chanted a psalm in such a restrained fashion that it seemed more like reading than singing, while the congregation stood listening to him. This is what Athanasius used to do at Alexandria.[5] When St. Ambrose improved on this older custom, he may have been the subject of some criticism as St. Basil had been at Caesarea before him.[6] At least when explaining Psalm LXVIII, he seems to allude to some objections as he discusses the introduction of music and chant into the temple at Jerusalem by Solomon, the driving out of the evil spirit that tormented Saul by David's playing on the harp, and the harmonies that rang through the house in the parable as the father of the prodigal celebrated his son's return.

Since he had grown up in an aristocratic milieu where music was considered to be an integral part of a youth's education, St. Ambrose was more favorably inclined towards it than St. Augustine.[7] The latter looked upon music as something rather vain and superfluous, whereas St. Ambrose had a high regard for it and was enthralled to hear the choral singing in his church.

St. Ambrose's innovations must have created something of a sensation in the other churches, but they came in time to imitate them.[8] For this, of course, there was need of more than the simple desire since the proper execution of musical works demands talents not possessed by all and a good deal of time for practice and other means as well.

Roman tradition, represented in the *Liber Pontificalis*, attributes the introduction of antiphonal singing at Rome to Pope Celestine I (422-432).[9] This is quite in keeping with Roman conservatism which would have waited for some decades before adopting such an innovation. But since the notice is due to the second editor of this work on the popes of Rome, there can be some questioning its authenticity. Still it seems that Celestine I, though he was born at Rome, spent some time in his youth with St. Ambrose at Milan.[10]

In the year 430, when he was presiding over a council being held at Rome, he declared while speaking against the doctrines of the Nestorians: "I remember that once on the Birthday of our Lord Jesus Christ, Ambrose of blessed memory had all the people sing in unison: 'Come, O Redeemer of the nations. Show Yourself, the offspring of a virgin, and let every age marvel, for such a birth alone befits God.' " The incident must have occurred at Milan since this hymn was not sung at Rome during the time of Pope Celestine, nor for centuries after.

The music which St. Ambrose introduced into his church was different from that which was to be heard at the time in the theaters. It was both new and religious in character. In his *Hexameron* he exhorts his subjects to take their pleasure "not in the harmful songs and the music of the stage which soften the mind for sensual loves but in the chants of the Church and the voice of the people singing in harmony the praises of God."[11]

Questions discussed by specialists are whether Ambrose personally composed the music which he introduced into his church at Milan, or whether others composed it under his direction, or whether, as seems more probable, he adapted to Latin hymns melodies that had already been used for some decades at Antioch and in other cities of the East.[12] The "Ambrosian" chant now used in the churches of Milan is preserved in manuscripts no earlier than the twelfth century. It is thus difficult to determine how faithfully the present manner of singing reflects that of the time of St. Ambrose. Some musical critics believe that Ambrosian, in comparison with Gregorian chant, is more primitive, freer, and more spontaneous. Others, however, are of a contrary opinion. To them it seems more elaborate. One of the greatest medieval authorities on chant, Guido d'Arezzo, thought that he perceived a certain harmony in the apparent lack of form and structure in the chants of the "sweetest Ambrose."

During the fourth century, poetry was much in fashion.[13] There was such a mania for it that everybody wrote poems. Pope Damasus, despite his many cares as bishop of Rome, continued to write verse because of the high regard that was felt for it, even though his own compositions were as dry as nails and without any play of the imagination.[14] At this time there were even handbooks on chronology and history written in verse. That Ambrose should have learned how to write poetry is, as a consequence, not at all surprising. But in contrast with many of his contemporaries, a careful examination of St. Ambrose's hymns will show that he possessed a certain poetic inspiration and inner fire that are essential to a real poet.

He composed hymns as a means of instructing his people in a way that they would appreciate and understand. Simple people as a rule do not retain long in their minds exact, formal instructions, or, as he called them, *violentiora praecepta.*[15] He therefore wrote hymns which they could sing, as heretics had already done before him.

During the siege of the basilicas in the spring of 386 his hymns proved to have an almost magical efficacy. Though already composed or even in use, in that atmosphere of tension and enthusiasm, they provided an outlet for the aspirations and feelings of the people. But Ambrose's poetic talents are to be seen in his other works as well. Many of the pages of his *Hexameron* are really prose poems.

He moreover possessed the essential requirements for writing poetry: a creative imagination, an absolute disinterestedness, an ardent enthusiasm, and the ability to see parallels between the world of the senses and of faith. In addition to this there were obvious reasons why he should have given poetical expression to truths which had urgent need of being taught. Among these could be listed the already existing practice of singing hymns during the course of the liturgical functions and the use which the Arians had made and were still making of poetry to spread their own teachings.[16]

In writing to the Ephesians, St. Paul urged these early converts "not to be drunk with wine but to be filled with the Holy Spirit," speaking to themselves "in psalms, and hymns, and spiritual canticles, singing and making melody" in their hearts to the Lord.[17] And in the same spirit he wrote to the Colossians:

"Let the word of Christ dwell in you abundantly, in all wisdom; teaching and admonishing one another in psalms, hymns, and spiritual canticles, singing in your hearts to God by his grace."[18] From the description which the Christians of Bithynia gave to Pliny of their meetings, we know that part of the liturgy consisted in singing a song "to Christ as God"—*carmen Christo quasi Deo*.[19] In the early third century in North Africa, as we know from Tertullian, the Christians at their evening services also sang hymns which they took either from the scriptures or which they had composed themselves.[20]

As we have already noted, heretics, and particularly the Arians, made use of hymns to spread their doctrines. The rapid diffusion of Arianism may be partially explained by the popularity of Arius's *Thalia*, a medley of verse and prose, in which he explained his notions about Christ in a manner that appealed to the masses. Ballads which he composed were sung *ad nauseam* by sailors, merchants, and travelers in the streets and harbors of the Mediterranean world. It is quite possible that Auxentius at Milan, among his other innovations, had introduced such Arian songs.

The first to attempt to compose hymns for the liturgical functions in the West was Hilary of Poitiers, but he failed in his endeavors, not so much perhaps because of the insensitivity of the Gauls, as because of the obscurity and heaviness of his works. At least this would seem to be the reason from the extant fragments, though there is some doubt about their authenticity.

Ambrose, on the other hand, was so successful in his own endeavors that his hymns began to be used throughout all the churches, and the term "Ambrosian" became synonymous with "hymn." His fame as a composer, which he enjoyed even in antiquity, as we know from the *Confessions* of St. Augustine, the Rule of St. Benedict, and the writings of St. Isidore of Seville, is ample proof of the fact that Ambrose must have written a number of them.

The fact that many hymns which he could not have written

have also been attributed to him is a further proof of his labors along this line.

In the edition of Ambrose's works published by the Maurists, twelve hymns are regarded as authentic; eighty-two others printed in an appendix are considered to be spurious. Just as more recent hymns have been introduced into the office, so the hymns of St. Ambrose, by being used first in the office at Milan and later in that of the Latin Church in general, have become common property.

Modern critics, as a rule, continue to be skeptical: they regard as authentic only the four hymns that can be expressly attributed to Ambrose from the testimony of St. Augustine. This has led them to minimize the poetic gifts of the bishop, even though these four poems deserve more attention than they have been willing to give them.

But now critics are beginning to realize that these four hymns cannot by themselves explain the renown which Ambrose has as an hymnographer.

St. Augustine was at Milan for only three years (384-387). In later life he does not seem to have been in contact with the church at Milan. In his *Confessions* he mentions only those hymns which were to be frequently heard in the basilicas at Milan. There could have been others, since his remarks about these four are simply made in passing. Further, in the following ten years, St. Ambrose could have composed a number of others.

A Milanese scholar has attempted to prove the authenticity of eighteen hymns. To support this he has collected the ancient evidence with respect to these hymns, the use which was made of them in the liturgy at Milan, and the resemblance which they bear in thought and expression to the known works of St. Ambrose.[21] Though his arguments have been questioned, there are other scholars who now believe that he has proved his point.

Like much other poetry, the hymns of St. Ambrose are not always immediately comprehensible. Art is as varied as life, and not every form of life is intelligible to all. There can be truly great art which demands a certain disposition in the recipient before it can be understood or appreciated. St. Ambrose's hymns are religious poetry. They are not necessarily intellectual in character, but they appeal strongly to the affections. They find their response in a heart that is not too preoccupied with worldly problems.

It should not be surprising that certain elements in fifteenth-century humanism contemned Dante, and that the Enlightenment of the eighteenth century failed to understand him. Something similar has happened to the poetry of St. Ambrose. If its thrill and charm are to be appreciated, it would be well to listen to these hymns as chanted in the office by a choir of well-trained Benedictine monks.

In his poetry, Ambrose expressed his most intimate thoughts and feelings, and he expressed them in a form acquired with a considerable amount of effort. His style was deliberately popular: his writing is facile, clear, and supple. At times his hymns are burdened by the heaviness of their thought, but elsewhere the inspiration is sustained. They are universal in their sentiments and simple in their perfection.

One of the best known hymns of St. Ambrose is the *Aeterne rerum Conditor*, which is recited in the Roman office at Lauds from the second Sunday after the Epiphany to Septuagesima Sunday, and from the Sunday nearest the first of October to Advent:

O Everlasting Architect,
  Who dost renew the day and night,
And by the seasons' change effect
  In sated hearts a fresh delight:

Behold! the Herald of the Day—
  Who as a lamp when light is gone,
Doth watches of the night display—
  Now wakes the splendors of the dawn.

And as he sings, the morning star
Dissolves the darkness of the sky:
The motley crews of night afar
From wonted paths of evil fly:

The weary sailor laughs once more,
The waves a softer song begin;
Yea, and the Church's Rock doth pour
Forth-gushing floods to drown his sin.

Arouse ye, then, as duty bids!
The Cock doth call to sleeping eyes;
He chides the heavy slumberous lids;
Rebukes the limbs that will not rise.

The clarion call of Chanticleer
Unto the sick brings health again;
The robber's sword is sheathed in fear;
And trust returns to fallen men.

Jesu! behold the wavering will,
And with a glance our fault reprove;
If Thou but look on us, the ill
We do dissolves in tears of love.

True Light, our hearts flood with Thy rays:
Let sleep from all our senses flee;
Thee let our voice first sing in praise,
Our hearts pay vows of love to Thee.[22]

A companion piece and sequel to the preceding hymn is the *Splendor paternae gloriae*, which is recited on Mondays at Lauds in the Roman office. It is a morning hymn to the Blessed Trinity, to Christ as the Light of the World, and contains petitions for help and guidance during the coming day:

O Thou the Father's Image blest!
  Who callest forth the morning ray;
O Thou eternal Light of Light!
  And inexhaustive Fount of Day!

True Sun! upon our souls arise.
  Shining in beauty evermore;
And through each sense the quic'ning beam
  Of the eternal Spirit pour.

Thee, too, O Father we entreat,
  Father of might and grace divine!
Father of glorious majesty!
  Thy pitying eye on us incline.

Confirm us in each good resolve;
  The tempter's envious rage subdue;
Turn each misfortune to our good;
  Direct us right in all we do.

Rule Thou our inmost thoughts; let no
  Impurity our hearts defile;
Grant us a true and fervent faith;
  Grant us a spirit free from guile.

May Christ Himself be our true food,
  And faith our daily cup supply;
While from the Spirit's tranquil depth
  We drink unfailing draughts of joy.

Still ever with the peep of morn
  May saintly modesty attend;
Faith sanctify the midday hours;
  Upon the soul no night descend.

Fast breaks the dawn, each whole in each,
  Come, Father blest! Come, Son most high!
Shine in our souls, and be to them
  The dawn of immortality.[23]

The *Rerum Deus tenax vigor* is found in the Roman breviary for None:

O strength, and stay upholding all creation,
Who ever dost Thyself unmoved abide,
Yet day by day the light in due gradation
From hour to hour through all its changes guide:

Grant to life's day a calm unclouded ending,
An eve untouched by shadows of decay,
The brightness of a holy deathbed blending
With dawning glories of the eternal day.

Hear us, O Father, gracious and forgiving,
And thou, O Christ, the co-eternal Word,
Who, with the Holy Ghost, by all things living
Now and to endless ages art adored.[24]

As a final example of St. Ambrose's verse, we may give a translation of the *Jesu, corona virginum,* which is recited at Lauds and Vespers on the feast of a virgin:

Thou crown of all the virgin choir!
  That holy mother's virgin Son!
Who is, alone of womankind,
  Mother and virgin both in one!

Encircled by Thy virgin band,
  Amid the lilies Thou art found;
For Thy pure brides with lavish hand
  Scattering immortal graces round.

And still, wherever Thou dost bend
  Thy lovely steps, O glorious King,
Virgins upon Thy steps attend,
  And hymns to Thy high glory sing.

Keep us, O purity divine,
  From every least corruption free;
Our every sense from sin refine,
  And purify our souls for Thee.[25]

Just as it is impossible to fully appreciate the poetry of Sappho without knowing Greek, or of Shelley without knowing English, or Leopardi without a knowledge of Italian, so it is impossible to appreciate the poetry of St. Ambrose unless one can read it in Latin, or, better still, hear it chanted in that ancient tongue. As we know from St. Augustine's description of the emotions which he experienced after his conversion, these poems must have had a powerful effect upon the faithful at Milan: "How I wept as I was deeply moved by the voices of Your Church sweetly swelling in the singing of Your hymns and canticles!"[26] And elsewhere he confesses that in trying to avoid the pleasure which he found in singing, he sometimes became excessively severe: "Sometimes, I could wish that all the sweet melody of the chants with which the psalms of David are accompanied were banished from my ears and from the whole Church. And then it seems to me safer to follow what I remember was often told me about Bishop Athanasius of Alexandria. He had the reader of the psalms modulate his voice so slightly that it was closer to speaking than to singing. But when I remember the tears which I shed at the singing in Your Church when I had first recovered my faith, and now when I am affected not by the singing, but by the words which are sung, if they are sung in a clear voice and with a suitable inflection, I again recognize the great advantages of this custom."[27]

Ambrose was also pleased to hear the singing of the faithful in the church. When the whole people were united in prayer and were alternately chanting the verses of the psalms, the voices of the men, women, and children were "like the sound of breaking waves."[28]

To the objection that the Apostle bids women to be silent in church, St. Ambrose replied that the chanting of psalms "is suitable for those of both sexes, and of any age."[29] When he was accused of influencing the people in this way, he confessed as much: "They say that I have bewitched the people with the hymns I have given them to sing. I do not at all deny it. This singing is something great, in fact there can be nothing more wonderful. For what can be more marvelous than a profession of faith in the Trinity as is daily done by the mouths of all the people?"[30]

At Milan the liturgy is celebrated in what is known as the "Ambrosian rite."[31] How much does this depend upon St. Ambrose? At least the antiphons and hymns are to be attributed to him. But do the prayers which are recited from the Ambrosian missal in more than a thousand churches in the diocese of Milan also come from his pen? In many instances this would be difficult, if not impossible to determine, but certainly some of them, especially those attached to the oldest feasts, may safely be ascribed to him.

When St. Ambrose became the bishop of Milan after the church there had been ruled by an Arian for almost twenty years, he must have had to make many reforms, and among these must have been some connected with the liturgy. As he himself observed, his lawful predecessor, Dionysius, had prayed to die in exile so that he would not have to see what the Arians had done to the Church at Milan. In his first years as bishop, Ambrose for the sake of peace must have limited himself to restoring old traditions. Later he was free to introduce changes that have since become famous.

An eighth-century pilgrim copied down three inscriptions in elegiac distichs composed by St. Ambrose, thus preserving them for posterity.[32] Though their number is limited, the great Roman archaeologist Giovanni Battista De Rossi was of the opinion that they were considerably better than many of those written by Pope St. Damasus. The first of these, in four lines, adorned the tomb of the bishop's brother Satyrus. The second, of ten lines, recalled the dedication of the basilica of the Apostles. This church, built in the shape of a cross on the Via Romana, was the one in which St. Ambrose placed the relics of the martyr Nazarius. The third and last of these inscriptions was the one within the baptistery adjoining the *basilica maior:* "This eight-apsed temple was built for sacred use. The font is also octagonal, worthy of the gift that it procures. It was fitting that the place destined for baptism, from which the people receive salvation from the light of the risen Christ, should be built according to this [sacred] number. . . ." The whole inscription comprises eight distichs, or sixteen lines. This was in keeping with Neoplatonic speculations according to which the number eight, the ogdoad, was a symbol of perfection. Eight-apsed baptisteries were found elsewhere as well. There is one near the Lateran basilica in Rome, another at Albenga, another at Ventimiglia, two at Ravenna, and others in France and Spain.

Finally, we have forty-two hexameters arranged in couplets that were composed by St. Ambrose.[33] These were copied down by French pilgrims and first published by François Juret, a canon of Langres, in the sixteenth century. The couplets were composed by St. Ambrose to serve as titles or explanations for twenty-one scenes from the Old and New Testaments which were painted on the walls of the Ambrosian basilica. Unfortunately, just as the primitive walls of the basilica have long since disappeared, so have the paintings. Nevertheless even the record of their former existence throws valuable light on the character of St. Ambrose. Whereas the intellectually-minded St. Augustine regarded paintings and sculpture as something superfluous, the bishop of Milan was of a more practical bent: the common people do not as a rule read books that could instruct them, but they can learn much from a beautiful statue or picture.

A caricature of Christ on the cross. The figure on the T-shaped cross is standing on a *suppedaneum,* or small platform, with its arms extended. The head, which is that of an ass, is turned towards another figure whose left hand is raised in the ancient attitude of adoration. The Greek below states: ΑΛΕΞΑΜΕΝΟϹ ϹΕΒΕΤΕ ΘΕΟΝ, that is, *'Αλεξάμενος σέβεται θεόν*—"Alexamenos adores his God." This famous graffito, which probably comes from the third century, was found in 1856 on a wall of an aula on the Palatine in Rome. See H. Leclercq, "Croix et crucifix," *Dict. Arch. chrét. et de Lit.,* III (1913), cc. 3050-56. The fragment of the wall containing this drawing was taken from the Palatine to the Museo Kircheriano. See E. De Ruggiero, *Guida* (Rome, 1879), p. 62. The drawing reproduced here was verified for Rohault by Father Tongiorgi, who was at that time the director of the Museo Kircheriano. The original is now found at the National Museum in Rome, Room XXXIX.

XVII
The Exile

o

The antipagan legislation of Theodosius. The Council of Capua. Valentinian II and Arbogast. Ambrose's hesitation. The usurpation of Eugenius. The pagan reaction. Ambrose leaves Milan. The battle of the Frigidus. The legacy of Theodosius.

The slaying of the spectators in the circus at Thessalonica and the public penance of the emperor on Christmas, 390, were events of no small moment. In the popular imagination, St. Ambrose assumed the figure of a John the Baptist confronting Herod, or of a prophet Nathan pointing his finger at David. The same is found in the fantasies of some modern historians who portray Theodosius as yielding to the bishop's every whim. But for the emperor's antipagan legislation of the year 391, there is no need to postulate any influence on the part of Ambrose. A decree given at Milan on February 24 ordered Albinus, the prefect of Rome, to forbid any kind of open pagan worship in the city: the temples must not be entered for the sake of offering a sacrifice or paying a visit. Serious penalties are provided for officials who might tolerate any infractions of this decree.[1]

On June 9, 391, a law was published at Concordia which was aimed at apostates from Christianity. It reaffirmed their incapacity to bear witness in court, to inherit, and their lack of civil status because of their infamy.[2]

While he was still in northern Italy, Theodosius received news of grave disorders in Egypt. The bishop, Theophilus, had obtained possession of a temple which he planned to convert into a church. In it a number of obscene cult objects were found.[3] To ridicule this aspect of some of the mystery religions, Theophilus had these objects paraded through the squares of the city. The pagans were naturally offended and rushed upon the Christians. In the ensuing conflict a good many were killed or wounded, though there were more casualties among the Christians than among the pagans. Helladius, one of the chiefs of the pagan party, later boasted that on this occasion he had killed nine Christians with his own hands. Theodosius intervened. In June, 391, he issued an order at Aquileia closing the pagan temples also at Alexandria.[4] According to Theodoret, Theophilus ordered the great statue of Serapis to be torn down, but no earthquake occurred as his worshipers had foretold when its head was struck off with an ax. Instead, an army of mice came running out of the open wooden trunk. The great god of the Egyptians was thus no more than a nest for mice![5] But it was not so easy to abolish the worship of Serapis. It was on this occasion that the library in the great Serapeum was sacked while the shattered pieces of the colossal statue of the god were burned in the amphitheater amidst the shouts of the people.

Finally, with a law of November 8, 392, Theodosius prohibited all pagan worship throughout the whole of the empire. This included acts of worship within the home. A fine of twenty pounds of gold was decreed for all those who would still offer sacrifices in temples that were not on their own private property.[6] This legislation marked the end of paganism. From this time on it survived only in the fields and country districts *(pagi)*. As the Christians had been accustomed to say for centuries when reciting the psalms of David, the ancient gods now became identified with the devils: "For all the gods of the Gentiles are devils."[7] Other riots occurred, if not on the same scale as at Alexandria. St. Augustine tells us that in Colonia Sufetana, a town in what is now Tunisia, sixty Christians were massacred by the pagans in retaliation for the destruction of a local statue of Hercules.[8] He further states, however, that it is not true that the Christians destroy pagan statues wherever they find them. These disturbances explain how it is that there were martyrs to the faith even during the reign of Theodosius, a most Christian emperor, and his sons. Deliberately mutilated statues of pagan divinities have been found also at Milan, but there do not seem to have been serious troubles in northern Italy except in isolated instances such as that of the three martyrs of Anaunia who were slain in 396 or 397 by the inhabitants of these Trentine valleys.[9]

In April, 391, Theodosius left Milan to take up his residence in the East. Valentinian was in Gaul, protected by Count Arbogast. His two sisters, Grata and Iusta, were staying in the imperial palace at Milan.

In the preaching and writings of St. Ambrose during these months, which include *On the Patriarchs (De Patriarchis), On Isaac and the Soul (De Isaac et anima),* and *On the Good of Death (De bono mortis),* there no longer shines forth that buoyancy so characteristic of the years of struggle against the Arians. From their contemplative spirit, from their reserve we come to appreciate his change of attitude: age and experience had made him more calm, more spiritual.[10]

Theodosius arrived at Constantinople on December 10, 391. From there he sent orders to Flavian, the bishop of Antioch, to attend the council which Pope Siricius had convoked at Capua. The sessions of this council, which was held in the early months of 392, were presided over by St. Ambrose. It is even probable that the council had been called at his suggestion. Ambrose insisted that Theodosius should see to it that the question of the schism at Antioch was resolved. Actually, the bishops of the West failed to realize that the split in the church in that ancient city could now be ignored: Evagrius, the successor of Paulinus, had very few adherents, while Flavian was recognized by almost all the Easterners. Since Flavian did not present himself as requested, the Council of Capua decided to refer the matter to the bishop of Alexandria. Again Flavian failed to appear. He went instead to Constantinople to persuade Theodosius to summon a council in the imperial city. Ambrose, highly resentful, complained and protested. He was afraid that there might be a return to the system of imperial rescripts. He insisted that the bishop of Alexandria should condemn Flavian if he did not make an appearance, and he then referred the matter to the bishop of Rome.[11] But, as a matter of fact, despite all his desires to regulate matters in the East, Ambrose's action again at this time produced no effects.

The Council of Capua was also concerned with the teaching of Bonosus, the bishop of Naissus (modern Nish in Yugoslavia). Since they were not able to condemn him *in absentia* as a heretic for denying the perpetual virginity of Mary, the bishops assembled at Capua commissioned the bishop of Thessalonica to make such a condemnation. Bonosus then accused Ambrose of meddling in matters that were of no concern to him by attempting to secure the condemnation of a bishop in a province so far from his own.

During these same months the political balance which had been restored through Theodosius's strenuous efforts was again upset. There were new claims to power and new wars.[12]

Ambrose could not easily remain within his church. The great events of the past years had given his person too much authority for that, had linked him solidly with the fortunes of the emperors, and as a consequence involved him also in the new political crisis.

In the winter of 391-392, Valentinian II had moved from Trier to Vienne on the left bank of the Rhone. Since he was now twenty-one years old, he believed that he should no longer be under the guardianship of Count Arbogast. The latter, however, deemed himself to be specially trusted by Theodosius. Rather than by any legitimate power which he had in the West, his prestige was maintained by the remembrance of his services during the campaign against Maximus and by his enlightened activity as general and diplomat. A Frank by birth, Arbogast continued to assign Franks to high posts in the army. All of these were pagans like Arbogast himself, and most were out of sympathy with Valentinian.

Because of these and other personal or political motives, some of which are not too apparent, there was an obvious break between the prince and his chief minister. The youthful Augustus felt as if he were a prisoner. He wrote frequently to his powerful relative, Theodosius; but the latter knew that it would be dangerous to give orders to Arbogast that he did not favor. He therefore sent no replies. If Valentinian were at Milan instead of in Gaul, the situation could certainly be clarified. Early in 392, he was presented with an excuse to take up his residence south of the Alps. An invasion of barbarians from beyond the Danube into the regions of Pannonia aroused a great deal of fear in Milan. The prefect of the praetorium and other authorities at Milan thought about sending a delegation to Vienne to invite Valentinian to bring his court to Milan and thus be in a better position to defend Italy. The delegation should have as its leader Ambrose. Then it was learned that Valentinian had himself already decided to come to Milan and that preparations had already been made for the journey. The proposed delegation thus seemed to be useless. It would be better to simply await Valentinian's arrival. But in the meantime, a serious quarrel broke out between the emperor and his prime minister. At a public meeting of the consistory Arbogast killed one of Valentinian's friends. When Valentinian then sent the count a decree depriving him of his office, Arbogast tore it up: the prince had not given him his command, and he was not going to take it away.[13] An attempt on the part of Valentinian to kill the rebel miscarried because of the intervention of a soldier of the guard.

For the time being Arbogast did not think of slaying Valentinian: it would be sufficient if he were kept from exercising any effective control over the government.

The young prince was anxious to set out for Pannonia, but his minister made any movement on his part impossible. Valentinian even wrote to Ambrose asking him to come to Gaul to baptize him.

Ambrose was also asked by the bishops of Gaul to use his influence in settling the disputes that had risen among themselves as the result of the Felician schism.

Despite the many reasons prompting such an intervention, the bishop of Milan was now much more prudent than he had once been. Nine years before he had not hesitated to intervene in a matter no less risky. Now, instead, he expressed his happiness to learn that the prince, as rumor had it, was himself coming to Milan, and that as a consequence he did not have to leave the city. Was his hesitancy due to a scruple about anticipating the decisions of Theodosius? or was it due to the fact that he had now renounced a field of activity really foreign to him and tasks which could only distract him from God and the care of souls?

Valentinian wrote again to the bishop, earnestly entreating him to come and establish peace between himself and the count. Ambrose hesitated no longer. It was now a question of settling a quarrel, of reconfirming the state of affairs desired by Theodosius. He left Milan and had already crossed the Alps when he learned that Valentinian had died on May 15, that he had in fact been found hanging with a rope about his neck in the imperial palace at Vienne.

Valentinian's two sisters waited in tears for the arrival of his body, which reached Milan some weeks later.

What had happened at Vienne? Had Valentinian been slain, or had he committed suicide? Had he yielded to an impulse of despair? Our sources are in little agreement about all this. In his funeral discourse over the dead prince, St. Ambrose stated that Valentinian had ardently longed to meet with him and that the news of his trip to Vienne had unfortunately hastened the prince's death. This implies that St. Ambrose was convinced that Valentinian had not killed himself but rather had been murdered. The crime was perhaps not directly due to Arbogast. Others could have committed the deed on their own initiative. The stage was then set so that whoever found the body would think that Valentinian had committed suicide. This was also the official version of what had happened.

Despite the gravity of the events, and despite the fact that he had taken Galla, the sister of the deceased, as his wife, Theodosius continued to keep aloof and undecided. And even Ambrose, with the scrupulous circumspection of an aged official, waited for his orders.

He finally received a letter from Theodosius. He answered it at once, asking the emperor to give detailed instructions about the state funeral.[14] In his letter, Ambrose takes pains to state that it was to Theodosius's credit that Valentinian had withdrawn from the heretical influence of his mother and that he had changed from being a persecutor to a loving son of the bishop. And if he mentions this, it is not to recall the insults endured but to bear witness to the prince's conversion. In this same letter he seems to excuse himself somewhat for having thought of going to Gaul to confer baptism on Valentinian. The request had not been reasonable since there were prominent and saintly bishops also in Gaul, but still it had been a means for Valentinian to show with great courtesy his love for Ambrose. He informs the emperor that a beautiful porphyry sarcophagus was ready to receive the body of Valentinian, and he ends his letter by referring to the intense sorrow of the two princesses.

During the funeral services, which were celebrated on a Sunday in August, 392, St. Ambrose preached a moving sermon. The bishop is sure the good prince's ardent desire for baptism has sufficed to save him.[15] He praises his courage, his spirit of justice, his chastity. Even he, the bishop, weeps with the prince's two sisters and consoles them. And he expresses his grief as if to the Lord in the following terms: "Bishops are better off when they are persecuted by the emperors than when they are loved by them."[16] He also describes the meeting in heaven of Valentinian with his brother Gratian, who had also perished in the flower of his youth, and with his father Valentinian I, who too had suffered for the faith.

In this sermon on the death of Valentinian, there is no reference to recent events in Gaul. From this it is thought that the *De obitu Valentiniani* must have been preached before the news reached Milan that Arbogast's troops had acclaimed the rhetor Eugenius as the new Augustus on August 22, 392. The acclamation took place perhaps at Lyons. Eugenius had been a professor of rhetoric at Rome, and later, possibly in 389, he had taken a position in the government under Valentinian. As soon as he had been proclaimed Augustus, Eugenius sent trusted messengers to Theodosius to inform him of his nomination and to let him know that Arbogast was not responsible for the death of Valentinian. He also made overtures to the bishop of Milan, but Ambrose refused to answer the letter which Eugenius had hastened to send him. The new Augustus was a Christian, a Roman by birth, and he had been previously acquainted with Ambrose at Milan. To consolidate his position, he now sought to win over the sympathies of the bishops of Gaul, many of whom were sent along with the embassy to Theodosius to help negotiate an agreement between the two. But Ambrose kept silent.

He did not, however, refuse to submit to the new ruler, and he could not have even if he had so wished, since Eugenius had already been proclaimed Augustus by the troops. All that was needed was that he should be accepted by the elder imperial colleague. Such an acceptance would validate any irregularities there may have been in his election. But early in 393, Theodosius proclaimed his nine-year-old son Honorius as Augustus of Italy. Then Eugenius, who claimed Italy for himself, made an open break with the emperor of the East. At the time Ambrose was busy with the Third Council of Milan.

Towards the end of 392, Pope Siricius had sent three Roman priests to Ambrose at Milan to let him know that the monk Jovinian and his eight companions had been condemned as heretics. This pseudo-monk taught that the equality of baptism among Christians induced an equality of merit among all individuals, whether they were married or not; that baptism frees one from the dominion of the devil and all temptations; and, finally, that fasting or feasting is a matter of complete indifference. Such teaching, of course, was the equivalent of an open attack on all asceticism and it threatened Christian morality at its very roots.[17]

Jovinian's doctrine, which was ostensively aimed at facilitating the acceptance of Christianity by the many newcomers who were entering the fold, actually denied the message of the Gospels by substituting a shadow for the substance. The effects of this scandalous teaching were already manifest at Rome: monks and virgins were renouncing their vows and getting married.[18]

It is quite understandable that news of this sort should have caused Ambrose a considerable amount of anxiety. Even though Siricius had notified the bishop of Milan of the excommunication of the heretics so that the sentence passed at Rome could be carried out in the northern city without delay, Ambrose convoked his own council to deal with the problem. This may have been due to a desire to affirm along with his own submission to Rome a certain autonomy for his own see, but account must also be taken of the gravity of the heresy and the danger it represented, especially in the eyes of such an ardent champion of virginity as St. Ambrose. It seems natural, then, that he wished to prevent the scandals which had occurred at Rome by solemnly condemning the teachings of Jovinian in a council at Milan as well. At this assembly, which was held in the beginning of 393, the following bishops were present: Sabinus of Piacenza, Bassianus of Lodi, Eventius of Pavia, Maximus of

Aemona, Felix of Como, Theodore of Octodurum, Constantius of Claterna, Geminian of Modena, and Eustatius of Tortona. We have two synodal letters of this council, one to Pope Siricius and the other to Anysius, still dealing with the question of Bonosus.[19]

Meanwhile the political situation was hastening to a climax. At Rome under the influence of a spirit of nationalism, the people were naturally opposed to the rule of an emperor residing in Constantinople. This hostility to the East was increased by a pagan reaction which set in after the publication of Theodosius's edicts proscribing the old religion. One of these, as we have already noted, was the edict issued at Constantinople on November 8, 392, forbidding even private forms of pagan worship throughout the empire.

While Theodosius was still undecided as to what he should do, and while his attitude towards the usurper in Gaul was still unknown, the Roman senate in the name of the city decided in favor of Eugenius. It then sent an embassy to him requesting the abrogation of the famous decrees of Gratian and inviting him to take possession of Italy. It must be remembered that Eugenius was a Roman and that he had taught for a long time in Rome before entering government service in Gaul. He was also, as has been already noted, a Christian, though probably more through expediency than conviction. The first request of the Roman senate was made perhaps in September and a second in November, 392, but Eugenius gave no answer, or at least deferred his decision on the matter. Instead, he wrote a second time to Ambrose. But the bishop still kept his peace. When he was asked the reasons for his silence, he replied that he did not speak out because he feared that the pagans would be able to win the new Augustus over to their side.[20] He saw that a struggle was inevitable even though Theodosius was so far away and always so dilatory in his decisions. He further realized that the very force of circumstances would give a religious cast to the contest: all those who had been offended by the decisively antipagan policy of Theodosius would naturally rally about Eugenius. But in the meantime Arbogast speeded up his military preparations. A fortunate campaign against the Franks in the winter of 392-393 enabled him to secure the boundaries of Gaul and to conclude an advantageous peace with these barbarians. Some of the Frankish leaders on this occasion asked Arbogast during the course of a banquet if he knew Ambrose. To this he replied: "I know the man and I am loved by him, and I have frequently dined with him." The Franks then observed: "This then, O Count, is the reason why you are victorious: You are loved by that man who tells the sun: 'Stop' and it stops." Paulinus, who records this incident, has done so in order that his readers may know "of the fame of this saintly man even among the barbarians."[21]

A new delegation sent from Rome to Vienne in Gaul under the leadership of Virius Nicomachus Flavianus, a cousin of Symmachus, now obtained a better reception. The confiscated assets of the pagan temples were restored, not however to the ancient priests, but to the pagan senators who asked for them. These in turn could devote them to their former use without implicating the government in the transaction. The grant was meant to be understood as a personal gift to deserving citizens. But at the same time Eugenius sent gifts also to the bishops.[22]

Amidst the many tribulations of this year 393, St. Ambrose was again assailed by St. Jerome. At the request of a wealthy patron, Jerome in his usual haste threw together his *De viris illustribus*. This work, which was published towards the end of 392, contains biographical sketches of one hundred and thirty-five Christian writers. In it Jerome speaks of himself at considerable length and lists all of his writings, even those which he only had in mind. At the same time this fiery monk of Bethlehem slurs the reputations of Sts. Cyril of Jerusalem, John Chrysostom, and Ambrose. Of the latter he writes: "Ambrose, the bishop of Milan, is still writing today. I shall therefore not say what I think of him lest in taking either side I should be condemned either for indulging in flattery or for telling the truth."[23] According to a modern historian, these lines are "a monument of malice and bad faith."[24] It would be interesting to know what Augustine said when he read them. Ambrose himself bore this cruel and unjust criticism in silence. Less than a year later, however, Jerome praised Ambrose's writings on virginity and widowhood. At the time he had to defend himself against some serious accusations that had been lodged against him at Rome, and Ambrose's writings served him in good stead in making his rebuttal.[25]

From Lyons, Eugenius sent an order to the Roman senate to restore the altar of Victory. In the summer of 393 he crossed the Alps with Arbogast and arrived at Milan in August. Before these new masters of the West reached the city, however, Ambrose had left it. To avoid meeting them he had gone into a voluntary exile that was to last for more than a year.

In a famous letter to Eugenius, the bishop justified his opposition and defined its terms.[26] He left Milan not because he was afraid: he knew perfectly well that the new Augustus would be extremely careful not to do any violence to a bishop, but he wished to show his disapproval of the sacrilege committed by Eugenius in acceding to the pagan requests by a public act, just as he had done before with Theodosius after the crime of Thessalonica:

"The cause of my departure was the fear of the Lord, towards whom I am accustomed to direct as best I can all my actions, nor do I ever turn my mind from Him or esteem any man higher than the grace of Christ. For I do no one an injury if I prefer God to all, and trusting in Him, I do not fear to tell you emperors what I think best. Consequently, just as I have not been silent with the other emperors, so I will not be silent with you, most gracious Emperor."

He then reviews the requests made by the pagans at different times and their rejection by Valentinian in 384, Theodosius in

389, by Valentinian again in 391, and finally by Eugenius himself in 392. He recalls in particular his own opposition to the petition brought by Symmachus and how he later did not hesitate to speak directly to Theodosius about the matter, since he was not speaking on his own behalf. He reminds Eugenius of his obligations before God: "Even if the power of an emperor is great, still remember, Emperor, how great God is. He sees the hearts of all. He searches into the innermost conscience. He knows all things even before they happen: He knows the secrets of your heart."

The bishop does not intend to criticize the generosity of the prince, he only wishes to defend the integrity of the faith. The continued obstinacy of the pagans in their requests should be an added reason for refusal. There are no excuses. He, the bishop, has long been silent. He has long kept his sorrow to himself. He has said nothing to anyone. But now he can no longer act as if he does not know what is going on.

When Eugenius first assumed the imperial authority, Ambrose did not answer his letters since he foresaw how it would all turn out. Nevertheless, when there was a question of interceding with the new Augustus on behalf of individuals who feared the change in the regime, he had written, since this was demanded by charity and by his office of bishop.

On the other hand, Ambrose is careful to avow his own complete and loyal subjection to the new master in the West. This civic loyalty of the bishop towards an emperor whom he saw to be in political and religious conflict with Theodosius is in itself quite interesting. The sole limit which he places on his deference is the law of God: if the emperor wishes to be honored, he should see to it that God is not deprived of the honor due to Him, since He is the author of every empire.

Thus this letter ends. We seek in vain to find in it an invitation to repentance like that which Ambrose had extended to Theodosius so persuasively in 390. Ambrose could see that

Eugenius was now at one with the pagan party. The implicit excommunication of the emperor in Ambrose's letter and departure from Milan clarified the situation still further.

The gifts which the sacrilegious emperor offered to the Church were refused. Eugenius in turn allowed free play to the pagan reaction at Rome and throughout Italy under the direction of Nicomachus Flavianus.[27]

The pagan temples were reopened and the offering of sacrifices taken up again. In the winter of 393-394 the generally forgotten feasts were restored. In March there was the procession of Isis, in April the Megalensian games in honor of Cybele, and from April 28 to May 6 the scandalous shows of the *Ludi Florales*. All the positions of honor in the state were reserved for pagans, and there was grief in the Church both in Rome and in Milan over the numerous apostasies.

This must have been a grave source of worry to the many Christian officials, and this in turn caused further anxiety to Ambrose as seems apparent from his first letter to Eugenius written early in 393. And, in a letter written that summer before his departure from Milan, the bishop rejoices with Irenaeus, who was probably some sort of an official, that he has suffered for Christ.[28]

During his absence from the city he felt it necessary to write to his clergy to strengthen them in their trials.[29] He knows that some say: What does it profit me to remain a cleric, to suffer injuries, to experience hardships, as if my fields were not sufficient to support me or as if I were not able to gain a livelihood in some other way? In the face of such temptations, Ambrose urges them to put up a stout resistance: They have not entered the clergy to secure a position. To abandon their state would be to leave heaven for earth. Rather, they should continue to serve the Lord, who is a good master.

At Bologna, where the bishop Eusebius was an intimate friend of his, Ambrose discovered the bodies of the martyrs Vitalis and Agricola in a cemetery of the Jews.[30] After this discovery, he distributed relics of these saints among different Italian cities.

For some days Ambrose remained at Faenza. Then, accepting the invitation of a Florentine widow, Juliana, he set out for Florence by way of the valley of Mugnone. After passing through Mugello he arrived at his destination, where he officiated at the solemn dedication of a basilica which Juliana had constructed. In one of his *opuscula* on virginity, the *Exhortatio virginitatis*, we have the sermon which he delivered on this occasion. In Florence, the bishop of Milan was the guest of a senator *(clarissimus)* Decens, and he repaid his host for his hospitality by restoring to life his young son Pansophius.[31] On his return from Florence towards the beginning of August, 394, Ambrose brought back with him to Milan a youth, Paulinus. He enrolled him among his clergy and appointed him his secretary. And later, this same Paulinus was to become the saint's first biographer.

Ambrose returned to his see because Eugenius had gone out to meet the forces of Theodosius. Before setting out with him, Nicomachus Flavianus and Arbogast had promised that on their return they would convert the great basilica of Milan into a barn and would force the clergy to enter into the ranks of the army.[32] But they did not return.

On their way the pagan leaders had raised statues of Jupiter along the Alpine passes and replaced the monogram of Christ on their standards with the image of Hercules Invictus.[33] Theodosius also multiplied his acts of piety.

Arbogast had concentrated his forces, composed chiefly of Franks and Alemanni, near Aquileia on the bank of the Frigidus (Vippacco) river, a tributary of the Isonzo. Theodosius in the meantime was bringing up masses of Goths, Alani, Huns, and Iberians from the Caucusus. These were under the command of the Goth Gainas, the vandal Stilicho, and the Goth Alaric who in the year 410 would make himself master of Rome.

The first day of the battle, September 5, 394, proved to be

extremely hard on the forces of Theodosius since the Goths under Gainas were completely beaten. Despite treason within the legions of Eugenius, the final outcome was still highly uncertain. Later Christian tradition described Theodosius as passing the night in prayer and having a vision of Sts. John and Philip on horseback announcing his ultimate victory.

The following day Arbogast again attacked. There were further defections from the ranks of Eugenius, possibly brought about by the gold of Theodosius. When the latter saw that his army was hindered from advancing as rapidly as it should by the narrowness of the defile and the confusion caused by the camp attendants, he leapt down from his horse and advanced alone in front of his forces crying: "Where is the God of Theodosius?" As Ambrose, who has recorded this, later explained: "Who could have said this unless he knew that he clung to Christ?" And, as he further notes, "By these words, Theodosius aroused all, and by his example he armed all."[34]

A wind blowing from the northeast favored Theodosius's troops. It was so strong that it not only blew clouds of dust into faces of Eugenius's troops but it even tore their shields from their hands. The Christians saw in this a manifest intervention of divine providence. God, as Ambrose later declared, was fighting on the side of Theodosius.[35]

The rout was complete. Even before the battle Nicomachus Flavianus had committed suicide since he had not been able to hold the pass of the Julian Alps near Ober Laibach. Two days after the battle, Arbogast also killed himself after being relentlessly pursued through the mountains. Eugenius was slain by the soldiers, probably on orders from Theodosius.

The emperor sent an official from Aquileia with a letter for the bishop of Milan to announce the victory and to ask him to give thanks to God. Ambrose carried the imperial letter to the altar so that the faith of Theodosius might speak out more eloquently than the bishop himself during the sacrifice. As a matter of fact, in his letter Theodosius expressed some surprise that

Ambrose had left Milan and had showed obedience to Eugenius.

The bishop answered at once stating that he had never despaired of the cause of Theodosius and giving his reasons for going into exile.[36] He was anxious for the emperor to grant pardon to the conquered, and he therefore wrote him a second letter. He then went in person to Aquileia. As the bishop knelt before him, Theodosius raised him to his feet and then in turn knelt before him since he regarded his own victory as a work of God and the fruit of Ambrose's prayers.

In his sermons during the last months of 394, St. Ambrose expressed his joy over the great Christian victory which had once again reunited the empire in peace under the scepter of a Christian prince. But the great emperor had by this time completed his work. His battles were over; he had conquered Christ's enemies; and with his ever more Christian laws he was striving to infuse a new life into the not yet exhausted organism of the Roman empire. And then God called His faithful servant to his reward: after only three months in Milan, Theodosius died on January 17, 395.

On Sunday, February 25, the fortieth day after the death of the emperor, Ambrose preached his funeral oration in the cathedral before the princes, the court, the armed forces, and the people. It was largely political in character. Proclaiming himself to be the defender of the name of Theodosius and the protector of Honorius, Theodosius's youngest son and his successor in the West, Ambrose earnestly entreated the soldiers and all those present to remain faithful to the family of the deceased emperor.

Among the blond Goths who witnessed the solemnity of the services and listened to the thin voice of the great bishop was Alaric.

In the course of his sermon, Ambrose outlined a course of political action for Honorius. He suggested that he follow the example of his father, who had been so solicitous for the Church and for its bishops, who had also been so kind and merciful. As he was accustomed to do, Ambrose directed more of his attention to the future than to the past. He then praised the dead emperor, a truly Christian prince, and one whom he had himself loved so much.

In the Christianity of Constantine there had been too many shadows, whereas that of Theodosius marked the consecration of the Roman empire to Christianity.

In this discourse, St. Ambrose describes at some length how Helena, the mother of Constantine, found the Cross of Christ and other instruments of His passion. This is the earliest evidence that we have for the famous undertaking of this noble woman.[37] In his life of Constantine, Eusebius of Caesarea mentions the pilgrimage which the aged Helena made to the sacred sites in Palestine with youthful vigor, but he has nothing to say about the invention of the Cross. On the other hand, he does recall the decisions taken by Constantine with Bishop Macarius of Jerusalem at Nicea in the summer of 325 for freeing the places sanctified by Christ's passion from the pagan structures erected at the time of Hadrian.[38] Helena probably arrived in Jerusalem in 326 (or 327). In a catechetical instruction of the year 347, St. Cyril of Jerusalem speaks of the finding of the true Cross and the distribution of fragments of it throughout the world, but he says nothing about its being the work of St. Helena.[39]

When St. Ambrose pronounced the funeral oration of Theodosius, seventy years had not yet passed since the time of Helena's pilgrimage. In the presence of members of the imperial family he took pains to insist upon the humble origins of the Augusta whom Constantius Chlorus had found working in an inn either in Serbia or in the Middle East (*bona stabularia . . . ideo illam Christus de stercore levavit ad regnum*—" a good innkeeper . . . and thus Christ raised her from the dung to a kingdom").[40] To remind the Christians of her time, too ready for compromises, that Christianity had sprung from a Cross, St. Helena had numerous excavations made until she at last found three crosses. From the title that it had borne was recognized the Cross of Christ. After further searching, the nails also were found.

Helena had one of these nails worked into a bridle for the emperor's horse and another set in a jeweled crown for his head. Ambrose looked upon this as a symbol of the conversion of the Roman empire, and he used it to draw up a happy synthesis of his own political teaching: "Fair is the nail of the Roman empire which rules over the whole world and adorns the head of emperors, thus making those who had been persecutors heralds of the faith. . . . And why was a nail placed on a bridle unless it was to check the haughtiness of emperors, to restrain the licentiousness of tyrants who neighed like horses in their evil desires since they could with impunity commit adultery? What shameful deeds we have heard of the Neros and Caligulas and of the rest who had no sacred object upon their bridle? . . . For power was carried headlong into vice, and rulers defiled themselves like beasts in their unrestrained lust. They did not know God, but the Cross of Christ has held them in and called them back from an impious fall. It has lifted up their eyes so that they might seek Christ in heaven. They have cast off the cloak of wickedness and taken on the bridles of faith and devotion, following Him who says: 'Take up my yoke upon you. . . . For my yoke is sweet, and my burden light.' "[41]

Finally, in his peroration on this solemn occasion, St. Ambrose cites a sentence from Isaias: "Kings will walk in thy light."[42] Gratian and Theodosius, he continues, "will walk before the others, not now surrounded by the weapons of their soldiers but by their own merits, not now clothed with a purple garment but with a robe of glory."

XVIII
The Saint

o

Stilicho and the barbarians. Their relations with the bishop. Ambrose's services in the Church. The new episcopal sees. His last labors. Death and life.

The political activity of the bishop of Milan may be said to have come to an end with his funeral oration for Theodosius. After the death of his great friend, Ambrose lived for only two more years: God spared him the sorrow of seeing the sack of Rome by the barbarians.

On his deathbed, Theodosius entrusted Stilicho with the task of continuing his work by appointing him as the guardian of Honorius and Arcadius. The former, only eleven years old at the time, was the Augustus at Milan, and the latter, who was eighteen, the Augustus at Constantinople.

Since Jerome describes him as being "half-barbarian" *(semi-barbarus)*, the Vandal Stilicho may have had a Roman mother. In 384 he gained a place within the imperial family when he received as his wife from Theodosius the emperor's niece Serena. When still an infant she had lost her father, and had been reared in the imperial palace.

A break soon took place between the two capitals. Rufinus, the prefect of the East, aimed at ruling over Macedonia and Dacia as well as over his own provinces. Stilicho, on the other hand, maintained that these dioceses should depend upon the court of Milan according to the last wishes of Theodosius. During the course of this dispute, the Gothic troops that had assisted Theodosius in the battle of the Frigidus rebelled since they had not received the rewards they had expected. In the spring of 395 under the leadership of Alaric they set about sacking the Balkan peninsula as far as Constantinople. Rufinus then attempted to persuade Alaric to attack the West, but the Goth, fearing the forces of Stilicho, turned aside instead to devastate Greece.

Stilicho came up with an army, but the court of the East, to obviate a preponderant Western influence, asked for the restoration of the Eastern troops still at his disposal. Stilicho, pretending to obey, sent back the barbarian troops under Gainas. But when these arrived at Constantinople on November 27, 395, they slew Rufinus.

Eutropius, the new prefect of the East, and Stilicho, finally convinced of the grave danger created by the dispute over Macedonia and Dacia, reached an agreement by setting up a new prefecture, which they called Illyrica, for the two dioceses. Alaric was named the *magister militum* of this new prefecture.

In 395 barbarian Huns invaded Syria and threatened Palestine.[1] At Bethlehem the two famous monasteries ruled over by Paula and Jerome were abandoned, and a ship was even hired to carry the religious back to the West. Jerome and his companions went to the coast and were prepared to embark as soon as the danger appeared to be imminent. But the storm settled for the time being and the monks and virgins were able to return to their convents.

In 397 wars and invasions broke out again on a still larger scale. In 401 Alaric with his Goths pushed on as far as Milan. Stilicho forced him to retire and defeated him in 402 at Pollentia (near Cuneo, in Piedmont) and again in 403 at Verona. In 404 the court of Honorius left Milan for good and fixed its residence at Ravenna. In 406 Stilicho had to stem the onslaught of a huge mass of Ostrogoths who had even invaded central Italy under the leadership of Radagaisus. They were exterminated by Stilicho at Fiesole, only a few miles from Florence. Meanwhile other barbarians were ceaselessly crossing the Rhine.

Upon the death of Arcadius in 408, Alaric resumed hostilities against the Eastern empire, perhaps with the approval of Stilicho. Then he suddenly turned again towards the West fearing he would be betrayed by the court at Ravenna. He then demanded an enormous sum in compensation for the expenses sustained in his campaign in the East. Since Stilicho advised paying the demands, he was suspected of treason. Honorius issued an order for his arrest. He was seized at Ravenna on August 22, 408, and put to death. All of his friends and relatives experienced the same fate.[2]

On August 24, 410, Alaric breached the Aurelian wall and entered Rome, abandoning the city to the soldiers to pillage. Some of the churches, however, were spared since Alaric was a Christian even if an Arian.

Among those captured was Galla Placidia, the last of the children of Theodosius the Great. Many Christians, both men and women, fled even to the East. During this period of desolation St. Jerome interrupted his commentary on Ezechiel to express his grief over the fall of Rome.[3]

Stilicho was the last lord of the empire with whom Ambrose had anything to do. There has been a great deal of discussion about the true character of this brave barbarian. It is certain that he was not preoccupied with the welfare of the Church in the same sense that Theodosius had been. Even though he was himself a Christian, he seems to have been somewhat inclined to favor pagans. Nevertheless he faithfully carried out the last orders of Theodosius, granting a reduction in taxes and promulgating the amnesty which Theodosius had already arranged.

A law of March 23, 395, confirmed in solemn fashion the

privileges of the Church.[4] At the same time, however, it seems that this law and two others of January, 397, betray a widespread reaction against the privileged position which Theodosius had granted to the Christian churches.

As for Ambrose, even these last years were not without their worries. This may be deduced from two incidents recorded by his biographer Paulinus.

Cresconius, a man who had been accused of serious crimes and condemned to the beasts, sought asylum in a church. Stilicho and Eusebius, the prefect of the praetorium, ordered the soldiers to drag him out. Powerless to prevent this sacrilegious violation of the right of sanctuary, Ambrose prostrated himself before the altar and remained there a long time weeping. But the beasts in the amphitheater vindicated the bishop. Leaving Cresconius unharmed, they hurled themselves at the spectators. Stilicho repented the violence he had used and asked pardon of the bishop.[5]

A former slave of Stilicho, after being freed of a demoniacal possession by Ambrose, entered into the service of the Church in the Ambrosian basilica.[6] In the beginning of 397, he was convicted of having procured for various individuals false documents which supposedly appointed them to military or civil posts. Of his own accord, and also because of the intervention of the bishop, Stilicho freed those who had been thrown into prison for using these documents. Though he did not want to punish the principal culprit, he did protest to the bishop in such a way as to give the impression that he was responsible for the scandal that had been caused by a minister of the Church. Ambrose punished the forger by handing him over again to be the sport of the evil spirit, but still he must not have been too happy about Stilicho's way of acting.

The bishop was now more than ever occupied with God and the immediate interests of the Church. He was surrounded by a halo of marvels: revelations, miracles, and ecstasies.

In 395 he had the body of the martyr Nazarius brought to

the basilica of the Apostles from the garden outside the walls of the city where it had been buried. Paulinus, who was present, relates that when the tomb was opened, the martyr's head was seen to be perfectly preserved, while his blood was so fresh that it would seem to have been shed that very same day.[7]

After the body of St. Nazarius had been placed on a bier, the bishop went to pray at the tomb of another martyr hidden in the same garden, St. Celsus. Those who followed him realized that this was the first time that Ambrose had prayed at this spot. According to Paulinus, this indicated that the place of burial of a martyr had been revealed to him.

On the occasion of these translations the bishop cured individuals possessed by devils. Nicentius, a pensioned official, was suffering from the gout. One day as he approached the altar to receive communion, Ambrose accidentally stepped on his foot. At his cry of pain, the bishop not only excused himself but proceeded to cure him; and, as a matter of fact, Nicentius never again suffered from the ailment.[8]

The bishop's fame even reached out to the regions beyond the Danube. About the year 396, Fritigil, a queen of the Marcomanni, a German tribe living between the Elbe and the Oder rivers, wrote to Ambrose so that she might be instructed in the Christian faith. She was converted; and St. Ambrose in return for the gifts she sent addressed a letter of instructions to her and advised her to persuade her husband to make a treaty of peace with the Romans. Then Fritigil aspired to know the bishop in person and set out to find him. Unfortunately, when she arrived at Milan, Ambrose was already dead.[9] Although the saint felt that he was now old, he did not rest. He continued to act as metropolitan for northern Italy, far beyond the boundaries of his province of Liguria.[10]

The respect and veneration which he enjoyed at court made it possible for him to found new episcopal sees, since many cities were still without bishops.

In his own province he added to the four already existing

sees of Bergamo, Lodi, Pavia, and Vercelli, the new sees of Como and Novara, and perhaps also of Aosta and Ivrea. In Aemilia there were bishops at Bologna, Modena, Parma, and Piacenza. These also had recourse to Milan, for example, with respect to the date on which to celebrate Easter. The bishops of Flaminia, in Ravenna, Imola, Forli, Forlimpopoli, and Claterna, were also to a certain extent dependent upon Milan, but about the year 410 these bishoprics began to be suffragans of the new metropolis of Ravenna.

In the regions now known as Piedmont and Liguria there were only the bishops of Genoa and Tortona. Ambrose probably founded new sees at Ast, Acqui, and Alba, while he prepared the ground for that of Turin, which was founded in 398 by his successor Simplicianus.

In the province of Venice there are seven episcopal sees: Brescia, Altino, Trent, Aemona, Concordia, Padua, and Verona. In the fifth century these depended upon the new metropolis of Aquileia. At the time of St. Ambrose, the bishop of Milan exercised a real jurisdiction also over these churches. In 381 Ambrose presided over the discussions at the Council of Aquileia; in 385 he sent instructions to Vigilius the new bishop of Trent; in 388 he went to preside over the election of the new bishop of Aquileia; and in 395-396 he received the petition of the virgin Indicia and wrote a letter reproving her bishop, Syagrius of Verona.

His influence stretched out even into the dioceses of Pannonia and Dacia and perhaps even into Macedonia. This predominance of Milan beyond the Venetian and Istrian provinces was, however, only the effect of Ambrose's personal prestige. It still continued under Simplicianus, so much so that the bishops of a council held at Carthage in 397 had recourse to him, as did the bishops at the Council of Turin of 398, and those of Spain at the Council of Toledo of 400. The bishop of Milan had obviously come to be regarded as a higher arbitrator. But when the imperial residence was moved from Milan to

Ravenna in 404, the importance of Milan as an ecclesiastical center decreased and almost disappeared.

Ambrose always kept up an intense correspondence. Writing to Sabinus of Piacenza, he makes a laudatory defense of the decision of the cultured millionaire Anicius Paulinus and his wife Therasia to leave the world and retire to a life of asceticism in the neighborhood of Nola: "What will the other lords say," he asks, "when they hear this? They will say that it is unsufferable that one of such a family, of such a race, of such talent, of such great eloquence should leave the senate. And those very individuals who shave their hair and their eyebrows if they celebrate the sacred mysteries of Isis say that it is a base crime if ever a Christian, aiming at a more perfect observance of his holy religion, changes his garment."[11]

Paulinus, who had been born at Bordeaux, was originally, like Ambrose, a member of a very noble Roman family that owned vast properties in Italy, Gaul, and Spain. In his own right, he had been governor of Campania in 379. With his wife Therasia he dedicated himself to an ascetical life. Giving his possessions to the poor, he came to Nola where St. Felix was buried. There he built a number of basilicas and died in 431. In a letter written in 395 or 396, Paulinus declares: "Although I was baptized at Bordeaux by the bishop Delphinus and ordained a priest at Barcellona by Lampius, . . . I still consider the venerable Ambrose as my spiritual father. It was Ambrose who instructed me in the mysteries of the faith, who still gives me the advice I need to carry out my duties as a priest worthily, and who has done me the favor of enrolling me among his clergy, so that wherever I may happen to be, I am always regarded as a priest of the Church of Milan."[12] Nothing is known as to when or where he made the acquaintance of the bishop. Their correspondence has completely disappeared.

The longest of all the extant letters of St. Ambrose is the one which he wrote in 396 to the Church of Vercelli.[13] Limenius, the bishop of the city, had died and a successor had to be elected.

This provoked some hearty disputes among the faithful, encouraged perhaps by apostate monks who, after staying some time in Milan, had become preachers of the destructive doctrines of Jovinian.

These false followers of Christ, St. Ambrose writes, are worse than Epicureans: they are wolves lying in wait for the flock, proclaiming the uselessness of abstinence, of fasting, of virginity. The bishop to be elected by the people of Vercelli should be free from every vice, should possess all those virtues which these new Epicureans despise. This is a rule which should be observed in every church, but particularly at Vercelli where the memory of the saintly bishop Eusebius is still very much alive, who was the first to combine the priestly with the monastic life in the West. The thought of Eusebius reminds Ambrose of his own predecessor Dionysius and the exile he suffered for the faith. Since one of the qualifications in a candidate for the episcopacy was that he should have advanced beyond the stage of neophyte, Ambrose makes a digression to explain his own election.

The fact that he makes no mention of Limenius is rather surprising. Limenius was the deceased bishop whose position had to be filled. He had taken part in the Council of Aquileia in 381 and had quite probably baptized Ambrose himself in 374. Was the omission of any reference to him due to a lack of zeal on his part in combating the followers of Jovinian? The letter ends with earnest exhortations to the people, to the virgins, married women, husbands, mothers of families, and masters of slaves that they should all lead truly Christian lives.

Still this letter was not enough. It was perhaps towards the end of 396 that St. Ambrose had to go personally to Vercelli. Honoratus, the new bishop whom he installed there, seems to have been a member of the Milanese clergy whom Ambrose had himself trained. Returning from Vercelli, Ambrose stopped at Novara. There he prepared the ground for the erection of a new episcopal see, even foretelling the election of its first bishop, Gaudentius (397/8-418). The latter in turn told Ambrose that he would not be consecrated by him.

In February, 397, he was at Pavia for the election of Profuturus, the new bishop of that city. From there he returned to Milan, sick and broken. During his last weeks he dictated his exposition of Psalm XLIV to his secretary Paulinus, but he was unable to complete it.[14]

Ambrose was not really old; he was only sixty-two. He had frequently spoken to his flock about death, and he had said that a man has nothing much to gain from a long life. He accepted as his own the teaching of Seneca on the contempt of death. This Roman Stoic had taught that death is not an evil, is not a punishment, since it is a law of nature.[15] But the Christian bishop went even farther than the pagan philosopher: if for Seneca death was not an evil, it was also not a good; for Ambrose, on the other hand, it was a gain. Seneca in his writings maintains that earthly things, including men, do not perish but only change. But actually, though he speaks with great clarity about death, he becomes dangerously hesitant when he speaks about the hereafter. Following the example of St. Paul, Ambrose puts a decisive stop to the waverings of the human mind in this regard: if life is changed, it is not taken away; to die is only to change one's mode of existence, and for the better if faith is not an illusion. This, then, is why Ambrose constantly exhorted his subjects not to allow themselves to become too much entangled in wealth, earthly possessions, and perishable affections.[16]

Then, too, the bishop knew the meaning of death from the fact that he had helped so many to die well.

To his friends it seemed impossible that Ambrose should also have to die. He had been a bishop for twenty-two years in one of the largest cities of the empire. He had been in intimate contact with the emperors, and had shown himself to be their master even as he was of the ordinary faithful. He had been the support of the lowly, a saint who had practiced the greatest austerities towards himself but who had also given most generously of himself in the service of others. It seemed that the Church and the empire could simply not do without him.

When Stilicho learned that Ambrose was dying, fearing that his death would mean the destruction of Italy, he sent the leading nobles of the city to the bishop. When they asked Ambrose to pray to God that He might cure him he replied: "I have not lived among you in such a way that I would be ashamed to live still longer, but neither do I fear to die since we have a good Lord."[17] St. Augustine in later years liked to repeat this saying as an example of Christian calm in the face of death.[18]

One day Castus, Polemius, Venerius, and Felix, who were at the time deacons, were speaking in a very low voice in the room where Ambrose lay ill. Making some conjectures about his possible successor, they mentioned the fact that Simplicianus was old. Though the bishop was at a considerable distance from them, he heard what they were saying and repeated three times: "He is old, but good."[19]

On Good Friday, April 3, 397, he entered into his agony. At five o'clock in the evening he stretched his arms out in the form of a cross and thus, moving his lips in prayer, he remained until the end. Some days before he had seen the Lord Jesus smiling upon him and calling him unto Himself.

During the night, Honoratus, the bishop of Vercelli, who happened to be sleeping in the room above, heard himself called three times. He arose, obtained the Blessed Sacrament, and placed it upon the tongue of Ambrose as his Viaticum. After swallowing the host, he breathed his last. It was the dawn of Holy Saturday.

Ambrose had toiled incessantly throughout his life. Despite his weak health, he fasted every day with the exception of Saturdays and Sundays. He passed many hours of the day and night in prayer. He wrote practically all of his many works with his own hand. His house was open to all. He was so diligent in the ministry that after his death it took five bishops to carry on his work.

His slight and fragile body was endowed with all the energy

of the ancient Romans. Perhaps too there was in him, at least on certain occasions, something of their stubbornness and severity.[20] There also may have been in him a keen desire not only to be loved but also to be esteemed and applauded by the crowds.

But more than Roman was his disinterestedness, his love of the cross. In the fourth century even pagans had at times to smile at the ambitions of certain ecclesiastics who got nothing but honors and temporal gains from their faith. In contrast to such individuals, Ambrose felt that he could not bear the person of the poor and suffering Christ among men unless he became poor himself, unless he also bore the fatigues of the day. And he did bear witness to the faith. From certain of his pages it would seem that he did not even consider the imminent downfall of the Roman empire as being possible. However, it is difficult for us to imagine that he did not see how transitory would be many of his public achievements.

Less than half a century after his death, his city and church would be devastated by hordes of barbarians; all the Christian legislation that he had toiled so hard to bring about would seem to fall with the empire.

Ambrose never yielded to a spirit of mistrust. Then as now it was easy to see how little the Gospel and Christianity could change the natural course of human events. This great bishop believed that the kingdom of God is not of this world, that the life of a Christian and of the Church transcend natural hopes and aspirations. And thus it was that he was not scandalized either by evil or by sorrow.

He was a man who was easily moved to tears; he ardently longed for martyrdom; and with unflinching faith he bore the many crosses that the Lord laid upon him. He was never discouraged by criticism or opposition. He stoutly resisted the mighty in this world in his defence of the rights of God, but his weapons were only tears and prayers. Later legends put a scourge in his hand, not because he ever used it, but simply as a symbol of his activity against the pagans and the last of the Arians.[21] He earnestly entreated his people to receive daily communion so that they might find in it the strength and courage that they would need each day.

"Everyone is in the power of the Lord, and Christ is everything to us. If you wish to cure a wound, He is the physician. If you are burning with a fever, He is a fountain. If you are weighed down with sin, He is justice. If you need help, He is strength. If you fear death, He is life. If you long for heaven, He is the way. If you are fleeing from darkness, He is light. If you are looking for food, He is nourishment. 'Taste,' therefore, 'and see that the Lord is sweet, and blessed is the man who hopes in Him.' "[22]

He had given to the Lord all his possessions and all his time, and he only asked in return: "Preserve, O Lord, your gift, guard that favor which you bestowed on me even when I was fleeing from it. For I knew that I was unworthy to be chosen a bishop since I had given myself to this world. . . . Yet since I have undertaken some toil for Your holy Church, safeguard this fruit lest You allow him whom You called when he was lost to the priesthood to perish as a priest. Grant first that I may know how to have heartfelt compassion for sinners, . . . that I may not be proud in reproaching them, but that I may weep and grieve with them."[23]

The name and memory of St. Ambrose has remained in benediction throughout all succeeding centuries. Men of all times have come to look upon that great figure of the bishop of Milan who, at the end of the ancient world, stood as the living symbol of the power of Rome ennobled by the new Christian virtues of humility, sweetness, and love.[24]

Early fourth-century mosaic in the floor of the primitive oratory north of Aquileia.

According to Rudolf Egger, this scene of a cock fighting with a turtle indicates the victorious struggle of light (the cock) over darkness (the turtle, which dwells in darkness, in Tartarus). It could also indicate the victory of the true doctrine of the Catholics over the shadowy teachings of the heretical Arians. The amphora on the pedestal is the prize to be awarded to the winner. See G. Brusin-P. L. Zovatto, *Monumenti paleo-cristiani di Aquileia e di Grado* (Udine, 1957), pp. 44-47.

Notes

o

PREFACE

1. E. Waugh, *Helena: A Novel* (Boston, 1950), p. 116.

2. H. Bremond, "Discours de réception à l'Académie française," quoted at length by H. Leclercq in "Historiens du christianisme," *Dict. d'Arch. chrét. et de Lit.*, VI (1925), c. 2710.

3. H. Lietzmann, *A History of the Early Church*, IV, trans. by B. L. Woolf (London, 1951), p. 96.

CHAPTER I

1. Ambrose, *Expl. Ps. XLV* 21. A list of Ambrose's works is given in an appendix.

2. Augustine, *Enarr. in Ps. XXXII* 2.10. The same concept is already found in Origen, *Contra Celsum* 2.30, and in Melito of Sardis, quoted by Eusebius in *Eccl. Hist.* 4.26.

3. A. Momigliano, "Genesi storica e funzione attuale del concetto di Ellenismo," in *Contributo alla Storia degli studi classici* (Rome, 1955), p. 186. In too many other works, on the other hand, the tradition of the Enlightenment, as found in Voltaire and to a great extent in Gibbon, persists. According to this tradition, Christianity may have "opened up heaven, but it destroyed the empire." Momigliano in the work just cited, p. 333, has shown that the only basis for such a contention is historical prejudice.

4. The only extant source for the early years of St. Ambrose is the *Vita Ambrosii* composed by his secretary Paulinus in 422. For a critique of this life, see M. Pellegrino in *La Scuola Cattolica*, LXXXIX (1951), pp.

151 ff.; F. Homes Dudden, *The Life and Times of St. Ambrose* (Oxford, 1935), p. 715; J. R. Palanque, *Saint Ambroise et l'empire romain* (Paris, 1933), pp. 409-416.

5. Paulinus in *Vita Ambr.* 3 has the following: *posito in administratione praefecturae Galliarum patre eius Ambrosio natus est Ambrosius.* From this, practically all of Ambrose's biographers have concluded that Ambrose's father was praetorian prefect in Gaul. This is the only evidence we have, however, that there ever was an Ambrose as prefect in Gaul. Since he could not have been prefect before the summer of 337, nor after the spring of 340, Palanque sets the date of Ambrose's birth in the first months of 339. In *Ep.* 59.3, Ambrose himself helps to fix the chronology of his life. He here states that he was living in the midst of a peril from a barbarian invasion: *nos autem obiecti barbaricis motibus et bellorum procellis in medio versamur omnium molestiarum freto.* A few lines further on he mentions the fact that he has already completed his fifty-third year. Palanque believes that the letter must have been written in 392, when there was a barbarian invasion of Pannonia (*op. cit.*, pp. 542-543). Baronius, Rauschen, and Faller, on the other hand, hold that the letter was written in 387 (cf. *Enc. Catt.*, I [1948], pp. 984 ff.), since in the summer of that year Maximus invaded Italy, the court of Valentinian II fled from Milan to Thessalonica, and the barbarians overflowed into the Balkans (cf. *Apol. David* 27). They would therefore place the birth of St. Ambrose in the fall of 334. But his father could not have been prefect of Gaul in that year (see W. Ensslin, "Praefectus praetorio," *Realen. der class. Alter. XXII*.2 [1954], c. 2496). In that case, Paulinus's words should be understood in the sense that Ambrose's father was not actually the prefect of Gaul but one of the high imperial functionaries stationed there. Palanque has more recently held that the prefecture may have been unoccupied in the years 334-337 (*Historia*, IV [1955], pp. 258 ff.). Even if the post of the prefect was itself vacant, the fiscal and administrative offices at Trier must have continued to function, and Paulinus's description of the position held by Ambrose's father seems to favor such a situation in 334. Moreover, if Ambrose was already forty years old in 374, his election to the episcopacy seems to be more plausible. For the *gens Aurelia*, see G. B. de Rossi, *Roma sotterranea*, III (Rome, 1877), p. 24; H. Delehaye in *Anal. Boll.*, XLVIII (1930), p. 193. Ambrose's family was probably related to that of Symmachus (see Ambrose, *De exc. fratris* 1.32; Symmachus, *Ep.* 1.63; 3.30-37). The Ambrosian distichs for the basilica of St. Nazarius preserved in the Dresden codex are subscribed *Aur. Ambrosius episc.* (See G. B. Pighi in *Aevum*, XVIII [1944], p. 17, and the studies of A. Silvagni cited there.)

6. See M. Rampolla del Tindaro, *Santa Melania giuniore* (Rome, 1905), p. 180 ff.

7. Ammianus Marcellinus 27.11.1.

8. Ausonius, *Ep.* 24.115.

9. Ambrose, *Exh. virgin.* 12.

10. Athanasius, *Vita Antonii* 2. See R. T. Meyer, *St. Athanasius: The Life of Saint Anthony* (Westminster, Md., 1950), p. 107, n. 14.

11. Augustine, *Confess.* 8.6.

12. Cf. Ambrose, *De fide* 5.5.56-57, where he defends the mother of the sons of Zebedee in the following fashion: *nesciunt enim materna viscera patientiam. . . . matrem considerate, matrem cogitate.*

13. Paulinus, *Vita Ambr.* 3.

14. Ambrose, *Exh. virgin.* 12; see also *De virgin.* 3.7. These are the only places in which Ambrose mentions his sister. The traditional date of Soteris's death, the *dies natalis,* is Feb. 11, 304. Her feast was later changed to the tenth. She was buried in a hypogeum on the Via Appia next to the cemetery of Calixtus. See Delehaye, *Martyr. Romanum scholiis historicis instructum* (Brussels, 1940), p. 56.

15. Jerome, *Ep.* 82.2: *ab ipsis, ut ita dicam, incunabulis, catholico sumus lacte nutriti.*

16. Augustine, *Confess.* 1.11.

17. Origen, *Comm. in Matth., XXVII* 15.

18. Augustine, *Sermo de urbis excidio* 7 (PL 40:722). This took place during the reign of Arcadius (395-408).

19. John Chrysostom, *Homil. XXIII in Act. Apost., IV* (PG 60:181-2). St. Ambrose had reason to deplore the same evil attitude at Milan: *scio quosdam dicere quod ad mortem sibi lavacri gratiam vel paenitentiam reservent (Exp. evang. Luc.* 7.221); *redempti animae promittitur et nemo festinat. . . . Christus gratiam dispensat et cum fastidio convenitur (De Helia* 84).

20. See Leclercq, "Neophyte," *Diction. d'Arch. chrét. et de Lit.,* XII (1935), cc. 1103-1107; P. de Puniet, "Catechumenat," *Diction. d'Arch. chrét. et de Lit.,* II (1925), cc. 2579 ff.

21. Augustine, *Confess.* 1.11.

22. Ambrose, *De paenit.* 2.73.

CHAPTER II

1. The splendid buildings of Rome in the fourth century are represented in a model made by Paul Bigot, a copy of which is to be found in the University of Pennsylvania Museum in Philadelphia. For Ambrose's life at Rome, see Paulinus, *Vita Ambr.* 4: *postea vero cum adolevisset et esset in urbe Roma constitutus cum matre vidua et sorore.* Some German scholars, though without sufficient evidence, maintain that Ambrose stayed at Trier until he was about twelve years old. See G. Schnürer, *Kirche und Kultur im Mittelalter* (Paderborn, 1927), p. 22; F. J. Dölger, "Der erste Schreibunterricht in Trier nach einer Jugenderinnerung des Bischofs Ambrosius von Mailand," *Antike und Christ.,* III (1932), pp. 62-

72. According to a tradition, the origin of which is not well known, the house of the Ambrosii at Rome was near the Piazza Argentina on what is now the Via Sant' Ambrogio. At No. 3 on this street is a small convent of the Benedictines. See G. Trezzi in *Ambrosiana: Scritti di storia, archeologia ed arte pubblicati nel XVI centenario della nascità di s. Ambrogio* (Milan, 1942), pp. 333 ff.

2. Ambrose, *Hexameron* 6.38.

3. Julian, *Misopogon* 351cd. On Julian, see J. Bidez, *La vie de l'empereur Julien* (Paris, 1930); G. Ricciotti, *Julian the Apostate,* trans. M. J. Costelloe, S.J. (Milwaukee, 1960).

4. On the Roman schools, see H. I. Marrou, *A History of Education in Antiquity,* trans. G. Lamb (New York, 1956).

5. Quintilian, *Instit. orat.* 1.3.16-17.

6. Augustine, *Confess.* 1.13.

7. *Ibid.,* 1.9. In *Ep.* 133.2, he notes that whipping was one of the lightest punishments employed in the schools.

8. Vegetius, *De re milit.* 2.19.

9. For Jerome's youthful studies at Rome, see F. Cavallera, *S. Jérôme,* I (Louvain, 1922), pp. 7 ff.

10. Jerome, *Ep.* 39.1: *si graece loquentem audiisses, latine eam nescire putares.*

11. Quintilian, *Instit. orat.* 1.9-12.

12. Augustine, *Confess.* 1.13,17.

13. *Ibid.,* 1.13: *illa inania . . . amabam.*

14. For St. Ambrose's quotations and imitations of classical Greek and Latin authors, see the indices to his works in the *Corp. Script. Eccl. Latin.* He was particularly familiar with Virgil. Though he quotes him directly only three times, he is constantly imitating him. Some 418 definite imitations, 220 being from the *Aeneid* have been counted, and there are some 248 other probable imitations, 183 being from the *Aeneid.* See M. D. Diederich, *Virgil in the Works of St. Ambrose* (Washington, 1931); H. Hagendahl, *Latin Fathers and the Classics* (Göteberg, 1958), pp. 347-372.

15. On the rhetorical schools, see J. Carcopino, *Daily Life in Ancient Rome,* ed. H. T. Rowell (New Haven, 1940), pp. 114-131.

16. On the university at Constantinople, see G. Boissier, *La fin du paganisme,* I (Paris, 1891), pp. 201 ff.

17. Petronius, *Satyr.* 1-4.

18. Augustine, *Confess.* 9.2.

19. Ammianus Marcellinus 14.6.18.

20. Ambrose, *Hexam.* 6.1; *Explic. Ps. I, praef.* 9; *Exp. evang. Luc.* 8.3. St. Jerome, on the other hand, was opposed to teaching music to a Christian girl: *surda sit ad organa; tibia lyra et cithara cur facta sint nesciat* (*Ep.* 107.8, on the education of Paula).

21. Paulinus, *Vita Ambr.* 4,9. There is no reason why a young man would not joke in this way, but for a contrary opinion, see Palanque, *S.*

Ambroise, pp. 482-483. In connection with this text, see Ambrose, *De virginibus* 3.1, which gives the discourse of Liberius. M. Klein, *Meletemata Ambrosiana* (Koenigsberg, 1927), pp. 9-15, has shown that this discourse is really the work of St. Ambrose.

22. The date of Marcellina's reception of the veil is disputed. It may have been on Dec. 25, 352, or on Jan. 6, 353. From the way St. Ambrose describes it, we may conclude that even if at Rome in 353 there were already two distinct feasts, the Nativity and the Epiphany, at Milan in 377, when St. Ambrose published his *De virginibus*, there was only one, that of the Epiphany on Jan. 6. According to him, when he was preaching in 377, Marcellina received the veil from Pope Liberius on a feast of the Epiphany. See E. Caspar, "Die Marcellina-Predigt des Liberius und das römische Weihnachtsfest," *Zeitschr. f. Kirchengesch.*, LXXXVI (1928), pp. 346-355; Lietzmann, *Petrus und Paulus in Rom*, II (1927), p. 107 ff.; Palanque, *S. Ambroise, op. cit.*, p. 483; Dudden, *St. Ambrose, op. cit.*, p. 3; A. Paredi, in the collection of essays *S. Ambrogio nel XVI centenario* (Milan, 1940), pp. 126-130.

23. Basil, *Regulae fusius tractatae, interr. XII* (PG 31:947-50).

24. St. Nilus, *Narratio* 2 (PG 79:601,3). This work is perhaps not from the pen of St. Nilus but from that of an anonymous fourth-century author. See M. Disdier, "Nil l'ascète," *Dict. de Théol. Cath.*, XI (1931), c. 667.

25. Philostorgius 3.22 (PG 65:509).

26. Sulpicius Severus, *Hist. sacra* 2.38.

27. On the history of Arianism, see G. Bardy, "La crise arienne," in Fliche-Martin, *Histoire de l'église*, III (Paris, 1947), pp. 69-176.

28. See P. Batiffol, *La paix constantinienne* (Paris, 1929), pp. 303 ff.; H. M. Gwatkin, *The Arian Controversy* (Cambridge, 1889), pp. 4-5; E. Buonaiuti, *Sant' Ambrogio* (Rome, 1932), pp. 12 ff. A. Harnack notes that Arianism, if it had been victorious in the Greek-speaking world, would have destroyed the religious character of Christianity, leaving only its cosmology and moral teaching. See his *History of Dogma*, trans. from the 3rd German ed. by E. Speirs and J. Miller, IV (London, 1898), p. 43.

29. Socrates 1.34; Athanasius, *Apol.* 86; A. Piganiol, *L'empire chrétien* (Paris, 1947), p. 60; Batiffol, *Paix*, p. 379.

30. Athanasius, *Ep. ad Serapionem de morte Arii* (PG:25:685-689). Athanasius was not in Constantinople at the time of Arius's death, but received his information from a priest of his see, Macharius, who was there at the time. St. Ambrose describes the death of Arius in his *De fide* 1.124 in the following terms: *effusa sunt enim et Arii viscera—pudet dicere ubi —adque ita crepuit medius prostratus in faciem, ea, quibus Christum negaverat, foede ora pollutus.* See also *Gesta conc. Aquil.* 15.

31. L. Duchesne, *Early History of the Christian Church*, trans. from the 4th French ed. (London, 1912), pp. 159 ff.

32. Judges 19:27 ff.

33. Athanasius inserts the letters of Pope Julius in his *Apologia contra*

Arianos. See Batiffol, *Paix,* pp. 416-425; Caspar, *Geschichte des Papsttums von den Anfängen bis zur Höhe der Weltherrschaft,* I (Tübingen, 1930), pp. 151-154.

34. Athanasius, *Hist. Arian. ad mon.* 20. See Bardy, "Crise arienne," p. 137.

35. Hilary, *Frag. hist.* 1.6: *indignus ecclesia ab episcopis, dignus exilio a rege est iudicatus* (PL 10:631). See Duchesne, *op. cit.,* p. 205.

36. For St. Dionysius and his commemoration in the Milanese liturgy, see Paredi in *Scritti storici e giuridici in memoria di A. Visconti* (Milan, 1955), pp. 341-349. Socrates states that three hundred bishops took part in the Council of Milan (*Hist. Eccl.* 2.36). Baronius, on the contrary, reports a list of only thirty bishops who signed the decrees. Caspar is probably right in preferring the smaller figure (*Geschichte,* I, p. 588).

37. Ammianus Marcellinus 15.7.10.

38. For the friendship of Julian and George of Cappadocia, see Bidez, *Julien,* p. 25; Ricciotti, *Julian,* p. 17. For the advantages of Macellum, see Gregory of Nazianzus, *Orat.* 4.22 and Sozomen 5.2.

39. Duchesne, *Early History,* II, p. 215; Ricciotti, *Julian,* pp. 182-184.

40. Carcopino, *Daily Life,* pp. 9-11, 65.

41. Ammianus Marcellinus 16.10.4-17.

42. E. Amann, "Libère," *Dict. de Theol. Cath.,* IX (1926), cc. 631-659; V. Monachino, "Liberio," *Enc. Catt.,* VII (1951), p. 1270. The four famous letters of Liberius in exile preserved among the works of St. Hilary are now considered authentic even by Catholic scholars. See B. Altaner, *Patrology,* trans. H. Graef (New York, 1960), p. 414. For the difficulties from the viewpoint of style, see Caspar, *Geschichte,* I, p. 185.

43. N. Turchi, *La religione di Roma antica* (Bologna, 1939), p. 307.

44. M. A. Kugener, "Les brimades aux IVe et Ve siècles de notre ère," *Rev. de l'Univ. de Bruxelles* (1905), pp. 345-356. See also Marrou, *A History of Education in Antiquity,* trans. Lamb (New York, 1956), pp. 314 ff.; A. J. Festugière, "Discours de Libanius relatifs à l'école," *Antioche païenne et chrétienne* (Paris, 1959), pp. 433 ff.

45. Augustine, *Confess.* 3.3.

46. *Ibid.,* 2.3.

47. St. Jerome, *Ep.* 22.7.

48. *Ibid.,* 7.4.

49. *Codex Theodosianus* 14.9.1.

50. Augustine, *Confess.* 3.2.

51. Symmachus, *Ep.* 2.46. See also F. Lot, *The End of the Ancient World and the Beginning of the Middle Ages,* trans. P. and M. Leon (New York, 1953), p. 155; S. Dill, *Roman Society in the Last Century of the Western Empire* (reprint of the 2nd edition [1899], New York, 1960), pp. 143 ff.; and A. Segré, *Byzantion,* XVI (1942-43), pp. 393-444.

52. Augustine, *Confess.* 1.19.

53. *Ibid.*, 6.8.

54. Tertullian, *De spectaculis* 20.

55. Chrysostom, *Homil. contra ludos et theatra* 1.2.

56. Ambrose, *Enarr. in Ps. XL* 24.

57. Ambrose, *Ep.* 20.17. See also *De Abraham* 2.11.78, where he notes that men are more tempted in the flesh than women.

58. Ambrose, *De instit. virg.* 4.

59. Jerome, *Comm. in Ezech.* 40.5.

60. Athanasius, *Hist. Arian. ad Monach.* 44.

61. For the fall of Hosius, see G. Madoz, "Osio," *Enc. Catt.*, IX (1952), p. 407 and Caspar, *Geschichte*, I, pp. 181 ff. The latter shows some bias in excusing Hosius while roundly condemning Liberius for the same weakness. See also V. C. de Clercq, *Ossius of Corduba. A Contribution to the History of the Constantinian Period* (Washington, 1954).

62. Athanasius, *Apolog. ad Constant.* 33.

63. Athanasius, *Hist. Arian. ad Monach.* 77.

64. Hilary, *Contra Constant. Imper.* 13.

65. See Duchesne, *Early History*, II, p. 223.

66. Sozomen 4.14. See also Batiffol, *Paix*, p. 479.

67. Ammianus Marcellinus 21.16.18.

68. Ambrose's account of the humble antecedents of the mother of Constantine in his *De obitu Theod.* 42 are interesting: "She was a good hand about the stable *(bona stabularia)* who so earnestly sought the manger of her Lord, a good hand who recognized the groom *(stabularium)* who cured the wounds of the one wounded by robbers, a good hand who preferred to be counted as dung in order to gain Christ. And this is why Christ raised her from the dung to the kingdom, etc."

69. Bidez, *Julien*, p. 83.

70. Julian, *Message to the Senate and the People of Athens* 275b.

71. Gregory of Nazianzus, *Orat.* 5.23.

72. Ammianus Marcellinus 15.8.17.

73. For Julian's adventures in Gaul, see Bidez, *Julien*, pp. 161 ff.; Ricciotti, *Julian*, pp. 77-127.

74. Gregory of Nazianzus, *Orat.* 5.16; Bidez, *Julien*, p. 197.

75. For the relationship of the Ambrosii with the Aurelii Symmachi, see Ambrose, *De excessu fratris* 1.32, where the saint, turning towards his dead brother, says "your relative" in referring to Avianius Symmachus. The orator, Quintus Aurelius Symmachus (340-402) also, in writing to his brother Celsinus Tatianus, calls Satyrus, St. Ambrose's brother, *frater communis*. See Symmachus, *Ep.* 1.63.

76. Ammianus Marcellinus 22.5.2-3.

77. On the Christian martyrs of Julian's reign, see P. de Labriolle in Fliche-Martin, *Hist. de l'égl.*, III (Paris, 1947), p. 187.

78. Bidez, *Julien*, p. 314.

79. *Ibid.*, p. 261.

80. *Ibid.*, 363; Ricciotti, *Julian*, pp. 194-200. *Cod. Theod.* 13.3.5; Julian, *On Christian Teachers* 422a-424a.

81. Augustine, *Confess.* 8.2.

82. Ammianus Marcellinus 22.10.7.

83. Cyril of Alexandria, *Contra Iulianum acclamatio* 3.

84. On Julian's chastity, see Ammianus Marcellinus 25.4.2; Libanius, *Orat.* 18.179. The emperor also mentions it himself in his *Misopogon*, but indirectly.

85. Julian, *Ep.* 112 (Bidez, p. 192).

86. Theodoret 3.3; Sozomen 5.10; Gregory of Nazianzus, *Orat.* 4.87.

87. Ambrose, *Ep.* 40.12,15.

88. Bidez, *Julien*, p. 306; Ricciotti, *Julian*, pp. 223-226.

89. *Cod. Theod.* 9.17.5.

90. Theodoret 3.25, and Sozomen 6.2, report the legend that when Julian was dying he gathered blood from his wound in his hand and tossed it toward heaven with the cry: "Galilean, You have conquered!" Philostorgius 7.15, on the other hand, states that he reproached his favorite sun god with the words: "Helios, you have ruined me!" On the question as to whether or not it was a Christian that struck him with the lance, see Ricciotti, *Julian*, p. 254.

CHAPTER III

1. Themistius, *Orat.* 1.

2. *Cod. Theod.* 13.3.6.

3. Ammianus Marcellinus 25.10.13; Piganiol, *L'empire chrétien* (Paris, 1947), p. 148.

4. For the Christianity of Valentinian I, see A. Solari, *La crisi dell'impero romano*, I (Milan, 1933), p. 10.

5. Zosimus 4.2. See also Sozomen 6.6; Philostratus 7.7, Theodoret 3.16.

6. Ambrose, *De obitu Valent.* 55: *militiam sub Iuliano et tribunatus honores fidei amore contempsit.* See also *Epp.* 17.16; 21.2,5,7.

7. Piganiol, *L'empire chrétien*, pp. 197 ff.

8. Ammianus Marcellinus 29.3.4,6,9.

9. See A. Alföldi, *A Conflict of Ideas in the Late Roman Empire* (Oxford, 1952).

10. Ambrose, *De obitu Valent.* 55.

11. Palanque, *S. Ambroise*, p. 13; Ensslin, "Praefectus praetorio," *Realen. der class. Alter.*, XX.2 (1954), cc. 2435 ff.

12. Jerome, *Comm. in . . . Galatas* 2.11: *aliquoties cum adulescentulus*

Romae controversias declararem et ad vera certamina fictis me litibus exercerem, currebam ad tribunalia iudicum et disertissimos oratorum tanta inter se videbam acerbitate contendere ut, omissis saepe negotiis, in proprias contumelias verterentur et ioculari se invicem dente morderent.

13. Ammianus Marcellinus 30.4.1-22.

14. Symmachus, *Ep.* 2.41,87; 4.68.

15. Ammianus Marcellinus 18.5.3.

16. Augustine, *Confess.* 6.10.

17. Ambrose, *Ep.* 52.

18. Ammianus Marcellinus 27.7.5.

19. *Ibid.*, 27.11.1; see also 28.1.31; 29.6.9; 30.3.1; 30.5.4-11; *Corp. Insc. Lat.*, VI, 1751, 1753, 1736; O. Seeck, "Chronologia Symmachiana," *Monum. Germ. Hist., Auct. Antiq.*, VI.1 (Berlin, 1883), pp. CII-CIV; *idem, Geschichte des Untergangs der antiken Welt*, V (Berlin, 1913), pp. 35-36; E. Stein and Palanque, *Histoire du Bas-Empire*, I (Paris, 1959), p. 178.

20. Paulinus, *Vita Ambr.* 5.

21. Palanque, *S. Ambroise*, p. 483.

22. M. Rostovtzeff, *The Social and Economic History of the Roman Empire* (Oxford, 1926), pp. 463-470.

23. Ambrose, *De interp. Iob* 4.21.

24. Cf. *Codex Iustinianus* 11.52 and 69.

25. Ambrose, *De Abraham* 1.19: *discant homines coniugia non spernere, nec sibi sociare impares.*

26. Symmachus, *Ep.* 5.12; Jerome, *In Sophon.* 1.2-3. See A. E. R. Boak, *Manpower Shortage and the Fall of the Roman Empire in the West* (Ann Arbor, 1955).

27. For the persecution of Diocletian, see Batiffol, *Paix*, pp. 160 ff.; H. Gregoire, *Les persécutions dans l'empire romain* (Brussels, 1950), pp. 66-82. G. E. M. de Ste. Croix, "Aspects of the Great Persecution," *Harvard Theol. Rev.*, XLVII (1954).

28. Rostovtzeff, *op. cit.*, p. 456.

29. *Ibid.*, p. 469.

30. *Ibid.*, p. 469.

31. Batiffol, *Paix*, pp. 36, 520.

32. Lactantius, *De mort. persecut.* 44.

33. On the various theories with respect to Constantine's conversion, see Palanque in Fliche-Martin, *Histoire de l'église*, III, pp. 24-33. See also Alföldi, *The Conversion of Constantine and Pagan Rome* (Oxford, 1948); Pio Franchi de' Cavalieri, *Constantiniana* (Studi e Testi 171: Vatican City, 1953).

34. According to J. Moreau, *Lactance: De la mort des persécuteurs*, II (Paris, 1954), pp. 457 ff., the so-called "Edict of Milan" was a letter of Licinius addressed to the governor of Bithynia.

35. Batiffol, *Paix*, pp. 348-356.

36. Jerome, *Contra Ioan. Hieros.* 8: *Praetextatus homo sacrilegus et idolorum cultor solebat ludens beato papae Damaso dicere: Facite me Romanae urbis episcopum et ero protinus christianus.*

37. Firmicus Maternus, *De err. prof. rel.* 28.

38. Ammianus Marcellinus 30.9.5: *postremo hoc moderamine principatus inclaruit, quod inter religionum diversitates medius stetit, nec quemquam inquietavit.*

39. See, for example, Augustine, *Enarr. in Ps. XXXIV* 2.8: *ubicumque invenerint Christianum, solent insultare, exagitare, irridere: vocare hebetem, insulsum, nullius cordis, nullius peritiae.*

40. Hilary, *Contra Aux.* 6.

41. Sulpicius Severus, *Vita Martini* 6.

42. A description of this trial is given in "*Altercatio Heracliani cum Germinio*," edited by C. P. Caspari in *Kirchenhistorische Anecdota*, I (Christiania, 1883), pp. 131-147. See also Palanque in Fliche-Martin, *Hist. de l'égl.*, III, p. 226.

43. See the sentiments on labor expressed by Cicero, *De off.* 1.42; *Pro Flacco* 18; *Pro domo* 33; Valerius Maximus 5.11.10; Seneca, *De benef.* 6.18; Suetonius, *Claudius* 22. However, there is also another side to this story as has been shown by A. T. Geoghegan in *The Attitude Towards Labor in Early Christianity and Ancient Culture* (Washington, D.C., 1945).

44. Tertullian, *Apolog.* 46.

45. See, for example, John Chrysostom, *In Ep. II Cor., Hom.* 12.5; *In evang. Matt., Hom.* 38.5; *In Hebr., Hom.* 2.2.

46. De Rossi, *Inscriptiones Christianae Urbis Romae*, I (Rome, 1857), p. 49 (no. 62).

47. Jerome, *Vita Malchi* 1.

48. Jerome, *Ep.* 77.3-4.

49. Jerome, *Ep.* 147.

50. Jerome, *Ep.* 22.32.

51. Jerome, *Ep.* 22.13,16,28.

52. Jerome, *Ep.* 52.5,6,11.

53. Jerome, *Ep.* 22.14; cf. Proverbs 6:27.

54. Eusebius, *Eccl. Hist.* 7.30.14. See De Labriolle, "Le 'mariage spirituel,' " *Revue Historique*, CXXXVII (1921), pp. 217 ff.

55. See, for example, the condemnation of Libanius, *Orat.* 2.32, of "the men dressed in black, who eat more than elephants, and who, under the influence of drink, weary the hands of slaves who pour wine for them amidst the sound of singing." For the pagan reaction to Christianity, see Palanque in *Hist. de l'égl.*, III, pp. 355 ff., and especially De Labriolle, *La reaction païenne. Étude sur la polémique antichrétienne du Ier au VIe siècle* (Paris, 1934).

56. On the events connected with the election of Pope Damasus, see

Duchesne, *Early History of the Christian Church*, II (London, 1912), pp. 450 ff.; Palanque in Fliche-Martin, *Hist. de l'égl.*, III, pp. 232-233; Caspar, *Geschichte des Papsttums*, I (Tübingen, 1930), p. 198.

57. Ammianus Marcellinus 27.3.12-13.

58. The Latin translation of "Hegesippus" (edited by V. Ussani in *Corp. Script. Eccl. Lat.*, LXVI [Vienna, 1932]) was made without much concern for exactness. The translator adds and substracts from the original as he pleases. There are serious doubts as to whether this can be attributed to St. Ambrose, especially since the vocabulary is quite different from that of his known works. In his introduction, the translator states that he has already made of summary of the four books of Kings. See De Labriolle, *History and Literature of Christianity*, trans. Herbert Wilson (New York, 1924), p. 267.

59. Paulinus, *Vita Ambr.* 8: *vade, age non ut iudex sed ut episcopus.*

CHAPTER IV

1. For the history of Roman Milan, see A. de Marchi, *Le antiche epigrafi di Milano* (Milan, 1917), pp. 183 ff.

2. Plutarch, *Caesar* 17.

3. A. Calderini, *Storia di Milano*, I (Milan, 1953), pp. 217-415.

4. Peiper, *Ordo urbium nobilium* (Leipzig, 1886), p. 146:

> *Et Mediolani mira omnia: copia rerum,*
> *innumerae cultaeque domus, facunda virorum*
> *ingenia, et mores laeti, tum duplice muro*
> *amplificata loci species, populique voluptas,*
> *circus et inclusi moles cuneata theatri;*
> *templa, Palatinaeque arces, opulensque moneta,*
> *et regio Herculei celebris sub honore lavacri,*
> *cunctaque marmoreis ornata peristyla signis,*
> *moeniaque in valli formam circumdata limbo,*
> *omnia quae magnis operum velut aemula formis*
> *excellunt, nec iuncta premit vicinia Romae.*

See Calderini, *La "Forma Urbis Mediolani" nell'anno bimillenario di Augusto* (Milan, 1937).

5. Idem, *L'anfiteatro romano* (Milan, 1940); A. De Capitani d'Arzago, *Il circo romano* (Milan, 1939).

6. Paulinus, *Vita Ambr.* 34.

7. See De Marchi, *Antiche epigrafi*, p. 83.

8. Ambrose, *Enarr. in Ps. XXXIX* 4; *Expos. Ps. CXVIII* 16.45.

9. Claudius Mamertinus, *Panegyricus genethliacus Maximiano Augusto dictus* II, in G. Baehrens, *XII Panegyrici latini* (Leipzig, 1911), p. 284, see also p. 295.

10. De Marchi, *Antiche epigrafi*, p. 316.

11. *Ibid.*, pp. 215 ff., for the inscriptions on the Milanese corporations.

12. Pliny, *Ep.* 4.13.3.

13. J. Vendryes, "La religion des Celtes," in *Les religions de l'Europe ancienne*, III (Paris, 1948), p. 276.

14. Ambrose, *Enarr. in Ps. XXXIX* 4.

15. For these inscriptions, see *Corpus Inscr. Lat.*, V: 5870, 5824, 5970, 6087.

16. For this and the following letters, see G. Ghedini, *Lettere cristiane dai papiri greci del III e IV secolo* (Milan, 1923), pp. 236, 225, 283; "Paganesimo e cristianesimo nelle lettere papiracee greche dei primi secoli dopo Cristo," *Atti del IV Congresso Internazionale di Papirologia* (Milan, 1936), pp. 344, 342.

17. G. Vitelli and D. Comparetti, *Papiri Fiorentini*, I-III (Milan, 1906-1915), n. 332.

18. *Papiri Greci e Latini*, I-VI: Pubblicazioni della Società Italiana di Papirologia (Florence, 1912-1920), n. 1161.

19. B. P. Grenfell and A. S. Hunt, *The Amherst Papyri*, I-II (London, 1900-1901), n. 144.

20. F. Savio, *Gli antichi vescovi d'Italia dalle origini al 1300, descritti per regioni. La Lombardia I: Milano* (Florence, 1913).

21. See the protocol in Optatus of Milevis, *De schismate* 1.23-24; see also Palanque in Fliche-Martin, *Hist. de l'égl.*, III, p. 37.

22. Athanasius, *Ep. ad episc. Aegypti et Libyae* 7; *Hist. Arian. ad monach.* 75.

23. Ambrose, *De Spiritu Sancto* 3.59.

24. Hilary, *Contra Constantiam* 11. In *Contra Auxen.* 8, Hilary states that Auxentius was ordained a priest at Alexandria in a church under the charge of Gregory of Cappadocia. Athanasius mentions the fact that Auxentius came to Milan from Cappadocia in 355.

25. Hilary, *Contra Auxen.* 12.

26. The Roman council which condemned Auxentius was held between 368 and 373. It published the decree *Confidimus quidem* (J. D. Mansi, *Sacrorum Conciliorum nova et amplissima collectio*, III [Florence, 1759], p. 459; *Patrologia Latina*, XIII [Paris, 1845], c. 347). According to Bardy, *Rev. Bénéd.*, XLV (1933), p. 197, and M. Richard, *Anal. Bollan.*, LXVII (1949), p. 179, the council met in September, 371. From an examination of Basil's letters, Richard concludes that the Milanese deacon Sabinus went to Caesarea, not at the request of Pope Damasus or the council, but at the suggestion of Athanasius to whom he had brought the decree of the Roman synod.

27. The deacon Sabinus is probably the same person who later became bishop of Piacenza and took part in the Council of Aquileia in 381. See F. Lanzoni, *Le diocesi d'Italia*, II (Faenza, 1927), p. 816.

28. Ammianus Marcellinus 21.16.3.

29. For the administration of the provinces in the fourth century, see Piganiol, *L'empire chrétien* (Paris, 1947), pp. 319 ff.

30. Ambrose, *De paenit.* 2.73.

31. Ambrose, *De Cain et Abel* 2.38.

32. Ambrose, *In Ps. CXVIII* 20.39.

33. *Ibid.*, 8.25.

34. Ambrose, *De paradiso* 56.

35. Cf. Ambrose, *Ep.* 19.4; *De exc. fratr.* 13.

36. For the religious policies of Valentinian and Valens, see A. Nagl, "Valentinianus I," *Realen. der class. Alter.*, VII A,2 (1948), cc. 2198-2201.

37. Ambrose, *Ep.* 18.14.

38. For St. Zeno, see A. Grazioli in *La Scuola Cattolica,* LXVIII (1940), pp. 207 ff.

39. E. Griffe, *La Gaule chrétienne,* I (Paris, 1947), pp. 207 ff.

40. Ambrose, *Ep.* 21.2.

41. *Cod. Theod.* 3.14.1 (of the year 370 or 373).

42. Duchesne, *Early History of the Christian Church, II,* pp. 309-318; Batiffol, *Le siège,* pp. 89 ff.

CHAPTER V

1. Jerome, *Ep.* 1.15; Caspar, *Geschichte,* I, pp. 204-205.

2. Damasus, *Ep.* 1 (*Patr. Lat.* 13:347); Caspar, *Geschichte,* I, p. 593.

3. Rufinus, *Hist. sacra* 2.11; see also Ambrose, *Ep.* 63.64-65; *Exp. evang. Luc.* 8.73.

4. Paulinus, *Vita Ambr.* 6. Ambrose's voice was naturally weak, as we know from the following texts: Ambrose, *De sacramentis* 1.6.24: *sed interim secundum fragilitatem vocis nostrae, et secundum temporis rationem satis sit hodie de sacro fonte libasse mysteria;* Augustine, *Confess.* 6.3.3: *quamquam et causa servandae vocis, quae illi facillime obtundebatur, poterat esse iustior tacite legendi.*

5. Our knowledge of St. Ambrose's physical appearance is derived in part from the examination made of his remains at the time of their exhumation along with those of Sts. Gervasius and Protasius. According to the *Acta apud Sanctam Sedem super iudicio de identitate sacrorum corporum Ambrosii . . . Gervasii et Protasii invent. Mediol. die VIII Aug. MDCCCLXXI* (Rome, 1873), the three bodies measured 5′ 4⅛″, 5′ 11¼″, and 5′ 11$\frac{3}{16}$″ respectively (163, 181, and 180 cm.). The right eyesocket of the skull of the first skeleton was about ⅛″ (3 mm.) lower than the left. This explains why in portraits of the saint the right eye is also a bit lower. Further details about his appearance may be derived from Ambrose's description of his brother, who was often taken for the saint himself. See A. Ratti, "Il piu antico ritratto di s. Ambrogio," in *Ambrosiana:*

Scritti vari pubblicati nel XV Centenario dalla morte di s. Ambrogio (Milan, 1897). At Milan the saints buried near St. Ambrose are always referred to in the order Protasius and Gervasius.

6. The contrary opinion of Von Campenhausen, *Ambrosius*, p. 27, is not convincing.

7. For ecclesiastical celibacy at Milan in the fourth century, see Ambrose, *De offic.* 1.248, 217; *Ep.* 63.62; *De viduis* 65. See Dudden, *St. Ambrose*, pp. 124-125. The rule of celibacy, however, was not as yet absolute. See the inscription of the priest Probus who died at Milan in 368 cited by Calderini in *Scritti storici e giur. in mem. di Aless. Visconti* (Milan, 1955), p. 198.

8. Leclercq, "Mariage," *Dict. d'Arch. chrét. et de Lit.*, X (1931), c. 1973, gives the ages of men and women at the time of their marriage as recorded on inscriptions. Ninety-four out of 156 women were married between the ages of fifteen and twenty. Fifty-one out of eighty-four men were married between the ages of twenty and thirty-one.

9. Paulinus, *Vita Ambr.* 6: *cum alloqueretur plebem, subito vox fertur infantis in populo sonuisse Ambrosium episcopum.*

10. I Tim. 3:6. See Canon 10 (Canon 13 in the Greek text) of the Council of Sardica. Cf. H. Hess, *The Canons of the Council of Sardica* (Oxford, 1958), pp. 103-108.

11. Jerome, *Ep.* 69.9: *heri catechumenus, hodie pontifex; heri in amphitheatro, hodie in ecclesia; vesperi in circo, mane in altario; dudum fautor histrionum, nunc virginum consecrator.* Jerome may here be alluding to Ambrose's election as bishop. The whole of *Ep.* 69 (between 396-400) was written (erroneously) to refute the interpretation which both Ambrose of Milan and Pope Siricius of Rome had given to the Pauline text that a bishop should be *unius uxoris vir* (Ambrose, *De offic.* 1.50.247). In *Ep.* 112, Jerome (again erroneously) rejects the interpretation which Augustine maintained should be given to the Pauline text (Gal. 2:11) that was the source of the Antiochian controversy. Augustine (*Ep.* 82.24) states that his interpretation of the text was also that of Ambrose and Cyprian. Ambrose's pronouncement on this text has been lost. It may have been in a commentary on the Epistles of St. Paul no longer extant at the time of Cassian, or it may have been in a homily which Augustine heard him deliver at Milan. Augustine was aware of the fact that the *Commentary on Thirteen Pauline Epistles*, known since the time of Erasmus as *Ambrosiaster* (Pseudo-Ambrose), was not the work of the bishop of Milan.

12. Ambrose, *Ep.* 63.68-70.

13. Matt. 4:19.

14. Ambrose, *Ep.* 63.65: *quam resistebam ne ordinarer!*

15. Paulinus, *Vita Ambr.* 7-9: *contra consuetudinem suam tormenta iussit personis adhiberi. . . . philosophiam profiteri voluit. . . . publicas mulieres publice ad se ingredi fecit. . . . egressusque noctis medio civitatem, cum Ticinum se pergere putaret, mane ad portam civitatis Medio-*

lanensis quae Romana dicitur invenitur. . . . in possessione cuiusdam Leontii clarissimi viri aliquando delituit.

16. Paulinus, *Vita Ambr.* 8; Ambrose, *Ep.* 21.7; Rufinus, *Hist. eccl.* 2.11.

17. Ambrose, *Ep.* 21.7: *pater pietatis tuae quietem futuram spopondit, si electus susciperet sacerdotium.*

18. Ammianus Marcellinus 26.1.7. On leap years February 24th was counted twice.

19. Rufinus, *Hist. eccl.* 2.11.

20. Cf. Ambrose, *Ep.* 21.7; Rufinus, *Hist. eccl.* 2.11; Paulinus, *Vita Ambr.* 9.

21. For the criticism of Ambrose by the Arian Palladius, *amicali gratia suffragio tantum humano passim creareris indigne,* see F. Kauffmann, *Aus der Schule des Wulfila, Auxenti Dorostorensis epistula im Zusammenhang der Dissertatio Maximini contra Ambrosium* (Strasbourg, 1899), p. 86. See also Von Campenhausen, *Ambrosius,* p. 30.

22. The episcopal consecration of St. Ambrose took place on Sunday, December 7, 374, and not 373, as too many still maintain. The day of the month is indicated by the very ancient feast at Milan: *VII idus dec. ordinatio beati ambrosii epi.* See the *Sacramentarium Bergomense,* ed. A. Paredi (Bergamo, 1962), p. 48. For the year 374, see O. Faller in *Ambrosiana* (Milan, 1942), pp. 97-112. After giving the bibliography on this difficult problem, Faller points out the mistake made by the copyist in the Oxford codex of the *Chronicon* of St. Jerome. Fr. Halkin in *Anal. Boll.,* LII (1934), p. 400, had already corrected Palanque in this same regard. For the tenth year of Valentinian's reign, that is 374, Jerome therefore mentions among other items: *post Auxenti seram mortem Mediolani Ambrosio episcopo constituto omnis ad fidem rectam Italia convertitur* (*Griechische Christl. Schrifst.,* XXIV [Berlin, 1913], p. 247).

23. Paulinus, *Vita Ambr.* 9: *postulavit non se nisi a catholico episcopo baptizari.* This text indicates that Ambrose was baptized by a bishop, but we have no direct information as to who this was.

24. From the fact that Ambrose venerated Simplicianus as a father, some like Baunard in his unhistorical biography of Ambrose have concluded that Ambrose most probably received baptism from Simplicianus. See A. Baunard, *Histoire de saint Ambroise* (2nd ed., Paris, 1872), p. 41. For the texts, see Ambrose *Ep.* 37.2: *in eo tamen quoniam et veteris affectum amicitiae, et quod plus est, paternae gratiae amorem recognosco . . .* ; Augustine, *Confess.* 8.2.3: . . . *Simplicianum, patrem in accipienda gratia tua tunc episcopi Ambrosii, quem vere ut patrem diligebat.* Such a conclusion, however, goes directly against the statement of Paulinus. St. Augustine's words may be explained in the sense that Simplicianus had been charged with the instruction of Ambrose for his reception of baptism and had continued his instructions after his consecration as bishop. Baronius, the Maurists, and a number of others have maintained that Simplicianus was a priest of Rome and that Ambrose

had known him as a youth. They base their belief on a remark made by Ambrose which, however, can be understood in several different ways (*Ep.* 65.1. See note *c* in *Patr. Lat.*, XVI, c. 1221 on this text). It is much more likely that Simplicianus was an elder of the Church of Milan.

25. Limenius is mentioned as the consecrator of Ambrose in an old calendar of Vercelli. See M. A. Cusano, *Discorsi historiali concernenti la vita e le azioni del vescovi di Vercelli* (Vercelli, 1676), p. 311; R. Pasté in *Ambrosius* (Milan, 1938), pp. 289-295; (Milan, 1940), pp. 53-55. If this evidence is accepted, the fact that St. Ambrose makes no mention of Limenius in *Ep.* 63 is even more surprising.

26. Paulinus, *Vita Ambr.* 38: *aurum omne atque argentum quod habere poterat, Ecclesiae vel pauperibus contulit. praedia etiam . . . donavit Ecclesiae.*

27. *Ibid.*, 38: *reservato usufructu germanae suae.* See also Ambrose, *De exc. fratris* 59. For the family possessions in Africa, in addition to the troubles with Prosper and Satyrus's voyage to Africa, there is the fact that after the death of St. Ambrose Paulinus remained for some years at Milan or Florence and then, about the year 405, moved to Africa as the *defensor et procurator ecclesiae Mediolanensis*, that is, as the administrator of the property which the Milanese church had in Africa as its legacy from its bishop. See *Praedestinatus* . . . 88 (*Patr. Lat.*, LIII, c. 617). For the possessions of the family in Sicily, there is Satyrus's stay there in January, 378, on his return from Africa. See Ambrose, *De exc. fratris* 1.36, 79 (see pp. 169-170), and the letter of Gregory the Great of August, 591, to the Bishop of Milan, Laurentius II, in which he states that he has received his complaints about the patrimony of the Milanese church in Sicily, the revenues of which had been wrongfully collected by agents of the Roman church. See *Monum. Germ. Hist., Registrum episcop.*, I, p. 98; Ph. Jaffé, *Regesta Romanorum Pontificum* (2nd ed., Leipzig, 1881), 1149; Savio, *Gli antichi Vescovi di Milano* (Florence, 1913), pp. 249-250.

28. Ambrose, *De exc. fratr.* 1.20: *gubernasti fratris domum.*

29. Luke 5:69.

30. Ambrose, *Exp. evang. Luc.* 8.70: *magna vis, magnum pondus in verbis.*

31. Ambrose, *De offic.* 2.128.

32. Paulinus, *Vita Ambr.* 38.

33. Possidius, *Vita August.* 27.4.

34. Sulpicius Severus, *Dialog.* 1.25: *exemplum beati Ambrosi episcopi praeferebat, qui eo tempore consules et praefectos subinde pascere ferebatur.* According to St. Ambrose, "the Lord does not forbid our taking part in the banquets of pagans" if there is a sufficient reason for so doing (*Exp. evang. Luc.* 5.18). He vividly describes scenes at pagan feasts in *De Cain* 1.4, 14; *De Helia* 8.25; *In Ps. XXXVII* 30. The count Arbogast frequently dined with St. Ambrose. See Paulinus, *Vita Ambr.* 30.

35. Paulinus, *Vita Ambr.* 38: *nudus atque expeditus miles.*

36. Basil, *Ep.* 197 (*Patr. Graec.* 32:709 ff.). In the first edition of this work (1940), as in other lives of the saint, it was stated that St. Ambrose wrote to Basil in 374 asking him to search for, and send to Milan, the body of the former bishop of Milan, Dionysius, who had died in exile in some unidentified spot in Asia Minor. Basil received the delegation that had been sent out from Milan for this purpose in the spring of 375. He then added to the group a priest of his own church who accompanied them to the borders of Cappadocia and Armenia where the body of St. Dionysius was buried. Later Basil wrote to Ambrose attesting the authenticity of the relics in the following terms: "The priest of our church in the presence of many priests, deacons, and laymen took the holy relics from the tomb and gave them to your brethren. Receive them, then, with as great a joy as was the sadness of those who gave them up. Let no one dare to criticize or doubt: here you have the unconquerable athlete. He had a separate tomb. No other body was buried with his. The same Christians who received him as their guest in life and buried him in death have taken up his body with tears since they believe that they are losing a father and protector. There is thus no question of fraud, or lie, or error" (Basil, *Ep.* 197.2). This constitutes the second paragraph of Basil's letter, but since it is missing in the best codices and is preserved in only one, the *Codex Paris., Suppl. Graec. 1020,* A. Cavallin has maintained with good reason in *Eranos,* XLIII (1945), pp. 136 ff., that this is an addition to the original letter. St. Ambrose refers three times to St. Dionysius. In the spring of 386 he mentions him in passing in the course of a sermon (*Sermo contra Auxent.* 18), and in 396 in a letter to the Church of Vercelli at greater length, where he dwells upon his heroism and death (*Ep.* 63.22). In this same letter he states that Eusebius of Vercelli and Dionysius in their exile *non desiderarunt patrium sepulcrum* (*Ep.* 63.68-69). But never, as far as we know from his own writings, did Ambrose ask for, or receive, the body of Dionysius. The fact that he expressly states that neither Eusebius nor Dionysius "longed for a burial in their fatherland" has led me, after a good deal of hesitation, to suppress this paragraph from Basil's letter in the body of the text. In my attempts to settle this problem I have had recourse to the sound scholarship of D. J. Gribomont, of the Abbey of St. Jerome *in Urbe* at Rome. He has had the kindness to reply that paragraph 2 of Basil's letter may be an addition contemporaneous to that of paragraph 1. The matter is not yet decided. The doubts raised by the Swedish scholar are still serious.

The first definite evidence that we have for the cult of the body of St. Dionysius, or a part of it, at Milan is the stone of 475 (*Corp. Insc. Lat.,* V, p. 620, n. 7, and n. 6183a). This was studied by Delehaye in *Bull. de la Classe de Lettres de l'Acad. Royale de Belgique,* Ser. 5, XV (1929), pp. 313 ff.

37. *The Sixth Book of the Select Letters of Severus*, ed. and trans. by E. W. Brooks, II, part II (London, 1904), p. 304. See also Von Campenhausen, *Ambrosius*, p. 31.

38. Ambrose, *De offic.* 1.1-20.

39. Augustine, *Confess.* 6.3.3.

40. Ambrose, *Ep.* 18.7.

41. Th. Schermann, *Die griechischen Quellen des Ambr. de Spiritu Sancto* (Munich, 1902), p. 92.

42. Ambrose, *Ep.* 2.3-4.

43. Ambrose, *De Cain* 2.6.22. Cf. *De offic.* 1.31.163-64.

44. Ambrose, *In Ps. CXVIII* 12.28. For St. Ambrose's exceptional interest in the scriptures, see J. Huhn, "Bewertung und Gebrauch der heiligen Schrift durch den Kirchenvater Ambrosius," *Historisches Jahrbuch*, LXXVII (1958), pp. 387-396.

45. Dudden, *St. Ambrose*, pp. 113 ff.

46. Augustine, *Confess.* 6.3.3. See also Paulinus, *Vita Ambr.* 38.

47. Ambrose, *Ep.* 47.1-2.

48. Eusebius, *Eccl. Hist.* 6.43.11.

49. Ammianus Marcellinus 27.3.7; cf. 14.6.14.

50. Ambrose, *De offic.* 2.76-78.

51. Ambrose, *De Nabuthe* 8.40.

52. Ambrose, *De offic.* 2.102.

53. For episcopal interventions, see Gregory of Nazianzus, *Ep.* 198, 199; *Oratio* 43.56-57; Basil, *Ep.* 389.

54. Possidius, *Vita August.* 19; see Dudden, *St. Ambrose*, pp. 121 ff.

55. Ambrose, *De offic.* 3.59.

CHAPTER VI

1. Carcopino, *Daily Life*, pp. 76-100.

2. Ambrose, *De viduis* 14.84.

3. See, for example, Martial 6.7; 6.39; Juvenal 6.26-30; 11.185-189.

4. Seneca, *De benef.* 3.16.2.

5. Papinianus, *Dig.* 48.5.6.1: *adulterium in nuptam committitur.*

6. Ambrose, *Hexam.* 5.19.

7. Rostovtzeff, *Social and Economic History*, p. 471.

8. Ambrose, *De Nabuthe* 5.26; *De Helia* 18.66.

9. Ephesians 5:25.

10. 2 Cor. 12:14.

11. Hippolytus, *Philosoph.* 9.12.

12. De Labriolle in Fliche-Martin, *Hist. de l'égl.*, III, pp. 299-369.

13. Sulpicius Severus, *Vita S. Martini* 6. St. Ambrose makes practically no mention of monasticism at Milan, though he does refer to it in *Ep.* 63.7-9 and *Enarr. in Ps. XXXVI* 49. See also Augustine, *Confess.* 6.6.15;

De moribus eccl. cath. 33.70; Gregory of Tours, *Hist. Franc.* 10.31.3; Griffe, *Gaul chrétienne*, I, p. 206.

14. *Cod. Theod.* 12.1.63. Cf. Jerome, *Chron., ad ann.* 377.

15. Orosius 7.32.6, 33.1.

16. Libanius, *Orat.* 30.8.

17. Eunapius, *Lives of the Sophists* 472.

18. See the idyllic descriptions of the monks of Syria by St. John Chrysostom in Festugière, *Antioche païenne et chrétienne* (Paris, 1959), pp. 329-346.

19. See the critical edition of the *De virginibus* edited by O. Faller with a valuable commentary in *Florilegium Patristicum*, XXXI (Bonn, 1933). For the *De lapsu virg. cons.*, see M. Schanz, *Geschichte der römischen Litteratur*, IV.1 (Munich, 1914), p. 345; Dudden, *St. Ambrose*, pp. 707-708. It seems that the author of the *De lapsu virg.* made use of the *De lapso* of Bachiarius. See J. Duhr, *Le "De lapso" de Bachiarius* (Louvain, 1934), pp. 45 ff.

20. A. E. Burn, *Niceta of Remesiana* (Cambridge, 1905), p. CXXXIII.

21. Ambrose, *Exhort. virginitatis* 4.19.

22. Ambrose, *De virginitate* 28.

23. Ambrose, *De virginibus* 1.56. See R. Thamin, *Saint Ambroise et la morale chrétienne au IVe siècle* (Paris, 1895), pp. 346 ff.

24. Ambrose, *Exp. evang. Luc.* 8.75.

25. Ambrose, *De virginitate* 77.

26. Among the citations from, or reminiscences of, Plato in Ambrose are the following: *De Abraham* 2.54 for the *Phaedo: De virginitate* 111, for the *Symposium.* See also *De bono mortis*, 19-21; *De Isaac* 78; *De fuga* 51.

27. *De virginibus* 1.64-67. In *Ep.* 22, written in the spring of 384, St. Jerome praises highly the *De virginibus* of St. Ambrose. In 1929, T. L. Lefort found a brief treatise on virginity among the Coptic manuscripts of the *Bibliothèque Nationale* in Paris which seems to be an authentic work of St. Athanasius. St. Ambrose certainly made use of the general plan of the work for his *De virginibus.* The originality of St. Ambrose's work remains even if he used this writing of St. Athanasius as a model, who composed other works also on virginity. See Lefort in *Muséon*, XLVI, L (1929, 1933); *Anal. Bolland.*, LXVII (1949), p. 151.

28. Aelius Spartianus, *Hadrianus* 18.10: *lavacra pro sexibus separavit.* See also Cassius Dio 69.8.2; Mau, "Bäder," *Realen. der class. Alter.*, II (1896), c. 2750.

29. Thamin, *Saint Ambroise*, pp. 343-363. For charity as the dominant theme of Christian preaching in the first centuries and chastity in the fourth, see W. Lecky, *History of European Morals from Augustus to Charlemagne*, II (3rd ed., New York, 1929).

30. Ambrose, *De virginibus* 1.32, 60.

31. *Ibid.*, 1.57.

32. Ambrose, *De virginitate* 25.

33. Buonaiuti, *Sant' Ambrogio* (Rome, 1923), p. 73; *Ricerche religiose,* IV (1928), p. 185. See also G. La Piana, "Ambrogio, santo," Encic. Ital., II (1929), p. 800.

34. Ambrose, *De virginitate* 35-37.

35. Ambrose, *De virginibus* 1.34-35.

36. Ambrose, *Exp. evang. Luc.* 8.4-5; see also *De viduis* 9.57.

37. I Tim. 2:13-14.

38. Tertullian, *De cultu femin.* 1.1.

39. Clement of Alexandria, *Stromata* 3.9.

40. *Acta Thomae*, ed. M. Bonnet (Leipzig, 1883), p. 11, n. 12.

41. Mansi, *Sacrorum Conciliorum nova et amplissima collectio,* III (Florence, 1759), pp. 1095 ff.

42. Ambrose, *De instit. virg.* 25 ff. In *Hexam.* 5.18, however, he states the opposite: *Adam per Evam deceptus est, non Eva per Adam. quem vocavit ad culpam mulier, justum est ut eum gubernatorem assumat; ne iterum feminea facilitate labatur.* The expression *nihil muliere perfidiosius* of *Ep.* 19.17 is a quotation from Flavius Josephus.

43. Jerome, *Ep.* 107.11: *scio praecepisse quosdam, ne virgo Christi cum eunuchis lavet, nec cum maritatis feminis: quia alii non deponunt animos virorum, aliae tumentibus uteris, praeferunt foeditatem. mihi omnino in adulta virgine lavacra displicent, quae seipsam debet erubescere, et nudam videre non posse.*

44. Mansi, *op. cit.*, II, p. 569, Can. 30.

45. Cyprian, *De habitu virg.* 19: *quid vero quae promiscuas balneas adeunt, quae oculis ad libidinem curiosis pudori ac pudicitiae corpora dicata prostituunt? quae cum viros atque a viris nudae vident turpiter ac videntur, nonne ipsae illecebram vitiis praestant? . . . spectaculum de lavacro facis.* See J. Zellinger, *Bad und Bäder in der altchristlichen Kirche* (Munich, 1928), Carcopino, *Daily Life*, p. 258.

46. Ambrose, *De virginibus* 2.31.

47. *Ibid.*, 1.14-16; 2.36.

48. Firmicus Maternus, *De err. profan. relig.* 28.6.

49. Lk 9:55.

50. Ambrose, *Exp. evang. Luc.* 7.27-28: *Deus quos dignatur vocat et quem vult religiosum facit.* The same idea may be found in *Exp. Ps. CXVIII* 22.32: *ego te [Domine] quaesivi, sed invenire non possum, nisi tu volueris inveniri. et tu quidem vis inveniri, sed vis diu quaeri, vis diligentius indagari.*

51. Augustine, *De dono persev.* 19.49; *De gratia Christi* 46.51; *Contra sec. Iuliani respons.* 1.135,138; 2.85.

CHAPTER VII

1. Ammianus Marcellinus 29.6.5.

2. *Ibid.*, 29.6.7.

3. *Ibid.*, 30.5.15-19; 6.1-6.

4. Socrates 4.31.10 says that he made a law authorizing the keeping of two wives simultaneously. Others now say that he cannot be accused of bigamy. See J. Rougé in *Cahiers d'histoire des Universités de Clermont, Lyon, Grenoble*, III (1958), pp. 6-15.

5. See Ensslin "Valentinianus II" in *Realen. der class. Alter.*, VII A,2 (1948), c. 2207.

6. *Ibid.*, cc. 2097-2137.

7. Gregory of Nazianzus, *Orat.* 43.46.

8. Ammianus Marcellinus 29.1.32.

9. *Ibid.*, 29.2.4.

10. *Ibid.*, 31.2.1-11; Piganiol, *L'empire*, pp. 165 ff.

11. For Ulfilas, see J. Zeiller, *Les origines chrétiennes dans les provinces danubiennes* (Paris, 1918), pp. 440-460.

12. For the number of the Goths, see Eunapius, frg. 49-55.

13. Nagl, "Valens," *Realen. der class. Alter.*, VII A,2 (1948), cc. 2118-2126.

14. Ammianus Marcellinus 31.16.6.

15. Ambrose *De exc. fratr.* 1.37,38,21-22.

16. For the many problems connected with the date of Satyrus's voyage, see Faller in *Corp. Script. Eccl. Lat.*, LXXIII (Vienna, 1955), pp. 81-89.

17. See Batiffol, *Le siège*, pp. 21-23; Caspar, *Geschichte*, I, pp. 201-202.

18. Cassiodorus, *Variarum* 2.29; Gregory I, *Ep.* 1.80; see also Savio, *Gli antichi vescovi di Milano* (Florence, 1913), pp. 897 ff. The Arab invasion of Sicily in the ninth century destroyed everything.

19. Ambrose *De exc. fratr.* 1.1; 1.8; 1.31; 1.70.

20. The inscription is in elegiac distichs:

URANIO SATYRO SUPREMUM FRATER HONOREM
MARTYRIS AD LAEVAM DETULIT AMBROSIUS
HAEC MERITI MERCES UT SACRI SANGUINIS UMOR
FINITIMAS PENETRANS ADLUAT EXUVIAS

Corp. Ins. Lat., V, p. 617, 5. The cult of St. Satyrus was not introduced into the Milanese liturgy, however, until after the Carolingian Age. See Paredi, *Sacramentarium Bergomense* (Bergamo, 1962), p. xviii.

21. Ambrose, *Exp. evang. Luc.* 10.10. He published the complete work in 390, but included in it sermons and instructions given in earlier years.

22. Ambrose, *De offic.* 2.136; *Ep.* 82.9. It should be noted that the greater number of women saved by Ambrose from the barbarians, of the provincials freed from slavery, were probably Arians. All the more significant, then, is this charitable gesture.

23. Ambrose, *De offic.* 2.136-138.

24. Ambrose, *Ep.* 82.9.

CHAPTER VIII

1. Ambrose, *De virginibus* 1.1.1-4: *liber enim non erubescit. . . . ego quoque muta diu ora laxabo . . . post triennium. . . . ac fortasse miretur aliquis cur scribere audeo, qui loqui non queo.* Cf. Cicero, *Ad Fam.* 5.12.1.

2. Paulinus, *Vita Ambr.* 11; see also Zeiller, *Les origines*, p. 309.

3. Socrates 4.31.17; see Seeck, "Justina," *Realen. der class. Alter.*, X (1919), cc. 1337-1338.

4. Ambrose probably alludes to these Arian intrigues in *De virginitate* 11, delivered on June 27, 377 (or 378). See Zeiller, *Les origines*, p. 336.

5. For Gratian's trip to Rome in 376 or 377, see M. Fortina, *L'imperatore Graziano* (Turin, 1953), p. 72; Piganiol, *L'empire chrétien*, p. 204.

6. See Faller, "Ambrogio, S.," *Enc. Catt.*, I (1948), c. 988.

7. Batiffol, *Le siège*, pp. 39 ff.; see also Caspar, *Geschichte*, I, pp. 205, 594. For the text of the decree, see Mansi, *Sacrorum Conciliorum nova et amplissima collectio*, III (Florence, 1759), p. 624. It is possible, and even probable, that Ambrose had already returned to Rome in the years 375-377.

8. The *Ordinariorum sententias* is not the text of the letter to the bishops but an instruction on the law for the prefect of the city. See *Collectio Avellana* 13, in *Corp. Scrip. Eccl. Lat.* XXXV.1 (Vienna, 1895), pp. 54-58.

9. Batiffol, *Le siège*, pp. 49-50.

10. Ambrose, *De fide* 2.139-140.

11. *Ibid.*, 3.141-142. St. Jerome, however, without mentioning Ambrose by name, questions the value of a comparison of the Goths with the Gog of Ezechiel. See *Quaest. Hebraicae in Genesim*, ed. Lagarde (Leipzig, 1868), p. 14.

12. The edict of toleration issued by Gratian in the fall of 378 is recorded in Socrates 5.2 and Sozomen 7.1, but is not found in the Theodosian Code. See Rauschen *Jahrbuecher der Christlichen Kirche unter dem Kaiser Theodosius dem Grossen* (Freiburg i. B., 1897), p. 30.

13. For Theodosius, see Ensslin, *Die Religionspolitik des Kaisers Theodosius des Grossen* (Munich, 1953).

14. The enemies of Count Theodosius tried to ruin his son as well. See Ambrose, *De obitu Theod.* 53.

15. Ambrose, *Ep.* 2.10-11, 27-28.

16. Ambrose, *Ep.* 1.1.

17. For the troubles at Antioch following the edict of toleration see Socrates 5.4; Sozomen 7.2. The chronology given here follows that of Faller. See the preface to *Corp. Scrip. Eccl. Lat.* LXXVIII (1962). In dating the different relations which Ambrose had with Gratian, Faller agrees with Rauschen and Ensslin in opposition to Palanque.

18. Ambrose, Ep. 1.3: *scripsisti tua totam epistolam manu, ut et ipsi apices fidem tuam pietatemque loquerentur.* Some hold that Gratian at this time also asked for a second copy of the *De fide*. See H. Glaesener, "L'empereur Gratien et saint Ambroise," *Rev. d'Hist. Eccl.*, LII (1957), pp. 474 ff.

19. Ambrose, *De Spir. Sancto* 1.20.

20. *Cod. Theod.* 13.1.11.

21. *Cod. Theod.* 16.5.5; see Ensslin, *Die Religionspolitik*, p. 10.

22. *Cod. Theod.* 16.1.12. Ensslin has shown that the emperor's sickness and baptism did not take place before the edict but ten months after it. According to him, "das Problem der Kircheneinheit in jenen Tagen ein Politicum erster Ordnung war" (*Die Religionspolitik*, p. 13).

23. *Cod. Theod.* 16.1.2.

24. Gratian's movements during the early months of 380 are hard to determine. Almost all authorities place the letter of Ambrose to Gratian at the beginning of 379, but Palanque gives good reasons for placing it in the first months of 380. See his *S. Ambroise*, pp. 501-502.

25. *Cod. Theod.* 15.7.4,8,9.

26. See Ensslin, *Die Religionspolitik*, pp. 18, 28.

27. *Cod. Theod.* 16.5.6.

28. Some pages of Palladius's *Contra Ambrosium* are preserved in a work of the same name published about the year 383 by a certain Maximus, a bishop of the Goths. This work was copied at the beginning of the sixth century on the margins of the leaves of Codex Parisinus 8907 and later edited by Kauffmann in *Aus der Schule des Wulfila* (Strasbourg, 1899). See Faller, *Ambrosius: Opera* in *Corpus Script. Eccl. Lat.*, LXXVIII (Vienna, 1962), pp. 9* and 329; *Clavis Patrum*, nos. 688 and 692. G. Haendler, *Wulfila und Ambrosius* (Stuttgart, 1961) could be called a modern *Contra Ambrosium*.

29. Ambrose, *De fide* 5.192 ff.

30. Jerome, *Interpret. Libri Didymi de Spir. Sancto, Praefatio.* See Cavallera, *S. Jérôme*, I, pp. 134 ff. Did Jerome publish his translation of the *De Spiritu Sancto* of Didymus and the homilies of Origen on Luke to make the speculations of the Greeks known in the West as he claims? Not at all, according to Bardy: "*Pas le moins du monde, mais ses traductions ont pour but de raconter les méfaits littéraires de s. Ambroise*" (*Rev. d'Hist. Eccl.*, XLVIII [1953], pp. 826 ff.). He then goes on to state that Jerome's observations on Ambrose, Cyril of Jerusalem, and John Chrysostom "*sont des monuments de méchanceté et de mauvaise foi.*" St. Augustine and Rufinus, on the other hand, praise this work of Ambrose.

31. Bardy and Palanque in Fliche-Martin, *Hist. de l'égl.*, III, pp. 285-292.

32. Gregory of Nazianzus, *Carmen de vita sua* 1684-1686.

33. *Cod. Theod.* 16.1.3.

34. The *Gesta Concilii Aquileiensis* are printed among the letters of St. Ambrose after *Ep.* 9. The documentary evidence for the Council of Aquileia of 381 deserves to be more accurately studied. It may be said, however, that the criticisms made by C. G. Starr in *Civilization and the Caesars* (New York, 1954), p. 372, are without foundation or at least exaggerated. Starr maintains that Ambrose used physical force to condemn Palladius and Secundianus, basing this allegation perhaps on Kauffmann, *Aus der Schule des Wulfila* (Strasbourg, 1899), p. XXXV, where the latter states that the two were constrained to remain by force. But Maximus's

opusculum *Contra Ambrosium* does not say this, and it would have if such had been the case.

35. This is the general tenor of Ambrose, *Ep.* 10.

36. Ambrose, *Ep.* 11.2.

37. For Palladius's attack on Ambrose, see Kauffmann, *Aus der Schule des Wulfila* (Strasbourg, 1899), pp. 86 ff.; Batiffol, *Le siège*, pp. 27 ff.

38. Ambrose, *Ep.* 13.4: *praestolari utique etiam nostram super eo sententiam debuerunt; non praerogativam vindicamus examinis, sed consortium tamen debuit esse communis arbitrii.*

39. Ambrose, *Ep.* 14.

40. Batiffol, *Le siège*, pp. 141 ff.

41. Paulinus, *Vita Ambr.* 18.

42. Ambrose, *De incarnationis Dominicae sacramento.*

43. Cavallera, *S. Jérôme*, pp. 60 ff.

44. Paulinus, *Vita Ambr.* 10. The words *orantis et imponentis manus* that appear in this passage could be understood also as the imposition of hands upon one who was ill and not simply of one offering the Holy Sacrifice. Many of Ambrose's biographers refer the illness which he mentions in *Ep.* 15.10 to this stay in Rome, but it more likely occurred at Milan. See Palanque, *S. Ambroise*, pp. 103, 507.

45. See H. Brewer, *Das sogenannte athanasianische Glaubensbekenntnis, ein Werk des hl. Ambrosius* (Paderborn, 1909); P. Schepens, "Pour l'histoire du symbole Quicumque," *Rev. d'Hist. Eccl.*, XXXI (1936), pp. 548-569. Many others, however, deny that he wrote it. See Altaner, *Patrology*, pp. 319-321.

CHAPTER IX

1. Paulinus, *Vita Ambr.* 37. The court of Justina came from Sirmium to Milan in 378 at the latest. See Ensslin, "Valentinian II," *Realen. der class. Alter.*, VII A,2 (1948), c. 2208.

2. De Labriolle in Fliche-Martin, *Hist. de l'égl.*, III, pp. 385-392. A. D'Ales, *Priscillien et l'Espagne* (Paris, 1936).

3. Sulpicius Severus, *Chron.* 2.47.6.

4. At Milan *per libidinem et potentiam paucorum cuncta venalia erant* (Sulpicius Severus, *Chron.* 2.49.3).

5. Seeck, *Regesten der Kaiser und Päpste für die Jahre 311 bis 476 n. Chr.* (Stuttgart, 1919), pp. 248 ff. For the Council of Rome in 382, see Caspar, *Geschichte*, I, pp. 247 ff.; Ensslin, *op. cit.*, p. 40.

6. Ambrose, *Ep.* 17.3; see also Palanque, *S. Ambroise*, pp. 117 ff.; Piganiol, *L'empire chrétien*, p. 228.

7. Paulinus, *Vita Ambr.* 26, in reporting the request of Symmachus in 384, specifies two things: *de repetenda ara Victoriae et sumptibus caeremoniarum.*

8. Ambrose, *Ep.* 17.10.

9. *Cod. Theod.* 16.7.3.

10. Ambrose later explicitly stated that the measures taken against the pagans were not suggested by him to Gratian (*Ep.* 57.2). He also maintained that freedom of conscience and freedom of worship were not abolished by these decisions (*Ep.* 18:16). Gratian must have abolished his title of *pontifex maximus* in January, 379. See Alföldi, *A Festival of Isis in Rome* (Budapest, 1937), p. 36; Piganiol, *L'empire,* p. 228; Stein and Palanque, *Histoire du Bas-Empire,* I (284-476) (Bruges, 1959), p. 524. Ambrose's influence on Gratian's legislation deserves further study. See M. Roberti, *Cristianesimo e diritto romano* (Milan, 1935); R. T. Troplong, *De l'influence du christianisme sur le droit civil des Romains* (Paris, 1855).

11. Ambrose, *Ep.* 15 and 16.

12. Possidius, *Vita August.* 57.

13. Ambrose, *De Abraham* 84-89.

14. Sozomen 7.25.

15. Ammianus Marcellinus 31.10.18.

16. C. Barbagallo, *Roma Antica,* II (Turin, 1932), p. 870, expresses great surprise at the statements of Augustine and Orosius, but see on the other hand Lot, *End of the Ancient World,* p. 161.

17. Rostovtzeff, *Social and Economic History,* p. 481. Nevertheless, the devastation caused by the barbarian invasions in the fifth century was certainly one of the principal reasons for the loss of the West, that is, for the fall of the Roman empire. See R. M. Haywood, *The Myth of Rome's Fall* (New York, 1958), an interesting, competent, but at times overly optimistic work. St. Augustine saw a "decline" in the empire. See, for example, *Enar. in Ps. XXVI* 2.18; *Sermo* 81.9; 105.8 ff.; see also Jerome, *Ep.* 60.16; 121.11.

18. Socrates 5.11; Sozomen 7.13. According to St. Ambrose, Gratian was slain at a banquet. See *Enar. in Ps. LXI* 17 ff., but the interpretation is not obvious, and the testimony of the historians seems more credible. See Glaesener in *Rev. d'Hist. Eccl.,* LII (1957), p. 485.

19. Our only source of information on this first mission of St. Ambrose to Trier is his *Ep.* 24. With this may be compared Rufinus, *Hist. eccl.* 2.15: *Valentinianus in Italia degens fratris nece atque hostis metu perterritus simulatione oblatam pacem a Maximo simulans ipse quoque libenter amplectitur.* In addition to the excellent pages of Palanque and Dudden on this mission, see the accurate "Appunti" of Calderini in *Miscellanea G. Galbiati,* III (Milan, 1951), pp. 111 ff., and Ensslin, "Valentinianus II," *Realen. der class. Alter.,* VII A,2 (1948), c. 2210. The fact that Ambrose went from Milan to Trier by way of Mainz indicates that he crossed the

mountains over the Splügen (the *Cuneus aureus*) and Chur (*Curia*) passes.

CHAPTER X

1. See Alberto de Capitani d'Arzago, *La chiesa maggiore di Milano* (Milan, 1952), pp. 4 ff.; Calderini, "La tradizione letteraria più antica sulle basiliche milanesi," *Rend. R. Ist. Lomb.*, LXXV (1941-42), pp. 69 ff.

2. Ambrose, *Hexam.* 3.5.24.

3. Paulinus, *Vita Ambr.* 26; Ensslin, "Valentinianus II," *Realen. der class. Alter.*, VII A,2 (1948), c. 2212.

4. Juvenal 2.149-152.

5. Suetonius, *Vespas.* 3.

6. W. W. Fowler, *The Roman Festivals of the Period of the Republic* (London, 1899); Turchi, *La religione di Roma antica* (Bologna, 1939), pp. 77-113. H. Bloch, "The Pagan Revival in the West at the End of the Fourth Century," in Momigliano, *The Conflict Between Paganism and Christianity in the Fourth Century* (Oxford, 1963), pp. 193-218.

7. Turchi, *La religione*, p. 112; E. T. Silk and B. C. Wells, *Descriptive List of Papyri from the Temple . . . at Dura Europos* (New Haven, 1934), p. 295. See A. D. Nock, "The Roman Army and the Roman Religious Year," *Harv. Theol. Rev.*, XLV (1952), pp. 187-252.

8. See the study of G. Pomarès on the letter of Pope Gelasius against the Luperci in *Sources Chrétiennes*, LXV (Paris, 1959).

9. Ambrose, *De offic.* 3.45-49.

10. Ammianus Marcellinus 14.6.19; see also Symmachus, *Ep.* 2.7.

11. Turchi, *La religione*, p. 277. See also Franz Cumont, *Les religions orientales dans le paganisme romain* (4th ed., Paris, 1929).

12. H. Rahner, *Griechische Mythen in christlicher Deutung* (Zurich, 1945).

13. Pliny, *Nat. hist.* 7.55 (56).

14. Tertullian, *De praescrip. haer.* 40.

15. Augustine, *De civit. Dei*, 6.7.

16. Apuleius, *Metamorph.* 11.27: *tacenda quaedam gerens.* Plutarch, however, does mention some of the obscenities connected with the rites (*De Iside et Osiride* 36); see also Augustine, *De civit.* Dei 7.21. The temples of Isis were popular places for amorous intrigues. See Juvenal 6.489; Cumont, *Religions orientales*, p. 84.

17. M. J. Vermaseren, *Der Mithrasdienst in Rome* (Nijmegen, 1951); G. Becatti, *Scavi di Ostia II: I Mitrei* (Rome, 1954); R. Meiggs, *Roman Ostia* (Oxford, 1960), pp. 370-377. For the Mithraeum at Milan, see Calderini, *Storia di Milano*, I, p. 268. For the famous Mithraeum at Angera, see *ibid.*, pp. 179 ff. See also *Enc. Catt.*, VIII (1952), pp. 1147 ff.

18. Jerome, *Ep.* 107.2.

19. Juvenal 3.62-65; 6.553; 9.22.

20. Augustine, *Tract. in Ioan.* 7.1.6: *et ipse Pilleatus christianus est.* See De Bruyne, "Un texte de s. Augustin sur le culte de Cybèle," *Theolog. Revue,* XXX (1931), p. 227.

21. H. Dessau, *Insc. lat. sel.,* no. 1259. See De Labriolle, *Le réaction,* pp. 349 ff.; Th. W. J. Nicolaas, *Praetextatus* (Nijmegen, 1940).

22. *Corp. Insc. Lat.,* VI: 564.

23. Philostratus, *Apollonius of Tyana* 4.40.

24. F. van der Meer, *Augustine the Bishop,* trans. B. Battershaw and Lamb (New York, 1961), pp. 47 ff., 405 ff.

25. Mt. 11:12.

26. *Relatio Symmachi,* to be found after Ambrose, *Ep.* 17.

27. Ambrose, *Ep.* 17.

28. Ambrose, *Ep.* 18.

29. Turchi, *La religione,* p. 311. The statue of Victory, however, continued to remain on its original site. It was perhaps destroyed in the fire started by Alaric in 410.

It should be noted that Ambrose's struggle was against paganism and not against pagans. At his funeral there was a great crowd not only of Christians but also of pagans and Jews (Paulinus, *Vita Ambr.* 48).

CHAPTER XI

1. The date of the second mission to Trier, and consequently of *Ep.* 24, has been much discussed. The way in which St. Ambrose approached these two missions makes it appear to me that they were not too far apart. Rauschen, Campenhausen, De Labriolle, and most recently V. Grumel in *Rev. des Études Byzant.,* IX (1951), pp. 154 ff., place it at the end of 384. Ensslin in *Realen. der class. Alter.,* VII A,2 (1948), c. 2210, places it in the summer of this same year. Palanque has consistently maintained it was in the summer of 386. See Stein-Palanque, *Histoire du Bas-Empire,* I, p. 526. According to Grumel, an agreement was reached between Maximus and Theodosius in the summer of 384 (cf. Zosimus 4.37). The court at Milan was thus forced to recognize Maximus. In October, 384, Ambrose was sent to Trier to begin the necessary negotiations. These were continued by others after Ambrose was expelled from the city. The agreement between Valentinian and Maximus in 384 is recorded in the Chronograph of 452 *(Monum. Germ. Hist., Auct. Ant.,* IX.1, p. 646).

2. See De Labriolle in Fliche-Martin, *Hist. de l'égl.,* III, pp. 385 ff.; Caspar, *Geschichte,* I, p. 219.

3. Palanque, *S. Ambroise,* p. 174, literally interprets the phrase used by Paulinus in *Vita Ambr.* 19 to mean that Ambrose "excommunicated" Maximus. Batiffol, *Le siège,* p. 66, on the other hand, draws attention to

the fact that St. Ambrose in his letter speaks only of refraining from "communicating with the bishops" who were with Maximus.

4. Ambrose, *Ep.* 24.12. From a phrase of a council held at Toledo, De Labriolle concludes that Ambrose must have composed a work against the Priscillianists which opened the eyes of Paternus, the bishop of Braga. See De Labriolle in Fliche-Martin, *Hist. de l'égl.*, III, p. 390.

5. Antonio Ferrua, "Damaso I," *Enc. Catt.*, IV (1950), pp. 1136-1139.

6. Cavellera, *S. Jérôme*, pp. 108 ff.

7. Jerome, *Ep.* 39.6.2.

8. *Ibid.*, 27.2: *scio te cum ista legeris, rugare fontem, et libertatem meam rursus seminarium timere rixarum; ac meum, si fieri potest, os digito velle comprimere, ne audeam dicere quae alii facere non erubescunt.*

9. Jerome, *Ad interpret. libri Didymi de Spir. Sancto, praef.* In *Ep.* 22, of 384, and in the *Chronicon* of 380 St. Jerome speaks favorably of Ambrose. See Cavallera, *St. Jérôme*, I, p. 117; II, pp. 86-88; F. X. Murphy, *Rufinus of Aquileia* (Washington, 1945), p. 146, n. 32.

10. *Ep.* 19, which Ambrose wrote to Vigilius, probably the bishop of Trent, is perhaps also from the year 385. In it he lays down a program of pastoral activity: a bishop should teach the faithful the duties of hospitality, the obligation of paying a just wage, the horror of usury, and warn them especially about the dangers coming from marriages with women of a different race or religion. To prove his point, he retells at some length the story of Samson.

11. See *Exp. evang. Luc.* 8.57-59.

12. For the chronology of the events at Milan in 385-386, see Seeck, *Geschichte des Untergangs der antiken Welt*, V (2nd ed.; Stuttgart, 1921), pp. 201 ff. Before Seeck, all of St. Ambrose's biographers described two almost identical persecutions, one of the year 385 and the other of the year 386. Seeck's chronology has been adopted by Palanque and others. Still more recently Ensslin, a specialist in the history of the fourth century, in his biography of Valentinian II (*Realen. der class. Alter.*, VII 2,A [1948], cc. 2204-2232) has re-examined all the sources for this period. He has accepted Seeck's chronology but has refined it in a number of places. The principal documents from the saint's life and letters are as follows:

1) Ambrose, *Ep.* 21, to Valentinian, in March, 386.
2) Ambrose, *Sermo c. Auxen.*, delivered on Sunday, March 29, 386.
3) Ambrose, *Ep.* 20, to Marcellina, in April, 386.
4) Ambrose, *Ep.* 22, to Marcellina, in June, 386.
5) Paulinus, *Vita Ambr.* 13.

13. At Milan when Ambrose became bishop there were three basilicas in which the people could congregate in addition to the small cemeterial chapels: the new basilica *(nova)*, which was the largest, the old basilica *(vetus)*, and the Portiana. The latter was outside the walls of the city. During his episcopacy, St. Ambrose constructed the Ambrosian basilica

and the basilica of St. Nazarius, also known as the basilica of the Apostles at the Roman gate. The events of 385-386 evolved about the first three basilicas. In his account of these events, it is not always perfectly clear as to which of these basilicas Ambrose is referring. It is useless to try and go beyond the wording of his letters, and I have, as a consequence, left some ambiguity also in the text. Attempts to identify the three basilicas with still extant churches are even less fruitful.

Savio, for example, after a long and learned discussion identifies the Portian basilica with the basilica of *S. Vittore al Corpo*, the *vetus* with the basilica of Sts. Nabor and Felix, formerly located on the site of the present garrison of Garibaldi, the *nova* with St. Thecla, which was on the site of the cathedral square. See Savio, *Gli antichi vescovi d'Italia dalle origini al 1300: La Lombardia: Parte I: Milano* (Florence, 1913). Professor Calderini, in a more recent study, has suggested that the *nova*, or *maior*, within the walls, was the cathedral located on the site of the present square of the modern cathedral and was known as St. Thecla, the *vetus* was located on some unidentified spot within the walls, and the Portiana "very likely" is to be identified with the present basilica of St. Lawrence, at least as far as the site is concerned, although a centuries-old tradition has located it on the site now occupied by *S. Vittore al Corpo*. St. Ambrose, *Sermo c. Auxen.* 17-18, usually cited for one or other of these locations, does not seem to contribute much to a solution of the problem. According to C. Cecchelli, the *vetus* must have been at the center of the city in the immediate vicinity of the *basilica nova*. See Calderini, Chierici, Cecchelli, *La Basilica di San Lorenzo Maggiore in Milano* (Milan, 1952), pp. 244-248.

14. Rufinus, *Hist. eccl.* 2.16.

15. Ambrose, *Ep.* 21.18.

16. Paulinus, *Vita Ambr.* 12.

17. Ambrose, *Ep.* 21.

18. Ambrose, *Exp. evang. Luc.* 7.49-53.

19. For the events of Holy Week, 386, see Ambrose *Ep.* 20, to Marcellina

20. *Ibid.*, 20.4: *ego tamen mansi in munere, missam facere coepi.*

21. Ambrose, *Sermo c. Auxen.* 2 ff. According to Ambrose, *imperator enim intra ecclesiam non supra ecclesiam est* (*ibid.*, 36). The same principle is expressed in his letter to Valentinian, *Ep.* 21.10: *legem enim tuam nollem esse supra Dei legem. Dei lex nos docuit quid sequamur, humanae leges hoc docere non possunt.*

22. Ambrose, *Ep.* 20.9.

23. Ambrose, *Ep.* 20.19. See C. Ferrini, "Postille giuridiche all' epistola XX di s. Ambr. diretta alla sorella Marcellina," in *Ambrosiana*, VI (Milan, 1897), p. 9: "The statement that the emperor *domum privati nullo iure potest temerare* may seem to be strange when compared with the other

which states that all things belong to him. But it should be remembered that the latter was a theoretical principle whereas numerous imperial constitutions protected individuals from the treasury, and that in any case the "peace of the home" was a very ancient concept recognized in numerous ways in every period, and one which was revived in Roman law in later years through Germanic influences upon Latin traditions."

24. Ambrose, *Ep.* 20.26: *erat autem dies quo sese Dominus pro nobis tradidit, quo in ecclesia paenitentia relaxatur.* Rauschen, Von Campenhausen, Palanque, Manser, and Dölger hold that this was on Good Friday. F. Probst, M. Ihm, K. Schenkl, Dudden, I. H. van Haeringen, the Milanese, naturally, and finally H. Frank, *Ambrosius und die Büsseraussöhnung in Mailand* (Münster, 1938), pp. 136-173, hold that it was on Holy Thursday. See Paredi in *S. Ambrogio nel XVI centenario* (Milan, 1940), pp. 139 ff.

25. Ambrose, *Ep.* 22; Paulinus, *Vita Ambr.* 14; Delehaye, "Quelques dates du Martyrologe Hiéronymien," *Anal. Boll.*, IL (1931), pp. 30 ff.; P. Courcelle, "L'invention et la translation des Saints Gervais et Protais," in *Recherches sur les Confessions de Saint Augustin* (Paris, 1950), pp. 139-155.

26. See Delehaye, "*Les origines du culte des martyrs* (2nd ed.; Brussels, 1933); L. Hertling, S.J., and E. Kirschbaum, S.J., *The Roman Catacombs and Their Martyrs*, trans. Costelloe (2nd ed.; London, 1960), pp. 65 ff.

27. See Delehaye, *Les légendes hagiographiques* (3rd ed.; Brussels, 1927); Am. ed., *The Legends of the Saints* (New York, 1962), pp. 153-155; J. C. Lawson, *Modern Greek Folklore and Ancient Greek Religion* (Cambridge, 1910).

28. Plutarch, *Theseus* 36.1-9; *Cimon* 8-9.

29. Hertling-Kirschbaum, *Roman Catacombs*, pp. 65 ff.

30. Ricciotti, *Julian*, p. 211.

31. Delehaye, *Origines*, p. 65. At Milan, however, in the fourth century the Roman system of computing Easter was not followed but that of Alexandria. See Leclercq, "Pâques," *Dict. Arch. chrét. et de Lit.*, XII (1938), c. 1564.

32. Augustine, *De opere monach.* 28.36: *tam multos hypocritas sub habitu monachorum usquequaque dispersit, circumeuntes provincias, nusquam missos, nusquam fixos, nusquam stantes, nusquam sedentes; alii membra martyrum, si tamen martyrum, venditant.*

33. *Cod. Theod.* 9.17.7: *humatum corpus nemo ad alterum locum transferat; nemo martyrem distrahat, nemo mercetur.* From St. Jerome, *Adv. Vigilant.* 7-8, we know that this priest, a friend of Paulinus of Nola, not only fought against clerical celibacy and argued against sending alms to the monks of Palestine, but he also protested against the vigils celebrated at the tombs of the martyrs and the worship of their relics. The sympathy which some non-Catholic scholars feel for Vigilantius is understandable. See Cavallera, *S. Jérôme*, I, pp. 306 ff.

34. *Collectio Avellana* XXXIX, pp. 88-90. See Palanque, *S. Ambroise*, p. 169; Batiffol, *Le siège apost.*, p. 64.

35. Seeck, "Aelia Flaccilla Augusta," *Realen. der class. Alter.*, VI (1909), cc. 2431-2433.

36. See, for example, Ensslin, "Valentinianus II," *Realen. der class. Alter.* VII A,2 (1948), c. 2221.

37. Augustine, *Confess.* 9.7.16.

CHAPTER XII

1. See Ambrose *Ep.* 22.1: *Dominae sorori, vitae atque oculis praeferendae, frater;* and *De virginibus* 3.7.37: *constituta in agro, nulla socia virgine.* A medieval tradition locates Marcellina's villa on the plain north of Milan between Carugate and Brugherio, twelve miles from the city.

2. *Ibid.* 20.1: *significaveras quod te exagitarent somnia tua.*

3. Ambrose *Ep.* 20.26: *tunc agnovi quod Deus vermem antelucanum percusserat.* Cf. Jonas 4:7.

4. For the reading of Jonas, see Paredi, "*La liturgia di s. Ambrogio*" in *S. Ambrogio nel XVI centenario* (Milan, 1940), pp. 138 ff.

5. Cf. Ambrose, *Ep.* 20.27.

6. Ambrose, *Sermo Contra Auxen.* 34: *hymnorum quoque meorum carminibus deceptum populum ferunt.* For St. Ambrose's fame as a preacher, see Gaudentius of Brescia, *Tract.* 16.9.

7. Augustine, *Confess.* 6.3; *et eum quidem in populo verbum veritatis recte tractantem omni die dominico audiebam. . . . erubui non me tot annos adversus catholicam fidem, sed contra carnalium cogitationum figmenta latrasse.*

8. For the way Ambrose edited his sermons see Ambrose, *Ep.* 47.1; M. Schanz, *Geschichte der römischen Litteratur*, IV.1 (Munich, 1914), p. 319.

9. Despite Ambrose's harsh words for pagan authors, it should be remembered how deeply he was imbued with classical culture. See p. 382. Even St. Augustine, for all his genius, was not actually interested in the arts and sciences. He did not believe that history or scientific chronology exercised any control on Scripture. Such gaps are in large part to be explained by the general ignorance of the age. See De Labriolle "S. Ambroise" in Fliche-Martin, *Hist. de l'égl.*, III, pp. 411-415. For numerous texts from St. Ambrose on the relationship between the culture of the ancient world and Christianity, see Dudden, *St. Ambrose*, pp. 15 ff.

10. De Labriolle, *St. Ambroise*, pp. 179-183.

11. Clement of Alexandria, *Stromata* 5.4.

12. Origen, *De princip.* 9.16-17.

13. Ambrose, *De Isaac* 1 ff.

14. Ambrose, *De paradiso* 2.11.

15. E. Pasteris, *L'esamerone* (Turin, 1937), pp. xxiv-xxix. For the sources of the *Hexameron*, see Klein, *Meletemata Ambrosiana* (Königsberg, 1927).

16. Ammianus Marcellinus 18.3.9; 22.15.29; 23.6.67; 23.6.88.

17. Ambrose, *Hexam.* 3.2-4. Cf. III Kings 20.28; Ps. 83.7; 32.17; 79.14; 41.2.

18. For the monks living on the islands, see Rutilius Namatianus, *Itiner.* 5.439-526.

19. Ambrose, *Hexam.* 3.21-24.

20. *Ibid.*, 4.1-3. Cf. Mal. 3.4; Ps. 71.19; Job 9.7; Phil. 2.7; John 1.9.

21. *Ibid.*, 5.22.

22. *Ibid.*, 5.36.

23. *Ibid.*, 5.50-52.

24. *Ibid.*, 5.62-63. Cf. Luke 2.24; Vergil, *Aeneid* 4.17-18; I Tim. 5.14; I Cor. 7.8.

25. Ambrose, *Hexam.*, 5.64-65. Cf. Vergil, *Georgics* 4.206.

26. *Ibid.*, 5.88.

27. *Ibid.*, 6.56.

28. *Ibid.*, 6.68.

29. *Ibid.*, 6.75-76. Cf. Gen. 2:2; Isaias 66:2 (Septuagint).

30. Cf. Courcelle, *Récherches sur les Confessions de saint Augustin* (Paris, 1950), pp. 93-138. See P. Hadot and Courcelle in *Revue des Études Latines*, XXXIV (1956), pp. 202-239, for two other studies on Plato and Plotinus in the sermons of St. Ambrose and for new aspects of his Platonism; and C. Mohrmann, *Études sur le latin des chrétiens*, II (Rome, 1961), pp. 300 ff. Also, Courcelle, *Orpheus*, IX (1962), pp. 21-34; H. Ch. Puech, Hadot, *Vigiliae Christianae*, XIII (1959), pp. 204-234.

31. See the prologue to this treatise in Faller, *Ambrosius: Opera VII, Corp. Script. Eccl. Lat.*, LXXIII (Vienna, 1955). It is to Faller's particular credit that his long studies have demonstrated the authenticity of this work. For the recent objections of K. Gamber, see the reply of B. Botte in *Bulletin de Théologie ancienne et médiévale*, VIII (1958), no. 513.

32. Ambrose, *De sacram.* 1.17. Cf. Matt. 3.16.

33. *Ibid.*, 3.13. See also F. Petit, "Sur les cathéchèses post-baptismales de s. Ambroise," *Revue Bénéd.*, LXVIII (1958), pp. 256-264. On the different categories of people to whom St. Ambrose directed his preaching, see J. Mesot, *Die Heidenbekehrung bei Ambrosius von Mailand* (Schöneck-Beckenried, 1958). For the general background see V. Monachino, *La cura pastorale a Milano, Cartagine e Roma nel secolo* IV (Rome, 1947); B. Parodi, *La catechesi di sant' Ambrogio* (Genoa, 1957); Courcelle, "Anti-Christian Arguments and Christian Platonism from Arnobius to St. Ambrose," in *The Conflict between Paganism and Christianity in the Fourth Century*, edited by Momigliano (Oxford, 1963), pp. 151-192.

34. Cassiodorus, *Instit. divin. et human. lect.* 20.

CHAPTER XIII

1. Augustine, *Confess.* 2.3.7.

2. *Ibid.*, 5.8.14. Cf. *Cod. Theod.* 14.9.1 for a law of March 12, 370, fixing the status of the universities and containing rigorous measures with respect to students at Rome, including the permission to beat and expel those who did not retain the proper attitude.

3. Augustine, *Confess.* 5.8.15.

4. *Ibid.*, 5.12.22-23.

5. *Cod. Theod.* 13.3.11. Cf. J. J. O'Meara, *The Young Augustine* (London, 1954), pp. 116 ff., where the recent studies of Courcelle are discussed. See J. B. Bury, *History of the Later Roman Empire*, I (New York, 1958), p. 46: "The supply of provisions, consisting of corn, oil, wine, salt, pork, mutton, necessary to feed a soldier for a year, was calculated, and was called an annona."

6. Augustine *Confess.* 6.3.4.

7. Ambrose, *De fide* 1.42, 85.

8. This legend was reported by Nicholas de Cusa in his *Apologia doctae ignorantiae*, cited in Migne, *Patrol. Lat.*, XVI (Paris, 1845), c. 536 (from the Maurists) in the note to Ambrose, *De fide* 1.41.

9. Augustine, *Sermo* 339 and 340.

10. Augustine, *Confess.* 5.13.23; 14.24.

11. *Ibid.*, 6.1.1; 2.2. Cf. John 4:14.

12. *Ibid.*, 6.2.2.

13. See J. Quasten, " 'Vetus Superstitio et Nova Religio': The Problem of *Refrigerium* in the Ancient Church of North Africa," *Harvard Theol. Rev.*, XXXIII (1940), pp. 253-266; Leclercq, "Refrigerium," *Diction. d'Arch. chrét. et de Lit.*, XIV.2 (1948), cc. 2178-2190; E. Josi "Refrigerio," *Enc. Catt.*, X (1953), pp. 627 ff.; Delehaye, *Sanctus* (Brussels, 1927), pp. 135-140.

14. Hertling-Kirschbaum, *The Roman Catacombs*, pp. 107 ff.

15. Paulinus of Nola, *Carmina* 27.549-553. As an excuse for this habit he alleges the *rusticitas* of the people which leads them to worship their stomachs as a god: *adsueta diu sacris servire profanis, ventre Deo.*

16. Paulinus of Nola, *Ep.* 13.11-15.

17. Augustine, *Ep.* 29.10.

18. Zeno, *Tractatus* 1.15.6.

19. Gaudentius of Brescia, *Tractatus IV in Exod.* (*Corp. Script. Eccl. Lat.*, LXVIII, p. 42).

20. Ambrose, *De Helia* 17.62: *videtur enim non amare imperatorem qui pro eius salute non biberit. . . . et haec vota ad Deum pervenire iudicant sicut illi qui calices ad sepulchra martyrum deferunt atque illic in vesperam bibunt; aliter se exaudiri posse non credunt. Stultitia hominum, qui ebrietatem sacrificium putant, qui existimant illis ebrietatem placere*

qui ieiunio passionem sustinere didicerunt. See also Augustine, *Ep.* 22.3 and Van der Meer, "The Feasts of the Dead," in *Augustine the Bishop,* pp. 498-526.

21. Augustine, *Ep.* 29.8: *nihil nos nec brevius nec verius posse afferre adversus eos qui dicunt, 'Quare modo?' nisi et nos dicamus, 'Vel modo!'*

22. Augustine, *Confess.* 6.15.25.

23. *Ibid.,* 6.3.3-4.

24. *Ibid.,* 6.4.6. Cf. II Cor. 3.6.

25. *Ibid.,* 9.7.15.

26. *Ibid.,* 8.12.29: "*Tolle, lege; tolle, lege.*" For the endless discussions on the definitive crisis, see Marrou, "La querelle autour de 'Tolle, lege'," *Rev. d'Hist. Eccl.,* LIII (1958), pp. 47-57.

27. For the location of Cassiciacum, see G. Morin, "Où en est la question de Cassiciacum?" *Scuola Cattol.,* LXV (1927), pp. 51-56; F. Meda, "Ancora il Cassiciacum di s. Agostino," *ibid.,* pp. 198-202. Both of these authors defend the modern Cassago. The villa of Verecundus would correspond to the site of the present palace Visconti Modrone and the building for the baths of Verecundus with the house of Padulli. Cassago is about twenty-one miles from Milan in the center of Brianza.

28. Augustine, *Confess.* 9.6.14.

29. *Ibid.,* 9.11.28.

30. The thesis that Augustine remained a Platonist even after his baptism and that consequently there was no real conversion at the time of his baptism was sustained by Thimme and later by P. Alfaric, *L'evolution intellectuelle de saint Augustin* (Paris, 1918). This has been refuted by C. Boyer, *Christianisme et neoplatonisme dans la formation de s. Augustin* (Paris, 1920; *idem,* "La conversion de s. Augustin," *Scuola Catt.,* LXV (1927), pp. 401-414.

31. Augustine, *Confess.* 6.2.2.

32. Augustine, *Ep.* 209.2-7, 9-10. See also Van der Meer, *Augustine the Bishop,* pp. 230-231.

33. Possidius, *Vita August., ad init.*

34. Augustine, *Confess.* 9.12.32.

35. Augustine, *Oper. imper. c. Iulian.* 6.21.

36. Cf. Batiffol, *Le catholicisme de s. Augustin* (Paris, 1920), pp. 4 ff.; J. Tixeront, *History of Dogmas,* II (St. Louis, 1914), pp. 355 ff.; A. Harnack, *History of Dogma,* trans. from the 3rd German edition by J. Millar, V (London, 1898), p. 48. Harnack was of the opinion that Augustine would perhaps never have written *The City of God* except for the impressions he had received from Ambrose. The bishop of Milan is explicitly cited by St. Augustine at least one hundred and fifty times. See Van der Meer, *Augustine the Bishop,* pp. 570-572: "It may be said that in all practical matters Augustine had a quite definite model before his eyes—his father in Christ Ambrose. . . . But, above all, in really practical matters he followed Ambrose in detail, if with all the warmth of his own heart and all

the variability of a sensitive nature utterly foreign to that of his examplar. . . . It was not Italy that was his model, but Ambrose. This silent adherence to the first of the Latin Fathers is one of the most striking and informative features in the total picture of Augustine the spiritual genius." Recent critics have also noted that while Augustine did not prefix "Aurelius" to his own family name, this *praenomen* is to be found in the oldest manuscripts, as it is also found already in Orosius (*Lib. Apol. de lib. arb.* 1.4) and in Claudianus Mamertus (*De statu animae* 2.9). C. Cavedoni in *Archivio dell'Ecclesiastico*, II (Florence, 1865), pp. 559-562, tried to prove that Augustine took the name Aurelius from Ambrose as a sign of his spiritual sonship, just as Cyprian added to his own name the *praenomen* Caecilius which he took from the saintly priest of Carthage who converted him (Jerome, *De viris illust.* 67).

37. Ambrose's good sense, which avoided the scruples of the pedants and the laxity of the tepid, made a lively impression on Augustine. See, for example, the reference made to him on the question of fasting, which to the surprise of Monica was not observed at Milan on Saturdays (Augustine, *Ep.* 36.32).

Some of the practical solutions given by Augustine to various problems seem to have been inspired by Ambrose. Compare, for example, Augustine's *In Ps. XXXIII, enarr.* 2.9 with Ambrose's, *De paenit.* 1.31. See P. Rollero, *La "Exp. evan. sec. Luc." di Ambrogio come fonte della esegesi agostiniana* (Turin, 1958), p. 137: "Ambrose was not only the one who introduced Augustine to exegesis and sacred oratory, but he was a guide to whom the bishop of Hippo had frequent recourse in his various works."

CHAPTER XIV

1. For the political developments of 387-389, see Ensslin, "Valentinian II," *Realen. der class. Alter.*, VII A,2 (1948), cc. 2222 ff. In *Ep.* 49, to Severus, bishop of Naples, Ambrose laments the fact that he is embroiled in a sea of troubles. It should be dated in the fall of 387. See p. 380, n. 5. The praise which Symmachus gives to a bishop Severus in *Ep.* 7.51 is probably to be referred to this same bishop. See *Mon. Germ. Hist., Auct. Antiq.*, VI.1 (1883), p. 191.

2. Zosimus 4.44.

3. Ambrose, *De offic.* 2.150-151.

4. Ambrose, *Ep.* 40.23.

5. Cf. Pacatus, *Panegyr.* 34-35; Zosimus 4.45-47; Orosius 7.35. See also A. Solari, *La crisi dell'impero romano: II. Gli ultimi Valentiniani* (Milan, 1933), pp. 67-79. Solari is, however, too partial to the pagan historian.

6. Ensslin, *Die Religionspolitik*, pp. 55 ff. A minute analysis of the

events is given by Petit in *Libanius et la vie municipale à Antioche au IV siècle* (Paris, 1955), pp. 238 ff.

7. Sozomen 7.23.

8. Ambrose, *Ep.* 40.25: *me petente, liberasti plurimos de exsiliis, de carceribus, de ultimae necis poenis.*

9. Ambrose, *Exp. evang. Luc.* 9.32.

10. Sozomen 7.25; Theodoret 5.18. See also Gregory of Nazianzus *Orat.* 20.49-50 for a similar attitude taken by Basil towards the prefect of the East.

11. Ambrose, *Ep.* 40. K. Barth goes too far in tracing Luther's fanatical prejudice against the Jews and in other matters as well to this stand taken by St. Ambrose. See his "Ambrosius und die Synagoge zu Callinicum," *Theologische Zeitschrift aus der Schweiz,* V (1889), pp. 65-86. Caspar in *Geschichte,* I, pp. 276-277, is much more reasonable: although Ambrose was the bishop of Milan rather than of Rome, this episode is an essential factor in the development of papal power. In the seventeenth century, the well-informed Godefroy Hermant did not dare to criticize the saint. He added, however, two pages of incidents in the life of Gregory the Great whose attitude towards the Jews was just the opposite of that of St. Ambrose. See *Vie de s. Ambroise* (Paris, 1678), pp. 355 ff. See also M. Simon, "Le antisémitisme chrétien" in *Verus Israel* (Paris, 1948), pp. 239-274; R. Wilde, *The Treatment of the Jews in the Greek Christian Writers of the First Three Centuries* (Washington, D.C., 1949); and J. E. Seaver, *Persecution of the Jews in the Roman Empire* (Lawrence, Kansas, 1952).

12. Ambrose, *Ep.* 41.

13. Socrates 6.2.6-8. See Ensslin, *Religionspolitik,* p. 3; Palanque in Fliche-Martin, *Hist. de l'égl.,* III, p. 448, n. 1.

14. Pacatus, *Panegyr.* 4 (G. Baehrens, *XII Panegyrici latini* [Leipzig, 1911], p. 93).

15. *Cod. Theod.* 16.5.18. See De Labriolle in Fliche-Martin, *Hist. de l'égl.,* III, p. 523, n. 7, for the ever increasing severity of the laws against the Manichees. The increased harshness of the legislation gives support to the accusation of gross immorality which Augustine, *De haeres.* 46, makes against them.

16. Paulinus, *Vita Ambr.* 25.

17. Ambrose, *Ep.* 57.4. Rauschen and Palanque date this third legation at the end of 389. See Palanque in Fliche-Martin, *Hist. de l'égl.,* III, p. 517, n. 2; *idem, S. Ambroise,* p. 536. Others on the other hand, such as Tillemont and Seeck, place it a year earlier.

18. *Cod. Theod.* 12.1.123.

19. *Ibid.,* 16.2.27; cf. Ensslin, *Religionspolitik,* pp. 69-70.

20. *Ibid.,* 16.3.1.

21. Rufinus, *Hist. Eccl.* 2.22-23; Cavallera, *S. Jérôme,* I (Louvain, 1922), pp. 142 ff.; Murphy, *Rufinus of Aquileia* (Washington, 1945), p. 146.

22. Ambrose, *Ep.* 51; *De obitu Theodos.* 28-34; Paulinus, *Vita Ambr.* 24; Augustine, *De civ. Dei* 5:26; Ensslin, *Religionspolitik*, pp. 67-75. The chronology of Ensslin is here followed. M. R. P. McGuire in his excellent review of Palanque, *Saint Ambroise*, in the *Catholic Historical Review*, XXII (1936-1937), pp. 304-318, also holds for the spring of 390.

23. Theodoret, *Hist. Eccl.* 5.17 gives the "reported" number slain as 7,000. This figure seems to be somewhat high. He was writing about the year 450. Caspar sets the figure at about 2,000 (*Geschichte*, I, p. 277), and Piganiol at about 3,000 (*L'empire*, p. 257).

24; Augustine, *De civ. Dei* 5.26; Ensslin, *Religionspolitik*, pp. 67-75. The

24. Ambrose, *Ep.* 51.

25. *Cod. Theod.* 9.40.13. cf. B. Biondi, "L'influenza di s. Ambrogio su la legislazione religiosa del suo tempo," in *S. Ambrogio nel XVI centenario* (Milan, 1940), p. 387 ff. Many jurists regard this law as the *penance* imposed by St. Ambrose upon Theodosius. The fifth canon of the Council of Elvira from about the year 304 imposed seven years of penance upon a woman who would strike her servant so hard that she would die within three days. The twenty-second canon of the Council of Ancyra of the year 314 imposed a penance for life upon those who were guilty of willful murder. They were to be allowed to receive communion only at the end of their life. See C. J. Hefele, *A History of the Christian Councils, from the Original Documents, to the Close of the Council of Nicea*, translated by Wm. R. Clark (2nd ed., Edinburgh, 1883), pp. 140, 220. Since Theodosius was the emperor, his case was obviously something quite special. See Ambrose *Ep.* 51.17: *si credis, sequere; si, inquam, credis, agnosce quod dico: si non credis, ignosce quod facio, in quo Deum praefero.*

26. See R. Paribeni, *L'Italia imperiale* (Milan, 1938), p. 623: "Neither Napoleon reconciled with God on the desolate ocean rock, nor Henry IV waiting as a suppliant about the moat of Canossa are historical facts that can be compared with the importance of Ambrose's victory. A leader whose absolute power was recognized by all civilians and who till then had no one above himself, one who possessed the highest post in eternal and triumphant Rome and whose prestige had been enhanced by imported concepts of Oriental despotism, yielded before the unarmed representative of a supernatural power that Rome had failed to understand for nearly three centuries and which it had tried to suppress by means of shameful tortures." Although Von Campenhausen makes a number of unfair criticisms of St. Ambrose, this Protestant historian admits that in this instance "the power and freedom of the clergy proved here to be a bastion of public freedom and law" (*Ambrosius*, p. 271). Barbagallo in *Roma antica*, II (Turin, 1932), p. 834, has unfortunately called this Christmas of 390 a "sad" day. On the prejudices of Gibbon, see Meda in the review *Sant' Ambrogio*, I (1939), pp. 273-280.

According to Paulinus, *Vita Ambr.* 8.24, Theodosius reminded Ambrose of the fact that David had not only committed murder but also adultery.

Ambrose then advised him: "Imitate the penance of David!" But this incident may depend upon the questionable authority of Paulinus.

Finally, it must be noted that Ambrose's stand towards Theodosius after the slaughter at Thessalonica was something quite new. When Valentinian I, about the year 370, married Justina after divorcing Marina, the mother of Gratian, no ecclesiastical authority excommunicated the emperor, even though his act has been the source of serious scandal (see Socrates 4.31). Similarly, in 372, when Valens, an Arian and a persecutor of the Catholics, assisted at the celebration of the Eucharist in the church at Caesarea, St. Basil made no protest, and he even accepted the offerings which Valens brought to the altar. See Batiffol, *Le siège*, pp. 73-74.

Paulinus, after his account of the public penance performed by Theodosius, goes on to say: *cuius correctionis profectus secundam illi paravit victoriam (Vita Ambr.* 24). These words have been interpreted in different ways. Older biographers of St. Ambrose took them as referring to Theodosius: "The profit he gained from this correction prepared him for a second victory," that is, a victory over Eugenius after his first victory over Maximus. This is the way it was interpreted by Placidus, a twelfth-century monk of Nonantola in his *Liber de honore ecclesiae* 60 (*Mon. Germ. Hist., Libelli de lite,* II [1892], p. 594): *propter hanc [Theodosii] humilitatem victoriam ei de Eugenio tyranno Dominus dedit.* This also was the interpretation of Tillemont, but Palanque, *S. Ambroise,* p. 244, and Ensslin, *Religionspolitik*, p. 75, take the words as referring to St. Ambrose. According to this interpretation, the first victory would be the settling of the trouble at Callinicum, and the second the penance performed by the emperor after the massacre at Thessalonica. The older interpretation seems to be much better. The more recent interpretation is little in keeping with Ambrose's character and scarcely Christian. If this had been Paulinus's intent, he would have expressed it more definitely.

CHAPTER XV

1. See Jacobus de Voragine, *The Golden Legend,* trans. and adapted by Granger Ryan and Helmut Ripperger, I (New York, 1941), p. 28.

2. For St. Ambrose's Christological definitions, see Faller, "Ambrogio, Sant'," *Encicl. Catt.*, I (1948), c. 996.

3. Ambrose, *De incarnat. Dom. sacram.* 54-56. For his teaching on the efficacy of baptism of desire, see *De obitu Valen.* 51-53.

4. See Huhn, *Das Geheimnis der Jungfrau Mutter Maria nach dem Kirchenvater Ambrosius* (Würzburg, 1954); *idem, Ursprung und Wesen des Bösen und der Sünde nach der Lehre des Kirchenvaters Ambrosius* (Paderborn, 1953); C. W. Neumann, *The Virgin Mary in the Works of St. Ambrose* (Fribourg, 1962); W. Seibel, *Fleisch und Geist beim heiligen Ambrosius* (Munich, 1953). St. Ambrose was well aware of the more seri-

ous problems of Christian theology, though he did not as a rule take time to investigate them. See, for example, his *De paradiso* 9.41: *esset enim aptior huius querellae locus, quod cum omnia possit Deus, hominem tamen perire sit passus.*

5. For Ambrose's ideas on the primacy of the bishop of Rome, see the letter *Provisum* of the Council of Aquileia addressed to Gratian, Valentinian, and Theodosius (Ambrose, *Ep.* 11.4). Cf. Batiffol, *Le siège*, pp. 24 ff.; B. Citterio, *Lineamenti sulla concezione teologica della chiesa in s. Ambrogio* (Milan, 1940). Some see an evolution in his thought on this matter. In 382, his *De incarnat. Dom. sacram.* 32, he explains the promise of the primacy to Peter (Matt. 16.18-19) as a primacy of honor and of faith but not of jurisdiction. On the other hand, in 395, he states that where Peter is, there is the Church: *ubi Petrus ibi ecclesia, ibi nulla mors sed vita aeterna (Enarr. in Ps. XL 30).* For this famous text, see Batiffol, *Le siège*, pp. 26-27. For the earlier text, see J. Ludwig, *Die Primatworte, Mt 16, 18-19, in der altkirchlichen Exegese* (Münster, 1952), pp. 65-68; A. Rimoldi, *L'apostolo san Pietro* (Rome, 1958), pp. 114-126. For St. Ambrose's own relations with the bishop of Rome, see Citterio in *La Scuola Cattolica* LXXVIII (1940), pp. 64-70; Batiffol, *Le siège*, pp. 26-30, which still contains valid observations despite what may be read in Caspar, *Geschichte*, I, p. 287. For Palladius, see Kauffmann, *Aus der Schule des Wulfila* (Strasbourg, 1899), p. 86.

6. See Dudden, *St. Ambrose*, pp. 500-501.

7. See Thamin, *Saint Ambroise et la morale chrétienne au IV*[e] *siècle. Étude comparée des traités "Des devoirs" de Cicéron et de saint Ambroise* (Paris, 1895), and the introduction to the Italian translation of the *De officiis* of Ambrose by A. Cavasin in the series *Corona Patrum Salesiana* (Vol. V, Turin, 1938).

8. See Ambrose, *De Abraham* 2.2-6; 2.7,37; *In Ps. CXVIII* 2.13; *Ep.* 28.1; *De bono mortis* 45; cf. De Labriolle, *St. Ambrose*, p. 203; Hagendahl, *Latin Fathers and the Classics* (Göteborg, 1958), p. 372. On the "spoil of the Egyptians," see C. N. Cochrane, *Christianity and Classical Culture* (New York, 1944), pp. 360 ff.

9. For a more comprehensive view of St. Ambrose's moral teaching, see D. Löpfe, *Die Tugendlehre des heiligen Ambrosius* (Sarnen, 1951). (Thamin is concerned almost exclusively with the *De officiis.*) For his teaching on marriage, see W. J. Dooley, *Marriage According to St. Ambrose* (Washington, D.C., 1948).

10. *De offic.* 1.132: *natura ius commune generavit, usurpatio ius fecit privatum.* Cf. F. Sala, "La dottrina di s. Ambrogio," *Conferenze santambrosiane* (Milan, 1897), p. 146; S. Calafato, *La proprietà privata in s. Ambrogio* (Turin, 1958); L. Orabona in *Aevum*, XXXIII (1959), pp. 495 ff. A. Amati wrote some pleasant nonsense on the "socialism" of St. Ambrose in *Rendiconti del R. Ist. Lomb. di Scienze e Lettere (Milan,* 1897), pp. 764 ff. On the other hand, the study of I. Seipel, *Die Wirtschaftset-*

ischen Lehren der Kirchenväter (Vienna, 1907) chapter IV, is still useful.

11. Ambrose, *Ep.* 37.9: *non igitur natura servum facit, sed insipientia; nec manumissio liberum, sed disciplina.*

12. Paulinus, *Vita Ambr.* 41.

13. Ambrose, *De Tobia* 36.

14. Ambrose, *De Nabuthe* 21.

15. Basil, *Hom. in illud Luca Destruam*, etc. (PG 31 [1885], c. 268).

16. Ambrose, *Hexam.* 5.27.

17. *Ibid.*, 6.47.

18. *Ibid.* 5.58. From these lines it may be concluded that St. Ambrose, like the scriptures, had a high regard for children: "The inheritance of the Lord are children: the reward, the fruit of the womb" (Ps. 126:3). It was a commonplace in monastic literature, however, that children were a burden. Cf. Festugière, *Antioche païenne et chrétienne* (Paris, 1959), p. 184. Tertullian thought that famines, wars, and earthquakes were a providential remedy for the problem of overpopulation (*De anima* 30).

19. Ambrose, *Hexam*, 5.18-19.

20. Ambrose, *De virginitate* 32. Cf. I Cor. 7:27.

21. Ambrose, *Ep.* 63.32; *De Cain* 2.21. Cf. I. Cor. 7:5.

22. Ambrose, *De Helia* 46-68.

23. *Ibid.*, 62. Cf. Augustine, *Confess.* 6.2.2.

24. Leclercq, "Périodeute," *Dict. d'Arch. chrét. et de Lit.* XIV (1939), cc. 369-379; B. Kötting, *Pereginatio religiosa* (Münster, 1950), p. 378.

25. C. J. Hefele, *A History of the Councils of the Church*, trans. H. N. Oxenham, II (Edinburgh, 1876), p. 404: *Can. IV: additum etiam est, ut, quia multi, sub specie peregrinationis, de ecclesiarum conlatione luxuriant, victura (victuaria) non omnibus detur (dentur).*

26. Ambrose, *Ep.* 82.9-10. See F. Martroye, "Une sentence arbitrale de s. Ambroise," *Rev. Hist. de Droit Franç. et Étranger*, Ser. 4, VII (1929), pp. 300-311. Ambrose's solution to the problem was not exactly juridical. It was a compromise and shows his own disinterestedness.

27. Ambrose, *Ep.* 83.2. Cf. Possidius, *Vita August.* 57.

28. Ambrose, *Ep.* 5 and 6, perhaps of the years 395-396. Cf. Martroye, "L'affaire *Indicia*: Une sentence de saint Ambroise," *Mélanges Paul Fournier* (Paris, 1929), pp. 503-510.

29. The *De lapsu virginis* should apparently be attributed to Niceta of Remesiana. See Dudden, *Ambrose*, p. 155; Burn, *Niceta of Remesiana* (Cambridge, 1905), p. cxxxiii.

30. Symmachus, *Ep.* 9.147.

31. Ambrose, *Ep.* 25, of uncertain date.

32. Ambrose, *De paenit.* 1.31.

33. Van der Meer, *Augustine the Bishop*, pp. 53-54.

34. For the excessive pessimism of St. Augustine, see Pierre Charles, S.I., "L'element populaire dans les sermons de saint Augustin," *Nouv. Rev. Théolog.*, LXIX (1947), pp. 649-650.

35. From the chant sung after the Gospel on Abraham's Sunday celebrated during Lent at Milan: "*Respice Domine ad fragilitatem generis humani et require vulnera quae curasti; quia quantum circa nos pietatem impenderis, amplius, quibus miserearis, invenies. Extende quaesumus medicas manus: et quod infirmum est, cura; quod dubium est, repara; quod integrum, fide perseverante, conserva.*" See *Missale Ambrosianum* (Milan, 1954), *Dominica III in Quadragesima, antiphona post evangelium.*

36. J. H. Newman, "Essay XI," *Essays Critical and Historical,* II (London, 1873), p. 233.

CHAPTER XVI

1. For the origins of antiphonal singing in the church at Antioch, see L. Eisenhofer, *Handbuch der katholischen Liturgik,* I (Freiburg i.B., 1932), pp. 222-223. For St. Ambrose's contributions to church music see H. Anglés, "Latin Chant before St. Gregory," in the *New Oxford History of Music,* II (Oxford, 1954), pp. 58-72.

2. Basil, *Ep.* 207.

3. Socrates 6.8.

4. Augustine, *Confess.* 9.6-7; Paulinus, *Vita Ambr.* 13. Paulinus, who wrote about the year 422, may have had before him the *Confessions* of St. Augustine, written in 397.

5. Augustine, *Confess.* 10.33.

6. For the hostility to singing in the West, see *Niceta of Remesiana,* ed. Burn (Cambridge, 1905), p. 68: *scis nonnullos non solum in nostris, sed etiam in orientalibus esse partibus, qui superfluam nec congruentem divinae religioni aestiment psalmorum et hymnorum decantationem. sufficere enim putant quod corde dicitur, lascivum esse si hoc lingua proferatur.* See Ambrose, *In Ps. CXVIII* 7.26.

7. St. Augustine thought that music was *per se* something rather useless. See his *De doctr. Christ.* 2.18.28. The *study* of music could, however, be of some use. His work *De musica* deals with rhythm.

8. Ambrose, *Contra Auxen.* 34: *hymnorum quoque meorum carminibus deceptum populum ferunt.* Isidore of Seville, *De eccles. offic.* 1.7: *antiphonas Graeci primi composuerunt, duobus choris alternatim concinentibus. . . . apud Latinos autem primus idem beatissimus Ambrosius antiphonas constituit, Graecorum exemplum imitatus.*

9. *Liber pontificalis,* ed. Duchesne, I (Paris, 1886), pp. 230-231.

10. Mansi, *Sacrorum Conciliorum . . . collectio,* IV, p. 550.

11. Ambrose, *Hexam.* 3.5.

12. Roy Jesson, "Ambrosian Chant," in *Gregorian Chant,* ed. W. Apel (Bloomington, Ind., 1958), pp. 465-483; Huglo, Agustoni, Cardine, Moneta Caglio, *Fonti e paleografia del canto ambrosiano* (Milan, 1956). Among the oldest Eastern hymns found in the liturgy of Milan is the prayer to

the Virgin Mary: *Sub tuam misericordiam confugimus.* This prayer has been found in an Egyptian papyrus of the third century. See C. H. Roberts, *Catalogue of the Greek and Latin Papyri in the John Rylands Library* (Manchester, 1938), no. 470. The text of the papyrus is remarkably close to that used at Milan and at Constantinople. The prayer found in the Roman and Coptic liturgies has variant readings. See the comparisons made by P. F. Mercenier in "La plus ancienne prière à la Sainte Vierge," *Les Questions Liturg. et Paroiss.* (Louvain, 1940), pp. 33-36.

13. See Ferrua, "Educazione alla poesia nel IV secolo," *Civiltà Cattolica,* LXXXVIII.3 (1937), pp. 513-522.

14. Ferrua has published a critical edition of these poems, *Epigrammata damasiana* (Vatican City, 1942).

15. Ambrose, *In Ps. I* 10: *violentiora praecepta non permanent.*

16. See Athanasius, *De decr. Nicaen. syn.* 16; Bardy in Fliche-Martin, *Hist. de l'égl.*, III, pp. 75-76; J. Quasten, *Patrology,* III (Westminster, Md., 1960), pp. 11-13. Even before Arius, the Gnostics Valentine in Egypt and Bardesane in Syria made use of hymns to spread their heretical doctrines.

17. Ephesians 5:18-19.

18. Colossians 3:16.

19. Pliny, *Ep.* 10.96.

20. Tertullian, *Apolog.* 39; *De orat.* 28.

21. See L. Biraghi, *Inni sinceri e carmi di s. Ambrogio* (Milan, 1862); G. M. Dreves, *Aurelius Ambrosius, der Vater des Kirchengesanges: Eine hymnologische Studie* (Freiburg i.B., 1893); A. Steier, "Untersuchungen über die Echtheit der Hymnen des Ambrosius," *Jahrbücher für Klassische Philologie, Supplbd.,* XXVIII (1903), pp. 549-662. A. S. Walpole, *Early Latin Hymns* (Oxford, 1922). Walpole accepts eighteen hymns as coming from St. Ambrose. The four cited by St. Augustine are *the Aeterne rerum Conditor* (*Retract.* 1.21), *Iam surgit hora tertia* (*De nat. et grat. contra Pel.* 63), *Deus Creator omnium* (*Confess.* 9.12.32), and *Intendi qui regis Israel* (*Sermo* 372). A recent study has been made of the Ambrosian hymns by M. Simonetti in *Atti della Accad. Naz. dei Lincei: Memorie,* IV (1952), pp. 341-484, and *Innologia ambrosiana* (Alba, 1956), but his work does not replace that of Walpole, which he does not seem to have known. For the poetical technique of Ambrose, see M. P. Cunningham, "The Place of the Hymns of St. Ambrose in the Latin Poetic Tradition," *Studies in Philology,* LII (1955), pp. 509-514. W. Bulst, *Hymni latini antiquissimi LXXV, psalmi III* (Heidelberg, 1956), lists fourteen Ambrosian hymns which he regards as authentic. For Latin hymns in general, consult John Julian, *A Dictionary of Hymnology* (London, 1892), and O. J. Kuhnmuench, S.J., *Early Christian Latin Poets from the Fourth to the Sixth Century* (Chicago, 1929). For the hymns of the liturgy, see M. Britt, O.S.B., *The Hymns of the Breviary and Missal* (rev. ed., New York, 1936).

22. Translated by H. T. Henry. See his article, "The Hymn *Aeterne rerum Conditor,*" *American Ecclesiastical Review,* XV (1896), pp. 349-376.

23. Translated by Edward Caswall, *Lyra Catholica* (London, 1849), reprinted in Kuhnmuench, *Early Christian Latin Poets*, pp. 118-120.

24. Translated by J. Ellerton and F. J. A. Hart, reprinted in Britt, *op. cit.*, pp. 37-38; reprinted in Kuhnmuench, *op. cit.*, p. 124.

25. Translated by Caswall, reprinted in Kuhnmuench, *op. cit.*, p. 120.

26. Augustine, *Confess.* 9.6.14.

27. *Ibid.*, 10.33.50.

28. Ambrose, *Hexam.* 3.23.

29. Ambrose, *Enarr. in Ps.* I 9.

30. Ambrose, *Contra Auxen.* 34.

31. See Paredi, in *S. Ambrogio nel XVI centenario* (Milan, 1940), pp. 71-157; "Messali ambrosiani antichi," in *Ambrosius* (Milan, 1959), n. 4, pp. 1-25; A. A. King, "Rite of Milan: Ambrosian Rite," in *Liturgies of the Primatial Sees* (Milwaukee, 1957), pp. 286-453.

32. See Pighi in *Aevum*, XVIII (1944), pp. 16 ff. For the third of these inscriptions see also Dölger, "Zur Zymbolik des altchristlichen Taufhauses," in *Ant. und Christ.*, IV (1934), pp. 153-187; O. Perler, in *Riv. di Arch. Crist.*, XXVII (1951), pp. 145-166. According to Perler, the eight distichs that adorned the baptistery were the fruit of long and earnest reflections.

33. These hexameters were published by S. Merkle in *Röm. Quartalschr.*, X (1896), pp. 185-222. According to Faller, "in thought, language, and style, they are entirely Ambrosian." See Faller, "Ambrogio, S.," *Enc. Catt.*, I (1948), p. 999.

CHAPTER XVII

1. *Cod. Theod.* 16.10.10: *nemo se hostiis polluat, nemo insontem victimam caedat, nemo delubra adeat, templa perlustret.*

2. *Ibid.*, 11.39.11.

3. Socrates 5.16; Sozomen 7.15; Theodoret 5.22.

4. *Cod. Theod.* 16.10.11.

5. Theodoret 5.22; Socrates 5.16. See also Rufinus, *Eccl. hist.* 2.25; G. Lazzati, *Teofilo d'Alessandria* (Milan, 1935).

6. *Cod. Theod.* 16.10.12. On these various laws see Ensslin, *Religionspolitik des Kaisers Theodosius*, pp. 75 ff. Ensslin maintains that Seeck and Stein exaggerate in attributing them all to Ambrose's influence.

7. Ps. 95.5: *quoniam omnes dii gentium daemonia.*

8. Augustine, *Ep.* 50; Duchesne, *Early History of the Christian Church*, II, p. 512.

9. Paulinus, *Vita Ambr.* 52. See Delehaye, *Origines*, p. 334.

10. For the "evolution" of the bishop, see Palanque, *S. Ambroise*, pp. 254 ff. The same may be noted in St. Jerome. In 402 in his letter to Laeta he is rigoristic in his advice on the education of Paula (*Ep.* 107). In another letter, however, written after the sack of Rome in 410, he is sur-

prisingly moderate in his opinions on how to educate Pacatula: she should be favored with gifts, flowers, dolls, and caresses (*Ep.* 128). As Thamin has observed, "The years have given to our saint the instincts of a grandfather" (*S. Ambroise*, pp. 398-399).

11. Ambrose, *Ep.* 56, of March, 392. The problem of Flavian was settled in the East by the Council of Caesarea in Palestine held in 393. Nevertheless in 398 the bishops of the West assembled at Rome still refused to recognize him. See Batiffol, *Le siège*, pp. 279 ff.

12. Details of the political crisis in 392 are taken chiefly from Ambrose's *De obitu Valentiniani.* See Faller in *Corp. Script. Eccl. Lat.*, LXXIII (1955), pp. 101* ff.; Calderini in *Storia di Milano*, I (Milan, 1953), pp. 354 ff.; Ensslin, "Valentinianus II," *Realen. der class. Alter.*, VII A,2 (1948), cc. 2226 ff.

13. Zosimus 4.53; Philostorgius 11.1; John of Antioch, fragm. 187. See *Corp. Script. Eccl. Lat.*, LXXIII (1955), p. 103.

14. Ambrose, *Ep.* 53.5.

15. Piganiol, *L'empire chrétien*, p. 262, n. 77, states that Valentinian could not have entered heaven since he was not baptized. But this is contrary to Ambrose's explicit teaching on the baptism of desire. St. Jerome, *Ep.* 60.15, declares that Valentinian was already dead when hanged, thus ruling out the possibility of suicide.

16. Ambrose, *De obitu Valent.* 39: *felicius episcopos persequuntur imperatores quam diligunt.* The sentence could also be translated: "The emperors are more fortunate when they persecute the bishops than when they love them."

17. See Ambrose, *Ep.* 52; Siricius, *Optarem* (in Ph. Jaffé, *Regesta Romanorum Pontificum* [2nd ed., Leipzig, 1881], p. 260). Jerome, *Adv. Iovinianum libri duo*; Palanque, *S. Ambroise*, pp. 260-262; Cavallera, *S. Jérôme*, pp. 151 ff.; Fr. Valli, *Gioviniano* (Urbino, 1954).

18. Augustine, *De haeres.* 82: *ita ut quaedam virgines sacrae provectae iam aetatis in urbe Roma ubi haec docebat eo audito nupsisse dicantur. Idem, Retract.* 2.48: *tantum valuit in urbe Romana ut nonnullas etiam sanctimoniales de quarum impudicitia suspicio nulla praecesserat, deiecisse in nuptias diceretur, hoc maxime argumento cum eas argueret dicens: Tu ergo melior quam Sarra, melior quam Susanna sive Anna? . . . Hoc modo etiam virorum sanctorum sanctum caelibatum commemoratione patrum coniugatorum et comparatione frangebat.*

19. Mansi, *Sacrorum Conciliorum . . . collectio*, III, p. 689; Hefele-Oxenham, *History of the Councils*, II, pp. 391-393; Palanque in Fliche-Martin, *Hist. de l'égl.*, III, p. 475. The year of this council at Milan which condemned Jovinian is still disputed. Tillemont, Ihm, and Hefele-Oxenham, place it in 390, Rauschen in 392, and Palanque in 393. Recently Neumann has again suggested the year 390, but his arguments are not conclusive. See *The Virgin Mary in the Works of St. Ambrose* (Fribourg, 1962), pp. 144-153.

20. Ambrose, *Ep.* 57.11.
21. Paulinus, *Vita Ambr.* 30.
22. Ambrose, *Ep.* 57.8.
23. Jerome, *De viris illust.* 124: Ambrosius, *Mediolanensis episcopus, usque in praesentem diem scribit, de quo, quia superest, meum iudicium subtraham, ne in alterutram partem aut adulatio in me reprehendatur aut veritas.* In comparison with the four lines which Jerome devotes to St. Ambrose may be placed the twenty-seven which he dedicates to himself.
24. Bardy in *Revue d'Histoire Ecclés.*, XLVIII (1953), p. 828.
25. St. Jerome, *Ep.* 49.14 (in *Patr. Lat.* this is *Ep.* 48).
26. Ambrose, *Ep.* 57.
27. The only epigraphical evidence that we have for the pagan reaction during the reign of Eugenius is an inscription discovered at Ostia in 1938. It was set up in 393-394 to commemorate the restoration of a temple of Hercules. See Bloch, "A New Document of the Last Pagan Revival in the West," *Harv. Theol. Rev.*, XXXVIII (1945), pp. 199-241.
28. Ambrose, *Ep.* 29, to Irenaeus.
29. Ambrose, *Ep.* 81, to the clergy of Milan.
30. Paulinus, *Vita Ambr.* 29.
31. *Idem.*, 28. In the sermon which he preached at Florence on the occasion of the dedication of the basilica, St. Ambrose declared: *Paulus non potuisset ad tantam apostolatus sui pervenire gratiam, si fuisset alligatus coniugii contubernio* (*Exhort. virgin.* 22). For St. Ambrose's stay in Florence, see G. B. Ristori, "Della venuta e del soggiorno di s. Ambrogio in Firenze," *Archivio Storico Italiano*, Ser. 5, XXXVI (1905), pp. 241-275. He holds, however, that Ambrose remained at Florence for more than a year. See also G. Anichini, "S. Ambrogio e la chiesa di Firenze," in *Ambrosiana* (Milan, 1940), pp. 339 ff. That Paulinus was originally a member of the Church of Florence is a reasonable conjecture of different biographers of St. Ambrose.
32. Paulinus, *Vita Ambr.* 31.
33. See Augustine, *De civit. Dei.* 5.25-26.
34. Ambrose, *De obitu Theod.* 7.
35. See Ambrose, *Epp.* 61 and 62.
36. Ambrose, *Ep.* 61.1: *arbitratus es, beatissime imperator, quantum ex augustis litteris tuis comperi, me longe abesse ab urbe Mediolanensium, quia res tuas crederem a Deo destitui. sed non ego ita imprudens, aut virtutis et meritorum tuorum immemor abfui, ut non praesumerem coeleste auxilium pietati tuae adfore*, etc.
37. Ambrose, *De obitu Theod.* 41-51. There is no reason for denying the authenticity of this passage in the oration. It may not have been delivered at the time of the funeral, but, as Faller has indicated, could have been added when Ambrose was preparing the work for publication. See *Corp. Script. Eccl. Lat.*, LXXIII, p. 117.
38. Eusebius, *Vita Constant.* 3.30. For the pagan structures at Jerusalem,

see Jerome, *Ep.* 58.3. See also L. Voelkl, *Der Kaiser Konstantin* (Munich, 1957), pp. 158-160.

39. Cyril of Jerusalem, *Catech.* 13.4. St. John Chrysostom, Rufinus, and Socrates mention the finding of the Cross after St. Ambrose, but instead of the discovery of the title, they give the cure of a woman as the way it was identified. See Leclercq, "Hélène, Impératrice," *Dict. d'Arch. chrét. et Lit.*, VI (1925), c. 2130. An inscription of the year 359 on a stone slab used for a *refrigerium* that was found in a village near Algiers indicates that at this time relics of the true Cross were being venerated. See Leclercq, "Agape," *Dict. d'Arch. chrét. et Lit.*, I (1924), c. 828, fig. 178; E. Diehl, *Inscriptiones Latinae Christianae*, I (Berlin, 1925), no. 2068.

40. Ambrose, *De obitu Theod.* 42.

41. *Ibid.*, 48-51. St. Ambrose's use of the text *sanctum quod super frenum* was criticized by St. Jerome in his commentary on this passage in Zacharias (14.2): *audivi a quodam rem sensu quidem pio dictam, sed ridiculam, clavos Dominicae crucis e quibus Constantinus augustus frenos equo suo fecerit, sanctum Domini appellari.*

42. Isaias 60:3.

CHAPTER XVIII

1. Jerome, *Ep.* 77.8; A. Penna, *S. Girolamo* (Turin, 1949), p. 206.

2. See S. Mazzarino, *Trattato di storia romana,* II (Rome, 1956), p. 519.

3. Jerome, *Commentarium in Ezech.* 7.21: *quod absque lacrymis et gemitu videre non possumus.*

4. *Cod. Theod.* 16.5.25.

5. Paulinus, *Vita Ambr.* 34. The right of asylum was by this time spread throughout the Christian world. As early as 392, however, we have edicts for the East which were intended to suppress abuses connected with this right.

6. Paulinus, *Vita Ambr.* 43.

7. *Ibid.*, 33; see also Delehaye, *Origines*, p. 79.

8. Paulinus, *Vita Ambr.* 44.

9. *Ibid.*, 36.

10. Palanque in Fliche-Martin, *Hist. de l'égl.*, III, 471-477; Grazioli, "La giurisdizione metropolitana di Milano a Verona all'epoca di s. Ambrogio," *Scuola Cattolica*, LXVIII (1940), pp. 373 ff. Symposius, a bishop of Astorga in Spain who had been excommunicated by a synod held at Saragossa in 395, came to St. Ambrose at Milan and received from him the terms of his readmission into the Church. See Mansi, *Sacrorum Conciliorum . . . collectio*, III, p. 1005; Caspar, *Geschichte*, I, p. 280.

11. Ambrose, *Ep.* 58.3.

12. Paulinus of Nola, *Ep.* 3.4; see A. Baudrillart, *San Paolino vescovo di Nola* (Rome, 1908), p. 45.

13. Ambrose, *Ep.* 63; see Savio, *Gli antichi vescovi d'Italia: Il Piemonte* (Turin, 1899), p. 421. Ambrose's trip to Novara and Vercelli is witnessed by the legendary but not wholly unfounded *Vita Gaudentii.* See the *Acta Sanctorum* for April 3rd.

14. It was while he was taking down Ambrose's commentary on Psalm XLIV that Paulinus saw a ball of fire descend upon the head of the saint, enter his mouth, and make his face shine like snow (*Vita Ambr.* 42).

15. C. Marchesi, *Seneca* (Milan, 1934), pp. 351 ff. Martial 10.47 has the same regard for death: no fear of, but also no desire for, it.

16. See Ambrose's, *De bono mortis,* two sermons of the year 391, and *De fuga saeculi,* a homily delivered in 394.

17. Paulinus, *Vita Ambr.* 46.

18. Possidius, *Vita August.* 27.

19. Paulinus, *Vita Ambr.* 46.

20. On Ambrose's authoritarian ways, see *De offic.* 1.72: He did not want to have a certain priest among his clergy, even though he was zealous, because of his awkward gestures. He forbade another to appear before him because he thought he had an insolent way of walking. Sozomen 8.6 contains the account of a Milanese deacon, Gerontius, who was suspended by Ambrose. He went off to Constantinople where he made friends at court and soon succeeded in being elected bishop of Nicomedia. He was consecrated by the bishop of Caesarea in Cappadocia. Ambrose wrote to Nectarius asking him to depose Gerontius, but Nectarius was unable to carry out the request. Only after the death of Ambrose was he eventually deposed through the efforts of St. John Chrysostom. See Batiffol, *Le siège,* pp. 282-291. For a complete spiritual profile of St. Ambrose, see the careful study of U. Pestalozza, *La religione di Ambrogio* (Milan, 1949).

21. G. Calligaris, "Il flagello di sant'Ambrogio e le leggende delle lotte ariane," *Ambrosiana* (1897), p. XIII. The earliest representation of St. Ambrose with a scourge is the bas-relief on the Porta Romana at Milan, which dates from the year 1171.

22. Ambrose, *De virginitate* 99.

23. Ambrose, *De paenit.* 2.73.

24. For the tomb of St. Ambrose, see Biraghi, *I tre sepolcri santambrosiani* (Milan, 1864); L. Beltrami, "La basilica ambrosiana primitiva e la ricostruzione compiuta nel sec. IX," *Ambrosiana* (1897), p. X.; Paredi, "La tomba di S. Ambrogio," *Diocesi di Milano,* I, No. 11 (December, 1960), pp. 8-13.

After the death of St. Ambrose, in the early hours of Holy Saturday, April 4, 397, his body was carried into the basilica *maior,* where it remained until Easter morning. Then it was transferred to the Ambrosian basilica and buried there in a loculus under the high altar alongside another loculus in which had been placed the bodies of the martyrs Gervasius and Protasius.

About the year 835, the three bodies were taken from their sepulchers and placed in a single porphyry urn by the archbishop Engelbert II. This was found on January 13, 1864, along with the empty loculi. On August 8, 1871, the urn was opened. It was two-thirds full of clear water, at the bottom of which were the three skeletons. Earlier at the end of the fifth, or at the beginning of the sixth century an identification of the remains had also been made. See De Capitani d'Arzago, *Antichi tessuti della basilica Ambrosiana* (Milan, 1941), pp. 98-102.

Chronology

o

303, February 24 Edict of persecution published at Nicomedia
305, March 1 Abdication of Diocletian and Maximian
311, April 30 Galerius publishes at Nicomedia the edict which brings the persecution to an end
312, October 29 Constantine enters victoriously into Rome
313, February Meeting of Constantine and Licinius at Milan
313, June 13 Licinius publishes at Nicomedia the famous rescript which is usually called "the Edict of Milan"
325, Summer The Council of Nicea
328, June 8 Athanasius is elected bishop of Alexandria
331, Birth of Julian the Apostate
334, Birth of St. Ambrose at Trier
335, Council of Tyre. Athanasius is exiled to Trier. Death of Arius
337, February 6 Election of Pope Julius I
337, May 22 Death of Constantine the Great
337, November 23 Athanasius returns to Alexandria
339, March 18 Athanasius is expelled from Alexandria by command of Constantius II
340, Death of Constantine II
340, Mary, the sister of Pachomius, founds the first monastery for women at Atribi in upper Egypt
341-342, Athanasius at Rome and at Milan
343, Council of Sardica
346, May 9 Death of Pachomius, founder of Egyptian cenobitism.

347 (about) Birth of St. Jerome at Stirdon

350, January 18 Death of Constans. Usurpation of Magnentius

351, September 28 Battle of Mursa. Gallus is made Caesar

352, April 12 Death of Pope Julius

352, May 17 Election of Pope Liberius

353, January 6 Marcellina receives the veil at Rome (or in 354)

354, November Gallus is assassinated at Pola. Julian comes to Milan where Constantius II is in residence

354, November 13 Birth of St. Augustine

354, Birth of St. John Chrysostom

355, January-May Council of Milan. Exile of bishop Dionysius. Installation of Auxentius at Milan

355, June Julian at Athens

355, September-October Discussion of Constantius II with Pope Liberius at Milan. Exile of Liberius to Beroea. Felix elected and consecrated pope at Milan

355, November 6 Julian elected Caesar at Milan. He marries Helena, the daughter of Constantine the Great and Fausta

356. January 17 Death of St. Anthony, the father of anchoritism

356, February 8 Athanasius forced to flee from Alexandria. He takes up his residence with the monks of the Thebaid

357, Athanasius writes the life of Anthony

357, April 28-May 29 Constantius II at Rome

358, August 2 Return of Liberius to Rome

359, May 22 Fourth formula of Sirmium. Council of Rimini

359-367 (about) Stay of St. Jerome in Rome

360, March (about) Julian is acclaimed Augustus at Paris

360 (about) St. Martin retires to an hermetical life at Ligugé near Poitiers

361, November 3 Constantius II dies at Mopsucrene

361-362, Julian's decree of tolerance. Athanasius returns to Alexandria. The laws with respect to teaching in the schools

363, February 12 Prohibition of funeral processions during the day. Athanasius again exiled

363, June 26 Death of Julian. He is succeeded by Jovian

364, February 16-17 Death of Jovian

364, February 27 Election of Valentinian I at Nicea

364, March 28 Election of Valens, Augustus for the East

365, Athanasius, who had returned to Alexandria after the death of Julian, is again exiled by Valens

365 (about) Ambrose and Satyrus got to Sirmium as lawyers in the offices of the prefect of the praetorium

365, November 22 Death of the antipope Felix

366, Altercatio Heracliani laici cum Germinio episcopo Sirmiensi

366, September 24 Death of Liberius. Election of Damasus and of Ursinus. Riots at Rome

367 (about) Jerome goes from Rome to Trier. Augustine goes to Madaura to study grammar

367, August 24 The eight-year-old Gratian is elected Augustus at Amiens

368 (about) Ambrose and Satyrus are elected to membership in the council of the prefect

368, A Roman council condemns Auxentius of Milan

370 (about) Ambrose is appointed *consularis* of Liguria-Aemilia, with his residence at Milan

371, Process of Isaac against Pope Damasus

371-372, St. Martin, consecrated bishop of Tours, founds the monastery of Marmoutier

372, Conspiracy of Theodore against Valens

373, May 2 Athanasius dies at the age of seventy-seven

374, October (about) Death of Auxentius. Election of Ambrose

374, November 30 Baptism of Ambrose

374, December 7 Episcopal consecration

375, November 17 Death of Valentinian I at Brigetio

375, November 22 The four-year-old Valentinian II is proclaimed Augustus

375-376 (about) First disturbances caused by Ursinus and Julian Valens at Milan

377, Publication of the *De virginibus* and the *De viduis*

377 (about) The Goths cross the Danube. Journey of Ambrose to Sirmium for the election of Anemius

377, Revolt of the Goths at Marcianopolis

377 (about) Publication of the *De paradiso, De Cain,* and *De virginitate*

378, Melania the Elder founds a monastery of fifty virgins at Jerusalem. Death of Satyrus

378, February (or May) Gratian defeats the Lentienses at Argentaria (Harbourg, near Colmar)

378, June-July Gratian marches to the Balkans

378, August 9 The disaster at Hadrianople. Death of Valens

378, Autumn Edict of tolerance

378, September-October Council of Rome

378, October-November Gratian asks for, and receives from, Ambrose the first two books of his *De fide*

378, Autumn-Winter The court of Valentinian II is transferred from Sirmium to Milan. Gratian remains in Sirmium

379, January 1 St. Basil dies at Caesarea in Cappadocia at the age of forty-nine

379, January 19 Gratian nominates Theodosius Augustus at Sirmium

379, Spring Arian agitation at Milan. Sequestration of a basilica

379, June-July Gratian heads towards Milan by way of Aquileia

379, July Letter of Gratian to Ambrose and his reply (*Ep.* 1)

379, July 31 Gratian arrives at Milan

379, August 3 Revocation of the edict of tolerance

379, September Gratian returns to Trier

379, Final months St. Ambrose publishes the last three books of his *De fide*

380, January Letter of Gratian to Ambrose

380, February 28 Edict of Thessalonica

380, March Reply of Ambrose to Gratian

380, April Meeting of Ambrose with Gratian at Milan

380, November Entrance of Theodosius to Constantinople. Gregory of Nazianzus becomes bishop of the city

380, End of the year Arian controversies at Milan. Second disturbance caused by Julian Valens

381, March Editing of the *De Spiritu Sancto*

381, May-September Council of Constantinople. Nectarius becomes bishop of the city. Correspondence of Ambrose with Theodosius in the name of the Council of Aquileia

382, First months *De incarnationis Dominicae sacramento*

382, Summer Council of Rome. Ambrose at Rome. Jerome also there with Epiphanius. First petition of the Roman senate

382, Winter Death of Acholius, bishop of Thessalonica

383, January 16 The six-year-old Arcadius is proclaimed Augustus Maximus proclaimed Augustus in Britain

383, Summer Augustine arrives at Rome

383, August 25 Gratian slain at Lyons

383, End of the year First mission of Ambrose to Trier. Lack of provisions at Rome. Expulsion of foreigners from the city

384, Summer Second petition of the Roman senate. The legation of Symmachus to Milan for the Altar of Victory. Treaty of Theodosius with Maximus (see Zosimus 4.37). Letters of St. Ambrose to Valentinian (Epp. 17-18)

384, October Second mission of Ambrose to Trier

384, Autumn Augustine nominated professor at Milan

384, November-December Treaty of Valentinian with Maximus

384, December 11 Death of Pope Damasus. Election of Pope Siricius

385, Spring First struggle with the court because of the intrigues of Justina and Auxentius

385, August Jerome leaves Rome for the East. With Paula he visits the monks of the Nitria

385, Monica joins Augustine at Milan

385, Execution of Priscillian and his followers. Letter of St. Ambrose to the bishops of Aemilia (Ep. 23)

386, Spring Struggle renewed with the court. Council of bishops at Milan. Siege of the basilicas. Antiphonal singing. The sermon *Contra Auxentium*. Letter to Valentinian (*Ep*. 21). The *De Iacob*. Letter of Maximus to Valentinian

386, April 2 Holy Thursday. The end of the conflict. Letter to Marcellina (Ep. 20)

386, June 17-19 Discovery and transfer of the bodies of the martyrs Gervasius and Protasius. Second letter to Marcellina (Ep. 22)

386, Summer Conversion of Augustine and his withdrawal to Cassiciacum

386-389, Paula builds at Bethlehem a monastery for men, a convent for women, and a hospice for pilgrims

387, First months The *In Ps. LXI enarratio*

387, March-April Revolt at Antioch

387, April 19-24 The homilies of the *Hexameron*

387, April 24 Baptism of Augustine

387, June Homilies on Job and David: *Apologia David; De interpellatione Iob et David*

387, Summer Maximus invades Italy. Valentinian II flees to Thessalonica

387, Summer Monica dies at Ostia. Augustine returns to Rome

388, July 28 Death of Maximus at Aquileia. Augustine returns to Africa. Death of Justina

388, December Question of Callinicum. Letter to Theodosius (*Ep.* 40) and to Marcellina (Ep. 41)

389, Sermons against riches and on fasting: *De Helia et ieiunio; De Tobia; De Nabuthe*

389, June 13-September 1 Stay of Theodosius in Rome

389 (about) The *De paenitentia.* Visit of Persian nobles to Milan

389, Towards the end of the year Third petition of the Roman senate for the restoral of paganism

390 (about) Publication of the *Expositio evangelii secundum Lucam*

390, April Massacre at Thessalonica

390, September Council of bishops at Milan. Letter of Ambrose to Theodosius (Ep. 51)

390, October-December (about) Penance of Theodosius

390, Christmas Absolution of Theodosius

391, February 24 Antipagan edict for Rome

391, June 16 Antipagan edict for Egypt. Destruction of the Serapaeum

391, Augustine ordained to the priesthood at Hippo by Valerius

391, Final months Fourth petition of the Roman senate in favor of paganism

392, First months Council of Capua

392, March Letter of Ambrose to Theophilus of Alexandria. The veiling of Ambrosia: *De institutione virginis*

392, May 15 Death of Valentinian II at Vienne
392, August 22 Eugenius proclaimed Augustus
392, September Letter of Ambrose to Theodosius with respect to the burial of Valentinian II. *De obitu Valentiniani*
392, End of the year Fifth and sixth petitions of the Roman senate, to Eugenius, for the re-establishment of pagan worship. Condemnation of Jovinian at Rome
393, January 10 The nine-year-old Honorius proclaimed Augustus
393, First months Third Council of Milan. Condemnation of Jovinian. Letters of Ambrose to Pope Siricius (*Ep.* 42) and to the bishops of Macedonia (*Ep.* 56 bis)
393, Summer-autumn Eugenius and Arbogast invade Italy. Ambrose leaves for Bologna. His letters to Eugenius (*Ep.* 57) and the clergy of Milan (*Ep.* 81). Discovery at Bologna of the bodies of Sts. Vitalis and Agricola
394, March-July Stay of Ambrose at Florence. The *Exhortatio virginitatis*. Pagan reaction at Rome
394, Beginning of August Ambrose returns to Milan
394, September 5-6 Battle of the Frigidus. Death of Eugenius. Suicide of Arbogast. Letters of Ambrose to Theodosius (*Ep.* 61-62)
394, End of the year Preaching on Psalms XLV, XLVII, XLVIII. Paulinus and his wife Therasia consecrate themselves to a life of asceticism
395, January 17 Death of Theodosius at Milan
395, February 25 *De obitu Theodosii*
395, March Sermons on Psalms XXXV-XL
395, Discovery and transference of the bodies of Sts. Nazarius and Celsus
395-396, The question of Indicia. Letters to Syagrius of Verona (*Ep.* 5-6)
396, Cresconius dragged from a church. Correspondence with Fritigil
396, Letter to the church of Vercelli (*Ep.* 63)
396, Augustine consecrated bishop of Hippo
397, February-March Trouble caused by a former slave of Stilicho. Journey of Ambrose to Pavia. Editing of his commentary on Psalm XLIII
397, April 4 Death of St. Ambrose. Simplicianus succeeds him

397, November 8 Death of St. Martin. His burial on the 11th

397, Augustine publishes his *Confessions*

399, November 19 Death of Pope Siricius. Election of Anastasius

400, Summer Letter of Pope Anastasius to Simplicianus inviting him to condemn Origen and his writings

400, August 15 Death of Simplicianus. Succession of Venerius

402, February or March Stilicho forces Alaric to lift the siege of Milan

402, December 19 Death of Pope Anastasius. Election of Innocent I

404, Ravenna replaces Milan as the imperial place of residence

406, Stilicho at Fiesole defeats the Alani, Vandals, and Ostrogoths under the leadership of Radagaisus

408, August Stilicho is put to death

410, August 24 Alaric sacks Rome

419, September 30 Death of St. Jerome

430, August 28 Death of St. Augustine

452, Attila destroys Aquileia, devastates Pavia and Milan

Works of Saint Ambrose

o

There were several editions of individual works of St. Ambrose in the fifteenth century. A good list of these is given in the *Indice Generale degli Incunaboli delle Biblioteche d'Italia,* I (Rome, 1943), nos. 423-433. The first edition of all the works was that printed in three volumes by J. Amerbach at Basel in 1492. A celebrated but not outstanding edition is that of Erasmus of Rotterdam, which was printed at Basel in 1527. Jacques Du Friche and Nicholas Le Nourry, Benedictines of the Congregation of St. Maur, published an epoch-making edition in two folio volumes at Paris in 1686-1690. This "Maurist" edition was reprinted at Venice in 1748-1751 and again in 1781-1782. Migne again reprinted this Maurist edition in his *Patrologia Latina* at Paris in 1845. They form volumes 14-17 of the *Patrologia Latina,* which is here cited as PL.

P. A. Ballerini edited the works again in six volumes, which were published at Milan in the years between 1875 and 1883. Ballerini's work, which is here cited as B, is based upon the Maurist text but with editions and variants from a number of manuscripts found at Milan.

The Maurist text was also reproduced in a smaller format at Paris in 1836. The four volumes of this edition are cited as Par.

A new critical text of the works is being published in the *Corpus Scriptorum Ecclesiasticorum Latinorum* at Vienna. Seven volumes have thus far appeared. They are cited as CSEL.

For the critical value of these various editions, one should consult the different histories of Latin literature or manuals of patrology. Very useful is the list given by E. Dekkers in *Clavis Patrum Latinorum* (2nd ed., Bruges, 1961), pp. 27-40.

DE ABRAHAM LIBRI II
PL 14, 419 (441); B 1, 365; Par 1, 192; CSEL 32, 1, 501.
From about the year 378.

APOLOGIA DAVID (PRIMA)
PL 14, 851 (891); B 2, 73; Par 2, 1; CSEL 32, 2, 229.
From the summer of 387.

CONTRA AUXENTIUM INTER EPISTOLAS: POST EP. 16
From 386.

DE BONO MORTIS
PL 14, 539 (567); B 1, 501; Par 1, 264; CSEL 32, 1, 703.
About the year 391.

DE CAIN ET ABEL LIBRI II
PL 14, 315 (333); B 1, 247; Par 1, 127; CSEL 32, 1, 339.
From about 377-378.

EPIGRAMMATA
B 5, 689. Diehl, *Insc. Lat chr. vet.*, I (Berlin, 1925), nos. 1800, 1801, 1841, 2165. Pighi in *Aevum*, XVIII (1944), pp. 15-22.

EPISTOLAE
PL 16, 876 (913); B 5, 319; Par 4, 203; See the English translation: M. M. Beyenka, *Saint Ambrose: Letters:* Fathers of the Church, (New York, 1954).

EXAMERON LIBRI VI
PL 14, 123 (133); B 1, 1; Par 1, 1; CSEL 32, 1, 3. See the English translation: John J. Savage, *Saint Ambrose: Hexameron, Paradise, and Cain and Abel:* Fathers of the Church, XLII (New York, 1961).
From about 387-390.

DE EXCESSU FRATRIS LIBRI II
PL 16, 1289 (1345); B 5, 21; Par 4, 140; CSEL 73, 207.
Of February, 378.

EXHORTATIO VIRGINITATIS
PL 16, 335 (351); B 4, 349; Par 3, 306.
From 394.

EXPLANATIO PSALMORUM DUODECIM

PL 14, 921 (963); B 2, 157; Par 2, 41; CSEL 64, 3-397.

From 394 to 397.

EXPLANATIO SYMBOLI, A QUODAM EXCEPTA

PL 17, 1155 (1193); B 6, 277; CSEL 73, 1-12.

EXPOSITIO PSALMI CENTESIMI DUODEVICESIMI

PL 15, 1197 (1261); B 2, 435; Par 2, 213; CSEL 62, 3-510.

About the year 389.

EXULTET

Misc. Giov. Mercati, 1, 219; Misc. Bernareggi, 394.

DE FIDE LIBRI V

PL 16, 527 (549); B 4, 573; Par 3, 342; CSEL 78.

The first two books from 378, the last three from 380.

DE FUGA SAECULI

PL 14, 569 (597); B 1, 537; Par 1, 283; CSEL 32, 2, 163.

From about 394.

GESTA CONCILII AQUILEIENSIS. INTER EPISTOLAS: POST EP. 8

From 381

HEGESIPPUS: FLAVII IOSEPHI LIBRORUM DE BELLO IUDAICO VERSIO LATINA

B 6, 9; CSEL 66 (1932).

Before 374. Perhaps spurious.

DE HELIA ET IEIUNIO

PL 14, 697 (731); B 1, 687; Par 1, 358; CSEL 32, 2, 411; J. A. Buck, *Patristic Studies,* XV, Washington, 1929.

From about 389.

HYMNI

PL 16, 1409 (1473); 17, 1171 (1209); B 5, 665; 6, 853; Par 4, 200; A. S. Walpole, *Early Latin Hymns,* Cambridge, 1922; M. Simonetti, *Innologia Ambrosiana,* Alba, 1956; W. Bults, *Hymni latini,* Heidelberg, 1956.

DE IACOB

PL 14, 597 (627); B 1, 569; Par 1, 300; CSEL 32, 2, 3.

Probably from 386.

DE INCARNATIONIS DOMINICAE SACRAMENTO

PL 16, 817 (853); B 4, 875; Par 4, 69.

From 382.

DE INSTITUTIONE VIRGINIS

PL 16, 305 (319); B 4, 315; Par 3, 289.

From 392.

DE INTERPELLATIONE IOB ET DAVID LIBRI IV

PL 14, 797 (835); B 2, 5; Par 1, 415; CSEL 32, 2, 211.

Probably of 388-389.

DE IOSEPH

PL 14, 641 (673); B 1, 617; Par 1, 326; CSEL 32, 2, 73.

About 388.

DE ISAAC VEL ANIMA

PL 14, 501 (527); B 1, 457; Par 1, 243; CSEL 32, 1, 641.

About 391.

EXPOSITIO ESAIAE PROPHETAE (FRAGM.)

PL 44, 384. 410. 436, 632; B 2, 895; CSEL 42, 164. 205. 251; 60, 559-567; *Corpus Christianorum,* XIV, Turnhout, 1957, pp. 403-508.

LEX DEI SIVE MOSAICARUM ET ROMANARUM LEGUM COLLATIO

Th. Mommsen, *Collectio librorum iuris antiustinianaei,* III. Berlin, 1890, pp. 107-198; Johannes Baviera, *Fontes Iuris Romani Antejustiniani,* II, Florence, 1940, pp. 543-589. Cf. *Clavis Patrum,* no. 168; G. Galbiati in *Ambrosiana,* Milan, 1942, pp. 91 ff.

EXPOSITIO EVANGELII SECUNDUM LUCAM LIBRI X

PL 15, 1527 (1607); B 3, 9; Par 2, 425-3, 135; CSEL 32, 4, 3-528; *Corpus Christianorum,* XIV, 1957.

From about 390, from homilies of the years 377-389.

DE MYSTERIIS

PL 16, 389 (405); B 4, 427; Par 3, 332; CSEL 73, 87.

From about 391.

DE NABUTHE

PL 14, 731 (765); B 1, 725; Par 1, 377; CSEL 32, 2, 469; M. R. P. McGuire, *Patristic Studies,* XV, Washington, 1927.

From about 389.

DE NOE

PL 14, 361 (381); B 1, 301; Par 1, 156; CSEL 32, 1, 413.

From about 377-378.

DE OBITU THEODOSII

PL 16, 1385 (1447); B 5, 121; Par, 190; CSEL 73, 369; M. D. Mannix, *Patristic Studies,* IX, Washington, 1925.

From the year 395.

DE OBITU VALENTINIANI

PL 16, 1357 (1417); B 5, 91; Par 4, 177; CSEL 73, 327; T. A. Kelly, *Patristic Studies,* XV, Washington, 1927.

DE OFFICIIS LIBRI III

PL 16, 23 (25); B 4, 21; Par 3, 137.

From 389-390.

DE PAENITENTIA LIBRI II

PL 16, 465 (485); B 4, 509; Par 4, 88; CSEL 73, 117.

From about 388-389.

DE PARADISO

PL 14, 275 (291); B 1, 197; Par 1, 101; CSEL 32, 1, 265.

From about 377-378.

DE PATRIARCHIS

PL 14, 673 (707); B 1, 655; Par 1, 345; CSEL 32, 2, 125.

From about 391.

QUICUMQUE

Cf. Clavis Patrum, No. 167; Berthold Altaner, *Patrology,* trans. Hilda Graef, London, 1960, pp. 319-321.

RELATIO SYMMACHI. INTER EPISTOLAS: POST EP. 17

DE SACRAMENTIS SERMONES VI, A QUODAM EXCEPTI

PL 16, 417 (435); B 4, 457; Par 4, 119; CSEL 73, 13.

From about 391.

DE SPIRITU SANCTO LIBRA III

PL 16, 703 (731); B 4, 753; Par 4, 1.

Probably from 381.

DE SACRAMENTO REGENERATIONIS SIVE DE PHILOSOPHIA

B 4, 905; CSEL 11, 131.

DE TERNARII NUMERI EXCELLENTIA

PL 125, 821 (probably spurious).

TITULI

B 5,692; ed. S. Merkle, *Römische Quartalsch.,* X (1896) pp. 185-222; B 5, 692.

DE TOBIA

PL 14, 759 (797); B 1, 759; Par 1, 393; CSEL 32, 2, 519; L. M. Zucker, *Patristic Studies,* XXXV, Washington, 1933.

From about 389.

DE VIDUIS

PL 16, 233 (247); B 4, 241; Par 3, 250.

From 377.

DE VIRGINIBUS LIBRI III

PL 16, 187 (197); B 4, 189; Par 3, 224; O. Faller in *Florilegium Patristicum,* XXXI, Bonn, 1933; ed. Cazzaniga, 1948.

From 377.

DE VIRGINITATE

PL 16, 265 (279); B 4, 273; Par 3, 267.

From about 377.

VITA S. AMBROSII, AUCTORE PAULINO, EIUS NOTARIO

PL 14, 27 (29); B 6, 885; Par 1, 1; M. S. Kaniecka, *Patristic Studies,* XVI, Washington, 1928; M. Pellegrino, *Vita di s. Ambrogio,* Rome, 1961; R. J. Deferrari, *St. Ambrose. Theological and Dogmatic Works,* Washington, 1963.

The following works, falsely attributed to St. Ambrose, are usually included in the published editions of his writings:

Commentaria in XIII epistolas beati Pauli: PL 17, 45 (47); B 3, 373. The author, whose identity is disputed, is usually called "Ambrosiaster."

Apologia prophetae David altera: PL 14, 887 (930); B 2, 110; Par 2, 21; CSEL 32, 2, 359. R. H. Connolly, however, has defended the authenticity of this work in *The Downside Review,* LXV (1947), pp. 7-20; 121-130.

De lapsu Susannae, or *De lapsu virginis consecratae;* PL 16, 367 (383); B 4, 385; Par 3, 323; I. Cazzaniga has published a critical edition of this in the *Corpus Paravianum,* 1948.

Te Deum laudamus, perhaps composed by Niceta of Remesiana. See Altaner, *Patrology,* p. 459.

Plates

o

PLATE I

THE BEES

VBI EXAMEN APVM PVERI OS COMPLEVIT AMBROSI

The child lies in a crib upon a coverlet that falls down on the side in symmetrical folds. The legs of the crib are represented as resting upon rounded supports which would allow it to be rocked. Ambrose's father is standing at the foot of the crib wearing a tunic and cloak. Above the mouth of the child, and as if issuing from it, are a number of bees the size of birds. In the sky there are three banks of clouds sending forth flames. The episode is described in Paulinus, *Vita Ambr.* 3. For this type of prodigy, see H. Delehaye, *Les légendes hagiogr.* (Brussels, 1927), p. 32.

PLATE II

GOLD GLASS FROM BRESCIA

This fourth-century gold glass is now found in the Museo Civico of Brescia. It is 2 and 3/8 inches in diameter and of the finest workmanship. The two words on the disk are most likely the signature of the artist: "By Bounnerius the potter."

The woman has an open but thoughtful countenance. There is a delicate contour to her cheeks. The rather loose treatment of her hair is in marked contrast with the studied waves in her daughter's. The young girl is wearing a necklace of jewels. The boy is dressed in a tunic and the simple *praetexta.* See F. Odorici, *Antichità cristiane di Brescia* (Brescia, 1845), p. 59; A. Venturi *Storia dell'arte italiana,* I (Milan, 1901), p. 405; W. F. Volbach-M. Hirmer, *Frühchristliche Kunst* (Munich, 1958), p. 57, no. 61, where there is a beautiful reproduction of the glass in color. It is now incorporated into the jeweled cross of St. Julia, which comes from the seventh century.

PLATE III

JUSTINA

A sculpture found at Milan in 1846 in the excavation near the Via San Primo

A rich headdress surmounted by the *camauro,* decorated with a double roll of pearls which are extended down the nape of the neck. See Hayford Pierce and Royal Tyler, *L'Art byzantin,* I (Paris, 1932), plate 44. These authors date the work between the years 381-391 and identify it as a portrait of the empress Justina. Others, however, assign it to the fifth century. See Volbach-Hirmer, *Frühchristliche Kunst,* p. 58, no. 68; S. Vigezzi, *La scultura in Milano* (Milan, 1932), p. 59. The head is 10 and 5/8 inches high. It is found in the art collection of the Castello Sforzesco at Milan.

PLATE IV

THE ORDINATION

VBI OCTAVO DIE ORDINATVR EPISCOPVS

St. Ambrose, with his head surrounded by a nimbus, is vested in a chasuble. He stands between two bishops who have consecrated him, and he holds in his left hand a closed book. The bishop to the right of Ambrose holds an unrolled scroll in his left hand while he is giving a blessing in the Greek manner with his right. The other bishop also holds a closed scroll in his left hand. See Paulinus *Vita Ambr.* 9: "On the eighth day [after his baptism] he was consecrated bishop."

VBI OCTAVO DIE ORDINATVR EPS

PLATE V

SERENA WITH HER SON EUCHERIUS

Ivory Diptych in the Treasury of the Cathedral of Monza

This represents the second of two panels, each measuring 12-11/16 by 6-3/8 inches. The woman, Serena, was the niece of Theodosius and the wife of Stilicho. In this portrait she is dressed in a tunic known as an *interula*. This was a garment with close-fitting sleeves. She is also wearing a *stola*, a more ample tunic with short sleeves. Over the *stola* she is wearing the *palla*, a kind of long broad scarf corresponding to the *pallium* worn by men. Her hair is arranged like that of the Madonna in the mosaics of St. Mary Major's in Rome. In her left hand she is holding a handkerchief, and in her right a rose. The boy, who appears standing between his parents when the panels are opened, is wearing a sleeved tunic. He is also dressed in a *toga* that is fastened with a pin on his right shoulder. The tablets which he holds in his left hand symbolize the right of jurisdiction. His right hand, with the thumb and two first fingers extended, is like that of a judge when pronouncing a sentence.

This masterpiece was probably carved in an official workshop at Milan about the year 400. For a full description of the diptych, see H. Leclercq, "Diptyques (Archéologie)," *Dict. Arch. chrét. et de Lit.*, IV (1921), cc. 1100-04; Volbach-Hirmer, *Frühchristliche Kunst*, p. 57, no. 62. The diptych was given to the basilica of St. John the Baptist at Monza by Berengarius about the year 900.

PLATE VI

THE TRAY OF PARABIAGO

This tray was found in 1905 at Parabiago, fourteen miles from Milan, during the course of digging the foundations for a country home. The tray is of almost pure silver. It is 15 and 3/8 inches in diameter and weighs 7 pounds and 13 ounces. Until 1930 it remained unknown in the possession of the owner of the land on which it was found. It was then, through the interest of the engineer Guido Sutermeister and Professor Alda Levi, acquired by the state and became a part of the national heritage. The tray was cast all in one piece, including both the rim around and the pedestal beneath it. The figures have been polished off with a burin and the finer details marked with a chisel. The rim of the tray and the clothes and hair of the various figures have been covered with gold. From a merely technical point of view, the platter is an exceptionally fine example of ancient metalwork.

Cybele, the *Mater Idaea,* with her consort Attis at her side is mounting toward heaven in a chariot drawn by four lions. Around the divine pair are three Curetes performing a military dance. To the front of the central scene is Aeon, the youthful god of the Golden Age. He is standing within a zodiacal oval supported by Atlas. The cricket, lizard, and the serpent twined about the obelisk are also signs of the zodiac. Beneath the lions are four putti, or infants, symbolizing the four seasons. At the top of the tray may be seen the sun drawn in his chariot by four horses. He is preceded by a winged youth, the morning star. In front of this is the moon in a chariot drawn by two animals. She is preceded by the evening star. In the lower left part of the tray may be seen two figures. These are the divinities of springs and rivers. To their right are Oceanus, or Neptune, and his wife. Further still to the right is the goddess Tellus, the fruitful earth. She is resting on a cornucopia, while two putti are pointing at the central scene. See the text, pp. 221-225.

The tray is now found at the Soprintendenza alle Antichità della Lombardia, Piazza Duomo 14, Milan.

PLATE VII

ST. HELENA

Bust of St. Helena found on the front of her sarcophagus of red porphyry. The sarcophagus was originally located in the mausoleum of St. Helena on the Via Labicana, today the Tor Pignattara. Pope Anastasius IV (1153-54) had it brought to St. John Lateran's. It was broken during the course of further transfers. Pope Pius VI (1775-99) had it restored and placed in the Vatican, where it may now be seen in the Pio-Clementine Museum.

Some scholars maintain that this bust belongs to the original sarcophagus. Others, however, regard it as the work of the later restorers.

Since Eusebius does not mention St. Helena's discovery of the cross and nails of Christ's passion in his life of Constantine, some hold that this account is legendary. See J. Vogt, *Reallexikon für Antike und Christentum,* III (1957), cc. 372 ff. Many others, however, do not believe that this argument is sufficient to refute the evidence provided by St. Ambrose to the contrary. See, for example, P. de Labriolle in Fliche-Martin, *Histoire de l'église,* III, p. 364.

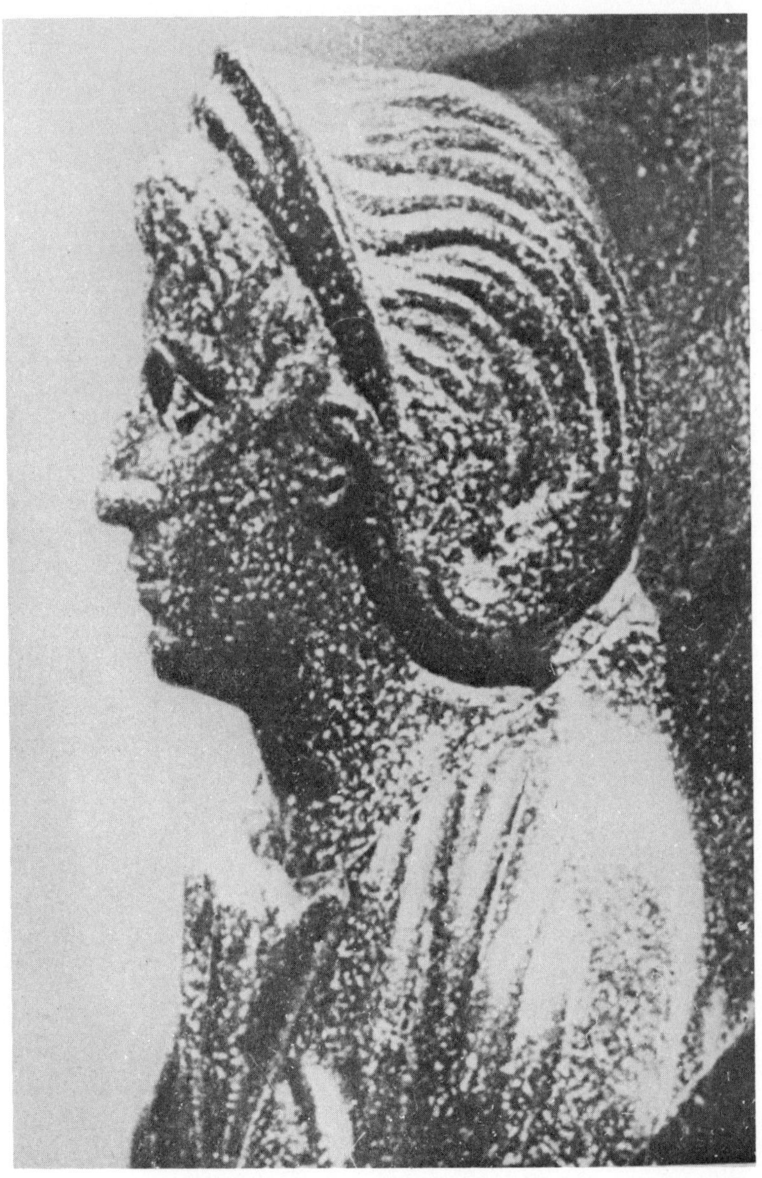

PLATE VIII

MAP OF MILAN

1. The *cardo*, or main cross street of an ancient city.
2. The *decumanus*, or main street of an ancient city.
3. Forum (?).
4. The *ecclesia maior*. See p. 406, n. 13.
5. Theater.
6. Thermae, or baths (?), on the Via Brisa.
7. Circus.

PORTA IOVIA
PORTA VERCELLINA
CORSO MAGENTA
VIA S. MARIA ALLA PORTA
LVINI
VIA ANSPERTO
THERMAE
VIA BRISA
BASILICA NABORIS ET FELICIS
VIA SANTA VALERIA
S. VALERIA
S. VITALE
MVRA DI MASSIMIANO
VIA CAPPVCCIO
CIRCVS
VIA MORIGI
PIAZZA MENTANA
VIA SAN
BASILICA PORTIANA
SAN VITTORE AL CORPO
PIAZZA SANT'AMBROGIO
S. VITTORE
BASILICA MARTYRVM
SANT'AMBROGIO
VIA CIRCO
VIA S. SISTO
PORTA TICINENSIS
CARROBBIO
VIA CESARE CORRENTI
PORTA TICINESE
ARENA
BASILICA PALATINA
S. LORENZO
CORSO DI
ARENA

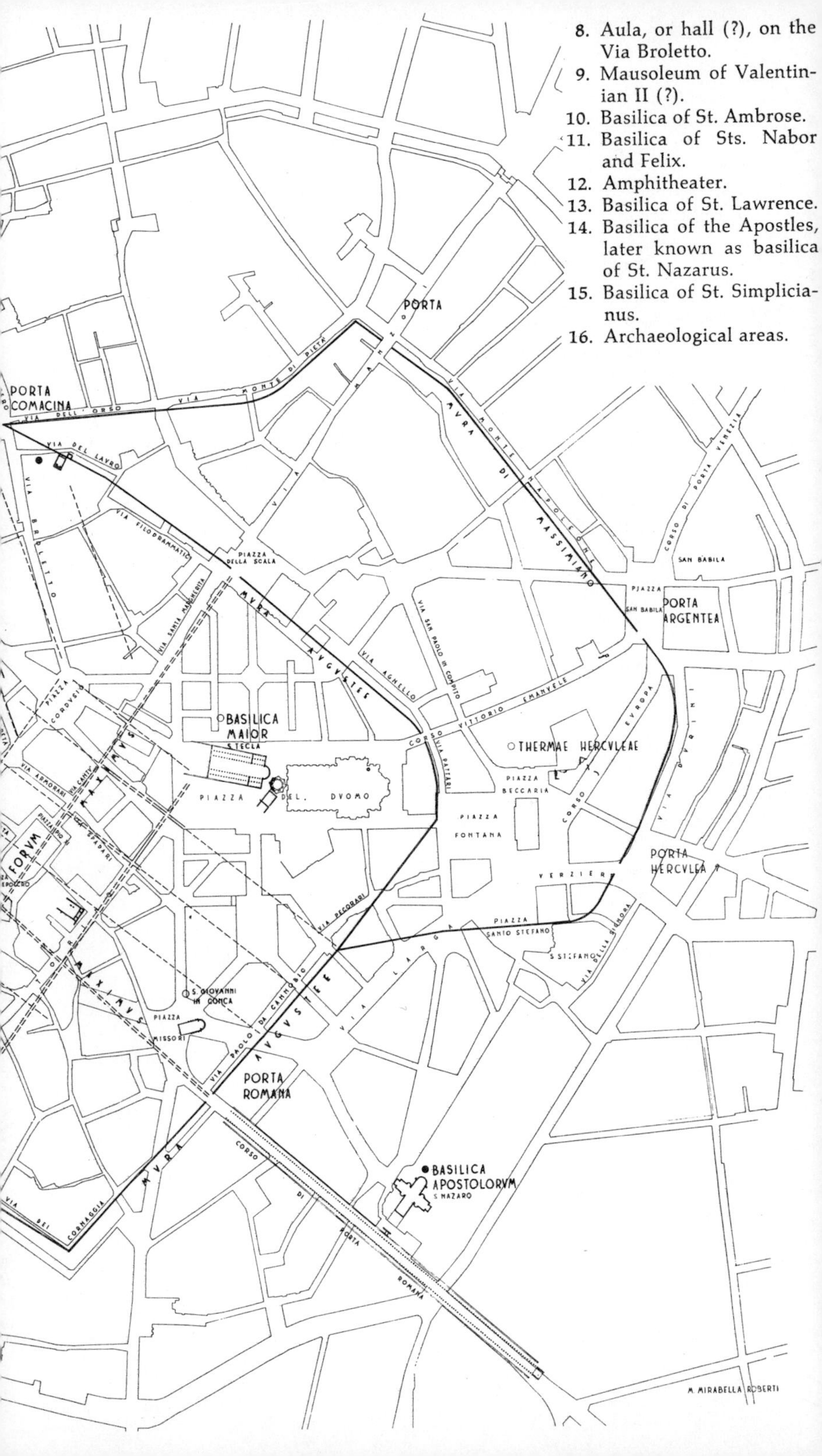

8. Aula, or hall (?), on the Via Broletto.
9. Mausoleum of Valentinian II (?).
10. Basilica of St. Ambrose.
11. Basilica of Sts. Nabor and Felix.
12. Amphitheater.
13. Basilica of St. Lawrence.
14. Basilica of the Apostles, later known as basilica of St. Nazarus.
15. Basilica of St. Simplicianus.
16. Archaeological areas.

PLATE IX

THE WOMAN WITH THE ISSUE OF BLOOD

Panel from the left side of the sarcophagus of St. Celsus.

The woman with the issue of blood for twelve years, dressed in a large, loose, and falling peplos, stoops to touch the hem of Christ's tunic. The latter, as He walks alone, suddenly turns His youthful head and asks, "Who touched Me?" In his commentary on Luke, St. Ambrose gives a lengthy exposition of this episode.

The sarcophagus, from the ancient basilica of St. Celsus, was carried into the neighboring church of St. Mary near Celsus on the Corso Italia in Milan. It is used as the *mensa* of the altar of the chapel of St. Basilides, which is located behind the altar of the Madonna, which newly married couples visit on their wedding day.

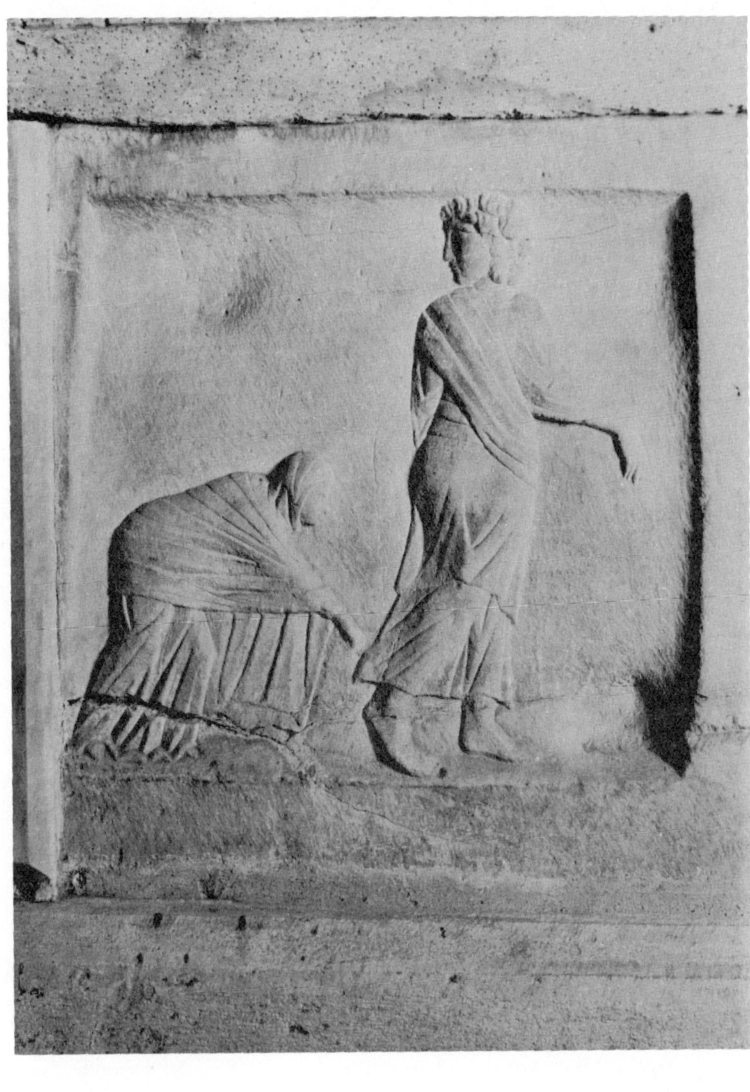

PLATE X

CHRIST BEFORE PILATE

Detail from the sarcophagus of Sts. Nabor and Felix. It was brought into the basilica of St. Ambrose at Milan in 1798 from the neighboring church of St. Francis, which stood over the site of the ancient chapel of Sts. Nabor and Felix.

Pilate is seated, dressed in a cloak and breastplate. The part of the relief representing the curule chair is broken off and lost. Covering his face with his left hand, he turns away in shame. At his side stands the messenger sent by his wife to tell him not to have anything to do with "that just man." In front of Pilate is a servant holding a pitcher in his right hand and in his left a dish. He is about to pour the water so that Pilate can wash his hands. Christ, represented as a beardless young man with long curly locks, is brought before Pilate by a soldier dressed in a tunic with long sleeves and having his cloak pinned at his right shoulder. He is holding on to the tunic worn by Christ.

St. Ambrose would pause to preach on such scenes. In his commentary on St. Luke he refers in a few exquisite lines to Pilate, "who washes his hands but does not lessen his guilt. For a judge should not yield to either envy or fear. . . . I think that he is an example of all those judges who condemn those whom they believe to be innocent" (*Expos. evang. sec. Luc.* 10.100-101).

On the front left side of the sarcophagus are two martyrs (Nabor and Felix, or Peter and Paul?) dressed in tunics and pallia. They are being led to martyrdom by two soldiers wearing tunics and military cloaks. The two groups of figures are connected by a third in the center. Two soldiers wearing helmets and breastplates, and with swords at their sides, are seated asleep, like those who watched at the sepulcher of Christ. Between them rises a cross planted on a spear, the symbol of the resurrection.

PLATE XI

IVORY OF THE RESURRECTION

The upper portion of the panel portrays the tomb of Christ as a round structure fitted with windows. In front of it two soldiers are sleeping. In the clouds above are the symbols of two of the evangelists: the calf of St. Luke and the man of St. Matthew. Both are fitted with triple sets of wings. See Ambrose, *De virginitate* 18.113-114.

In the lower portion of the panel are the holy women. They have come to the sepulcher and see the angel, who tells them that Christ has risen from the dead. See Ambrose, *De Isaac vel anima* 5.43. Others, however, interpret the seated figure as that of the risen Christ. On the twin doors of the sepulcher are carved incidents from the Gospels: Christ bidding Lazarus to come forth from his tomb; Zacchaeus in the fig tree, and Jesus curing the blind man. This diptych is also known at the Trivulzio Ivory since it is from the Trivulzian collection. It is now in the Castello Sforzesco at Milan. The ivory panel measures 12-1/8 by 5 and 5/16 inches. Some claim that the panel was carved in Syria, but both Alföldi and Volbach maintain that it was made during the fifth century in northern Italy. See Volbach-Hirmer, *Frühchristliche Kunst*, p. 61, no. 92.

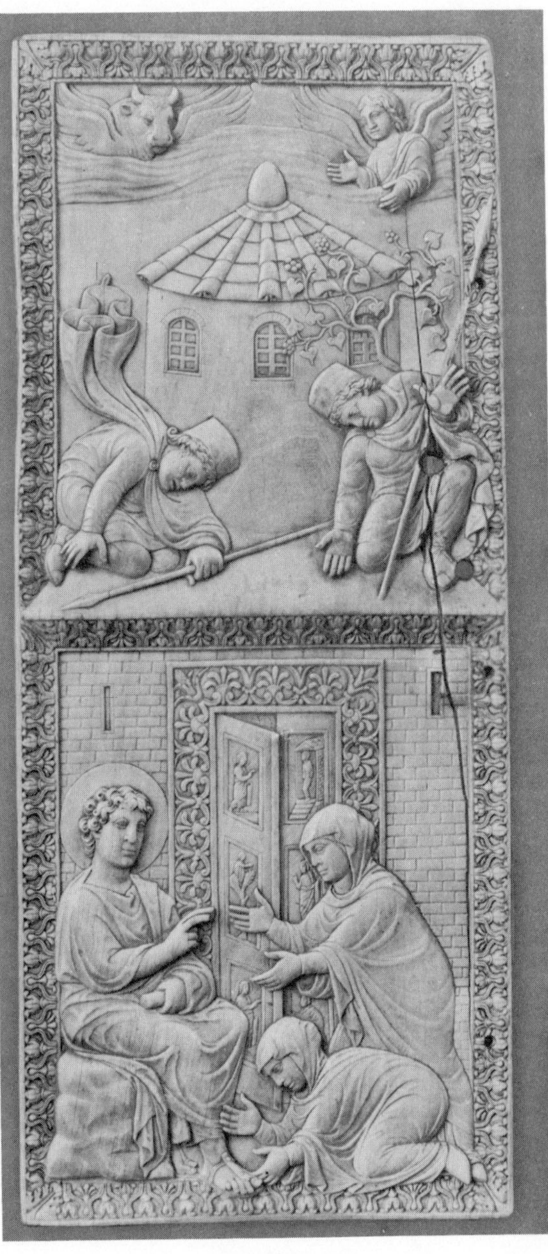

PLATE XII

CHRIST AND THOMAS

The right side of the front of the sarcophagus of St. Celsus. See Plate XV. Two women are going towards the sepulcher represented as a round tower with a conical roof. On the threshold of the door lies a piece of cloth, perhaps a shroud. The woman in front is pointing at it. The woman behind her is looking at the angel who announces the resurrection. The scene to the right represents the risen Christ, beardless and clothed in a tunic and pallium. His right hand is touching His head, while His left hand is drawing aside His garments so that Thomas can touch the wound in His side (John 20:27). This beautiful sarcophagus seems to be a few years later than the so-called Sarcophagus of Stilicho.

PLATE XIII

MOSAIC IN THE BASILICA OF ST. LAWRENCE

This mosaic may be seen in the chapel of St. Aquilinus in the basilica of St. Lawrence in Milan. The scene represents a man and woman standing with two seated children at their feet. Its significance is not known. According to F. Wittgens, *Glorie d'arte di Milano* (Milan, 1955), p. 18, "These strongly impressionistic mosaics may be compared with the famous mosaics of St. Mary Major's in Rome. They suggest that the pre-Justinian flowering of this art at Ravenna may have been due to Milanese masters whom the imperial court took with them to Ravenna when they moved there at the beginning of the fifth century." On the mosaics in the basilica of St. Lawrence, see C. Cecchelli in A. Calderini, G. Chierici, C. Cecchelli, *La Basilica di san Lorenzo Maggiore in Milano* (Milan, 1951).

PLATE XIV

ST. AMBROSE SLEEPING AT THE ALTAR

VBI SVPER ALTARE DORMIENS TVRONIAM PETIT

The altar is a gold cube resting on a gradine with a jeweled edge. Crosses may be seen traced on the two sides of the altar that are visible. A crown from which three jewels are hanging is suspended from the ceiling. St. Ambrose, with his head surrounded by a nimbus, is asleep. He is dressed in a chasuble and pallium and holds in his hands, which are resting on the altar, a tablet or a piece of parchment. The deacon behind the bishop touches him on the shoulder to awaken him. Behind the deacon, a lector standing on a jeweled platform continues to read from a book he is holding in his hand. According to Gregory of Tours, who relates this story, Ambrose was asleep for two or three hours, and during the course of this time he had conducted the funeral service for St. Martin. See his *De miraculis S. Martini* 1.5: *nam noveritis fratrem meum Martinum sacerdotem egressum fuisse de corpore, me autem ejus funeri obsequium praebuisse.* The incident is also portrayed in the twelfth-century mosaics in the apse of the basilica of St. Ambrose at Milan.

BISVBALTAREDOPIMENSTVRONIAMETT

PLATE XV

THE DEATH OF ST. AMBROSE

VBI ANIMA IN CAELVM DVCITVR CORPORE IN LECTO POSITO

St. Ambrose's body is laid out upon his bed. A richly adorned spread covers the corpse with the exception of the head, which is surrounded by a nimbus. The saint seems here to be represented with a beard. At the foot of the bed stands St. Honoratus holding his right hand to his face in grief. In the upper right corner, the hand of God surrounded by concentric circles appears in benediction, while three rays go out to meet the soul of the deceased (represented by a beardless youthful head), which is carried by the hand of an angel towards God.

VBIANIMAINCELVMD
V
CI
TVRCORPOREINLECTOPO
S

Index

o